LAW'S JUDGEMENT

Law's Judgement elucidates and defends a feature of contemporary law that is currently either overlooked or too glibly dismissed as morally troublesome or historically anachronistic. That feature is the abstract nature of law's judgement and its three components show that, when law judges us, it often does so in ignorance of our particular characters and abilities, on the one hand, and in ignorance of our context and circumstances, on the other. Law's judgement is thus insensitive to all or much that makes us the particular people we are. The book explores various connections between this mode of judgement and some of our most important legal and political values. It shows that law's abstract judgement is closely related to important juristic conceptions of personhood, responsibility and impartiality, and that these notions are not without moral significance. The book also examines the connections between modern law's judgement and three of our most important political values, namely, dignity, equality and community. It argues that, if we value particular conceptions of dignity, equality and community, then we must also value law's judgement. Illuminating these connections therefore serves a double purpose: first, it makes a case against those who counsel liberation from law's abstract judgement and, second, it redirects attention to the task of morally evaluating law's abstract judgement in its own terms.

[redacted]

Law's Judgement

William Lucy

• HART •
PUBLISHING
OXFORD AND PORTLAND, OREGON
2017

Hart Publishing
An imprint of Bloomsbury Publishing Plc

Hart Publishing Ltd
Kemp House
Chawley Park
Cumnor Hill
Oxford OX2 9PH
UK

Bloomsbury Publishing Plc
50 Bedford Square
London
WC1B 3DP
UK

www.hartpub.co.uk
www.bloomsbury.com

Published in North America (US and Canada) by
Hart Publishing
c/o International Specialized Book Services
920 NE 58th Avenue, Suite 300
Portland, OR 97213-3786
USA

www.isbs.com

First published 2017

British Library Cataloguing-in-Publication Data
A catalogue record for this book is available from the British Library.

ISBN: HB: 978-1-50991-328-2
ePDF: 978-1-50991-330-5
ePub: 978-1-50991-329-9

Library of Congress Cataloging-in-Publication Data

Names: Lucy, William, 1962- author.

Title: Law's judgement / William Lucy.

Description: Oxford [UK] ; Portland, Oregon : Hart Publishing, 2017. | Includes bibliographical references and index. | Description based on print version record and CIP data provided by publisher; resource not viewed.

Identifiers: LCCN 2017008721 (print) | LCCN 2017012714 (ebook) | ISBN 9781509913299 (Epub) | ISBN 9781509913282 (hardback : alk. paper)

Subjects: LCSH: Law and ethics. | Equity. | Law—Philosophy. | Justice.

Classification: LCC K247.6 (ebook) | LCC K247.6 .L83 2017 (print) | DDC 340/.112—dc23

LC record available at https://lccn.loc.gov/2017008721

Typeset by Compuscript Ltd, Shannon
Printed and bound in Great Britain by TJ International Ltd, Padstow, Cornwall

'[Al]though an aloof justice is bound at times to be harsh, an intimate justice, seeking to explore and grasp the boundaries of a private world, cannot in the nature of things be evenhanded. The law knows no magic that will enable it to transcend this antinomy. It is, therefore, condemned to tread an uncertain middle course, tempering the standard of the reasonable man in favour of certain obvious deficiencies, but formalising even its definitions of these'

Lon L Fuller, *The Morality of Law*, revised edn
(New Haven, Yale University Press, 1969) 72.

ACKNOWLEDGEMENTS

One incurs many debts when engaged in projects such as this and here I attempt to register those people and institutions that count among my principal creditors. The folk who helped (with information, or by reading, commenting on, chatting about and disagreeing with some or all of this book) are the most important creditors and this list, I hope, includes them all: Zenon Bankowski, David Cabrelli, Peter Cane, Colm O'Cinneide, Aoife O'Donoghue, Phil Handler, Dennis Klimchuk, Dino Kritsiotis, John Linarelli, Maks del Mar, Andrew Mason, Deirdre McCann, Christopher McCrudden, Richard Mullender, John Murphy, Ngaire Naffine, Jason Neyers, Shaun Pattinson, Hillel Steiner, Shaun Veitch, Jeremy Waldron, Neil Walker and Alexander Williams. Kit Barker, Ross Grantham, Dean Iain Scott, Neil Walker and Claudio Michelon also helped out by mobilising and/or explaining various forms of institutional support.

The institutions that made a very significant contribution to this project are: first and foremost, the Leverhulme Trust for the award of a Major Research Fellowship (MRF 2012-142) 2013–2015, which actually made it possible; the University of Durham, particularly its Law School and my colleagues therein, for providing an exciting, convivial and quite simply nice place to work; the IALS library, University of London; and the Law Schools at the Universities of Edinburgh and Western Ontario, for excellent hospitality and thus two enjoyable, productive visits. Portions of the book were delivered as talks at Edinburgh and UWO and I thank the audiences there (and in Brisbane, Canberra, Durham, Liverpool and Manchester) for their patience and attention. I now realise that the seeds of the project were planted a long time ago, during visits to the TC Beirne School of Law, University of Queensland and the College of Law at the Australian National University; both therefore bear some responsibility for what follows.

Parts of chapters two, three, five and six are drawn from sections of essays first published in the *Oxford Journal of Legal Studies* ((2005) 25 (1) 3–31 and (2009) (4) 787–804) and the *University of Toronto Law Journal* ((2011) (3) at 411–65). I am grateful to the publishers for permission to use this material. Finally, thanks to Bill Asquith, in particular, and to Hart Publishing in general, for their admirably efficient work on the book—if only all publishers were the same!

CONTENTS

1

Law's Judgement

> 'It is not easy—perhaps not even desirable—to judge other people by a consistent standard. Conduct obnoxious, even unbearable, in one person may be readily tolerated in another; apparently indispensable principles of behaviour are in practice relaxed—not always with impunity—in the interests of those whose nature seems to demand an exceptional measure'.[1]

> 'The lawyer's world is entire unto itself, the human pared away'.[2]

Law does many things. It can—insofar as it is published, clear, general, consistent and prospective—create and uphold a sphere of freedom since, if these conditions are satisfied, citizens will be able to predict when the law might affect them and take steps to avoid it. While not the only kind of freedom, freedom from legal liabilities and duties is undoubtedly worth having. Insofar as law embodies the formal virtues just noted, it can also allow long-term planning, and not just within the sphere of freedom from legal duties and liabilities. This is because clear, non-retrospective, general, consistent and facilitative bodies of law, like contract and trusts, allow citizens to create and project legal obligations far into the future, should they want to do so. The law can also, in many of its loftiest instantiations such as constitutional Bills and Charters of Rights and Freedoms, stand as the repository of some of a society's most important public values. But the law does something else, equally obvious and just as remarkable, and this is the focus of what follows. The law sets standards of behaviour for a whole community and even segments thereof. In doing so, it judges us.

The law judges us by assessing our conduct and its outcomes (and sometimes also our aims, intentions and cognitive status). The principal ways we stand before the law are as claimant or defendant in a contested private or public law action, or as accused or victim in a contested criminal case. As the accused in a criminal trial, prudence requires us—once the prosecution is close to proving its case—to account for our conduct, just as the victim must account for their accusation. As a claimant in either a public or private law trial we must make out our claim, while the defendant must account for their conduct as part of the process of rebutting the claimant's case. This process of giving an account of oneself before the law is

[1] A Powell, *A Question of Upbringing* (London, Arrow, 2005) 52.

[2] H Mantel, *Bring up the Bodies* (London, Harper Collins, 2015) 369.

clearly not a normal instance of explaining one's conduct, primarily because the explanation must be constructed within the categories of the relevant area of law. Such explanations are therefore usually tendered by lawyers on behalf of those being called to account, since if there is any skill a cadre of professional lawyers should have, it is expertise in the interpretation and disputation of the law.

The fact that, when either prudence or legal obligation demands, we must account for our conduct and that account has to take the form of, or be translatable into, legally relevant categories and standards, is both significant and obvious. These categories and standards constitute vast areas of legal doctrine (such as land and tort law, criminal and administrative law) and function as the thresholds against which our conduct is measured. That, after all, is why the word 'standard' is descriptively appropriate here. Moreover, this aspect of law's judgement pre-dates adjudication in an important sense: the law's standards are available in advance of particular judicial decisions about specific legal disputes.[3] They exist not just in the form of published precedents and statutes, but also in the tidier package we now know as the legal textbook. There is an undeniable sense in which many such texts are simply guides as to how and how not to behave. They are (usually voluminous) compendia of standards for acceptable legal behaviour.

Many questions can be asked of law's judgement. Some of these questions have been staple topics of legal philosophy for as long as that discipline itself has existed. We might wonder, for example, by what right the law judges us: in what sense, if any, can the law legitimately call us to account? Why, if at all, should we take its claims seriously? What, if any, obligations do such claims create? Besides these questions, which take us to the heart of one of the foundational issues of political and legal philosophy, there is a group of related questions that has traditionally been of more interest to jurists and lawyers than philosophers. First among equals in this group of questions is this: is law a rational means of judging us? It is common for the judgements of the appellate and some lower courts of the common law world to be published. When inspected, these judgements are very discursive and provide not just an answer to the specific legal question or questions raised in the dispute before the court, but also an analysis of other related cases in which courts in this and other jurisdictions have given judgement. These other judgements can be ancient or contemporary. Examination of the published judgements of the appellate courts in the common law world also reveals a minute concern not just with the detail of any legislative provision that is in play, but also often with its alleged point and legislative history. Clearly, the judges are working hard to support the conclusions they reach. One general question that can be asked of the work they do when deciding cases is: does it rationally justify the decisions they

[3] It is worth pointing out here that my spelling of 'judgement' bears no significance, save that I eschew the anachronistic lawyerly conceit of referring to law's judgement(s) as 'judgment(s)'. I thus align myself with what has been regarded as normal usage for some considerable time: see Sir E Gowers, *Fowler's Modern English Usage*, 2nd edn (Oxford, Clarendon Press, 1965).

come to? This question, in one form or another, has informed much of the best Anglo-American legal philosophy of the last four decades.[4]

In addition to questions about the legitimacy and rationality of law's judgement, we can ask a range of slightly narrower questions. These questions investigate the other properties law's judgement (or, more accurately, law's judgements) might have. So, for example, there is a great deal of interest in the degree, if any, to which judicial decisions differ from political or other normative judgements. There is also a question about the extent to which appellate court decisions are and can be predictable, given the fact that the courts often seem to develop the law in such cases. This question also serves to raise a concern about how, if at all, judicial decision-making in the common law world can abide by some of the requirements of the rule of law ideal.

Neither question about the legitimacy or the rationality of judicial decisions is of concern here. The family of slightly narrower questions about predictability and related issues is also set aside. This is certainly not to say that these questions are uninteresting. Rather, the fact that these questions are so interesting is part of the reason for ignoring them. They are ignored not because what follows aims to put tedious and dull questions centre stage, but because these very interesting questions have served to crowd out consideration of other equally interesting issues. I argue that one of these issues is the nature of law's judgement itself. This issue is often completely overlooked, the focus of much contemporary legal philosophy being instead upon the rationality or legitimacy or predictability of particular instances of law's judgement. These particular instances are a handful of judicial decisions which have been taken as exemplary and thus propelled to jurisprudential stardom: rare is the law student ignorant of *Riggs v Palmer*, or *Daniels and Daniels v R White's Lemonade and Tabard*, or *R v R*, or the *Snail Darter* case.[5] But all these cases, and almost all the other cases lawyers in the common law jurisdictions will ever come across, have features in common which are missed by most contemporary jurisprudential discussions of law's judgement. That, at least, is one of the guiding suppositions of this book.

These features are referred to with this compendious claim: law's judgement is abstract. This claim has at least two broad aspects, each of which can be further sub-divided. One aspect relates to *how* contemporary law *judges* us, the other to *how* contemporary law *sees* those it judges. The former is tackled in the remainder

[4] For a brief taster see N MacCormick, *Legal Reasoning and Legal Theory* (Oxford, Clarendon Press 1978; revised edn, 1993) and *Rhetoric and the Rule of Law* (Oxford, Clarendon Press, 2005); R Dworkin, *Taking Rights Seriously* (London, Duckworths, 1978) and *Law's Empire* (London, Fontana, 1986 and Oxford, Hart Publishing, 1998). That the question is not only of interest to Anglo-American jurists is clear from, *inter alios*, A Aarnio, *The Rational as Reasonable* (Dordrecht, D Reidel, 1987); R Alexy, *A Theory of Legal Argumentation* (Oxford, Clarendon Press, 1989) and K Gunther, *The Sense of Appropriateness* (Albany, SUNY Press, 1993).

[5] Respectively: 115 NY 506, 22 NE 188 (1889); [1938] 4 All ER 258; [1991] 4 All ER 481; and *Tennessee Valley Authority v Hill* 437 US 153 (1978).

of this chapter, which also sketches how our examination of law's judgement will proceed and why it should be thought significant. The latter aspect is the fulcrum of chapter two.

I. How Law Judges Us

When called to account by our nearest and dearest, it is normal to expect their judgement to be tempered not just with mercy but also by knowledge: not only of the conduct in question and its context, but knowledge of our character. We expect to be judged by those closest to us in all our particularity. We hope they know us and thus show a greater understanding of our deeds because of their knowledge of our characters or 'selves'. We are not strangers but intimates, with a history. Thus, those who know me best know that I am often tardy and, although they are rightly beyond excusing this inexcusable behaviour, they now plan with it in mind: I'm told, for example, to arrive for meetings earlier than they are actually scheduled to start. In addition, their judgement of this aspect of my conduct is in some sense mitigated or restrained by their knowledge of me; what they would invariably regard as inexcusable in others in most contexts, they sometimes tolerate in me in some contexts. My nearest and dearest clearly do not judge me by standards generally applicable to the rest of humankind.

The law does. Or, at least, it purports to judge me in the same way as it judges all its addressees. That is because bourgeois or liberal law's judgement is abstract.[6] This much becomes clear once we remind ourselves of three of bourgeois law's most distinctive features. The first feature can be labelled the presumptive identity component because bourgeois law usually sees its addressees not in all their particularity, but as *identical abstract beings*. Addressees of the law are identical in two respects according to this component: they are regarded as if they were the same in terms of those capacities, cognitive and physical, which enable humans to comply with achievable and intelligible legal standards; and they are taken to be identical in the sense of having the same entitlement to the same bundle of 'formal' rights and abilities. Bourgeois law's second feature is the uniformity component, which entails that, generally speaking, the law judges its addressees by reference to *general and objective standards equally applicable to all*. The idea that the same laws should apply to all addressees of the law is so powerful that it casts suspicion upon laws which apply to particular persons or groups. This requirement, once apparently called 'isonomy', is probably identical to some versions of the generality requirement of the rule of law ideal.[7] The limited avoidability component is the

[6] By 'bourgeois' or 'liberal' I mean only 'not feudal'. These terms are not used pejoratively here.

[7] On isonomy, see FA Hayek, *The Constitution of Liberty* (London, Routledge and Kegan Paul, 1960) 164–66. Neither of the two most influential accounts of the rule of law interpret its generality requirement expansively: see LL Fuller, *The Morality of Law* (New Haven, Yale University Press, revised edn, 1969) 49–51 and J Raz, *The Authority of Law* (Oxford, Clarendon Press 1979; 2nd edn, 2009) 213 and 215–16; contrast Hayek, ibid, 208–10.

third feature of law's abstract judgement. It highlights the fact that the application of the standards in play in the uniformity component is often mitigated only by a *limited number and range of exculpatory claims.*[8] Exculpatory claims are limited in range because they are subject to reasonableness standards. Thus, one can only rarely resist or deflect the law's judgement by averring, for example, that one lacks the fortitude or capacity to adhere to its standards. One is generally held to a reasonableness standard here and it usually matters not that one is unable to achieve such a standard.

In stating the three components, the qualifications used—'usually', 'generally speaking', 'often'—are deliberate. My claim is not that these three components are realised to the maximum degree across the whole of all or most current legal systems. Rather, it is that their significance in many legal systems and much legal thought is such that departures from them—which are in fact fairly numerous—are regarded as suspicious or problematic. Hence, laws which name particular addressees or which benefit particular groups are *prima facie* troublesome in most legal systems, even though many laws have the latter effect. There are also laws in most legal systems which attempt to take account of the context or character or particularity of a specific class of claimants or defendants but these, too, are often regarded as exceptional, as concessions to equity or mercy or some such allegedly non-legalistic virtue. In many legal systems the role played by the three components is that of fixed agitation points, against which departures must react and be tested. In most legal systems there is thus most likely a process of mediation between the three components, on the one hand, and their opposites or weaker versions of themselves, on the other.

Note that more or less 'pure' versions of law's abstract judgement are found in most current legal systems—common law, civilian or 'mixed'—and they function in private, public and criminal law. While these areas of law are indeed very different, the differences do not obviously impact upon the abstract nature of law's judgement, save perhaps to explain its more limited role in criminal as compared to public and private law.[9] It is also true that the purest form of law's abstract judgement is found in only some areas of public law and plays its principal role at the liability and conviction stages of private and criminal law. The selection,

[8] It is tempting to say these features show that law's judgement is also objective and there is at least one credible sense of 'objective' in which this is right (see M Kramer, *Objectivity and the Rule of Law* (Cambridge, Cambridge University Press, 2007) 38–45). However, the notion of objectivity when applied to law can have many other senses (all of which are dealt with in Kramer, ibid, and in K Greenawalt, *Law and Objectivity* (New York, Oxford University Press, 1992)) and is undoubtedly complex. Although some significant points about law's abstract judgement can be made using various senses of that term (see Greenawalt, ibid, Chs 6–8), this runs the risk of unnecessary complication.

[9] Insofar as liability judgements in the criminal law are also regarded as moral judgements, it might be thought that law's abstract judgement and its components, like reasonableness standards, are inappropriate. This, however, assumes a somewhat dubious picture of moral judgement, as will be noted below, as well as assuming an exaggerated distinction between private law judgements and moral judgements.

details and quantum of the remedy in private law and the sentence in criminal law are quite often (although certainly not always) tailored to the situation of the particular claimant and defendant in the former, and the precise circumstances of the accused, his conduct and its affect upon the victim, in the latter. Why the role of law's abstract judgement is limited in this way is an interesting question, but not one tackled here.

That law's abstract judgement is found in diverse areas of contemporary law should not be overlooked. I do not claim that the three components of law's abstract judgement have marked each and every legal system known to humankind. I claim only that law's abstract judgement is a more pronounced feature of liberal or bourgeois legal systems than it is of feudal legal systems. That its existence in the law has ebbed and flowed is plausible; so, too, might be the claim that it is now in terminal decline. The ultimate truth of these two claims is not questioned here. Moreover, the spirit of tidiness that informs these remarks demands that one other point be noted. It is a reminder, both substantive and terminological. The term 'law's abstract judgement' looms large in what follows. That it does so should not distract from the fact that it is nothing more than a shorthand way of referring to one, some or all of the three components just sketched. The substantive point follows on from this as a caution. It insists that the three components should not be taken as necessary and sufficient conditions of law's abstract judgement, for there is no intention here to foreclose the possibility of law's abstract judgement having additional components. These three components are simply the most important ones for our current purposes.

Our preliminary sketch of law's abstract judgement—hereinafter '*LAJ*'—can become less stipulative, and therefore more defensible, if it can be shown to describe something actually embedded in the law. That is the burden of the next two subsections. They elucidate the role *LAJ* plays in private law, public law and criminal law. Private law and criminal law are treated together because the three components of *LAJ* do similar work in both areas. For expository and substantive purposes, private and criminal law are therefore a good fit. As against those who insist that criminal law should be subsumed under the rubric of public law, my claim is this. There is indeed a perhaps trivial similarity in the 'public-ness' of both criminal and public law, namely, that the State is supposedly vividly present in each. But the State is assuredly not absent from private law, either as litigant, or as sponsor and guarantor of the court system and of the means of enforcing judgements. What makes public law public for our purposes is a far more banal, double-sided claim. First, the law in play in our discussion of public law is found in more or less fundamental constitutional provisions and the case-law surrounding them.[10] If any area of law is assuredly public law, then it is those provisions and

[10] But not all. Some 'public' law provisions in play below are found in 'ordinary' non-discrimination statutes. I have examined various ways in which public and private law might plausibly be distinguished in 'What's Private about Private Law?', Ch 3 of A Robertson and Tang Hang Wu (eds), *The Goals of Private Law* (Oxford, Hart Publishing, 2009) 47–75.

their associated case-law. Second, the public law of even the common law jurisdictions is far from uniform; complexity thus arises simply by virtue of difference and this provides another reason for treating public law separately from criminal law in what follows. Our category 'public law' is already a mixed-bag; it becomes too mixed to be coherent when criminal law is also added.

A. Private and Criminal Law

The third—limited avoidability—component of *LAJ* is best examined first, since this is the least complex and (perhaps) least interesting of the three. That private and criminal law recognise only a limited number of exculpatory claims is not news.[11] Nor is it particularly informative to highlight that these exculpatory claims are not easily available, being constrained by a variety of requirements. Almost as trite is the observation that some think the law's 'progress' from barbarism is marked by greater permissiveness and flexibility in its recognition of excusing conditions. The salient point, for current purposes, is that far fewer exculpatory claims are currently legally recognised than would be if defendants were judged by reference to all the detail of their context and particular attributes. If each defendant's conduct was judged not just against the law's general standards, but also by a fine-grained assessment of her particular capacities on this particular occasion, in these precise circumstances, then the grounds for excusing her conduct could multiply. To know the details of this particular defendant's character and situation at the time of, for example, a traffic accident might be to know that in some sense she could not have avoided it. And this, some assume, should generate either a complete or partial excuse. But, while factors such as these may be taken into account at the sentencing stage in the criminal law, they are almost completely irrelevant at the liability stage in private law.

That, when accepting exculpatory claims, the law rarely delves into the particularities of the defendant's context or character is reinforced by something else: such exculpatory claims are usually valid only if reasonable. Reasonableness requirements are the principal means by which the law treats those before it as abstract beings rather than as the beings they actually are. The third component of *LAJ* thus takes us to the core of the other two. All three are functionally connected since, both separately and combined, they serve to lead law's judgement away from particularity and toward abstraction.

The functional connection between the first two components becomes apparent as soon as we attempt to unpack them. The first, remember, is the presumptive identity component and it holds that the law regards those called before it

[11] In speaking of 'exculpatory claims' I do not intend to elide or even take a position on the plausibility of the oft-drawn distinction between justification and excuse. For some of the themes here see J Horder, *Excusing Crime* (Oxford, Clarendon Press, 2004) Ch 1 and 99–103.

as abstract beings. But what, exactly, does it entail? This, at the very least: that the law sees neither claimant nor defendant, neither accused nor victim, as the actual human beings they truly are, in all their detail and specificity. The law does not often see or even notice the specific set of abilities or experiences those being judged have, nor does it usually notice their different social, cultural, economic or ethnic backgrounds. Law's judgement is supposedly blind to these differences, treating Duke and pauper, man and woman, Christian and non-Christian, homo- and heterosexual, aesthete and philistine alike. And the law most obviously treats those brought before it alike, as the same, by assuming that all its addressees have the same bundle of formal legal rights.

Another way in which those judged by the law are treated as being both abstract and alike, is that all are usually held to the same general standards of conduct. This is the second—uniformity—component of *LAJ*. The standards are general in the sense that their content is the same and they apply to all those whom they address, applying whether or not particular addressees can actually live up to their requirements. Lack of interest in the specific capacities of particular individuals is, of course, the essence of reasonableness standards. The pass mark for examinations or driving tests is almost never set with a view of the abilities of particular candidates in mind. It is, rather, set with a view to assessing basic standards of competence anyone must achieve in order to succeed, provided it is possible for some to succeed. Whether or not specific candidates succeed, given their background, abilities and circumstances at the time of attempt, is irrelevant unless an exculpatory claim is triggered. This situation is obviously echoed in the law. Insofar as the law assumes all addressees can achieve the same standards of (usually reasonable) conduct, or embody the same standards of (usually reasonable) fortitude, it ignores obvious differences between them which actually determine whether or not they can achieve these standards on particular occasions. Holding those before the law to the same general standards is a means of treating them as abstract beings rather than as actual beings in all their particularity.

Most current legal systems contain standards for the assessment of a *defendant's* conduct or character that explicitly disregard the particularities of that individual, the context of their conduct, or both. Perhaps the most obvious private law example is the reasonable care standard in negligence and its cognates. In English and Scots law a defendant's conduct must be of the same standard as that of a reasonable person engaged in that kind of activity, a reasonable person being—by definition—reasonably competent. That the defendant cannot actually reach that standard is usually irrelevant.[12] There, are, however, some exceptional instances in which a judgement of negligence is influenced by the specific circumstances or particularities of a class of defendants. Child defendants are therefore sometimes held to a slightly different standard of care compared to that applied to most

[12] See *Nettleship v Weston* [1971] 2 QB 691 (UKCA); *Wilsher v Essex Area Health Authority* [1988] AC 1074 (UKHL); *Imbree v McNeilly* [2008] HCA 40.

adults.[13] There are also *dicta* in English negligence and nuisance cases suggesting that the level of a defendant's wealth will make a difference in the assessment of whether or not her conduct was reasonable.[14] Furthermore, in some jurisdictions it has been recognised that what is reasonably foreseeable for the purposes of establishing a duty of care in negligence can differ according to the ethnic and religious context of both claimant and defendant.[15]

If the requirement of reasonable care in negligence and the abstraction it involves sets a demanding standard, then the default standard of performance in contract law is even more stringent. It is not enough in many contracts for a defendant to have used reasonable endeavours to perform, since the standard of compliance is strict.[16] Thus, not only those unable to achieve a reasonable standard of performance are judged by a standard that is beyond them; so, too, are those capable of a reasonable level of performance. Both reasonableness and strict standards ignore the particularities and context of the individual being judged; both are therefore manifestations of *LAJ*.

A number of defences in English criminal law also rest upon assessments of reasonableness. The most problematic defence in recent years was the partial defence of provocation. To invoke this defence an accused had, *inter alia*, to establish that the alleged provocation was such as to lead any reasonable person to lose their self-control. A number of problems arose with this defence, both in terms of its rationale and its practical consequences. But one issue proved pre-eminently problematic: the determination of what a reasonable person is and how such a person behaves in specific contexts. Particularly fraught was the question of which physical features, character traits or habits of the accused should be regarded as pertinent to the alleged provocation.[17] The circumstances of the cases were usually such that endowing the reasonable person with one or other of these features made the putative provocation more rather than less salient. A substance abuser whose perception of the world is addled by abuse could well regard as provocation

[13] *McHale v Watson* (1966) 115 CLR 199 (HCAus); *Mullin v Richards and another* [1998] 1 All ER 920 (UKCA) and www.nytimes.com/2010/10/29/nyregion/29young.html (last accessed 3rd January 2017). Perhaps the first sustained analysis of the particular physical, psychological and other features of claimants and defendants regarded as salient by the American courts in determining tort liability was G Calabresi, *Ideals, Beliefs, Attitudes, and the Law* (Syracuse, Syracuse University Press, 1985) chs 2–4. Do not assume that the differential treatment of child defendants by the courts is unimpeachable: M Moran, *Rethinking the Reasonable Person* (Oxford, Clarendon Press, 2003) chs 2 and 3.

[14] *Knight v Home Office* [1990] 3 All ER 237 (UKHC); *East Suffolk Rivers Catchment Board v Kent* [1941] AC 74 (UKHL); *Goldman v Hargreave* [1967] 1 AC 645 (UKPC).

[15] See *Kavanagh v Aktar* (1998) NSWCA 779 (NSW, Aus); *Mustapha v Culligan of Canada Ltd* [2005] 138 ACWS 3rd 767 (Ontario, Can).

[16] *Rainieri v Miles* [1981] AC 1050, 1086 (UKHL). See also G Treitel and E Peel, *The Law of Contract*, 13th edn (London, Sweet and Maxwell, 2011) 834–36 and S Smith, *Contract Theory* (Oxford, Clarendon Press, 2004) Ch 10.

[17] Use of the past tense here is a result of the replacement of the provocation defence in English law by a statutory 'loss of control' defence (s 54–56 Coroners and Justice Act 2009, implemented 4 October 2010). For some vivid instances of the problems to which the defence gave rise in a number of jurisdictions, see *R v Morhall* [1996] AC 90 (UKHL); *Stingel v R* (1991) 171 CLR 312 (HCAus); *R v Thibert* [1996] 1 SCR 37 (SCCan).

conduct that in the eyes of others would be worthy of nothing more than laughter or a raised eyebrow. Of course, the greater the degree to which the reasonable person in provocation cases was endowed with the character, traits and habits of the accused, and situated as the accused was situated at the time, the less weight the reasonable person standard carried. The thrust of some decisions in England and elsewhere had been to all but obliterate, and then reaffirm, the distinction between a reasonable person standard and a subjective standard tailor-made for the particular accused. In England and Wales, at least, this process has been arrested as a result of ss 54–56 of the Coroners and Justice Act 2009 and subsequent case-law.[18]

A less prominent but equally interesting emerging issue in the criminal law is that of so-called 'cultural defences'.[19] While quite different in doctrinal terms, this issue has some resonance with recent developments in the provocation defence. This is found in the fact that cultural defences—whatever their particular form or detail—claim that the accused's conduct is either justified, excused or mitigated by the fact that it is right, reasonable or normal within a specific cultural group. The general claim by proponents of such defences is clear. It is that once account is taken of the accused's background and beliefs (and, perhaps, other features of their cultural context), then their conduct, which would ordinarily be contrary to the criminal law, is understandable and its culpability either reduced or eradicated.

Does private law treat *claimants* in the same way as it often treats defendants, namely, as abstract beings? Some doctrines suggest so. The law of contract, for example, only rarely awards damages for what can be called subjective losses which, on one view, are understood as those that arise from the specific non-market valuation claimants put upon performance.[20] Although different from one another in detail, the remoteness rules for damages in contract and tort seemingly ensure that claimants cannot claim for injury that results from their particular sensitivities. Insofar as such injury and the losses that result from it are not foreseeable by a reasonable person, they go uncompensated. Thus, while unlikely to be a goal of the remoteness rules, one of their practical effects is to treat claimants as abstract rather than actual beings. This effect is, however, almost completely negated with respect to some physical and psychological features of the claimant by the eggshell

[18] A list of problematic pre-2010 cases has to include *R v Smith (Morgan)* [2000] 4 All ER 289 (UKHL); *Luc Thiet Thuan v R* [1997] AC 131 (UKPC); *Jersey v Holley* [2005] 2 AC 580 (UKPC); and *R v Van Dongen* [2005] EWCA Crim 1728. On the changes effected by the 2009 Act and the status of the pre-existing law, see *R v Clinton* [2012] EWCA Crim 2; *R v Dawes* [2013] EWCA Crim 322; and *R v Gurpinar* [2015] EWCA Crim 178. A typically sure-footed overview is provided by D Ormerod and K Laird, *Smith and Hogan's Criminal Law*, 14th edn (Oxford, Oxford University Press, 2015) 576–604.

[19] An interesting introductory discussion is A Phillips, 'When Culture Means Gender: Issues of Cultural Defence in the English Courts' (2003) 66 *Modern Law Review* 510–31. Much more comprehensive is AD Renteln, *The Cultural Defense* (New York, Oxford University Press, 2004). One of the most vivid cases is *People v Kimura* No A-091133 (Sup Ct, LA County, 24th April 1985), on which see Renteln, ibid, 25.

[20] See *Ruxley Electronics and Construction Ltd v Forsyth* [1996] AC 344 (UKHL) and *Farley v Skinner* [2002] 2 AC 732 (UKHL).

skull rule in the law of negligence.[21] If the claimant has an unusual sensitivity to a particular process or form of treatment inflicted by the defendant in breach of a duty of care, the consequence being that the claimant is affected far more seriously than others would be, then the defendant cannot escape liability for the claimant's commensurately greater losses.[22] Much the same rule holds in the criminal law.[23]

By insisting tortfeasors and accused take their victims as they find them, the law is recognising some particularities of the actual claimant or victim before the court. There are other areas of private law—defamation, for example—in which the courts should in principle be willing to take seriously the claimant's cultural or religious context. It is surely right that a statement which clearly does not defame a non-Muslim can be defamatory when made about a Muslim. Alongside these instances in which the law recognises some aspects of a victim's particularity, there are doctrines which suppress other such aspects. In the tort and crime of battery, for instance, victims must display reasonable fortitude in light of the touching, buffeting and other non-consensual contact of everyday life.[24] The criminal law also rules out consent as a defence to some crimes whether or not the particular 'victim' consented, the animating notion of this prohibition being in part the idea that reasonable people will never agree to some forms of treatment by others.[25]

B. Public Law

My claim here is that the first two components of *LAJ* are central to some important constitutional and non-constitutional equality law provisions, while the third component is only a peripheral presence. An expansive survey of constitutional and equality provisions, along with their extensive layers of case-law, is not possible here. Rather, I concentrate upon a few very important provisions, chosen to highlight the first two components of *LAJ* at work. 'Work' here means—as it did in the discussion of private and criminal law—that the components operate as fixed agitation points against which departures must react and be tested. The claim is not that the outcomes of all (or even most) of the cases mentioned illustrate the two components being realised to the maximum degree. That would indeed be exceptional. The components are nevertheless almost always in play even when the outcomes of cases do a poor job of instantiating them; the components are still affirmed in such cases, although seemingly as obstacles around which judgements navigate. They can be honoured in the breach.

[21] The relevant psychological features, in the American cases, usually relate to matters of belief rather than psychological fortitude: see Calabresi (n 13) Chs 3 and 4. The eggshell skull rule is not, of course, confined only to negligence.

[22] A masterly treatment, although now slightly doctrinally outdated, is HLA Hart and T Honoré, *Causation in the Law*, 2nd edn (Oxford, Clarendon Press, 1985) 172–76.

[23] See *R v Blaue* [1975] 3 All ER 446 (UKCA) and the discussion in Hart and Honoré, ibid, 360–62.

[24] See *Re F* [1990] 2 AC 1 (UKHL) 72–73 (Lord Goff).

[25] See, for example, *R v Brown* [1994] 1 AC 212 (UKHL).

The first two components of law's abstract judgement feature in 'general', 'particularistic' and 'hybrid' equality regimes. The equal protection clause of Amendment XIV (1) of the US Constitution is a central instance of a general equality regime by virtue of its insistence that persons within states not be denied equal protection of the laws. No specific form of conduct which could constitute a denial of equal protection is mentioned, it being the job of the courts—and the Supreme Court in particular—to determine this on a case by case basis. Particularistic equality regimes, by contrast, address specific instances of unfair or discriminatory treatment one by one and usually prohibit such treatment only in specific spheres of activity or interaction. New Zealand equality law could perhaps be regarded in this way and the UK certainly used to have a particularistic equality regime. Hybrid regimes, unsurprisingly, combine elements of the other two: s 15 (1) of the Canadian Charter of Rights and Freedoms combines a non-exclusive list of types of discrimination with a general invocation of equality before and under the law, while the UK had a range of specific statutes (many of which were repealed and replaced by the Equality Act 2010)[26] in tandem with the general equality provisions found in EU law, the European Convention on Human Rights (ECHR) and the Human Rights Act 1998.

The uniformity component requires that the law judge its addressees by reference to general and objective standards equally applicable to all. The most obvious denial of this component consists of explicitly different laws for allegedly different groups. For most lawyers these are *prima facie* instances of direct discrimination. But the uniformity component can be denied in a less obvious yet still familiar way, by laws which, although they do not explicitly treat putatively different groups differently, affect one group far more adversely or far more beneficially than another. These are *prima facie* instances of indirect discrimination.[27]

General equality regimes like the equal protection clause of Amendment XIV currently have little difficulty in invalidating many directly discriminatory laws, such as those setting different age limits for men and women for the consumption of alcohol, and this is so regardless of the lower level of scrutiny used by the US Supreme Court in gender cases.[28] The old 'separate but equal' racial segregation cases, however, show that even an ostensibly strong, general equality regime need not always be interpreted as requiring that the same legal standards must apply to all. Of course, Amendment XIV is now interpreted quite differently, the court's current approach of subjecting racial classifications to strict scrutiny being one means of attempting to ensure that the same laws govern all.[29] Far more problematic

[26] For an overview of the 2010 Act and the relevant case law, see B Hepple, *Equality: The Legal Framework*, 2nd edn (Oxford, Hart Publishing, 2014) and K Monaghan, *Monaghan on Equality Law*, 2nd edn (Oxford, Clarendon Press, 2013).

[27] In using the direct/indirect distinction, I do not imply that it is unproblematic; its difficulties are not, however, central to the argument here.

[28] See *Craig v Boren* 429 US 190 (1976).

[29] The supposed originator of the separate but equal doctrine, *Plessy v Fergusson* 163 US 537 (1896), was laid to rest by *Brown v Board of Education of Topeka* 347 US 483 (1954) (Brown I) and 349 US

for the court have been instances in which the disproportionate adverse impact of particular laws has been challenged under the equal protection clause. Many different laws, including zoning regulations, preferential hiring requirements and educational admission tests, have been examined by the court on numerous occasions, with very different results.[30]

Among hybrid equality regimes, Canada has tackled the problem of apparently directly discriminatory laws in a number of important cases. A quartet of Supreme Court of Canada cases—*Andrews v Law Society of BC*; *Law v Canada*; *Nova Scotia (AG) v Walsh*; and *Gosselin v Quebec (AG)*[31]—show that, while the court takes a close look at laws treating some differently than others by, for example, setting welfare benefits at different levels for different age groups or by awarding survivor benefits only to those over a certain age, such laws will not automatically be discriminatory under s 15 (1) of the Canadian Charter of Rights and Freedoms. The test for compliance with s 15 (1) was clearly laid down in *Law* and was designed, in part, to ensure that not every instance of differential treatment will fail it. Although the court's approach to equality of impact could be characterised as a relatively cautious one, there being no presumption that all laws which treat addressees differently are suspect, there can be no suggestion that the court does not take seriously the idea of equal impact, or the uniformity component of juridical equality. In the UK, explicitly discriminatory laws, such as those prohibiting certain groups from working in particular ways or industries, have been repealed because they are incompatible with EU law.[32] In both jurisdictions, laws and practices which disproportionately affect specific groups have also been subject to scrutiny, raising very similar difficulties to those faced in the US cases.[33]

294 (1955) (Brown II). A fascinating account of Amendment XIV's interpretative history is provided by W Nelson, *The Fourteenth Amendment: From Political Principle to Judicial Doctrine* (Cambridge, Massachusetts, Harvard University Press, 1995).

[30] See *Village of Arlington Heights v Metropolitan Housing Development Corp*, 429 US 252 (1977); *Personnel Administrator of Massachusetts v Feeney* 442 US 256 (1979); and *Washington v Davis* 426 US 229 (1976). For an overview, see E Chemerinsky, *Constitutional Law*, 4th edn (New York, Wolters Kluwer, 2013) Ch 7.

[31] Respectively: [1989] 1 SCR 143; [1999] 1 SCR 497; [2002] 4 SCR 325; and [2002] 4 SCR 429. For discussion see R Sharpe and K Roach, *The Charter of Rights and Freedom*, 4th edn (Toronto, Irwin Law, 2009) Ch 15 and PW Hogg, *Constitutional Law of Canada*, 5th edn (Scarborough, Carswell, 2007) Vol II, Ch 55.

[32] See Sex Discrimination Act 1986, s 7 and Employment Act 1989, s 9 (both repealed by the Equality Act 2010, sch 27).

[33] The British position differs according to whether domestic, EU or ECHR principles held sway. For an instance of the former, see Sex Discrimination Act 1975, s 1 (1) (b) (repealed by the Equality Act 2010, sch 27); the EU position begins with Council Directive 97/80/EC of 15 December 1997 on the burden of proof in cases of discrimination based on sex (Burden of Proof Directive) [1998] OJ L14 and Council Directive 2000/43/EC of 29 June 2000 implementing the principle of equal treatment between persons irrespective of racial or ethnic origin (Race Equality Directive) [2000] OJ L180, while the European Court of Human Rights' (ECtHR) view of indirect discrimination is still well represented by *Abdulazizz, Cabales and Balkandali v UK* Series A No 42 (1985) 7 EHRR 471. Indirect discrimination is now explicitly identified in s 19 of the Equality Act 2010.

The second limb of the presumptive identity component, which insists that the law's addressees are identical in that each is equally entitled to the same bundle of formal legal rights and abilities, is in play in many equality provisions. Bans on interracial and same-sex marriage have been held unconstitutional under Amendment XIV and so, too, has the making of child custody decisions on the basis of race; the US Supreme Court has also held that the right to procreate is one enjoyed by all to the same degree.[34] The Court has ruled, in addition, that all must have the same access to the courts, that the voting rights of some citizens cannot be restricted, and that all are entitled to travel between states.[35] Access to public education cannot, the Court has held, be based exclusively on gender or race: these factors might be used, among others, in admissions processes but a blanket refusal to admit certain groups is almost always likely to be unconstitutional under Amendment XIV.[36]

In jurisdictions with either hybrid or particularistic equality regimes, cases of this type—which deal with civil rights—are likely to be covered by specific statutory provisions and have also, in some instances, been tackled by the courts. *AG v Quilter*,[37] a right to marry case decided by the New Zealand Court of Appeal, created a space for the presumptive identity component even while denying it and arriving at an outcome that few friends of equality could admire. The Court held that the Marriage Act 1955 could not be interpreted to include same-sex marriage. It concluded that this either did not make the Act incompatible with s 6 and s 10 of the New Zealand Bill of Rights Act 1990 and part II of the Human Rights Act 1993 or, if it did, that it was a form of incompatibility implicitly approved by the legislature. *Quilter* thus denied the presumptive identity component any role in this area of law, yet nevertheless implicitly affirmed that component's general importance via Tipping J's claim that New Zealand's specific anti-discrimination provisions 'gave substance to the principle of equality under the law'.[38] None of the other judges in the Court of Appeal disagreed with this claim and its significance, for present purposes, is this: there is almost no better way of attempting to ensure equality under the law than by taking the presumptive identity component seriously.[39]

The courts in a number of jurisdictions have also been vigilant with regard to interferences or restrictions upon equally distributed private law rights like, for example, the right to contract. This right is not one that can be exercised in

[34] See *Loving v Virginia* 388 US 1 (1967); *Palmore v Sidoti* 466 US 429 (1984); *Skinner v Oklahoma ex rel Willliamson* 316 US 535 (1942); and *Obergefell v Hodges* 576 US (2015).

[35] See, for example, *US v Guest* 383 US 745 (1966) and *Harper v Virginia Board of Elections* 383 US 663 (1966). These and the cases noted in n 34, above, can also be tackled under the due process clause of Amendment XIV, as 'fundamental rights' cases: see Chemerinsky (n 30) Ch 8.

[36] *US v Virginia* 518 US 515 (1996); *Gratz v Bollinger* 539 US 244 (2003); *Grutter v Bollinger* 539 US 306 (2003).

[37] [1998] 1 NZLR 523.

[38] ibid at 573.

[39] For an illustration, see my 'Equality Under and Before the Law' (2011) 61 *University of Toronto Law Journal* 411–65.

a discriminatory way, since the courts have regarded that as a practical denial of the entitlement of all to be able to enter into contractual and related arrangements.[40] Nor, for some courts, can the right be overly limited in the name of substantive equality. Thus courts in both general and hybrid equality regimes have held that contract-compliance provisions—terms inserted into contracts by one party, usually a government agency, designed to eliminate discrimination or reduce economic disadvantage—are, except for some fairly specific circumstances, incompatible with broader equality provisions.[41] In the UK, differential private pension entitlements have also been set aside as a result of conflict with EU law and the ECHR. These entitlements are, of course, contractual rights and, in the UK at least, they have traditionally been different for men and women, the retirement age for the former being 65 and the latter 60. The Courts have had no hesitation in pointing out the discriminatory character of these contractual terms and that has led to a uniform normal retirement age for men and women.[42]

Some—perhaps all—of the cases noted in this subsection can be cast in two roles simultaneously, as illustrations of *both* the uniformity and presumptive identity components. And, that being so, it might be inferred that the distinction between these two components is therefore infirm. The inference should be resisted, however, since a degree of overlap between the two components cannot show that they are identical. For the inference to be valid, each and every case subsumed under one component must also be appropriately subsumable under the other. But this seems unlikely, since one cannot convert, without remainder, the first limb of the presumptive identity component (which presumes that addressees of the law have the same physical and cognitive capacities) into the uniformity component (which holds that the same laws should apply to all). The former is about the nature of the law's addressees, while the latter is about the content of laws themselves: their reach is therefore quite different and there seems no obvious path in which a claim about the nature of law's addressees can be converted into one about the overall effect of a particular law or the law in general.

Finally, we come to the limited avoidability component. Its role in some equality provisions, although peripheral when compared with the other two components,

[40] In many jurisdictions the standard limitations on contracting included only age, intoxication and sanity. Where private law systems in the common law world did not include a non-discrimination constraint as a result of normal incremental development, such provisions were inserted as part of the process of 'constitutionalising' private law: see, for example, the Equality Act 2010 s 142 for an instance from the UK. An excellent cross-jurisdictional overview of the 'constitutionalising' process is D Friedmann and D Barak-Erez (eds), *Human Rights in Private Law* (Oxford, Hart Publishing, 2001).

[41] For the US position see *Ararand Constructors v Pena* 515 US 200 (1995); the EU position is stated in Case 31/87 *Gebroeders Beentjes BV v the Netherlands* [1989] ECR 4365; Case C-360/89 *Commission v Italy* [1992] ECR 1-3401; and Case C-513/99 *Concordia Bus Finland Oy Ab* v *City of Helsinki & HKL Bussilikenne* [2002] ECR I-7213.

[42] See *Barber v Guardian Royal Exchange* [1991] QB 344 1990; *Foster Wheeler Limited v Andrew Hanley and others* [2009] EWCA 1 WLR 235 and Equality Act 2010 s 61–63. On the often complex interplay between EU equality provisions and those in the ECHR, see S Besson, 'Gender Discrimination under EU and ECHR Law: *Never Shall the Twain Meet?*' (2008) 8 *Human Rights Law Review* 647–82.

is nevertheless significant. The component, remember, holds that the application of legal standards is mitigated only by a limited number and range of exculpatory claims. That the component operates within various equality regimes is plain: some such regimes allow no excuses or defences, however reasonable, for some forms of discrimination, while other forms of discrimination can be justified on tightly circumscribed and usually reasonable grounds.[43] None of the jurisdictions mentioned here recognise a 'I just like/can't help wrongfully discriminating' defence.

C. Two Points

The first makes explicit what was implicit in the preceding sketch of *LAJ*: it is not ubiquitous. It is more deeply embedded in some areas of legal doctrine than in others. A more expansive survey would surely disclose areas in which it has little influence.[44] Judged across entire legal systems, the abstract nature of *LAJ* is thus a matter of degree, of more or less. There is, moreover, undoubtedly a constant process of mediation between more and less abstract forms of judgement within areas of legal doctrine where *LAJ* is entrenched.

Although a pure form of *LAJ* is not ubiquitous, it is still probably rightly regarded as the focal meaning, or paradigmatic instance, of bourgeois law's judgement.[45] For, despite the many doctrinal departures from a pure and unyielding form of abstract judgement, the latter remains intact and central just because the former are usually regarded as exceptions. That they are seen as abnormal, as in need of justification, attests to the power the pure form of *LAJ* has over swathes of juristic thought.[46] This mixed picture might suggest that *LAJ* is actually in tension with a model of pure particularistic judgement, rather than being in tension with less abstract versions of itself. The question of that with which *LAJ* can and must be contrasted is the second point here. A number of considerations suggest that the tension cannot be understood as one between abstract judgement, on the one hand, and pure particularistic judgement, on the other.

First among these is that law surely is, in some significant sense, a matter of subjecting human conduct to *general* rules. And general rules are themselves unavoidably

[43] For the position in the UK, see S Fredman, *Discrimination Law*, 2nd edn (Oxford, Clarendon Press, 2011) 190–202 and Monaghan (n 26) Ch 13. The Equality Act 2010 broadly follows suit, containing the standard 'reasonable readjustment' provisions in relation to some forms of discrimination and to some contexts: see, for example, s 189 and schs 13 and 21.

[44] Two obvious examples are the sentencing stage in criminal law and the 'best interests of the child' principle in family law. Note that the latter ostensibly particularistic form of judgement is usually deployed not in relation to either claimant or defendant but rather to their offspring or ward.

[45] On focal meaning, see J Finnis, *Natural Law and Natural Rights*, 2nd edn (Oxford, Clarendon Press, 2011) 9–18, 277–81and 429–31.

[46] Evidence in support of this claim can be garnered from the critical response to cases such as *Morhall*, *Stingel* and *Thibert* (n 17) and *Smith* (n 18). Much the same responses are provoked by cases varying the standard of the duty in negligence.

a matter of abstraction, a means of setting aside or ignoring particularity. The rule 'drive on the right' applies to all drivers whatever their context or particular capabilities: it means drive on the right *regardless* of such matters. Some might deny that law and legal judgement must invoke general rules. Frederick Schauer, for example, suggests that

> disputes could … be *resolved* largely without reference to … rules imposing substantive constraint on the content of decisions. Having been empowered to resolve a dispute, the adjudicator would be authorised … to come to a conclusion as open-endedly as appropriate in the circumstances.[47]

While this is undoubtedly possible—an adjudicator could be empowered to resolve disputes however she likes, deciding one by flipping a coin, another by the reference to the height of the disputants, etc—it is important to see that general rules are nevertheless still in play here. First, as Schauer himself notes, 'empowering rules create the institutions of dispute resolution and empower certain officials to resolve certain sorts of disputes'.[48] These rules must surely be general to some extent if they are to perform their task. Second, the dispute here must, if genuine, have a subject-matter, a basis, and what else could that be except some or other standard of conduct for the disputants? If the dispute is not about whether one or other disputant did or refrained from doing something required or otherwise appropriate, then what could it conceivably be about? The dispute must revolve around either a standard of conduct, in which case the standard is likely to be general, or a contested matter of fact. A standard of conduct need not be general as a matter of necessity, since it is possible that a bespoke standard be created for and applied to no one but the disputants in question. Such a limited standard would be rare in a developed legal system. Furthermore, such a standard might, by virtue of its specificity, come into tension with some components of the rule of law ideal in such a legal system.

A second consideration showing it is implausible to regard *LAJ* as being in tension with pure particularistic judgement is both banal and true. It is that the idea of pure particularistic judgement is *prima facie* senseless. If this is judgement based upon all the specificities, physical and mental, of those being judged, and responsive to the context and all the relevant circumstances of their conduct, without recourse to any general rule or standard, then it is hard to see how anything is being judged. If the reply here is: 'the person before us' then it invites this question: 'against what standard?' If we allow (as we surely must) that judgement assumes a standard against which conduct or character or both are assessed, then

[47] F Schauer, *Playing by the Rules* (Oxford, Clarendon Press, 1991) 10 (emphasis added). It will be clear to anyone that the conception of rules in play in the picture of law's abstract judgement developed here is much the same as Schauer's conception of rules as entrenched generalisations: ibid, chs 2–5. For an additional, lighter-touch discussion of the same issue, see F Schauer, *Profiles, Probabilities, and Stereotypes* (Cambridge, Massachusetts, Harvard University Press, 2003).

[48] Schauer, *Playing by the Rules*, ibid.

this problem of intelligibility disappears, but we face another difficulty. This is that extremely fine-grained responsiveness to the character and context of those whose conduct is being judged can undermine the power of the standard against which they are assessed.

Suppose, for example, that the pass mark for an examination is 40 per cent. If, in assessing whether a candidate has failed, we have recourse to much more than the bare figure of their examination performance, taking into account and allowing marks for all the aspects of the candidate's character and context that affected their preparation for and performance in the examination, then the pass mark itself plays a relatively minor role in judging performance. Indeed, as the range of factors taken into account to explain and mitigate a 'failed' performance expands, so the weight of the standard embodied in the pass mark declines. While its weight cannot diminish to zero, provided the standard is still in force, it can get close to that if a massive number of factors can serve to turn a mark of less than 40 into a mark of 40. The rule that the pass mark is 40 persists, but the ways of getting 40 far exceed what was once the primary way of achieving that mark, namely, by answering a sufficient number of questions at or above the pass level.

That *LAJ* must be contrasted with less abstract (but not pure particularistic) judgement prefigures another and related warning. It is that *LAJ* should not be flippantly contrasted with moral or ethical judgement. This is a mistake because there is no *a priori* reason why the models in play in one domain should not be similar or even exactly the same as those in another. Moreover, if the contrast is motivated by the thought that morality's judgement is always and ever particular, then that is surely questionable.[49] Morality's judgement is sometimes abstract and sometimes less abstract, at least as a matter of moral practice. We accept that, generally speaking, an important characteristic of some moral judgements is their generality and abstraction: we think, for instance, that some moral duties are owed by all human beings *qua* human beings to all human beings *qua* human beings. Of course, this is a euphemistic way of referring to such duties for, although agent-neutral in the sense that they are owed by all human beings regardless of their conduct or projects, they are almost never unspecific in terms of their subjects and objects. Thus, the agent-neutral duty to aid those in mortal peril is defined by the situation of both those who owe it and those to whom it is owed. The duty is not one actually owed to 'all human beings' but only to 'all human beings in mortal peril' by 'those able to do something about that'. This does not, however, entail that the judgement which gives rise to the duty is in any but the most trivial sense particularistic; rather, the judgement is simply less general than it might be.

In addition to fairly broad, agent-neutral duties, our moral lives also contain agent-relative duties rooted in our past conduct or arising from our context.[50]

[49] Schauer's reading of act-utilitarianism comes close to this: *Playing by the Rules* (n 47).

[50] See D Parfit, *Reasons and Persons* (Oxford, Clarendon Press, 1984) 143 and T Nagel, *The View from Nowhere* (New York, Oxford University Press, 1986) 152–54.

The judgements that give rise to these duties—the judgement that, for example, some of my duties to my children are more demanding than some of my duties to the children of strangers—are obviously more particular or less abstract than some of those that generate agent-neutral duties. Yet it is far from clear that one kind of duty and judgement clearly dominates the other: agent-neutral and agent-relative duties, and the more and less abstract judgements that generate them, are undoubtedly both significant parts of the moral landscape. This relatively complex view of moral practice might be contested at the level of moral philosophy. Some moral philosophers might, indeed, argue that it embodies a flagrant contradiction. Arguments to that end, interestingly, can come from two completely differently directions: that ordinary moral practice is contradictory either because all moral duties, and the reasons that support them, are general and invariable, or because all moral duties and their supporting reasons are in fact variable and context-sensitive.[51] Each claim resonates with a broader position about the place of general principles in moral reasoning, and each can imply a view of the role of reason and impartiality in morality and moral deliberation.[52] The complexities here are side-stepped in what follows, the book's only commitment on this topic being that moral practice, like law, embodies both more and less abstract models of judgement.

II. Why and How?

Why is *LAJ* worthy of further study? And, if it is, how should we go about studying it? My answer to the former question is not fully unpacked until the end of this book: only by engaging with the topic can we be sure that the engagement was worthwhile. But a more concrete answer than this is necessary for those impatient with the vague prospect that something interesting might eventually be uncovered. I also provide an answer to the latter question, since it is important to appreciate the parameters and methodological assumptions that frame the discussion in the remainder of the book.

A. Why?

There are at least four considerations that make *LAJ* worthy of our attention. The first holds that *LAJ* is historically significant. Its emphasis on generality and

[51] The eye of this intellectual storm was the dispute between moral particularists and their opponents. For an introduction to one version of particularism see J Dancy, 'The Particularist's Progress' in B Hooker and M Little (eds), *Moral Particularism* (Oxford, Clarendon Press, 2000) Ch 6 and his *Ethics Without Principles* (Oxford, Clarendon Press, 2004).

[52] On which see L Blum, 'Against Deriving Particularity' in Hooker and Little, ibid, Ch 9.

abstraction could be seen, by historically inclined lawyers, as generating a distinction between feudal (or medieval) law, on the one hand, and bourgeois (or liberal) law, on the other. If the former was made up of different legal incidences tied to a variety of fairly rigid roles, one's rights and obligations being determined by those roles, then the latter seems distinctive in its lack of such rigidity and because all addressees of the law are legally formally equal. Law's abstract judgement in part embodies the latter idea and this could plausibly be regarded as a constitutive characteristic of bourgeois law.

For our purposes, English feudalism had two principal features. It was a system of order in which, first, economic production and the status, opportunities and life chances, along with the legal rights, duties and other incidents, of most members of the community depended upon holding and granting interests in land. It was also, second, an order marked by the fact that some holders of interests in land exercised considerable private jurisdiction over others.[53] A consequence of these two features was that the legal system of feudal England explicitly and systematically distinguished between different categories of addressee and, as a result, upheld a rigid system of social stratification and entrenched social immobility. There was no genuine sense in which all addressees of the law were regarded as the same before it; nor were addressees of the law always bound by the same laws. The law recognised a number of different legal statuses and these determined one's legal rights and duties, liabilities and immunities, in a fairly rigid way. The legal 'sorts and conditions of men' included, *inter alia*, that of Earl and Baron, Knight, serf, member of religious order, Clergy, Alien and Jew.[54] These legal sorts and conditions were not open to one as different choices that might be made. Rather, one's legal status was usually set for life and almost entirely a consequence of one's social rank when born. The qualifications 'usually' and 'almost entirely' are necessary because some degree of mobility existed between some (but assuredly not all) sorts and conditions. This fact does nothing to undermine the judgement that feudal society was hierarchical and rigidly stratified; nor does it make implausible the

[53] The utility of the term 'feudalism' and its cognates (feudal, the feudal system, etc) has been and still is vigorously contested by some historians (the *locus classicus* is E Brown, 'The Tyranny of a Concept: Feudalism and Historians of Medieval Europe' (1974) 79 *American Historical Review* 1063–88). The simplistic characterisations of feudalism and feudal legality adopted in this book do not purport to be of use to historians, but accord with what some historians and some historically informed thinkers say: K Marx, *Capital* I, Vol. 35 *Marx-Engels Collected Works* (London, Lawrence and Wishart, 1996) 706–751 and *Capital* III, Vol. 37 *Marx-Engels Collected Works* (London, Lawrence and Wishart, 1998) Ch XLVII; P Anderson, *Passages from Antiquity to Feudalism* (London, New Left Books 1974) part 2, I; C Hill, *The English Revolution 1640* (London, Lawrence and Wishart, 1955) Preface; JGA Pocock, *The Ancient Constitution and the Feudal Law* (Cambridge, Cambridge University Press, 1987 (reissue)) 68–69 and chs IV and V. A brief, clear and non-technical account of tenure and related matters in the shift from early to late middle ages is C Brooks, *Law, Politics and Society in Early Modern England* (Cambridge, Cambridge University Press, 2008) 322–41.

[54] F Pollock and F Maitland, *History of English Law Vol. 1* (Cambridge, Cambridge University Press, 1968) 407.

claim that such 'social immobility and hierarchy ... suggest[ed] a view of rights as inherently unequal privileges enjoyed by the established estates'.[55]

One thing abundantly clear about many contemporary legal systems is that they lack the range of explicit statuses and ranks, and thus the differentiated bundles of legal rights, duties and other incidences attached to them, characteristic of feudal legal systems. While truncated echoes of the notions of due process of law, of equal standing before and under the law, and of impartial application of the law were not unknown to feudal legal systems, thanks mainly to the influence of Roman law, they are undoubtedly to the forefront of contemporary law's self-understanding. There is probably no single point at which this transition in the nature of law and its own self-understanding occurred; it was surely a gradual process that went hand in hand with the development of mercantile, capitalist economies. Indeed, the practical and emancipatory power of ideas about due process of law, equal standing, impartiality and equality of legal rights has been regarded as one of the principal drivers of the capitalist revolution.[56] Be that as it may, the core historical claim relied upon here is a minimal one. It is that *LAJ* and its near relatives (due process, generality, equal rights and impartiality) are more explicitly in play in the legal systems of contemporary and early capitalist societies than in that of feudal England. And this difference surely merits some attention.

The second reason why *LAJ* merits attention is that it seems deeply morally counter-intuitive. The initial response of almost all first year law students, and many ordinary people, to cases like *Nettleship v Weston* and other instances of strict liability, is that they just cannot be right.[57] The fact that the law holds those it judges to standards some cannot hope to achieve provides non-lawyers and would-be lawyers with a moral jolt. Such a jolt also arises from the related realisation that the law deliberately ignores much about the character, context and knowledge of those before it, so that makers of good faith mistakes and those not wilfully ignorant can often be trapped in the law's maw. Thus, convicting a mother for ritually scaring her sons, a relatively benign and common practice in their community, seems just as troubling as holding Mrs Weston to a standard with which she cannot comply.[58] *LAJ*'s capacity to deliver such moral jolts is part of what makes it interesting and an examination of its normative standing should throw informative light upon the grounds for these moral shocks. While *LAJ* is not the only aspect of bourgeois law with the capacity to generate moral disquiet, that

[55] NE Simmonds, *The Decline of Juridical Reason* (Manchester, Manchester University Press, 1984) 42.

[56] See M Tigar and M Levy, *Law and the Rise of Capitalism*, 2nd edn (New York, Monthly Review Press, 2000) parts IV and V and note O Gierke's bold claim ('[t]he intellectual force which finally dissolved the medieval view of the nature of human Groups [sic] was the law of nature') in *Natural Law and the Theory of Society Vol. I*, translated by E Barker (Cambridge, Cambridge University Press, 1934) at 35.

[57] *Nettleship v Weston* (n 12). Lest it be thought a mistake to call this form of liability strict see: T Honoré, *Responsibility and Fault* (Oxford, Hart Publishing, 1999) Ch 2.

[58] *R v Adesanya*, *The Times*, 16 July 1974 at 3. See also [1983] *Crim LR* at 720–21.

capacity certainly triggers a number (but not all) of the critical responses to *LAJ* sketched in the following paragraphs.

The third reason why *LAJ* is worthy of examination is that many jurists and philosophers think that there is a great deal wrong with it. Numbered among these jurists and philosophers are some of the leading thinkers of their time and their views therefore merit serious attention and interrogation. While it would be an exaggeration to say that these thinkers regard *LAJ* as the source of all bourgeois law's problems, they undoubtedly view it as deeply problematic. The charge-sheet is not, however, always drafted in such a way as to explicitly identify *LAJ* as a general target. Rather, some charges are against something ostensibly more general (bourgeois or liberal law) or much more specific (the conditions for liability responsibility in criminal law) than *LAJ*. Yet the effect of this rich and varied charge-sheet is just the same as if *LAJ* were explicitly named, for all of the complaints serve to undermine it also. We must be careful when delineating these charges to note overlaps and similarities without eliding significant distinctions. With that in mind, we can separate at least four different but sometimes related strands in the critique of *LAJ*.

The first takes us back to history, albeit in a rather different way than that already noted. This indictment holds that contemporary bourgeois law is in the grip of a significant historical transition. Although the underlying, substantive claim is the same in each case, this process has been described quite differently, three of the most interesting descriptions being that it is a shift from modern law to postmodern law, from autonomous law to responsive law, or from legal order to post-liberal legal order.[59] If these claims are true, and if our assertion that *LAJ* is a fundamental component of current law is also right, then the further inference that *LAJ* is an historical anachronism seems almost irresistibly tempting. Whereas law in the advanced capitalist countries may once have embodied *LAJ*, these societies have changed significantly since the birth of capitalism and so, too, it is claimed, have their legal systems. On this view, the legal systems of these societies are now taking a historically unique form in which *LAJ*, its cognates and many other features of bourgeois legality, are but residues soon to be completely transcended.[60] Law's abstract judgement is rather like the hovel left standing in a cityscape of gleaming new towers: it is of no value, save as a reminder of how far we have come.

[59] In the order stated, the three claims belong to B Edgeworth, *Law, Modernity and Postmodernity* (Aldershot, Ashgate, 2003); P Nonet and P Selznick, *Law and Society in Transition* (New Jersey, Transaction Publishers, 2005 (originally published in 1978)); and R Unger, *Law in Modern Society* (New York, Free Press, 1976). These writers are neither the first nor the only jurists to make this kind of claim. For a related and much earlier version, see E Pashukanis, *Law and Marxism: A General Theory* (London, Pluto Press, 1983; first published in Russian in 1924) Introduction, chs 2–4.

[60] It is therefore now appropriate 'to talk of the appearance of a discernibly new legal order, no less historically and sociologically distinctive than its predecessor': Edgeworth, ibid, vi.

The second strand, at its most abstract, holds that current law suppresses particularity and difference. What this means often depends upon the specific kind of difference in view, but in general terms the objection is that law serves to ignore many of the significant features of those before it.[61] We are what we are as a result of a complex web of experience, context and commitments. Our ethnic and cultural origins are manifold. We are men, women, or transgendered individuals; we are sons and daughters, mothers and fathers, employees and employers. We might share the same religious commitments, or have quite different ones, or none at all. We might be militant cyclists or campaigners for the environment; we could be active in the women's institute or have no interest at all in our communities. Some of us coach children's or adult's football teams while others are couch potatoes. We might be heterosexual or homosexual, hetero-phobe or homo-phobe, or any of the paths in between. But what we are—our distinct identities—is undoubtedly a product of what we have done and continue to do, and of where we have come from and of where we are. The critique in question holds that current law is incapable of recognising this seemingly undeniable truth. Furthermore, some aspects of current law, including *LAJ*, appear specifically designed to ignore much of what makes those that stand before the law the people they are, to filter out exactly this kind of information.

A specific version of this strand appears in those areas of Alan Norrie's work concerned with the criminal law. One of the principal overarching themes of Norrie's indictment of contemporary criminal law is that it is a morally insensitive means of assessing culpability. The way in which contemporary criminal law articulates the concepts it uses to assess culpability, and the way in which it distinguishes between factors which are and are not relevant to culpability, serve to suppress morally important features of the accused, their context and the context of the conduct in question. Norrie once thought this both regrettable and avoidable.[62] More general versions of this strand often put gender to the fore, the usual claim being that, despite its ostensible gender-neutrality, current law articulates and is informed by objectionably valorised notions of masculinity, on the

[61] Within the legal academy the intellectual inspiration of this line of thought has been deconstruction: chs 4–6 of D Cornell, *Philosophy of the Limit* (New York, Routledge, 1992) outline some of the challenges some versions of deconstruction present to current law. A similar task, more critically conducted, is the burden of J Balkin's 'Deconstruction's Legal Career' (2005) 27 *Cardozo Law Review* 719–40. A nuanced and admirably clear general treatment of some of the problems of abstraction (and categorisation) in current law is M Minow, *Making All the Difference* (Ithaca, Cornell University Press, 1990) Introduction and chs 1–3. The abstraction and universality of human rights law, which itself can be seen as a manifestation of law's abstract judgement, has been impugned in Hegel's name by C Douzinas, *The End of Human Rights* (Oxford, Hart Publishing, 2000) chs 10 and 12.

[62] See A Norrie, '"Simulacra of Morality?" Beyond the Ideal/Actuality Antinomies of Criminal Law' in A Duff (ed), *Philosophy and the Criminal Law: Principle and Critique* (Cambridge, Cambridge University Press, 1998) Ch 3 at 131–43 and contrast his *Punishment, Responsibility and Justice* (Oxford, Clarendon Press, 2000) 232. Chapters 1–2 and 9 of the latter are a fine statement of Norrie's view of the criminal law, that view being generalised in *Law and the Beautiful Soul* (London, The Glasshouse Press, 2005) chs 1–7 and *Justice and the Slaughter-Bench: Essays on Law's Broken Dialectic* (London, Routledge, 2016) part I.

one hand, and inappropriate images of femininity, on the other. This argument has been substantiated in numerous contexts, including criminal law and many areas of private and public law.[63] Mayo Moran's demonstration that tort law has recourse to normal but discriminatory standards of judgement when assessing the conduct of playing boys and girls, is one among a number of compelling examples.[64] This strand of critique can cut in two distinct directions. One is of a piece with the current point: the law should be more sensitive to those that stand before it and thus, at the very least, register the significance of gender in all its forms. The alternative takes the complaint closer to the territory of the following two strands, for the objection is not that the law fails to register all forms of gender, but that it ought not to register only one. If the law's standards of judgement are interpreted solely in light of a distinctly male world-view, then the law might work to the disadvantage of those who do not or cannot share that view. And that, of course, looks like a form of unfair or unequal treatment.

A third strand in the critique of *LAJ* holds that, although law is often a means of treating people equally, it is simultaneously and equally often a means of treating them unequally. Treating different people as if they were the same, or treating different people in exactly the same way, is in effect a form of unequal treatment.[65] *LAJ* functions in just this way and it seems, at least at an intuitive level, to raise a problem of fairness. While in no sense a uniquely contemporary critique of either law or *LAJ*, this indictment receives intermittent contemporary expression, often as part of a process of rediscovering forgotten critical discourses about law. It seems as powerful now as when first expressed. What is particularly interesting about this objection to *LAJ* is its status. We might wonder whether this complaint is indeed a genuine objection to *LAJ* which could in principle be answered, or whether it is in fact a truth about the nature of judgement based upon general rules or standards. We have already noted that the latter unavoidably entails some degree of abstraction: the application of general rules requires, seemingly by definition, ignoring some particularities of both agents and the conduct subject to those rules. This apparent truth stands alongside those that remind us that all general rules are both over- and under-inclusive. The way in which one regards this critical claim—as a general truth or as an objection that might be answered—will, of course, determine the path one takes in response to it. The substance and the correct understanding of this complaint are issues that constitute the backdrop to the discussion in almost all subsequent chapters.

[63] Chapters 6 and 7 of N Lacey's *Unspeakable Subjects* (Oxford, Hart Publishing, 1998) provide an overview of the ways in which contemporary feminism engages legal doctrine and theory, as does J Conaghan's *Law and Gender* (Oxford, Clarendon Press, 2013); for a discussion of the links between feminism, deconstruction and law's abstraction see her 'Violence, Ethics and Law: Feminist Reflections on a Familiar Dilemma', Ch 5 of S James and S Palmer (eds), *Visible Women* (Oxford, Hart Publishing, 2002).

[64] See Moran (n 13).

[65] The classic statement of the point is K Marx, 'Critique of the Gotha Programme' Vol. 24 *Marx-Engels Collected Works* 1874–1883 (London, Lawrence and Wishart, 1989) 86–87.

Fairness is also the crux of the fourth strand in the critique of *LAJ*. This indictment is both closer to the surface of common sense than others and is also specifically directed at *LAJ*; it has, indeed, already appeared in that guise in the sketch of the second reason why *LAJ* merits attention. Its juristic form is neither complex nor technical but simply a direct analogue of the common sense intuition outlined above. It therefore takes two related forms. One holds that, keeping defendants rather than claimants in mind, it is unfair for the law to hold them to standards of behaviour which they cannot achieve. If those standards are reasonableness or strict standards, then a group of defendants—including the accident-prone and clumsy, the dim-witted, the bad-tempered, the easily distracted and the hasty, the absent-minded and the selfish—are almost always going to be short-comers when judged against them.[66] The other, related form of this intuition holds that it is unfair not to excuse good-faith wrong doing. If someone acts in good-faith but contrary to the law, their conduct being a result of ignorance, it seems unnecessarily harsh to bring the law's power to bear upon them. Yet that power is indeed often brought to bear in just these situations. It might be thought that criticising short-comers and the innocently mistaken is troubling enough; utilising the blunt instrument of state power in such circumstances surely compounds the problem, adding injury to insult. At first glance, this strand of critique appears more than capable of undermining whatever moral credit *LAJ* might have or claim. Any adequate response to this critique must look closely at the law's conception of liability-responsibility, law's supposed impartiality and the role of mercy in the administration of law.

These four strands of criticism constitute a daunting charge-sheet. The indictments on it have been arranged in order of generality, the early charges requiring some degree of extrapolation in order to affect *LAJ*, whereas the latter charges are directed specifically at it. Not every indictment is tackled in what follows, nor will those that are tackled receive equal attention. The thesis that contemporary bourgeois law is in the grip of an historical transformation is set aside, principally because the broad generality of the various claims invoked to support it require a level of historical and historiographical competence that this author lacks. No effort is made to offer a blow-by-blow rebuttal of the remaining indictments. Rather, some charges are present only as brooding shadows, the effort being to offer a positive argument in favour of some or other aspect of *LAJ* rather than a negative argument against one or other indictment. My general argumentative strategy is an attempt to find value in *LAJ* regardless of the charges against it. While not a direct engagement with those charges, this strategy nevertheless serves to counter-balance the cumulative weight of those charges by showing that something positive can be said on behalf of *LAJ*.

The final reason why *LAJ* deserves attention has been hinted at in the preceding discussion and will be attested to in subsequent chapters. It is that an examination

[66] The term 'short-comer' belongs to Honoré (n 57) 16.

of this notion brings us into contact with a range of other interesting juristic and general values. *LAJ* appears closely connected to apparent virtues such as impartiality and dignity, equality and fairness, and might also function as a means of realising specific forms of community. That, at least, is one of the more general arguments that the remainder of the book seeks to substantiate. The argument is that these virtues or values are actually embodied in *LAJ* and provide it with significant normative support.[67] That this picture of the various normative sources and props for *LAJ* is coherent, rather than incoherent, is something I hope to establish in the course of chapters four, five and six.

It would be foolish to maintain that *LAJ* is the only feature of bourgeois legal systems significantly connected to such virtues as dignity, equality and community. But this putative web of connections does become particularly interesting when we recall the relative opprobrium in which law's judgement is held by many jurists and philosophers. The idea seems to be in bad odour, yet it keeps what appears to be morally respectable company. That is puzzling and it is one driver of the discussion that follows. It aims not only to examine the doubts about *LAJ*, but also to excavate and perhaps renovate some of the values it embodies.

B. How?

There are many ways in which law's judgement could be studied. The whole panoply of the human sciences could be mined for disciplinary frameworks, the utilisation of which might throw light upon the topic. The approach adopted here is jurisprudential or legal-philosophical, but that is to say little more than that some effort is made to clarify and interrogate law's judgement in a general way, not completely free from engagement with the legal doctrines in which it is found, but not primarily concerned with the elucidation and analysis of those doctrines.

There is an important constraint upon the jurisprudential approach taken here and it arises from a substantive claim. The claim, I hope, is uncontroversial and holds that law's judgement is an aspect of legal institutional design. By that term I refer both to procedural and substantive doctrines, on the one hand, and more general features of a legal system, on the other. The law of contract in England and Wales is a substantive doctrine of that legal system and an aspect of that jurisdiction's legal institutional design; so, too, are its system of precedent and the standard patterns of justification used by its appellate court judges when deciding hard cases. The way in which trials are organised and the nature of the court structure, along with procedural rules and rules controlling access to the courts, are also aspects of a jurisdiction's legal institutional design. Little weight should be placed upon the 'design' element of this phrase, particularly if it suggests the deliberate implementation of a detailed prior plan. In common law (and perhaps other) legal

[67] I draw no significant distinction in what follows between 'values' and 'virtues': I use the two terms as synonyms.

systems, features of institutional design are just as likely to have evolved piecemeal as to be the products of advanced planning.

Why should legal institutional design be thought interesting and what, if anything, is distinctive about this focus? Comparative legal institutional design can be interesting in a simple and obvious sense. Those who know the law of one jurisdiction are often intrigued and interested to know whether other jurisdictions face similar specific doctrinal problems as their own and how, if at all, they are resolved. Thus, the Law Commission for England and Wales was interested to know how other jurisdictions dealt with third party rights under contracts before recommending a change in domestic law.[68] This type of comparative interest is obvious because an interest in difference and diversity—in how others do, think and organise—is one that all but the dullest of sentient human beings display. That lawyers in one jurisdiction are interested in what lawyers in other jurisdictions say, think and do is no more surprising than wine-makers (or footballers) in one country being interested in the wine and oenology (or football) of other countries. The history of human beings suggests they have a reasonably high level of curiosity.

Legal institutional design is interesting in another way that is neither first and foremost comparative, nor so obvious. Here the question raised about some or other aspect of legal institutional design is this: what is its point, purpose or value? Answers to that question can often lead to a reinterpretation or reappraisal of the aspect of institutional design in question. The temptation among many contemporary jurists and legal philosophers is to assume that answers to this question must entail the construction of arguments from first principles. Such arguments have this shape: the jurist first establishes or, more usually, simply assumes the pre-eminence of one or other supposedly fundamental value. Having done that, the jurist then proceeds to show that the selected value either makes whatever aspect of legal institutional design is in question uniquely salient or, more rarely, shows it to be of little value at all.[69] Argumentation from first principles is unhelpful (i) if

[68] The Law Commission, Consultation Paper No 121, *Privity of Contract: Contracts for the Benefit of Third Parties* (London, HMSO, 1991) 139–67.

[69] There are many examples and the values invoked often vary according to the area of law or aspect of legal institutional design focussed upon. Even a brief list must include: efficiency (see W Landes and R Posner, *The Economic Structure of Tort Law* (Cambridge, Massachusetts, Harvard University Press, 1987) and R Posner, *Economic Analysis of Law*, 1st edn (Boston, Little Brown, 1972)); corrective justice (E Weinrib, *The Idea of Private Law* (Cambridge, Massachusetts, Harvard University Press, 1995) and J Coleman, *The Practice of Principle* (Oxford, Clarendon Press, 2001)); retributive justice (M Moore, *Placing Blame* (Oxford, Clarendon Press, 1997)); dignity (S Moreau, 'The Wrongs of Unequal Treatment' (2004) 54 *University of Toronto Law Journal* 291–326 and P Capps, *Human Dignity and the Foundations of International Law* (Oxford, Hart Publishing, 2009)); combinations of consent, autonomy and liberty (C Fried, *Contract as Promise*, 2nd edn (New York, Oxford University Press, 2015); R Barnett, 'A Consent Theory of Contract' (1986) 86 *Columbia Law Review* 269–321); and liberty and justice (TRS Allan, *Law, Liberty and Justice* (Oxford, Clarendon Press, 1993)). The recalcitrance of one well entrenched aspect of legal institutional design to complete normative explanation and justification is illuminatingly explored by N Duxbury, *The Nature and Authority of Precedent* (Cambridge, Cambridge University Press, 2008).

no single fundamental value makes a particular aspect of legal institutional design uniquely salient; and (ii) when aspects of legal institutional design are compatible with, or derivable from, more than one first principle. Argumentation from first principles can also become a distraction for jurists and legal philosophers insofar as their focus is indeed some or other aspect of legal institutional design. For such arguments often become a competition between rival first principles, the discussion mutating into a meta-level contest between allegedly fundamental values and the various ways in which their power over us might be established. At this point, matters of legal institutional design tend to fall from view.

What follows avoids immediate recourse to first principles. Our examination of *LAJ* aims to illuminate the values, if any, immanent within this aspect of legal institutional design or, at the very least, closely related to it. The values I examine are normative—part of our ethical, moral and legal fabric—but the candidates considered do not constitute an exhaustive list. This is in part because I have examined some additional candidates elsewhere and in part a result of the usual constraints of space and time.[70] Furthermore, my focus might be thought unforgivably narrow for another reason: I ignore non-normative sources of support for *LAJ*.[71] That is true, although the omission is excusable if one embraces a wide conception of 'the normative', as I do. That domain or, rather, family of domains, has this in common: each contains considerations pertinent to what we should do or think or how we should be. Conceived in this way, normative considerations are many and various, while ostensible non-normative considerations are relatively few.

My discussion of the values immanent within and supportive of *LAJ* is not in any sense foundational. It is not therefore concerned, as much moral philosophy is, with the epistemological or rational basis of those values. Rather, the principal burden is to elucidate those values and their relationship not just with this aspect of legal institutional design but also with one another. This is best understood as a matter of value cartography. It might be objected that elucidating these values, some of their *inter se* connections, and their relationship with *LAJ*, does not provide an argument in support of *LAJ* or those values. In one sense this is certainly true—there is no argument to show the rational necessity of those values. But there certainly is an argument in favour of *LAJ* here, if it is accepted that the values that inform it or support it are indeed valuable. If they are, and if they do indeed support *LAJ*, then that must provide some insight into *LAJ*'s normative standing.

[70] See my 'Abstraction and the Rule of Law' (2009) 29 *Oxford Journal of Legal Studies* 481–509.

[71] Arguments from efficiency and from convention might well support law's abstract judgement yet neither is considered here. The former are often mistakenly regarded as non-normative, even by their proponents, who also usually cleave to an implausibly robust distinction between 'positive' and 'normative' modes of argument (for standard discussions see the works by Posner and by Landes and Posner (n 69) and S Shavell, *Foundations of Economic Analysis of Law* (Cambridge, Massachusetts, Harvard University Press, 2004)). Arguments of the latter type might also seem to be non-normative, but this is a mistake on my view: for a brief and helpful treatment, see Finnis (n 45) 284–89. Both types of argument are ignored not because they are non-normative but because I lack space and time to examine them thoroughly.

That insight does not demonstrate the rational necessity of *LAJ* nor does it show *LAJ* to be normatively unimpeachable.

The effort to unearth the values immanent within and supportive of *LAJ* ensures that the approach in what follows is, so far as possible, made-to-measure rather than off-the-peg. By that I mean that the account of the normative bases of this aspect of legal institutional design should fit it in such a way as to take all its aspects and contours equally seriously, relegating none to the background. Thus we are likely to generate a sensitive and nuanced account of *LAJ* and its value(s). While this observation does not imply that some jurists and philosophers aim to offer blunt and clumsy accounts of an aspect of legal institutional design, it does suggest that some such accounts are indeed blunt and clumsy. One reason for this is that some accounts of some aspects of legal institutional design proceed thus: they move from first principles to the domain they seek to understand and study, reading the latter in light of the former. First principles here are assigned explanatory and normative priority and, if some aspects of the domain in question do not fit with those principles, then they are either overlooked or lopped-off in Procrustean manner. This, at least, is one plausible explanation of the wildly implausible or plain old counter-intuitive claims made by jurists seemingly immersed in the details of a particular aspect of legal institutional design.[72] Such accounts are akin to off-the-peg clothing—just as the latter are occasionally a poor fit for a particular human body, these accounts are sometimes a poor fit with the object domain they purport to explain and justify.

One way in which we can try to ensure a close fit between our normative and explanatory accounts of an aspect of legal institutional design, on the one hand, and that aspect of legal institutional design, on the other, is by embracing the participants' point of view as our principal methodological injunction. This claim invites two obvious questions: what on earth is it and why, if at all, is a methodological injunction that includes it necessary? The participants' point of view is the understanding of the point, meaning and value of a practice held by those whose conduct and beliefs constitute that practice. As a methodological injunction, attending to the participants' point of view requires that any account of any aspect of the social world must first and foremost attempt to accommodate the views of those whose conduct and beliefs constitute that aspect of the social world.[73] Thus an account of *LAJ* that seeks to follow this injunction must (i) access the views about the point and value of that aspect of legal institutional design of those whose conduct and beliefs constitute that aspect of legal institutional design; and (ii),

72 See, for example, Weinrib's thoughts on strict liability (n 69) at 177, 185 and 190.

73 For an account of this methodological approach in legal philosophy, see my *Understanding and Explaining Adjudication* (Oxford, Clarendon Press, 1999) Chs 2–3; for its role in philosophy of private law, see my *Philosophy of Private Law* (Oxford, Clarendon Press, 2007) 26–44; 'Method and Fit: Two Problems for Contemporary Philosophies of Tort Law' (2007) 52 *McGill Law Journal* 605–56; and 'The Crises of Private Law' in T Wilhelmsson and S Hurri (eds), *From Dissonance to Sense: Welfare State-expectations, Privatization and Private Law* (London, Dartmouth, 1998) Ch 7, 177–218.

in the first instance, attempt to accommodate and make sense of those views within its own theoretical account of that aspect of legal institutional design.[74] Whether or not it is possible to accommodate and make sense of participants' views and beliefs, and how far a theoretical account can depart from those views and beliefs, are not issues that can be settled in advance. Nor can the issue of what should be done when faced with a plurality of different views about the meaning and value of a practice among participants in that practice. These issues can only be plausibly addressed during the study of whatever aspect of the social world is in play.[75]

The content of this methodological injunction might seem so obvious as to require no explication, but it is certainly not the only approach to understanding and explaining the social world that has been developed in the practice and philosophy of the social sciences. Nor is it the only such approach to have been adopted within legal scholarship.[76] It is, however, dominant in what can be called legal doctrinal scholarship, in which an attempt is made, primarily for the benefit of lawyers, to chronicle and make consistent some chunk of legal doctrine. Thus legal treatises and textbooks are written by lawyers for lawyers from the perspective of lawyers. This in part explains why they seem so arcane to non-lawyers. But the law can be studied, catalogued and examined *regardless* of the perspective of lawyers, of those whose beliefs and conduct constitute the practice. We (lawyers) should neither assume this type of work out of existence, nor demean its value just because it departs from the participants' point of view.

The principal virtue of this methodological injunction is that it ensures that theoretical attempts to understand and explain an aspect of the social world begin close-in to that aspect of the social world. Or, more accurately, begin close-in to the views of the participants whose conduct and beliefs constitute that aspect of the social world. This is one means of trying to ensure that the aspect of the social world under study is taken seriously, at least if it is assumed that participants' views about the meaning and point of that aspect of the social world are *prima facie* reliable. That is not to say participants' views must be incorrigible guides to the nature, meaning and value of the aspect of the social world in question. It is, rather, simply a matter of assigning some presumptive weight to those views at the outset of the effort to provide a theoretical account of that aspect of the social world. Of course, if it can be shown that human beings are generally subject to false consciousness or are otherwise blind to the nature of the social reality that their conduct in part creates, then the participants' point of view becomes a means

[74] As compared to most participants' accounts of some aspect of social reality, a theoretical account (for current purposes) is simply a more general, more abstract and sometimes more technical attempt to understand and explain that aspect.

[75] Some general guidance as to how to proceed in the face of the latter issue is provided by Finnis (n 45) Ch 1 and 426–35.

[76] For a sketch of alternative approaches as they have appeared in some relatively recent legal philosophy, see my *Understanding and Explaining Adjudication* (n 73) part II.

of mystifying social reality rather than understanding it.[77] This book proceeds on the basis that participants' views have some presumptive weight in the attempt to understand and explain aspects of the social world. The justification for so proceeding is two-fold: first, this assumption is the default position of much legal scholarship and, second, alternative approaches which reject this assumption are in many ways more problematic.[78]

This book's emphasis upon one aspect of legal institutional design ensures that, although the approach adopted is broadly jurisprudential, it runs contrary to much contemporary legal philosophy and must strive to avoid the pitfalls of an older jurisprudential approach. Contemporary legal philosophy has been accused of being boring.[79] One ground for this complaint is that the self-consciously 'analytical' wing of contemporary jurisprudence appears obsessed with the finest minutiae of the alleged dispute between legion varieties of legal positivism, on the one hand, and increasingly scarce versions of legal idealism, on the other.[80] This is a jurisprudential battlefield upon which an ever more differentiated and finely drawn army is lined up to face a near non-existent opponent, the supposed 'dispute' being one in which things have not appreciably advanced for more than 30 years.[81] This obsession illustrates what sceptics about legal philosophy claim to have known all along: that the subject has little connection with law and our—citizens', lawyers', students'—actual experience of it. It also seems that some of the most interesting jurisprudential scholarship of the last three decades is not 'purely' jurisprudential, since it has taken as its subject various chunks of legal doctrine (which are but aspects of legal institutional design).[82] True, such scholarship has often brought to bear the frameworks and insights of contemporary and classical moral and political philosophy upon these chunks of doctrine, but sceptics about jurisprudence might hold that this is not what makes such scholarship interesting in the first place. What makes such work so interesting and so resonant throughout the legal academy is its actual engagement with the law.

If much contemporary legal philosophy has indeed lost sight of the law in all but the most abstract sense—that which presumably animates the question 'What is law?'—what ought jurisprudentially inclined scholars to do? Carrying on

[77] See Marx, '*Capital* I' (n 53) 81–94; 185–86; and 537–42; and '*Capital* III', ibid, 209 for a critical account of ideology that would warrant this conclusion in some circumstances.

[78] For some arguments to this end, see n 73 above.

[79] Or, more accurately, at least one distinguished jurist thinks it should strive to be interesting: R Dworkin, 'Hart's Postscript and the Character of Political Philosophy' (2004) 24 *Oxford Journal of Legal Studies* 1–37, 37.

[80] For one suggestion as to the point when most observers lost interest in this debate, see the book review by D Priel, (2006) 69 *Modern Law Review* 114–19, 114.

[81] R Dworkin, 'Thirty Years On' (2001–2002) 115 *Harvard Law Review* 1655–87.

[82] Just four (North American) examples will do: see the work of Weinrib, Coleman and Fried, above n 69, in conjunction with G Fletcher, *Rethinking the Criminal Law* (Boston, Little Brown, 1978). To these few many more books and essays, all of them more recent, could be added, some of them belonging to authors who also produce work that sceptics might place in the (allegedly uninteresting) 'contemporary analytical jurisprudence' category.

regardless is one option, at least until the sceptics' charge is satisfactorily proven. Another option is adopted here: we cast our troth in with proponents of the allegedly interesting jurisprudential project and focus upon illuminating some area of legal institutional design. The questions in this enterprise do not revolve around the existence conditions for law in general or for any conceivable legal system, but instead centre upon particular legal concepts and features of existing legal systems.

Now, questions about the nature of some legal concepts were, of course, the fulcrum of an older tradition of jurisprudence textbooks, few of which were captivatingly interesting.[83] Yet the fact that these texts often made some legal concepts—possession, title, property, promises, rights and duties, etc—appear quite dull does not mean that those topics are, after all, actually dull. They are not only the everyday currency of lawyers but also, in some senses at least, part and parcel of many accounts of how our collective life together should be lived. It should not be too hard to bring such notions to life. Nor should we accept that the study of these concepts sets the limit of jurisprudential enquiry: that must, at the very least, range across the whole territory of legal institutional design. That these early analytical jurists gave life to a dreary tradition of the study of legal concepts,[84] and that contemporary analytical jurists appear trapped in a relatively fruitless discussion of a grand conflict, are claims hard to deny. They provide the Scylla and Charybdis between which this book attempts to sail.

III. Prospect

Given what has already been said, the structure of the book is not in the least bit surprising. The remaining chapters tackle the following issues. Chapter two addresses the legal person, examining the forms it takes and sketching the nature of its relation with *LAJ*. The chapter distinguishes two ways in which the legal person operates in law and notes that these two need not always be compatible. The principal arguments the chapter makes are these: first, that the two broad senses of the legal person are significantly connected to *LAJ* and, second, that law's persons must be understood 'legalistically'. I do not rule out the possibility that other conceptions of the person also exist in the law, but I do not think that these, if they do exist, are either central or closely connected to *LAJ*.

Chapter three distinguishes three charges of unfairness that *LAJ* often generates. One of these charges relates to legal-liability responsibility, one raises the issue

[83] Two instances: J Salmond, *On Jurisprudence* (London, Sweet and Maxwell, 1st edn, 1902; 12th edn, by PJ Fitzgerald, 1966) and F Pollock, *A First Book on Jurisprudence* (London, Macmillan, 1st edn, 1896; 6th edn, 1929).

[84] Excellent overviews of this type of jurisprudential scholarship and its wider intellectual context are N Duxbury, 'Why English Jurisprudence is Analytical' (2004) 57 *Current Legal Problems* 1–51 and his 'English Jurisprudence between Austin and Hart' (2005) 91 *Virginia Law Review* 1–91.

of impartiality and the third invokes the idea of equity (or mercy). Each of these notions is complex and they demand scrupulous unpacking. The argument of this chapter is that, once these three notions are properly understood, two of the charges of unfairness against *LAJ* that they are often taken to license are seen to be bogus. The one remaining unfairness charge, premised upon the idea of equity, retains some weight. Thus we cannot say that *LAJ* is fair in every sense in which we use that word. The ways in which law's judgement may be said to be fair and impartial still leave some room for certain types of moral criticism of the law. But the burden of these types of moral criticism seems ultimately to require the replacement of law as we currently know it, and as we have known it, with an altogether more ethically sensitive means of judging our conduct and characters. That, at least, is the implication of the argument of chapter three.

The idea of dignity and its connection with *LAJ* is the fulcrum of chapter four. Two conceptions of dignity are examined, the aim being to determine the degree to which they inform *LAJ* in particular and law in general. It is argued that these two ostensibly different conceptions of dignity are not ultimately incompatible, that they overlap in an interesting way, and that that overlap constitutes one of a number of connections between dignity, on the one hand, and *LAJ* and the law, on the other. That both of these allegedly different conceptions of dignity inform various areas of legal doctrine as well as broader aspects of legal institutional design requires relatively little argument and is not particularly newsworthy, either as a matter of legal philosophy or of common sense. The point has significance only from the perspective of critics of *LAJ* since, if dignity is one of *LAJ*'s moral anchors, then *LAJ* cannot be utterly without moral value. Or, at least, it cannot be so if dignity itself is a morally significant idea. I do not show that it is, being satisfied only to note that many have regarded it as such. Dignity features first in the list of values that might inform or be embedded in *LAJ* because it is first and foremost an individualistic notion, those that follow being more closely tied to how we stand to one another as members of groups. The narrative arc informing chapters four to six is that of a move from individual to group.

Equality—another complex notion—informs chapter five. This chapter attempts to show the senses in which *LAJ* is egalitarian and to demonstrate the value these senses have. Much work has to be done simply to carve out conceptual space for these senses and to distinguish them from those that are dominant in much current legal and political philosophy. The latter are like a cuckoo in a nest, squeezing out all other conceptions of equality to such a degree that the capacity to even conceive of alternatives is almost lost. The chapter argues that two conceptions of equality can act as *LAJ*'s moral anchors and that both are plausible and significant. If that is so, then we have another argument with which to commend *LAJ* that also makes another important point: it shows that *LAJ* is normatively over-determined from within the realm of equality. Of course, the argument that *LAJ* can take normative sustenance from plausible and significant conceptions of equality does not show that *LAJ* is of pre-eminent moral or political value. It does, however, serve to impede the thought that it is of no moral or political value at all.

Chapter six explores possibly the most contested and troublesome notion to have recently preoccupied jurists and philosophers, namely, community. The argument I make is that *LAJ* can be understood as a means of realising a particular conception (or, more accurately, family of conceptions) of community. This is certainly not to say that *LAJ* is the only means of realising this notion of community; rather, the point is that it is one not insignificant means of realising and maintaining this form of community. Unsurprisingly, perhaps, that form of community is in significant ways egalitarian and thus overlaps with two of the conceptions of equality explored and recommended in chapter five. Some effort is made to show the value of this notion of community but the argument is not one from first principles. I argue instead that this notion of community provides a convivial habitat for the realisation of many ostensibly competing values. The point is that this conception of community is compatible with, and may even be required by, numerous different arguments from first principles.

In the course of attempting to make out the various arguments just sketched, all the chapters also aim to redress the balance of argument in favour of *LAJ*. The cloud of suspicion that hangs over *LAJ*, and some of the specific charges that inform it, serve as the negative background against which any positive argument in favour of *LAJ* has to be made out. The final chapter—chapter seven—recaps the arguments of previous chapters and reiterates the claim that *LAJ* is nowhere near as morally and politically problematic as critics lead us to believe. That a more measured and circumspect assessment of the various arguments supporting *LAJ* yields insight is assuredly a pitiful rallying cry. But, while it falls far short of inspiration, this claim is nevertheless true and important. It allows us to better judge a still crucial feature of our law and that, given law's capacity for realising both unparalleled harm and good, is significant. Robert Cover was right to maintain that legal interpretation takes place in a field of pain and death; law occupies and constructs that field and it is important we judge it scrupulously and critically.[85] The argument of this book serves to clear the ground for a scrupulous and critical judgement of law's abstract judgement.

[85] R Cover, 'Violence and the Word' (1986) 95 *Yale Law Journal* 1601–30.

2

Law's Persons

'[A]s a lawyer, I may have rather uninteresting conclusions to draw with respect to the concept of the person'.[1]

What is the connection between law's abstract judgement (hereinafter '*LAJ*') and the legal person? The hypothesis this chapter explores and seeks to substantiate is that the three components of *LAJ*, taken either in their most abstract form or as they are given particular expression in specific areas of legal doctrine, presuppose and construct a conception of the legal person. The way law judges us is therefore closely connected to the way law sees us. However, this hypothesis and the putative connections it envisages between *LAJ* and law's person might seem horribly misguided. The mistake is that of subsuming a minor puzzle—the nature of law's judgement—within the intellectual morass of the on-going discussion about the nature of the legal person.

In the common law world at least, the legal person has been subject to intermittent and apparently inconclusive examination for a period of more than 250 years. It is hard to be sure why interest in the topic ebbs and flows, but one possible explanation is a cross-generational pattern of realising and then forgetting the obvious point that the legal person is not necessarily a natural person.[2] There might once have been a necessary connection here, but the legal-cum-economic invention that is the incorporated association assuredly severed it.[3] Corporations are not natural persons—the kind of physically embodied human beings by which we are surrounded—yet they are certainly legal persons. How this is possible, and what it tells us about the legal person in general, has engaged a vast number of notable jurists and lawyers.[4] Advances in stem-cell as well as sperm- and egg-donor technology, alongside mooted changes in the regulation of abortion,

[1] R Tur, 'The "Person" in Law' in A Peacock and G Gillett (eds), *Persons and Personality* (Oxford, Blackwell, 1987) Ch 7, 116.

[2] In what follows I use the terms 'natural person(s)' and 'human being(s)' interchangeably as synonyms; I also flit, in a fairly promiscuous way, between singular—'the legal person', 'law's person'—and plural—'legal persons', 'law's persons'—the reasons for which will become plain as the argument unfolds.

[3] The tendency to assume that the corporation must be a product of industrial capitalism is confounded by the fact that it seems there was no necessary connection between natural personhood and legal personality in Roman Law. The Romans, too, had *something* like corporations: see PW Duff, *Personality in Roman Private Law* (Cambridge, Cambridge University Press, 1938) Ch V.

[4] F Hallis, *Corporate Personality: A Study in Jurisprudence* (London, Oxford University Press, 1930) is still one of the most comprehensive treatments of both common law and civilian jurists' views of

provide a contemporary impetus to re-examine the nature of the legal person.[5] Furthermore, one of the most interesting and relatively recent approaches to analysing the legal person has been the interrogation of not just its gender but its sex. The gender critique of the legal person has shown that this allegedly neutral, putative abstraction looks a great deal like a heterosexual adult man; in some legal contexts it therefore serves to disadvantage, *inter alios*, adult women. One aim of the task of 'sexing' the legal person has been to relocate the category of sex from the domain of the 'natural' to that of the social and conventional where law, of course, occupies a prominent role.[6]

That an entity does not have to be a natural person in order to be a legal person prompts three closely related observations. First, it reminds us that other natural things have at some points, in some legal systems, been accorded legal status and, second, that some contemporary jurists argue that natural things in addition to humans should have legal standing.[7] Both points confuse those inclined to assume that the legal person must be a natural person but, while we may now doubt the sense of, for example, putting animals on trial, we are all too familiar with the claim that features of the natural environment would be best protected by being accorded legal standing. Just as legal guardians (or *guardians ad litem* in some jurisdictions) can represent the interests of human beings unable to represent themselves, so too could environmental stewards represent the 'interests' of trees, animals, rivers and seas. The third observation is perhaps the most obvious: many legal systems have failed (and some still fail) to accord full legal standing to all human beings within their jurisdiction. Do not forget that it was not until 1882 that married women in England were legally entitled to hold property independently of their husbands and, of course, not until 1928 that the women of Britain had the same voting rights as British men.[8] Similar expansion of the

corporate personality and needs only be supplemented with F Cohen's 'Transcendental Nonsense and the Functional Approach' (1935) 35 *Columbia Law Review* 809–49. A more recent discussion is C Wells, *Corporations and Criminal Responsibility*, 2nd edn (Oxford, Clarendon Press, 2001). Not all jurists found the topic fascinating: John Austin thought it nothing more than 'a technical matter' (R Campbell (ed), *Lectures on Jurisprudence, or the Philosophy of Positive Law*, 3rd edn (London, John Murray, 1869) Vol 1 at 362).

[5] For an introduction to these and related issues, see A Alghrani and M Brazier, 'Re-positioning the Foetus in the Context of Research' (2011) 70 *Cambridge Law Journal* 51–82 and J Harris, *Enhancing Evolution* (Princeton, New Jersey, Princeton University Press, 2010). See also 'Mississippi's Ambiguous "Personhood" Amendment' www.nytimes.com/2011/10/31/opinion/mississippis-ambiguous-personhood-amendment.html?_r=2&hp (last accessed 3rd January 2017).

[6] An interesting general statement of the critique, albeit now somewhat dated, is N Naffine, *Law and the Sexes* (Sydney, Allen and Unwin, 1990). See also N Naffine and R Owens (eds), *Sexing the Subject of Law* (London, Sweet and Maxwell, 1997) and M Moran, *Rethinking the Reasonable Person* (Oxford, Clarendon Press, 2003).

[7] See EP Evans, *The Criminal Prosecution and Capital Punishment of Animals* (London, Faber and Faber, 1987); C Stone, *Should Trees Have Standing?* 3rd edn (New York, Oxford University Press, 2010); and S Wise, *Rattling the Cage* (New York, Perseus Books, 2000).

[8] Married Women's Property Act 1882; Representation of the People (Equal Franchise) Act 1928. Jeremy Bentham had long before written against the denial of legal personality to women in marriage (for an overview, see M Sokal, *Bentham, Law and Marriage* (London, Continuum, 2011) Ch 4).

category of legal person occurred elsewhere in the common law world at roughly the same time.[9] That this category has often been expanded to include more and more human beings, as well other natural and human-made entities, is significant and worth repeating. In one form or another, the struggle to expand this category has been a hallmark of some of the most momentous political changes of the last 150 years in both common law and civil law jurisdictions. In a world in which all natural persons are *ipso facto* legal persons of the exact same standing, that struggle would be almost otiose.

Can anything be gained from connecting *LAJ* to this contentious and much disputed topic? Yes. We will gain an appreciation of the ways in which *LAJ* both presupposes and constructs the legal person. That is worth knowing, if we think it important to understand the ways in which *LAJ* is implicated within the broader elements of legal institutional design. The argument to show that *LAJ* presupposes and constructs the legal person is the fulcrum of the following section and it is indirect. By that I mean that my aim there is first and foremost to show the ways in which law creates the legal person; having done that, I simply point to *LAJ*'s role in that process. Section II defends the general approach taken to the legal person in section I and, in so doing, shows how that approach resonates with *LAJ*. I do not claim that *LAJ* and the legal person are different sides of the same coin, but I do insist that they are closely and significantly related.

I. Persons in Law

Talk of 'the' legal person provokes a perfectly legitimate query: are all instances of 'legal person-talk' the same? Whether or not they are could be established only by a detailed examination of the various instances of such talk.[10] Yet such an examination implies, at the least, a tentative sense of what it is that we are looking for, of what might plausibly underpin all, many or some instances of legal person-talk. The hunch informing the discussion in this section is that much of this talk refers to one or other—or sometimes even both—of the following notions. One encompasses what can be called 'the person as presupposition', while the other is 'the person as consequence'. Both aspects of legal person-talk are unpacked below. I suggest, first, that the two aspects capture what is at stake in large swathes of such talk but are unlikely to be in play in every instance of legal person-talk; second,

[9] Two excellent accounts of different aspects of this process: RJ Sharpe and PI McMahon, *The Persons Case: The Origins and Legacy of the Fight for Legal Personhood* (Toronto, University of Toronto Press, 2007) and K Karst, *Belonging to America* (New Haven, Yale University Press, 1989). C Dayan's *The Law is a White Dog* (Princeton, New Jersey, Princeton University Press, 2011) provides a fascinating medley of the legal person's various expansions and contractions.

[10] In the remainder of this chapter, I use the terms 'person-talk' and 'legal person-talk' interchangeably.

that they are not always in harmony; and third, that both aspects of legal person-talk are closely connected to law's abstract judgement.

The claim that the legal person is a presupposition of a legal system is not mysterious. It means, first, that law is part of the enterprise of subjecting human conduct to the governance of rules and, second, that this enterprise makes some assumptions about the nature of the addressees of those rules. It is no exaggeration to say that those assumptions generate a picture of the legal person. The claim that the legal person is a consequence of the standards constitutive of many areas of law is equally plain and blunt. It holds that, once we have a good understanding of some substantive body of legal doctrine (the criminal law of some jurisdiction, for example), we also know how that body of doctrine thinks of or constructs its subjects.[11] The entities that populate the criminal law of any jurisdiction—the perpetrators and victims of the various offences it contains—are in a significant sense brought into being by that body of law. That the legal person is both presupposition and consequence of many *existent* legal systems highlights the point that it is a product of systems of law with which we are familiar. This is not a claim about the very nature of law, holding that any conceivable legal system must embody the legal person in these two ways. Or, at least, I offer no sustained argument to that end here. The discussion has two parts. They examine in more depth each of the elements of this double claim about the legal person, as well as some objections that might be made against each.

A. Presupposition

If law is part of the enterprise of subjecting human conduct to the governance rules, then what must be assumed about the nature of the addressees of those rules? One obvious assumption is that addressees of rules are in principle able to understand them. Addressees must, therefore, share the language of the rule-maker and that language must be used intelligibly by the rule-maker. The norm, in most jurisdictions with which we are familiar, is that many legal rules and directives take written form, but this is plainly not a necessary precondition of legality. Besides having language, law's addressees must also be assumed to be able to control their conduct in accord with the law. If addressees lack this capacity, then issuing behavioural directives is literally pointless. I can command the trees in my garden to drop all their leaves on the 14th of October every year, but I know full well that this command is silly. My trees lack the capacity to understand my commands and to regulate their leaf-fall on my say so. This discloses something important about the nature of rule by law for, if addressees are in principle capable of modifying their conduct so as to accord with legal rules, then those rules must be more than merely intelligible. They must also be made known in advance

[11] The point often holds for areas of procedural law too, but I take no steps to show this here.

and possible to comply with. If rules of law are not made known in advance, I cannot take steps to ensure compliance with them. But, even when made known in advance, compliance with a rule that is contradictory or otherwise impossible is itself impossible. A legal rule that commands its addressees to hover, unaided, above ground for eight hours every day is not one with which any human being could comply.[12]

Even so superficial a discussion as this shows that law's addressees must be assumed to have the capacity both to understand legal rules and to modify their conduct in accord with them. This picture is assuredly shallow, telling us little of interest about actually existing persons. What it does tell us is nonetheless significant, since assuming that addressees of the law can, in principle, understand the law and can, in principle, modify their conduct in light of the law also implies that addressees of the law are in some sense reasoning beings. This implication follows if we assume, as we do in all normal instances, that the cognitive capacity of being able to understand language can and does inform the capacity for conduct modification. Consider this scenario: while cycling I see a Stop sign and then stop cycling. It might seem pedantic to call this scenario a deliberative or reasoning process, but it certainly is, if this is a good description of what occurred: I saw the Stop sign, understood the content of its message, understood it as a sign directed to me, and then acted in accordance with it (although I might have chosen to ignore it). Of course, the 'process' here is a very quick one which, with experience, becomes almost automatic. More difficult and time consuming decisions—should I marry young and have children, or wait and pursue a career or other interests?—involve more by way of deliberation, with a greater number of options and considerations in play and in need of weighing, and have momentous consequences. But both the decision to stop at a Stop sign, and the decision about whether or not to have children, engage a capacity to reason, a capacity that the law assumes of its addressees.

This trite lesson—that the law assumes its addressees have and understand language, can deliberate in such a way as to assess what legal directives require of them, and then decide whether or not to act in accord with those directives—simply is the legal person understood as the precondition of legal regulation. This picture of the legal person henceforth bears the unfortunate but pleasingly short label '*PaP*', so as to distinguish it from the vision of the legal person that emerges in the following subsection. Yet the trite lesson, and the picture it paints, might be doubted by some. We could just about imagine, for example, a sceptic questioning the very starting point of our discussion and holding that, whatever law is about, it is not a matter of subjecting human conduct to the governance of rules. Rather easier to conceive is one who claims that, while law is indeed a matter of subjecting human conduct to the governance of rules, those rules are frequently morally and politically objectionable. More specific objections hit at *PaP* itself, it being claimed

12 From the initial assumption about law's goal to the implications that flow from that, this and subsequent paragraphs follow LL Fuller, *The Morality of Law* (New Haven, Yale University Press, rev ed, 1969) Ch II, 162–67 and 207–13.

either that this version of the legal person has little or nothing in common with existing natural persons, or that it becomes endowed with the traits and characteristics of a specific group of natural persons, to the disadvantage of other groups of natural persons. It could also be claimed that this version of the legal person is now an historical irrelevance. Given this charge-sheet, prudence might suggest that *PaP* be jettisoned. Should we take that step? Not until these doubts have been subjected to closer scrutiny.

The first, second and fourth doubts will be addressed here. Part of the third—the claim that *PaP* can become endowed with features of a group of actual persons to the disadvantage of other groups—is tackled in subsection B. The other part of the third doubt—that this picture of the legal person has nothing in common with actually existing persons—is one of the alleged vices discussed in section II.

Is it a mistake to regard law as a means of subjecting human conduct to the governance of rules? The assumption that it is precisely such a means generates the undoubtedly thin picture of the legal person just sketched. If law is not a means of subjecting human conduct to the governance of rules, then that picture presumably must change. But what might law be, if not a means of subjecting human conduct to the governance of rules? The temptation is to answer this question with a list of the many different potential or actual goals a legal system might have and, although interesting, this kind of answer is almost always beside the point. That is because any but the most bizarre entry on a list of the goals legal systems might serve will in fact be an aspect of the enterprise of subjecting human conduct to the governance of rules. Consider a now unfashionable single item list of the goals of law: law is a means of upholding the power of the economically dominant class in a capitalist society.

If we ask how a legal system might achieve this goal, it is implausible that it could be done without ever attempting to subject human conduct to the governance of rules, where rules are understood as being, at the very least, articulated general standards of conduct. The economically dominant classes' power can be upheld, for example, by the extraction of surplus labour and value from operators of the means of production.[13] But how is surplus labour and value extracted? It could be done in an *ad hoc* way, so that every owner of the means of production (or one of their agents) stands over every operator of the means of production and coerces them into working for a longer period than that for which they are paid. That is a possible but, of course, incredibly inefficient way of extracting surplus value. At its most inefficient, this system would require every owner of the means of production (or employer) to have a dual labour force, one operating the means of production, another standing over the operators of the means of production

[13] See K Marx, *Capital* I, Vol. 35 of *Marx-Engels Collected Works* (London, Lawrence and Wishart, 1996) at, for example, 581–83. N Geras, 'The Controversy about Marx and Justice' (1985) 150 *New Left Review* 47–85 remains a superb starting point on this issue and sparked much debate, a sample of which is: J McCarney, 'Marx and Justice Again' (1992) 195 *New Left Review* 29–36 and N Geras, 'Bringing Marx to Justice: An Addendum and Rejoinder' (1992) 195 *New Left Review* 37–69.

and extracting surplus labour from them. More efficient would be a system in which fewer overseers of labour hold and occasionally exercise sufficient power so as to act as a powerful incentive for labourers to provide surplus labour. And more efficient still would be a system of enforceable contracts between employer, on the one hand, and employee (or operator of the means of production), on the other, in which the rate of pay is calculated so as to ensure that surplus labour and its value accrues to the employer. This system of contracts could on its face be ostensibly fair, if both employers and employees were formally free to enter contracts or not, and ostensibly equal, so that neither had greater legal power than the other. It is also likely to be a *general* system in which the employer uses more or less the same contract for all employees or for all similar groups of employee and, as such, is therefore a means of subjecting human conduct to the governance of rules. What else are the contracts here, if not instances of subjecting human conduct to the governance of rules? Furthermore, the rules contained in these contracts might well be subject to additional rules, if a formal legal system exists, specifying when and which contracts are enforceable and how they will be interpreted. Again, if these rules of the formal legal system do not constitute an effort at subjecting human conduct to the governance of rules, what can they be?

I cannot show here that each and every possible statement of the goal or goals of a legal system is at some point subsumable under the rubric of 'subjecting human conduct to the governance of rules'. But, given the generality and abstraction of this account of law's purpose, it seems almost certain that all less general, less abstract statements of law's purpose or goals will be so subsumable. There is, perhaps, one exception to this point. It is what was dubbed above, without further explanation, the most bizarre statement of law's goal or purpose. This holds that law's goal is not to subject human conduct to the governance of rules. The strangeness of this claim is apparent as soon as we posit this goal for a legal 'system', that is, for an ostensibly coherent body of expressed general rules. It is tempting to carry on the previous sentence thus: 'intended to guide human behaviour' but that extension must be resisted by a proponent of the bizarre view. For, if the system of ostensibly coherent rules is to guide human behaviour, then it is a means of subjecting human conduct to the governance of rules. Yet, once that goal is eschewed we face a profound difficulty, namely, that of providing a rationale for a system of rules, coherent or not. If we have no interest in subjecting human conduct to the governance of rules, why have any system of rules (legal or otherwise) at all? Even a single rule system—do as the dice dictates[14]—is a means of subjecting human conduct to the governance of that rule and its built-in decision-mechanism. If we genuinely believe that law is not part of the enterprise of subjecting human conduct to the governance of rules, we must, for the sake of consistency, eschew reliance on any rules at all, except perhaps the rule that there are no rules.

[14] See L Rhinehart, *The Dice Man* (London, Talmy, Franklin, 1971).

Since it seems hard to deny that law is a means of subjecting human conduct to the governance of rules, we must consider how else critics might seek to undermine *PaP*. The second objection to *PaP*—the claim that, while law is indeed a means of subjecting human conduct to the governance of rules, those rules are often morally and politically objectionable—can be discussed by reference to the sceptical Marxist account of law's goal just invoked. Accept that account as true. The reaction of many of us to its truth would be this: that is a baleful situation. Thus, on being shown that a particular legal system functions so as to uphold the dominance of an economically dominant class, we would infer that this is regrettable and ought to be changed. Yet note that the objection here is to the moral and political quality of this particular legal system and is nowhere near specific enough to impugn *PaP*. The moral and political quality of particular legal systems can, presumably, be improved, but *PaP* will continue to feature in all such systems. Only if the objection in question is universal, holding that every legal system, and hence the very idea of law itself, always and ever serves to uphold the dominance of the economically dominant, might it also discredit *PaP*. Or, more accurately, it might discredit *PaP* if *PaP* is a precondition of the very idea of law (understood as a means of subjecting human conduct to the governance of rules).

This point brings us to another, not previously noticed objection to *PaP*, which occupies the space between the first and second objections. This objection does not deny that law is a means of subjecting human conduct to the governance of rules, nor does it take a view of the moral and political quality of those rules. Rather, it seeks to sever the connection between law understood as a means of subjecting human conduct to the governance of rules and *PaP*. The claim is that the latter simply does not follow, in anything like a direct or rationally secure way, from the former. Is this claim plausible? Not if *PaP* is an intelligibility condition of human communication and, therefore, of any attempt to subject human conduct to any kind of governance. By intelligibility condition I mean that *PaP*, or something that shares its features, makes communication possible. That is not to say that *PaP* is the only necessary intelligibility condition of communication: there might well be others. To see *PaP*'s importance, we need only imagine a world including a single human being and no other animate creatures. Genuine communication is impossible here because there is nothing else capable of either understanding the messages our singular human might transmit or of transmitting messages of its own. It could be claimed that this human being might transmit such messages to itself, but this involves a division of one into two—in which an 'earlier' or 'better' self directs a 'latter' or 'worse' self, for example—and thus mimics an instance of genuine communication. It is also true that our imaginary single human being attempting to govern itself by its own self-created rules looks a great deal like *PaP*. We can therefore hazard the claim that, in order to understand and transmit messages that take the form of rules, any being must have capacities like those the law assumes its addressees have: language competence, the capacity to understand communication and to deliberate about its meaning and requirements. We need not assume that only human beings have these capacities, although it does seem that we have them in a fairly refined and sophisticated form. These capacities might change or whither and they could perhaps be made redundant by technological innovation. But, given humans as we currently know them, and technology as it now exists, the claim that *PaP* is an intelligibility condition of communication seems eminently plausible.

If rules must be communicated, then *PaP* is also an intelligibility condition of the ideal of subjecting human conduct to the governance of rules. Much depends here on the contours of the notions of 'communication' and 'rules'. But it seems that any expressed directive—that is, a claim about what should or must be done or how something should or must be done—from one human being to another must, in order to qualify as such, be passed on to that other human being. And this is so whether the directive be in the form of words, other sounds or any of a vast range of gestures. Not all communication between human beings must take the form of directives and rules, even where the latter are understood as including but going beyond the former. For the category 'rules' includes within it not just singular directives of the kind 'Don't do that!', but also more general principles of guidance like, for example, 'whenever you are cycling on the road and see a Stop sign, you must stop' or 'when making Risotto one must stir the mixture frequently'. While it is a mistake to think that all human communication must be *about* rules, it is probably the case that all human communication *must follow* certain rules in order to be reliable and meaningful. Yet the initial claim of our discussion of *PaP* is not that human conduct must always and ever be subject to rules. It is, instead, the claim that law is a means of so subjecting it, and that, so understood, law assumes *PaP*.

It may now seem absurd to address the fourth doubt for, in showing that *PaP* is an intelligibility condition of subjecting human conduct to the governance of rules, the argument just offered surely undermines any effort to claim that *PaP* is an historical irrelevance. This would be true if the fourth doubt challenged *PaP* on its own terms. *PaP* is committed to a model of legal regulation in which (i) laws are communicated to addresses so as (ii) to be able to impact upon their deliberations as to what to do in (iii) the expectation that these laws will in most instances be followed. But the objection that *PaP* is an historical irrelevance renounces one or both of the latter two commitments. The renunciation works by adopting a model of law in which legal directives are engineered in such a way as to make either deliberation by addressees irrelevant or non-compliance impossible. Both possibilities can be achieved by various technological fixes that go beyond the setting and communication of legal rules, often resting upon a more inventive or imaginative assessment as to who are or should be the addressees of various legal rules.[15] Assume, for example, that we live in a jurisdiction that wishes to impose

[15] I have in mind the regulatory ideal-type labelled 'techno-regulation' by R Brownsword in 'Code, Control, and Choice: Why East is East and West is West' (2005) 25 *Legal Studies* 1–21. While one of the key works here is L Lessig, *Code Version 2.0* (New York, Basic Books, 2006), Brownsword's essay is one of the best and briefest overviews of the terrain.

a legal duty on car drivers to wear seat-belts.[16] One way in which this goal could be achieved would be in accord with all the precepts of the *PaP* model: enact and communicate a requirement that all car drivers must wear seat-belts, back it up by a sanction of one kind or another, and empower some or other agency to enforce this requirement and the sanctions attendant on breach. Clearly this approach would be unlikely to guarantee complete compliance, even if the deterrent effect of the sanction was massively severe.[17] Some addressees of this legal rule will not—for a variety of reasons, including simple forgetfulness—act in accordance with it.

Another, and some might think much smarter way of achieving this goal, has already been adopted in some jurisdictions: impose a legal requirement on car manufacturers to include on all their models a device which prevents car engines being started by a driver who is not wearing a seat-belt. It is true that this legal rule endorses the precepts of *PaP* when addressing manufacturers, but it does so in order to short-circuit those precepts when addressing motorists. Indeed, motorists are in no real sense the addressees of this legal rule, although they are its intended beneficiaries. Yet, as beneficiaries of the rule, they are allowed no space in which to deliberate whether or not to avail themselves of this benefit. The smartest kind of regulation can therefore make deliberation about compliance pointless and non-compliance impossible.[18] In so doing, it seemingly undermines *PaP* and its animating assumptions. The dust heap of history beckons. Should *PaP* be speeded on its way there or redirected along another path? Providing a compelling answer to this question will take us well beyond the confines of this book. Suffice it to say that, even if *PaP* is indeed destined, in the fullness of time, for history's scrapyard, it persists in the here and now.

Finally, note the relation between *PaP* and *LAJ*. It is the same as that between any area of substantive legal doctrine and *PaP*: the former presupposes the latter and *LAJ* is simply a constituent of the former. Since *LAJ*'s three components have no independent existence over and beyond the various legal doctrines in which they are found, things could not be otherwise. It might be thought that the limited avoidability component runs contrary to *PaP* insofar as it embodies strict liability. It seemingly does so if and when those who cannot comply with reasonableness standards are nevertheless held to them. And that looks like a denial of the agential capacities—the dual capacity to understand language and rules, on the one hand, and to conform one's conduct to rules, on the other—that define *PaP*. I say 'looks like' advisedly because this is genuinely a matter of appearance only. Once we

[16] The example is Lessig's: see 'The New Chicago School' (1998) XXVII *Journal of Legal Studies* 661–91, 668.

[17] Because deterrence, it seems, doesn't always work, even when the sanctions are massively severe. For a taster of the discussion, see J Sorensen, R Winkle, V Brewer and J Marquart, 'Capital Punishment and Deterrence: Examining the Effect of Executions on Murder in Texas' (1999) 45 *Crime and Delinquency* 481–93.

[18] The smartest type of regulation maximises compliance for minimal cost or, in the argot of regulatory theorists, combines 'economy' (minimal input), 'effectiveness' (maximal output) and 'efficiency' (the cheapest way of achieving the latter by the former): see Brownsword (n 15) at 2.

are familiar with the law's conception of capacity—it is a matter of 'can-general' rather than 'can-particular'—this apparent problem disappears.[19] That notion of capacity is one of the key issues in chapter three.

B. Consequence

The picture of the legal person that emerges as a consequence of the substantive rules of different areas of legal doctrine need not be uniform—different areas of doctrine might 'create' slightly different legal persons. This possibility rests on the idea that, while all substantive areas of a legal system might have the same very general goal—that of subjecting human conduct to the governance of rules, for example—each substantive area can also have its own unique 'subject-specific' goals. One common claim about private law, for instance, is that the goals of some areas of tort law include deterring and reducing the costs of accidents, while one of the goals of contract law is to facilitate the legal enforceability of some promises. Setting aside the details and the exact merits of these specific claims, most lawyers find this general kind of claim entirely plausible. It is taken for granted that different areas of substantive law have different purposes and goals. And, if indeed they do, it should come as no surprise that judges, when applying the specific rules and principles of some area of legal doctrine in hard cases, invoke those purposes and goals.

On most accounts of the nature of hard case adjudication, judges have choices to make about, *inter alia*, whether or not there is an available proposition of law to apply in the case in question; or about which interpretation of an agreed proposition of law should apply; or about which proposition of law, from a range of competitors, should apply.[20] These choices are often made by reference to an account of the point, purpose, value or goal of the legal rule in play, or by reference to an account of the point, purpose, value or goal of the general area of legal doctrine within which the dispute has arisen.[21] It seems likely that the legal person which emerges from this process will differ according to the substantive area of law in play. For, if (i) the rules of different substantive areas of law do indeed differ; and (ii) the goal(s) and values(s) underpinning those rules also differ; and

[19] On the two meanings of can, and on capacity in general, see T Honore, *Responsibility and Fault* (Oxford, Hart Publishing, 1999) chs 1–2 and 7.

[20] By 'hard cases', I have in mind the statement of N MacCormick, *Legal Reasoning and Legal Theory* (Oxford, Clarendon Press, rev edn 1993) Ch VIII; this is a more detailed statement than that provided in R Dworkin, *Taking Rights Seriously* (London, Duckworth, 1978) at xiv and 83 but is not incompatible with it. MacCormick's and Dworkin's views as to how hard cases should be decided are, of course, in some respects completely incompatible. While MacCormick's and Dworkin's views about the way in which hard adjudication should and does proceed have gone beyond these early works (see N MacCormick, *Rhetoric and the Rule of Law* (Oxford, Clarendon Press, 2005) chs V–VIII and R Dworkin, *Law's Empire* (Oxford, Hart Publishing, 1998; first published 1986)) chs 6–10, neither has explicitly recanted their initial characterisation of the nature of hard cases.

[21] Lord Atkin's decision in *Donoghue v Stevenson* [1932] AC 562 remains a classic example.

(iii) those rules are at some point interpreted according to their different underpinning goal(s), purpose(s) or value(s); and (iv) those rules serve, *inter alia*, to create the legal person, then (v) the legal person that emerges from the application and interpretation of different substantive sets of legal rules and their underpinning values might also differ.

This conclusion could count as an insight, but it also presents a problem for our current task. If we are to sketch the contours of the legal person that emerges as a consequence of the interpretation and application of legal doctrine, how might we manage the possible variability just noted? Of course, showing that variability is possible is not the same as showing that it is realised. While different substantive areas of law might in principle generate different pictures of the legal person, whether they do so as a matter of fact needs to be established by examining those areas of law. But we have neither time nor space to conduct anything like a thorough survey of even one area of substantive law, never mind a comparison of numerous areas. So, how to proceed?

The first step is to narrow our focus and, while accepting the possibility that the contours of the legal person created by various different areas of substantive law might differ, concentrate only upon one area of law. The second step is to avail ourselves of some of the excellent work already done on the legal person as created by legal doctrine, which we will henceforth dub '*PaC*' (an abbreviation of 'the legal person as a consequence of legal doctrine'). Some of this work is a little too superficial, simply by virtue of taking essay form: there is just not the space to engage in the sustained analysis that the topic deserves.[22] Furthermore, some of it, while undoubtedly interesting, tackles *PaC* in a very general way, attending more to philosophical and sociological thought about 'the person' than to the ways in which the law constructs it.[23] Fortunately, there is one exemplary treatment of *PaC* that escapes these limitations: Mayo Moran's *Rethinking the Reasonable Person*.[24] This is a scrupulous, sustained and theoretically informed analysis of the way in which some areas of tort law construct the legal person and a thorough elucidation of the rather different persons thereby created. Moran shows that different versions of *PaC* are created within one and the same area of law and that these different versions serve to benefit some classes of claimant and defendant over other classes of claimant and defendant. This is a particularly important finding, for it goes beyond the possibility of variability noted above. That type of variability exists *between different areas of law*. What Moran has shown is that the contours of the legal person can also differ *within one and the same area of law*. This kind of variability, as Moran demonstrates, is particularly troublesome on what might be called 'generic' rule of law grounds.[25]

[22] See Naffine and Owens (n 6).

[23] See N Naffine, 'Can Women be Legal Persons?' in S James and S Palmer (eds), *Visible Women* (Oxford, Hart Publishing, 2002) Ch 3, 69–90.

[24] Moran (n 6) (hereinafter referred to as '*RTRP*'). A related instance, with a broader legal-doctrinal focus, is D Herman, *An Unfortunate Coincidence* (New York, Oxford University Press, 2011).

[25] *RTRP* (n 6) 10.

Moran is most interested in those areas of tort law that determine when and how far three differently situated types of human being will be liable: the developmentally disabled defendant, the playing child defendant and the playing child claimant. Moran sometimes ranges wider than this, examining other areas of tort law and, occasionally, criminal law, but this need not concern us here. What is of upmost interest is how the law in these areas conceives of its addressees.

The developmentally disabled defendant is a human being 'who suffer[s] from cognitive or intellectual limitations, disorders, or disabilities'.[26] Oddly, these limitations and disorders, if permanent, are ignored by the law of tort when determining liability. This is the rule in *Vaughan v Menlove*,[27] which is commonly taken to show that 'someone of limited intelligence can be held liable … in a system that allocated liability based on fault'.[28] This position is reasonably well-embedded in the principal common law tort systems, although some, like the US, adopt it more wholeheartedly than others, such as Canada. Equally odd is the fact that many of the common law tort systems allow such limitations and disabilities like those that affect the developmentally disabled to negate or excuse liability when they are temporary. And temporary here can mean something quite fleeting—the sudden loss of consciousness resulting from hypoglycaemia—or something fairly long-term, such as a lack of appreciation and judgement resulting from youth.[29] There is a final oddity, namely, that the principal common law tort systems usually take account, to some extent, of the defendant's *physical* limitations: 'the physically disabled person is simply required to act reasonably in the light of his or her knowledge of the disability, which is treated as merely one of the circumstances under which the person acts'.[30]

The picture of the developmentally disabled person that emerges from tort law is not, therefore, a complex one. The disabilities, disorders and limitations under which this group of defendants undoubtedly actually labour in their daily lives are simply not registered by the law, with the result that members of this group may well be liable for conduct or its outcomes over which they had no control. This might not be particularly worrying in and of itself: much depends upon how we understand the general conditions of responsibility and legal-liability underpinning this area of law in particular and the legal system as a whole. But it becomes especially troubling when, as Moran points out, other groups of defendants with relatively similar kinds of disability are able to invoke those very same disabilities as excusing conditions. Hence, a sizeable dollop of apparent unfairness accompanies the inability of the principal common law tort systems to see the developmentally disabled defendant. For these legal systems, this group of defendants does not exist.

[26] *RTRP* (n 6) 20.
[27] (1837) ER 490 (CP).
[28] *RTRP* (n 6) 19.
[29] *RTRP* (n 6) 21. Two of many examples: *Mansfield v Weetabix* [1998] 1 WLR 1263 (CA) and *Buckley v Smith Transport* [1946] 4 DLR 721 (Ont CA).
[30] *RTRP* (n 6) 24.

The playing child defendant is, generally, recognised by the law and this means that the features children have in common are taken into account in determining their liability. In

> stark contrast to the treatment of mentally disabled defendants, courts and commentators addressing the application of the objective standard to the child defendant insist that the basis of liability in negligence actually requires taking account of the limitations of childhood.[31]

Nowhere is this more clearly seen than in the High Court of Australia's judgement in *McHale v Watson*,[32] in which the Court accepted that playing boys, simply by virtue of being playing boys, will be heedless of some of the risks their conduct creates for others. The Court in *McHale* regarded this lack of concern as a constitutive part of boyish childhood, and it has been followed in this by many other courts in numerous jurisdictions. This conclusion might seem admirably in accord with common sense, but it generates at least two reservations. One of these will be dealt with in the final part of this subsection, but the other must be tackled now. It highlights the supposed common sense appeal of the *McHale* decision and asks this question: why is this approach not extended across the board to *all* child defendants? For it is the case that neither the Australian courts, nor the courts of many other common law jurisdictions, have recognised childish heedlessness as an exculpatory factor when determining the liability of bullies, playing girls and children involved in adult activities.[33] This, again, is troubling, for why should only playing boys be generously treated by the law? If heedlessness is indeed a constitutive element of childhood, then it is presumably a constitutive element of all children's lives, whatever their gender and whatever they are doing (be it playing, working or bullying). The only variation one would expect in the courts' recognition of heedlessness as an exculpatory factor would relate to age and would, presumably, work this way: the older the child defendant, the less likely their heedlessness is to negate liability. That the actual variation we see in the law reflects nothing but gender, playing boys being treated more favourably than any other relevant group, is disturbing on generic rule of law grounds.

The picture tort law constructs of the playing defendant is, then, this: it is a boy and his boyish heedlessness is often recognised by the law as an excuse. Playing girls and children engaged in adult activities receive no such indulgence. What of the child claimant? The law sees such claimants, for they stand before the court, albeit in the form of their legal representatives. The interesting question is: which of the many features that child claimants have in common are recognised by the law? Moran's answer turns out to be just as troubling as the outcome of her discussion of the law's treatment of the developmentally disabled and the playing boy defendant. The principal cases here involve contributory negligence and the key issue is usually whether or not a child claimant's behaviour should negate or

[31] *RTRP* (n 6) 58.
[32] [1966] HCA 13.
[33] *RTTP* (n 6) Ch 3. But see *Mullin v Richards* [1998] 1 All ER 920 (CA).

reduce the liability of the defendant. A typical scenario is this: a child is attracted to a dangerous thing—an unattended horse, railway wagons, deep construction trenches—and is injured or killed as a result of playing with, in or upon that thing. Does the law recognise playing children as to some extent heedless and foolish, these being regarded as natural, constitutive elements of childhood and childishness? If it does, then the courts will reject defendants' claims that child claimants' contributory negligence must reduce or negate their—defendants'—liability. If the law does not recognise childish heedlessness as natural or normal, then its existence can only serve to undermine, by reducing or completely negating, the claims of child claimants.

Moran shows that the courts of the principal common law jurisdictions yet again seem to favour the playing boy. That is to say, they rarely accept that playing boy claimants act sufficiently negligently to reduce the liability of the defendant, even when they do as they have been expressly forbidden to do. Thus, despite having been told by his father not to ride on colliery rail wagons, and despite the widely known practice of employees of the defendant company chasing away playing children, the damages of the boy claimant in *Gough v National Coal Board*[34] were not reduced. The boy's apparent contributory negligence was regarded by the Court of Appeal as entirely normal behaviour; indeed, it seems that the Court would have regarded it as abnormal had any boy not been tempted to ride the coal wagons or had been able to resist that temptation. In this and other similar cases, the courts

> exonerate boys on the ground that they could not help but yield to dangerous temptation … [and] justify doing so on the basis that it is natural or normal for a boy to respond to seductive impulses. The boy is not responsible for yielding to the temptation because his action is dictated by his nature.[35]

The problem is that girl claimants are not similarly indulged.

This seems primarily to be a result of the courts' alacrity to impute greater knowledge of obvious dangers to girls than boys. Thus, the Canadian courts have held that a girl of eight should be aware of the danger of being struck by a car while coasting in winter, despite the city authority taking steps to warn drivers that this activity was prevalent on particular streets; that a girl of seven should be aware of the danger of being burned by a pile of furnace ashes dumped adjacent to a playground; and that girls of nine and 10 should be aware of the danger of drowning in a large, flooded excavation hole. The claim of the girls' estates in the latter instance was dismissed in part because workers for the defendant company had often chased playing children away from the site.[36] Although such activity by

[34] [1953] 2 All ER 1283.

[35] *RTRP* (n 6) 107.

[36] See, respectively: *O'Connell v Town of Chatham* (1949) 24 MPR 36 (NBCA); *Koehler and Koehler v Pentecostal Assemblies of Canada* (1956) 7 DLR (2d) 616 (BCSC); *Nelson v The Pas (Town)* (1969) 67 WWR 580 (Man QB). All three cases, and others besides, are scrupulously treated in Moran, *RTRP* (n 6) Ch 3.

employees of the defendant was regarded as having no effect at all upon the playing boy and his claim in *Gough*, it served to undermine the claim of the playing girls in the latter case. Tort law's picture of the playing boy claimant is, then, quite different to its picture of the playing girl claimant. While she is taken to be well aware of all the risks that beset play, and apparently as cautious as a risk-averse adult, he is assumed to be naturally heedless and perhaps even reckless. These two legal persons are chalk and cheese; it is no surprise that each has quite a different effect on the outcome of otherwise very similar cases.

The picture of *PaC* that emerges from Moran's study is not a flattering one, but it contains a number of important truths. One reminds us that *PaC* is not often explicitly embodied in the rules of legal doctrine but, rather, emerges as an inference from them. Another truth is that inferring the nature of the legal person in any particular area of doctrine is usually a matter, in common law systems at least, of scrutinising the judicial application and interpretation of doctrinal rules. Such application and interpretation is most evident in hard cases, where judges have choices to make in light of indeterminate legal materials. The interpretative pathways pursued by the courts in this process are not always commendable. Indeed, in the instances Moran examines, the interpretative pathways the courts have followed generate results that fall short of the law's own rule of law commitments.

This is because, as Moran makes plain, the courts understand the notion of 'reasonable' in tort law's reasonableness standard as a synonym for 'normal' rather than as a synonym for 'morally proper'.[37] This elision in part explains the courts' failure to recognise the developmentally disabled person, since such people are assumed—perhaps with good reason—to be numerically 'abnormal' and thus (almost by definition) 'unreasonable'. What is reasonable is what is normal and normal here, while it is never explicitly given a statistical or numerical basis in the courts, is taken to mean what is usual or common. It is, according to the courts, normal (or usual or common) for playing boys to be heedless of the risks their activities impose upon others. The law, the judges plainly think, must bend itself to this entirely normal feature of this kind of human being and it should do so regardless of our view of the moral propriety of such heedlessness. Similarly, the judges also think that it is normal or common or usual for girls, playing or not, to be attentive to risks and generally cautious. They are assumed to be 'naturally' heedful and attentive and, when particular playing girls prove to be heedless, their behaviour is regarded as unreasonable (or uncommon, unusual or otherwise abnormal). The consequence of the courts interpreting 'reasonable' and 'reasonableness' along these lines is plain: one group (playing boys) is indulged by the law, in the sense that their heedlessness is accepted as a naturally occurring factor that usually negates liability, while other groups (the developmentally disabled and playing girls) are not so indulged. The heedlessness of the developmentally disabled, which is perhaps as much a 'naturally occurring' factor for them as it is

[37] *RTRP* (n 6) 89–90.

for playing boys, is simply rejected by the courts as a exculpatory ground. And the suggestion that playing girls can be just as heedless as playing boys serves to show the very unreasonableness of such conduct, since the courts assume that girls are normally (usually, commonly) attentive and cautious.

Hence, although the very same doctrinal rules apply to all three of these groups, those rules have a very different impact upon members of different groups as a result of the interpretive framework in which they are construed. We cannot say—and Moran certainly does not—that the courts deliberately set out to advantage playing boys as against playing girls and the developmentally disabled. Rather, this result is an unintended consequence of an interpretive gambit that assumes what is reasonable is that which is normal, usual or common: '[r]easonableness is ordinariness on this view'.[38] The significance of this gambit as an interpretive choice becomes even more evident once we realise that it is a choice the courts do not always make: what is normal or usual or common or ordinary does not always serve to negate negligence.[39]

Does Moran's account of *PaC* serve to discredit it? It cannot discredit the very idea of *PaC*, if there are other areas of legal doctrine which embody conceptions of the person that raise none of the concerns Moran highlights. If we assume that there are such areas, then Moran's critique must actually be what it appears to be, namely, a critique of the way *PaC* has been constructed in a particular legal context. Moreover, it is not clear what an attempt to discredit the very idea of *PaC* would entail, except perhaps a denial that the law should invoke any conception of the person at all, be it in the process of application and interpretation or anywhere else.[40] Such a denial seems radically implausible. If 'things' akin to actual human persons are not in some sense the objects and addressees of the law, it is hard to see what the laws' objects and addressees could be. If law is not aimed at persons, their conduct and its outcomes, and their creations, what can it be aimed at? At this point *PaP* reappears: if law is in part about subjecting human conduct to the governance of rules, then humans, their conduct, creations and their consequences are presuppositions of the idea of law. It is here that *PaP* and *PaC* overlap, but we should not assume that they must always exist in a state of harmonious unity.

Indeed, if we keep in mind one aspect of the picture of *PaC* that Moran illuminates, and contrast it with *PaP*, it seems eminently possible that the two can conflict. The aspect of *PaC* in question is tort law's failure to see the developmentally disabled person. The rule in *Vaughan v Menlove*[41] supposedly shows that such disabilities are not a defence and this imposes a form of strict liability upon developmentally disabled defendants. They are in some instances liable even though

[38] *RTRP* (n 6) 90.

[39] See *Bolitho v City and Hackney Health Authority* [1998] AC 232 at 241–42 (per Lord Browne-Wilkinson) and *Lloyds Bank v Savory* [1933] AC 201.

[40] Some accounts of the nature of law appear to come close to this view: see Z Bankowski, 'How Does it Feel to be on Your Own? The Person in the Sight of Autopoiesis' (1994) 7 *Ratio Juris* 245–66.

[41] See *Vaughan* (n 27).

unable to understand the nature of their conduct or its consequences. But if developmentally disabled defendants lack this level of understanding, we should surely infer that they are inappropriate addressees of the law, on the ground that they lack one or other of the capacities of reason, understanding, or control of conduct assumed by *PaP*. In this respect, the developmentally disabled should be treated as akin to children. This conclusion is not one that should be glibly arrived at, since its consequence is so significant—the relegation of a person or group to a legal status quite different from the majority of law's addressees. It is a conclusion that must depend to a large degree on an assessment of a particular defendant's own capacities and abilities in light of a general rule about the nature of legal capacity. While such a rule will assuredly overlap with *PaP*, it would still need extensive elucidation before we could determine the exact degree of conflict between it and the *Vaughan* principle. Our first impression—that *PaC* and *PaP* appear to be in conflict here—is nevertheless still valid. That this impression is borne out in this instance cannot, of course, show that *PaC* and *PaP* always and ever conflict. Some degree of conflict is always in principle possible, given the way in which *PaC* emerges. The judicial elucidation of a conception of the legal person within a particular doctrinal framework and its constitutive values and purposes, might be influenced more by that framework than by *PaP*. If and when that is so, a conflict between *PaP* and *PaC* can arise.

Finally, note that the picture of the legal person which has emerged is neither particularly tidy nor pellucidly simple. It is a picture of the way in which the person is both presupposed and constructed in law that licenses this claim: there are, at the very least, two principal types of legal person. That claim needs slight amendment, for, although the person as presupposition is discernibly one type, the person as a consequence of legal doctrine can yield numerous apparently quite different persons. Furthermore, *LAJ* itself creates one such particular legal person. This cannot be a surprise since, if legal doctrine constructs law's persons in the way *PaC* suggests, then *LAJ* must be complicit in that process. That is because *LAJ* is embodied in legal doctrine: its three components can thus create a legal person in the same way as any other segment of law. Taken at their most general, *LAJ*'s three components provide a picture of law's persons: they are more or less identical equal rights bearers, all of whom are bound by the same general and relatively invariant standards. When filtered through the detailed doctrines of specific areas of law, *LAJ* creates the legal person in much the same way as Moran sketches, although the outcomes of that process need not be the same across all areas of law. The outcomes Moran highlights within tort law—the ways in which it sees playing children and the developmentally disabled—is simply an account of *LAJ* in action, it's components in some instances being ameliorated (playing boys), while being rigorously adhered to in others (playing girls). Here, and I assume in many other areas, *LAJ* and *PaC* are closely connected.

Since the combination of *PaP* and *PaC* provides a somewhat messy view of law's persons, it is worth reminding ourselves of its advantages. So far, two such advantages are apparent. The first is that this picture of law's persons allows lawyers to say most of what they need to say about the legal person and, furthermore, concedes that the many ways in which lawyers speak about the person are intelligible. Lawyers need not be embarrassed to note that 'the' legal person is multiform and not identical with natural persons. The second is that this account avoids many of the pitfalls of other accounts. One of these general alleged pitfalls—legalism—is the fulcrum of the following section. Another alleged failing of numerous accounts of the legal person has been dubbed 'functionalism'. Proponents of this view supposedly claim

> that in applying a legal term one must look to the legal consequences being prescribed by its authoritative use by a judge, and further, that it ... [is] an illusion to think that such legal terms ... [have] a *meaning* that determine[s] their correct use apart from such consequences.[42]

Some have indeed made this radically implausible double-claim, even though it is one thing to hold that the application and interpretation of legal concepts, words and ideas by judges has significant legal consequences, and quite another to assert that that is the only way in which such concepts, words and ideas can have meaning.[43] Many have rightly objected to that additional, astonishing claim and it is worth pointing out that our account of law's persons is assuredly not committed to it.[44] The meaning of 'person' as and when used by lawyers is indeed determined by their use of that term, but that, for our purposes, need not refer only—or even at all—to the legal consequences of such use. The conditions that determine how and when lawyers use that term need not be just one homogenous type but, rather, can include many different sets of such conditions. And, while some of those sets of conditions could include assessments of legal consequences, they can include much else besides. This is not therefore a path into the maw of functionalism.

II. Legalism, Abstraction and Other Vices

There is still one complaint about the legal person that has not been addressed. It holds that, when understood either as *PaP* or *PaC*, the legal person has little or nothing in common with real people and this, it is inferred, is a problem. The precise nature of this alleged problem is tackled below, in subsection B, where I suggest that it is unproblematic. When invoked as a complaint against the legal person, this putative problem is often but a token of a broader type of criticism of law's person. The malady this broader criticism highlights can be labelled

[42] M Moore, *Law and Psychiatry: Rethinking the Relationship* (Cambridge, Cambridge University Press, 1984) 46. Emphasis in original.

[43] See F Cohen, 'Transcendental Nonsense and the Functional Approach' (1935) 35 *Columbia Law Review* 809–49 at 835–49 ('the meaning of a definition is found in its consequences': 838).

[44] Moore (n 42) Ch 2 is one of a number who elucidate the implausibility.

'legalism' and that is the focus of subsection A. The argument there is again deflationary: I show that this alleged malady, in one form at least, is entirely benign. I also note that 'legalism' about the legal person is, in many ways, an echo of *LAJ*.

A. Legalism

The term 'legalism' has been used to characterise a baleful syndrome, few of the features of which are in play here.[45] For our purposes, the term refers only to a view about the legal person. The 'legalist' view of the legal person holds that the law has stipulative sovereignty when it comes to determining the contours of the legal person or, more accurately, legal persons. So understood, legalism about the legal person is not obviously a substantive position: it does not explicitly embrace any particular picture of the legal person but, rather, claims that it is ultimately the legal systems of particular jurisdictions that tell us what the legal person looks like. And particular legal systems can, of course, accommodate more than one picture of the legal person. This view of the legal person can be reduced to a handy slogan: the legal person is exactly what the law says it is (subject to some constraints). This slogan, because both relatively empty and tediously familiar—in the sense that many lawyers accept the law's stipulative or definitional sovereignty over many aspects of life and language—might seem so obvious as to be unworthy of statement or elaboration. That this thought is mistaken becomes evident once we appreciate that the view that the law has stipulative sovereignty over language and life coexists with another view. This view, common among lawyers and non-lawyers alike, insists that law should be responsive to *inter alia* ordinary common sense and moral sensibilities. These two views cannot stand coherently together when the law of a particular jurisdiction adopts a picture of the legal person that runs contrary to common sense or morality. When the law's alleged stipulative sovereignty bumps into its putative duty to accommodate common sense and/or morality, something has to give.

For some jurists it is the former that must yield, particularly when the conflict surrounds the notion of the person. Common sense and/or ordinary moral conceptions of the person should, it is said, be represented in the law and the vice of legalism consists of the inability to see that they already are. This, at least, is the charge made against legalism by Ngaire Naffine in *Law's Meaning of Life*.[46] Naffine aims 'to discover and evaluate the major influences on … [the] process

[45] J Shklar, *Legalism*, 2nd edn (Cambridge, Massachusetts, Harvard University Press, 1986) 1–3, 8–24, 113–23 and vii–xii.

[46] Naffine, *Law's Meaning of Life: Philosophy, Religion, Darwin and the Legal Person* (Oxford, Hart Publishing, 2009), hereinafter referred to as '*LML*'. Parts of the discussion in this and the following subsection draw upon my review of Naffine's book, 'Persons in Law' (2009) 29 *Oxford Journal of Legal Studies* 787–804. I'm grateful to the editor and publisher for permission to reproduce segments of that essay here.

of constituting legal persons and so [to] arrive at a better, more critical understanding of our legal natures'.[47] To that end, she identifies and critically evaluates four principal positions jurists have taken up on the issue of legal personality, one of which bears some resemblance to that just sketched. These positions, Naffine thinks, are all present in the law and yield incompatible views or conceptions[48] of the legal person which can pull in different directions in one and the same case.[49] The four views are 'legalism', 'rationalism', 'religionism' and 'naturalism'.[50] The former, according to Naffine, is distinct from the latter three because it either actually lacks or eschews any metaphysical basis for the legal person: '[f]or the Legalist, law is not engaged in ... metaphysical or natural boundary setting and so, potentially, law's person has no limits'.[51]

> By contrast, the Rationalists, Religionists and Naturalists all believe that the legal person is an expression of some important defining attribute of human nature and therefore it is important to go beyond law to work out what that nature is.[52]

The latter tendency is the hallmark of a metaphysical view of the legal person.

While it is clear that Naffine's characterisation of a legalist view of the legal person is similar to that sketched above, they are not identical. There are two points of difference. The first may be more apparent than real, appearances sometimes suggesting Naffine thinks—contrary to the view defended here—that the legalist view of the legal person has no limits or constraints. By this is meant the idea that legalists believe that absolutely anything can count as a legal person and that there cannot be more or less central or important instances of legal personhood. Naffine seems to ascribe this belief to legalists by virtue of remarks such as that, for them, law's person has 'no natural limits', 'no essence',[53] is 'empty of ... content'[54] and 'neutral';[55] thus 'anything goes'.[56] That being so, anything at all can be a legal person. However, Naffine also regularly qualifies these claims by holding that *almost* anything can be a legal person. 'Almost' because she highlights one limit on legal personhood for legalists: 'the ability to bear rights and duties'.[57] Not everything has this ability, if it is regarded as a pre-existing capacity: clouds of fog, sunshine and the North Wind are but some 'things' that lack it, if what is meant is something like 'capacity to exercise rights and discharge duties'. Nor is it clear

[47] *LML* (n 46) 13.
[48] In what follows I use the terms 'view' and 'conception', when speaking of the different views or conceptions of the legal person, interchangeably. I also sometimes speak of a view or conception in the singular and sometimes in the plural. This is because each view or conception really is, as Naffine shows in Chs 3–8, a family of related views, but constant use of the plural would be cumbersome on occasion.
[49] *LML* (n 46) 6–7.
[50] *LML* (n 46) 20.
[51] *LML* (n 46) 21.
[52] *LML* (n 46) 22.
[53] *LML* (n 46) 36.
[54] *LML* (n 46) 35.
[55] *LML* (n 46) 166.
[56] *LML* (n 46) 21.
[57] *LML* (n 46) ibid.

how this ability could be brought into being and conferred by law rather than pre-dating legal recognition, unless some human being is nominated to exercise the ability on behalf of these things. In the absence of a human being the verbs 'exercise' and 'discharge'—as in the North Wind exercising its rights or a bank of fog discharging its duties—are obviously misplaced. Thus, when Naffine says that, for legalists, the legal person 'is … a formal … device for enabling a being or entity to act in law, to acquire what is known as a 'legal personality': the ability to bear rights and duties',[58] interpretative charity demands we assume she has in mind the constraints that this ability implies. It is silly to imagine she accepts that the law confers rights and duties regardless of the abilities necessary to discharge them. A contemporary Caligula might impose a legal duty on a horse to educate his children, but this is as pointless as asking for the moon on a plate.[59]

What legalism presupposes of the legal person is therefore clearly more than nothing. For, while the legalist view is both that the legal person can take many different forms—this relative openness being legalism's principal intellectual virtue, for Naffine[60]—and that there can indeed be degrees of legal personhood, there are limits.[61] One limit is that legal persons must have the properties displayed by *PaP*, either directly or vicariously. This is because the agential capacities *PaP* assumes—for language, understanding, deliberation and conduct-modification—are very similar to those we would expect bearers of rights and duties to have. Only when faced with beings able to deliberate, to understand language and capable of modifying their conduct according to their deliberations are the verbs 'exercising' (as in rights) and 'discharging' (as in duties) appropriate. Another limit exists in the evident connection between *PaP* and actually existing human beings: the latter are the best and most familiar instances we know of beings capable of deliberation, understanding language and the modification of conduct in light of those two abilities. Any plausible legalism must accept these two limits and the legalism espoused here does so.

The second point of difference between Naffine's characterisation of legalism and the version defended here consists of what Naffine regards as legalism's main weakness: its failure to recognise the presence in law of other conceptions of the legal person. An understanding of law's person informed by the ways that concept is invoked and has truth in legal discourse shows that 'metaphysical meanings of the person, be they Rationalist, Religionist, Naturalist, have already entered the legal lexicon'.[62] If this is the case, then the legalist goal of 'retain[ing] the essentially

[58] *LML* (n 46) ibid.

[59] The real Emperor Caligula, of course, only aimed to have his horse Incitatus made consul, rather than appointed to an academic position: see Suetonius, *The Twelve Caesars*, translated by R Graves (London, Cassell, 1962) 157.

[60] *LML* (n 46) 45.

[61] An elegant and economical account of Roman law's degrees of personhood is provided by Tur (n 1) 116–18.

[62] *LML* (n 46) 41. This claim is buttressed by the argument that the legal person is a cluster concept: *LML*, ibid, 46–47.

legal character of law's person, and thus ... assert[ing] the intellectual and conceptual autonomy of law'[63] is thwarted. What legalists would regard as extra-legal conceptions of the person are already part of the law; to deny this is a serious case of 'intellectual and moral myopia'.[64] On what grounds can legalists resist this charge? They can deny what Naffine says they must deny, namely, the existence of rationalist, religionist and naturalist conceptions of the person in law. Not only is this denial possible, it is also textually grounded, for there are some legalists who do not deny what Naffine says they must. A plausible legalism can therefore acknowledge that legal systems contain numerous conceptions of the legal person while also affirming, subject to some limits, law's stipulative sovereignty on this matter.

To see this, we need only to pause over the just reported claims from Naffine. How, exactly, does the legalist claim about the 'essentially legal character of law's person' lead to a denial that 'metaphysical meanings of the person, be they Rationalist, Religionist, Naturalist, have already entered the legal lexicon'? One of legalism's main intellectual virtues, as Naffine notes, is its potential promiscuousness about the person, allowing many 'things' to be included under the rubric 'legal person'. Why, then, must legalists deny that rationalist, religionist and naturalist conceptions of the person play a role in law? It seems plain that Naffine thinks legalism is committed to this denial by virtue of another commitment it has, namely, to the 'intellectual and conceptual autonomy of law'. Legalists, she says, 'think that law *does not* and *should not* operate with a natural conception of the person'.[65] But there are no compelling grounds for ascribing this commitment to legalism. It is not a matter of logical necessity or coherence, as is plain from our statement of the legalist credo: it is neither unintelligible nor contradictory to hold that legalism's principal tenet is that the law has stipulative sovereignty over the contours of the legal person (subject to some constraints). This means that the law has the last word as to what the legal person looks like and opens the possibility that legal systems can contain a variety of different legal persons, not all of which resemble natural persons.

Saying that we know what the legal person is by virtue of what the law says about it, is plainly not to affirm that law is and must be intellectually or conceptually autonomous. The way in which we determine what the law says on any issue is ultimately by reference to the rule or rules of recognition of the legal system in question. Such a rule tells us what counts as law. In the UK, the rule of recognition tells us, among other things, that whatever the Queen in Parliament enacts, and whatever EU directives require, and whatever the appellate courts have decided, is law. With this pedigree test in mind, we can determine whether or not conception of the person X, Y or Z has a life in our legal system by examining its various materials. If no statute, no EU directive and no appellate court decision has recognised

63 *LML* (n 46) 42.
64 *LML* (n 46) 43.
65 *LML* (n 46) 20; emphasis in original.

conception X, nor is conception X a fair implication of any statute, directive or appellate court decision, then conception X is not part of our law.

A legal system's rule of recognition constructs a boundary between law and other realms. Yet there are no grounds to think, within the context of the legal systems with which we are familiar, that this boundary must be impermeable, so that the law cannot be informed by the ideas and knowledge of realms beyond itself. The latter thought is certainly contrary to lawyerly experience in the common law world, and not only because many common law legal systems have a doctrine of 'judicial notice'.[66] In addition to that, appellate courts in these jurisdictions accept that the law should correspond with ordinary language, common sense and moral sensibilities on generic rule of law grounds. Thus, if it is important that addressees of the law be able to know the law in advance, and if they ought to be able to plan their conduct on the basis of knowledge of the law, then neither legal language nor concepts can be too arcane. Furthermore, the demand that the language and concepts of the law be relatively intelligible to non-experts is even more pressing when juries are used as a means of resolving some legal disputes. If juries cannot understand the law, then how can their decisions about guilt and innocence be legitimate?

Legalism's claim about law's stipulative sovereignty need not rest upon any belief about the desirability of law's intellectual and conceptual autonomy. It rests only upon a claim that legal systems have rules of recognition serving, in many instances, to distinguish propositions of law from non-law propositions. Knowledge of these rules allows us, in most instances, to determine whether or not a particular conception of the person has a legal life, the rules themselves being more or less 'open' to other sources of knowledge and reason. But, while legalism need not be committed to a claim about intellectual and conceptual autonomy as a matter of coherence or intelligibility, it might be that some legalists have indeed espoused such a claim. And this may be the basis of Naffine's ascription. In order to determine the truth of this claim, we should consider all potential legalists in the history of legal thought about the person. Such a survey would generate a sure-fire answer to the question 'do legalists believe in the intellectual and conceptual autonomy of law?' Time and space make such a survey impossible. The most we can do is to examine the work of some of those legalists Naffine discusses.

It is prudent to spell out exactly what we are looking for and, as a result, to make absolutely explicit the way in which the belief in law's intellectual and conceptual autonomy (hereinafter 'the autonomy belief') has been interpreted in the previous few paragraphs. Prompted by Naffine's claims that legalists think the law should not embrace natural conceptions of the person,[67] and that they suffer from intellectual myopia in being unable to see that such conceptions are already part of the law,[68] I have taken that belief to mean that the law must reject non-legal ideas

[66] See E Morgan, 'Judicial Notice' (1944) 57 *Harvard Law Review* 269–94.
[67] *LML* (n 46) 20.
[68] *LML* (n 46) 43.

and notions, holding itself strictly separate from other realms of knowledge and belief.[69] The argument above sought to show that legalists need not be committed, as a matter of logic or plausibility, to the autonomy belief. Yet if some legalists have indeed affirmed the autonomy belief, then we cannot complain about Naffine regarding the belief as one of the tenets of legalism. Our complaint, rather, must be against those legalists who espouse this belief.

Who might we place upon this list? Not every legalist that Naffine cites affirms the autonomy belief. A close reading shows that neither Richard Tur nor Bryant Smith claim that the law must reject non-legal ideas and hold itself strictly separate from other realms of knowledge and belief.[70] They do, however, affirm the legalist slogan—that the legal person is what the law says it is—as well as associated legalist claims that there can be a plurality of legal persons recognised in law and that not all of these need be natural persons.[71] Our version of legalism is therefore embedded in some of the literature. But what of a stronger version of legalism, one which espouses *all* the claims just noted *and* the autonomy belief? Two of Naffine's sample legalists *appear* committed to this view—FH Lawson and Alexander Nekam—while a third almost certainly is.[72]

The latter instance is Hans Kelsen. It seems entirely appropriate, given what we know of the pure theory of law, that something like the autonomy belief will loom large within it. Since the theory is ostensibly 'free of sociological and psychological investigations and … separates law from morality',[73] it can embody a near relative of the autonomy belief and perhaps even, with only slight exegetical work, its identical twin. But, although the pure theory provides a hospitable domain for the autonomy belief, Kelsen's actual treatment of the legal person suggests some significant connections between that, the 'physical person' and real human beings. These connections cast doubt on the claim that Kelsen is unequivocally a strong legalist about the person. For, although it is tempting to regard Kelsen as holding that *anything at all* can be a legal person—he claims *inter alia* that the legal or juristic person is 'a complex of legal obligations and legal rights' and that 'the physical person [is] not the human being who has rights and obligations' but 'the personified unity of the legal norms that obligate or authorize one and the same

69 Interestingly, Shklar (n 45) regards this belief, or something strikingly similar, as constitutive of what she calls (at 7) 'analytical positivism'.

70 Tur (n 1); B Smith, 'Legal Personality' (1928) 37 *Yale Law Journal* 283–99. My argument that neither Tur nor Bryant espouse the autonomy belief cannot be supported by citation from their texts, unless I cite each in its entirety, since the belief simply does not feature in them.

71 See Tur (n 1) at 121–23; Smith, ibid, at 284; 291–95.

72 FH Lawson, 'The Creative Use of Legal Concepts' (1957) 32 *New York University Law Review* 909–25; A Nekam, *The Personality Conception of the Legal Entity* (Harvard Studies in the Conflict of Laws (Cambridge, Massachusetts, Harvard University Press, 1938) Vol III; H Kelsen, *Introduction to the Problems of Legal Theory* (Oxford, Clarendon, 1992) 46–52 and *Pure Theory of Law* (Berkeley, University of California Press, 1967) 168–91. The latter is the revised and expanded second edition of the former; I refer to it in what follows because the discussion of the person is altogether less cryptic.

73 J Raz, *The Authority of Law*, 2nd edn (Oxford, Clarendon Press, 2009) Ch 16 at 294.

human being'[74]—he also reminds his readers 'that human behaviour is the content of legal obligations and rights'.[75] So, while the physical person and the juristic person are not natural realities but legal constructions ('in this sense a physical person is a juristic person'),[76] both serve as loci of legal obligations and rights and such obligations and rights bite upon, are informed by, human behaviour. That is surely a significant constraint upon the content of the legal and physical person: at some point the obligations and rights both carry or reflect and must be informed by (real) human behaviour and, by extension, (real) human beings. If human behaviour is indeed the content of legal obligations and rights, then neither the legal nor physical person can be unintelligible from the perspective of human behaviour (and human beings).

Lawson's strong legalism is not a well-developed position and, unlike Kelsen's, does not derive from a general account of the nature of law. It emerges in a series of claims, made in an essay in which the legal person is not paramount. Lawson affirms

> the separateness and completeness of what we may call the legal plane … Legal personality is not the same as human personality, an estate in fee simple does not exist physically in the same way as the land over which it exists … Legal personality, estates and contracts are parts of a world of their own, which is in some way related to the world of fact but is separate from it.
>
> It is an artificial world … [and the lawyer] … must work with artificial concepts.[77]

Although not an absolutely unequivocal statement of the autonomy belief, principally because of the claim that legal concepts are 'in some way related to the world of fact', these remarks nevertheless come fairly close to being so. For if Lawson's insistence upon the 'separateness and completeness' of the legal plane is not a near relative of the autonomy belief, how else can it be interpreted? Once interpreted as being similar or identical to the autonomy belief, the question that must be answered is this: what reasons are there to favour this strong legalist view of the person?

None. Which is to say: there are no general reasons articulated in Lawson's essay to favour strong legalism. The position appears a plausible one for him to take only as a result of a distinction he affirms at the outset, but does not argue for. This is a distinction between the realms of law and fact and it must be admitted that some or other version of this distinction has a great deal of intuitive appeal for lawyers. We know that 'the law's' view of some matters is just not the same as the common sense or ordinary view; and we know that legal concepts do not occupy physical space in the 'factual' world in anything like the same way as giraffes and houses do.

[74] Kelsen, *Pure Theory* (n 72) at 172 and 174.

[75] Kelsen, *Pure Theory* (n 72) 172.

[76] Kelsen, *Pure Theory* (n 72) 174. For a masterly treatment of some of the additional complexities to which Kelsen's view of the legal person gives rise, see S Paulson, 'Hans Kelsen's Doctrine of Imputation' (2001) 14 *Ratio Juris* 47–63.

[77] Lawson (n 72) 913.

Insofar as Lawson has this probably quite complex but seemingly obvious idea in mind, we cannot fault him. The problem arises with what he appears to infer from this notion: a strong legalist view of the person. This view simply does not follow from that notion in anything like a direct way. This is quickly evident when we note that weak legalists can also affirm the very same distinction that is Lawson's starting point. The distance from that distinction to strong legalism seems great and Lawson gives us no indication as to how to close the gap.

Nekam's view of the legal person is more ambiguous than Naffine thinks—he is in no sense an unequivocal strong legalist. While Naffine rightly notes that Nekam sets and defends a boundary between real humans (or what he often calls things 'experimentally existing'), on the one hand, and the legal person (or 'the legal entity'), on the other, his defence of this distinction does not rest upon the autonomy belief. The legal entity, for Nekam, is 'an artificial and abstract concept of legal science' but this concept protects that 'which the community acknowledges [is] a socially important interest' and the beneficiary of that interest 'is always something in whose experimental existence the community believes'.[78] Hence, '[t]he legal entity is only a legal image of this beneficiary, its legal abstraction … possess[ing] only those characteristics which the abstraction of the law attributes to it'.[79] Although these remarks repeat the tenets of the legalist credo, nothing in them entails the autonomy belief. That belief certainly does not follow, without strain, from Nekam's insistence upon the legal entity's artificiality and abstraction, since neither of the latter traits require that the law hold itself strictly separate from non-legal beliefs and knowledge. Nekam's core claim is that the latter do not become legal beliefs and knowledge simply by virtue of being non-legal beliefs and knowledge; they can easily become incorporated into the law, but the law's stipulative sovereignty determines when and how this happens. Holding that law is distinct from other realms of knowledge and belief does not require, as a matter of consistency, also holding that law be strictly separate from, and thus cannot ever overlap with, that knowledge and those beliefs.

Of course, this argument construes Nekam's notions of 'artificiality' and 'abstraction' as synonyms for 'not commonsensical' or 'not everyday' or 'not ordinary'. And saying that some or many legal concepts are not identical with their common sense or everyday equivalents is not to say that legal concepts cannot ever overlap with these equivalents. The possibility of such an overlap—which Nekam surely allows by virtue of the claim that legal concepts protect and thus overlap with socially important interests—undermines the plausibility of the autonomy belief. Indeed, one cannot coherently affirm the latter in conjunction with the former. Is there another, more or equally plausible interpretation of 'artificiality' and 'abstraction' such that the autonomy belief follows directly from it? The temptation to interpret these two terms as being identical with the autonomy claim is not one that gains any support from Nekam's own text, for the simple reason that

[78] Nekam (n 72) 40.
[79] Nekam (n 72) 40.

the autonomy claim does not exist in it. Extra-textual reasons must therefore be found and we have so far been unable to unearth compelling general reasons in support of strong legalism.

Strong legalism about the person is an implausible position. It is not required as a matter of logical coherence or consistency, nor does espousing it allow us to see or say things that weak legalism about the person cannot register. Insofar as there are genuine strong legalists, their arguments in favour of that position are not compelling. Or, more accurately, the arguments used by the few putative strong legalists considered above are implausible. By contrast, weak legalism about the person—which holds (i) that the legal person is what the law says it is (subject to some constraints); (ii) that there can be many different legal persons in law; and (iii) that the legal person is not always a natural person—appears eminently plausible. Not only is it a logically coherent and informative position, it is also embedded in much of the literature and thought about the legal person, and seems to serve all our needs. There is nothing weak legalists cannot say about the person that can be said by strong legalists, save for the autonomy belief. But, in the context of discussions about the legal person, that belief seems unsupported by reason. Legalism about the person must therefore be interpreted as it has been from the beginning of the discussion in this subsection, as *weak* legalism. While weak legalism is the only legalism worth espousing, it must be noted that the version defended here is also *qualified*, as is evident from claim (i). That the legal person is what the law says it is, *subject to constraints*, bears reiterating because those constraints, identified in the opening pages of this subsection, feature heavily below.

Finally, a question: what, if anything, connects weak legalism about the person and *LAJ*? The common features are abstraction and stipulative sovereignty. Weak legalism holds that, subject to some constraints, the legal person is what the law says it is. The law need not therefore immediately and completely incorporate our ordinary or common sense understandings of the nature of persons, although it often and in many areas overlaps with those understandings. At best the legal person is, on a legalist view, a simulacrum of natural persons and no more. Many features of natural persons are ignored by, or do not register in, the legal person. *LAJ* is similarly unresponsive to some of our ordinary judgements—it ignores much that we might otherwise think relevant about the conduct, character and context of those it judges. In doing so, it asserts law's stipulative sovereignty in much the same way as legalism: the law says what is and is not relevant about conduct, character and context.

B. *PaP*, the Rationalist Legal Person and Human Beings

The problems tackled here arise from the qualified nature of my weak legalist position. I have already suggested that there is one obvious constraint upon legalist accounts of the person: such accounts must accord with *PaP*. Here I suggest another constraint, which is that *PaP* stands in an interesting relationship to actual human beings, such that this limits what can count as a legal person. Both claims can be challenged and I consider two quite different challenges in what follows. One belongs to Naffine: her attack on what she calls the rationalist legal person seemingly undermines *PaP* by showing that neither the rationalist legal person nor *PaP* are anything like actually existing human beings. The other challenge arises from John Finnis's work and comes from the opposite direction. Holding that *PaP*, and its relationship with real human beings, constrains the nature of the legal person might seem to Finnis an absurd half-way house. He argues that the legal person is paradigmatically the real human being, understood as practically reasonable human beings understand themselves. Yet, while real human beings have much in common with *PaP* and *PaC*, the latter are only echoes of what humans really are and that, Finnis might add, is regrettable. Each challenge is considered in turn.

(i) Against the Rationalist Legal Person (and PaP)

Naffine's sketch of the rationalist legal person shows that it has one very significant feature in common with *PaP*: rationality. Indeed, the latter is so significant in both these accounts of the legal person as to suggest that they are, despite different labels, one and the same. If that is indeed so, then Naffine's arguments against the rationalist legal person must also undermine *PaP*. To determine whether they are the same, we must remind ourselves of the rationality component of *PaP* and compare it to Naffine's rationalist legal person. We can then evaluate Naffine's arguments. The rationality component of *PaP* was not, however, sketched in any great detail above, primarily because nothing turned on the point. Since it is now moot, some elucidation is necessary but note that a *general* statement of this component may be of limited utility. For, like the other components of *PaP*, this one is embedded in different areas of substantive legal doctrine and can therefore be interpreted in different ways within them. A general statement of the component risks losing sight of its variability.

A demanding version of the rationality component would hold 'rationality' to mean something like this: the ability to discern and then act upon the most compelling reasons for any belief or conduct, thus entailing both the ability to recognise reasons and to sort and weigh them.[80] To act upon, or inform oneself on the basis of, the best possible or most compelling reasons implies that one has distinguished the general class of salient reasons from non-reasons and then identified those reasons within the class of salient reasons which are most powerful. Being rational in this sense is therefore not just a matter of being able to

[80] This sketch echoes my essay 'Adjudication' in J Coleman and S Shapiro (eds), *The Oxford Handbook of Jurisprudence and Philosophy of Law* (New York, Oxford University Press, 2002) Ch 6 at 229–32. For more general treatments of the topic see: R Nozick, *The Nature of Rationality* (Princeton: Princeton University Press, 1993) chs III–V; J Raz, *Engaging Reason* (Oxford, Clarendon Press, 1999) chs 4 and 5; D Parfit, *On What Matters* (Oxford, Clarendon Press, 2011) Ch 5.

recognise reasons, but also requires the ability to discriminate between best, better and worst within the class of reasons. Less demanding conceptions of rationality jettison one or more of the limbs of this demanding conception. Thus we can imagine a slightly less demanding conception of rationality entailing all limbs of the previous conception, except that which insists agents act or believe on the basis of the best possible or most compelling reasons. This conception therefore allows that the reasons for which agents act and believe might be regarded as compelling from their first-person perspective, but not actually be so when judged objectively. An ability to weigh and sort reasons is still implied here, for rational beings believe and act upon reasons that they take to be compelling. To arrive at that judgement, rational beings must be able to discriminate between better and worse, weightier and less weighty reasons. An even less demanding conception of rationality insists only upon the ability to recognise reasons and act upon, or come to beliefs in light of, them. No weighing or sorting is involved here, except a capacity to discriminate between reasons and non-reasons.

These three conceptions of rationality could be further refined, but that task need not be tackled here. This is because the principal conception of rationality in play in private and criminal law is a weak one, being identical with or a near relation to the least demanding conception just sketched. Which is to say: whenever the question of what can be called basic capacity arises within private and criminal law—the question of whether or not the agent in question has the cognitive traits necessary to be an addressee of the law—it is answered in a relatively undemanding way by the courts. To be an addressee of the law here, to be 'response-able',[81] is to have the general capacity both to recognise reasons and have reasons as the basis for one's beliefs and conduct. If this view is correct—and I have argued that it is elsewhere—then there seems no obvious reason why it should not also inform, or actually constitute, the rationality component of *PaP*.[82] Yet, if it does so, we are on a clear collision course with Naffine.

Naffine's discussion of the rationalist legal person has two parts. The first tackles what she regards as a robust or sophisticated version of the rationalist legal person, while the second examines some of the ways in which rationalists respond 'to the vicissitudes of reason'.[83] Her general statement of the rationalist view shows the point of impact between it and our understanding of the rationality component of *PaP*:

> legal persons [for rationalists] are, in essence, real flesh-and-blood human beings whose most important characteristic is their ability to reason and deliberate.... [W]e are fitting subjects who can assume rights and duties precisely because of our human-defining powers of deliberation which allow us to make intelligent choices and, importantly, to be held to account for those choices.[84]

[81] The term is John Gardner's. See his 'The Mark of Responsibility' (2003) 23 *Oxford Journal of Legal Studies* 157–71.
[82] See my *Philosophy of Private Law* (Oxford, Clarendon Press, 2007) chs 2–3.
[83] *LML* (n 46) 84.
[84] *LML* (n 46) 59.

Rationalists thus believe that 'it is the capacity for sophisticated, high-level reason which most defines law's person'.[85] Their person is a 'robust and sophisticated reasoner', 'a highly rational agent', displaying a 'capacity for sophisticated, high-level reason'.[86] Furthermore, rationalists engaged with the criminal law tend 'to pitch the reason of the defendant at a fairly high level … he appears a sophisticated reasoner: someone offering reasoned justifications for his actions'.[87] This is 'an intellectually vigorous, assertive and engaged individual'.[88] The primary difficulty here is a pervasive double exaggeration: on the one hand, Naffine exaggerates the level of rationality required of the rationalist legal person while, on the other, she exaggerates the range of that account. A consequence is that some of her objections to the rationalist legal person miss their mark. They cannot therefore impact upon *PaP*.

In a fit of levity one might think that on Naffine's view the rationalist legal person, while not a rocket scientist, is not far away from such high levels of rational acuity. And this, of course, is the problem. For, just as we have no such highly sophisticated reasoner in mind when articulating the rationality component of *PaP*, neither should rationalists when they sketch their conception of the person. The evidence Naffine relies upon in order to ascribe this sophisticated reasoner to rationalists does not bear the interpretation she puts upon it. Or, at least, this is certainly not the only, nor is it the best, interpretation that the evidence will bear. In fact, the sources Naffine relies upon are quite consistent with the weakest interpretation of *PaP's* rationality component. Rationalists therefore think the legal person must be rational and not non-rational. As such, the legal person must be able to recognise reasons and distinguish them from non-reasons, while also using reasons to inform their conduct and beliefs. This does not mean that the legal person must be pre-eminently rational, never making mistakes as to what they have reason to do and always and ever conducting themselves only on the basis of objectively compelling reasons. Nor does it mean that the legal person always and ever conducts themselves on the basis of the weightiest reasons they have for acting or refraining on some, most or all occasions. It does not even mean that the legal person always and ever conducts themselves upon the basis of reasons; rather, it need only require that the legal person has the general capacity to conduct themselves upon the basis of reasons and does so much of the time. Possession of this general capacity is quite consistent with failures to exercise it on particular occasions, just as my possession of the general capacity to sink six-foot putts is consistent with me missing some six-foot putts.[89] What, then, of the evidence upon which Naffine relies?

[85] *LML* (n 46) 59.
[86] *LML* (n 46) at 60, 69 and 59 respectively.
[87] *LML* (n 46) 72.
[88] *LML* (n 46) 66.
[89] This account of general capacity belongs to Honore (n 19) Ch 7.

Limiting our palette only to the philosophers of criminal law mentioned by Naffine who, after all, are said to pitch the rational capacities of the legal person particularly high, we find claims like this: (i) individuals should be respected and treated as capable of choosing their actions and omissions;[90] (ii) if individuals are not recognised as capable of independent agency—of choosing their actions and omissions—they can hardly be moral agents;[91] (iii) very crazy human beings lack rationality, an attribute essential to human beings, and so cannot be considered addressees of the law;[92] (iv) the law presupposes that its addressees are practical reasoners;[93] (v) human beings show an ability to use reasons and aspire to excellence in rationality;[94] (vi) they are or should be able to give accounts of themselves and their conduct in terms of reasons.[95] Save for the claim about the aspiration towards excellence in rationality, nothing here is incompatible with either the minimalist view of the rationalist legal person or the minimalist view of the rationality component of *PaP*. Furthermore, and again save for the claim about excellence in rationality, there is nothing here which requires that legal persons must be sophisticated reasoners, where the latter means more than that legal persons must be rational rather than non-rational. Of course, it might be objected that the term 'sophisticated reasoner' and its cognates ('robust reasoner', 'high-level' reasoner, 'intellectually vigorous' reasoner, etc) means nothing more than 'rational as opposed to non-rational'. Yet note what an odd and jarring stipulation this would be: it would be like claiming my toddler, just able to take a few steps, was an accomplished (or robust or sophisticated or vigorous) walker.

If the rationalist legal person is, as just suggested, rational in a weak sense, then two of the objections Naffine aims at it (and which might also undermine *PaP*) are robbed of power. One of these objections, that the law does not require sophisticated reason for every type of legal decision, is now simply irrelevant.[96] The rationalist legal person is not and need not be a sophisticated reasoner; it is thus no criticism of this view to show that the law does not require its addressees to be sophisticated reasoners. The other objection denies that human beings are as rational as some human beings like to think all (or some) human beings are.[97] This point might well be true, but it neither embarrasses rationalists nor undermines the rationality component of *PaP*, unless the claim being made is that human beings are generally and pervasively non-rational. That claim would clearly be a problem for rationalists and for *PaP*. There are some strands in John Gray's work, which Naffine invokes to make the point, that might support it. As Naffine

[90] *LML* (n 46) 63. In this paragraph I paraphrase the original sources as cited in *LML*, with a page reference to *LML*, rather than re-quote from the original sources.
[91] *LML* (n 46) 63.
[92] *LML* (n 46) 73.
[93] *LML* (n 46) 73.
[94] *LML* (n 46) at 75 and 74 respectively.
[95] *LML* (n 46) 75.
[96] *LML* (n 46) 83.
[97] *LML* (n 46) 76–79.

characterises Gray's view, it is in part that '[w]e gull ourselves into thinking that our actions are guided by rational thoughts'.[98] This is a difficult claim to verify, being akin to a classic invocation of false consciousness.[99] We might, of course, be in the grip of such false consciousness and consistently misunderstand some feature of social reality. But how do we, and how can we, know this? And, if we can know it, are not the usual canons of rationality invoked in the process of coming to know it? There are, of course, respectable Marxist answers to these questions but they are invoked neither by Gray nor Naffine.[100]

Moreover, if we stick to the relatively shallow level of appearances only, it seems that life in many contemporary, mainly democratic capitalist societies is minimally rational in many respects.[101] A minimal level of rationality not only informs some of our consumption choices—is it the cheapest, greenest, healthiest, tastiest, most stylish (or whatever) consumable available here and now? It surely informs some of our lifestyle choices and might well inform some of our political choices. It is also consistently invoked in the near endless cycle of self-reflection—about feelings, careers, commitments, body-image, health, etc—engendered in our culture and embodied in everything from daytime TV chat shows to blogs and 'problem' pages in newspapers and magazines. Whatever else one might say, these are societies in which reasons are often sought, given and interrogated.

In saying that Naffine exaggerates the range of the rationalist conception of the legal person, what is meant is this: she regards it as committed to holding that the rationalist legal person either: (i) exhausts the whole range of the category of legal person; or (ii) that it is the only locus of legal and moral significance. The adverse inferences Naffine draws from these two claims can undermine both the rationality component of *PaP* and the rationalist legal person simply because these two notions overlap so significantly. These adverse inferences can, however, be stopped in their tracks, since the two claims from which they begin are false. Neither rationalists nor defenders of the rationality component of *PaP* need claim either that the rationalist legal person (or the rationality component of *PaP*) exhausts the range of the category of the person; or that the rationalist legal person (or the rationality component of *PaP*) is the only locus of moral significance. Note that, if legal personality is regarded as the sole determinant of legal and moral significance, then there is no difference between these two possibilities. If legal

[98] *LML* (n 46) 77.

[99] Which I take to be a vital element of any critical account of ideology, such as that espoused by the mature Marx (n 13) 81–94; 185–86 and 537–42. For a brief account of the distinction between critical and non-critical accounts of ideology, see my *Understanding and Explaining Adjudication* (Oxford, Clarendon Press, 1999) 224–27.

[100] Marx doesn't feature in *LML* and appears only intermittently—and then usually on a standardised list of enlightenment *bêtes noires*—in J Gray's *Straw Dogs* (London, Granta, 2002), which is invoked by Naffine.

[101] And in ways additional to, and very different from, the 'intellectualist rationalization' taken to be a hallmark of modernity by M Weber: see HH Gerth and C Wright Mills (eds), *From Max Weber: Essays in Sociology* (New York, Oxford University Press, 1958) 139–40.

and moral significance is a function of factors including legal personality then, of course, the two possibilities are genuinely distinct. Although Naffine plainly thinks rationalists are committed to claims (i) and (ii), there is neither evidence nor good reason to suggest that they must be. Hence my claim that Naffine is in the grip of an exaggeration here.

As to claim (i), the evidence is unequivocal. Naffine apparently accepts, as do just about all of the rationalists whose work she invokes, that the rationalist legal person is the 'paradigmatic legal person', based upon the 'normal person',[102] the 'normal human being' or the 'typical subject of rights'.[103] The paradigmatic, normal or typical legal person, for rationalists, is 'the ideal legal actor. Less than ideal persons are those of diminished reason, or even of no reason at all'.[104] '[L]egal subjects are typically and ideally rational human beings'.[105] Michael Moore is one of many rationalists who accept that some human beings do not come close to being legal persons on the rationalist view.[106] There is little doubt, then, that the rationalist legal person is the usual legal person or, in yet another variant on the language already used, the central case or focal meaning of the legal person.[107] Does this mean that the rationalist legal person exhausts the category of the legal person? Plainly not. Accepting that there are normal, usual or typical instances of something does not commit one to the view that these are the only instances of that thing.[108] Holding that whiteness is a normal, usual or typical property of swans does not entail that all swans are white. Thus rationalists can quite consistently maintain that, while the usual or paradigmatic or central case of the legal person has features W, X, Y and Z, there are instances of legal personality in which one or more of these features are lacking.

Naffine wants to deny rationalists this option, but her attempt to do so is misconceived. Take, for instance, her objection that rationalists are inconsistent in not taking their view of the legal person to its alleged logical conclusion:

> There is a palpable reluctance among nearly all styles of Rationalist to take Rationalism to its logical conclusion and say that legal personhood disappears altogether in the complete absence of reason. Among lawyers it is hard to find anyone who will say that the

[102] *LML* (n 46) 66.
[103] *LML* (n 46) 67.
[104] *LML* (n 46) 67.
[105] *LML* (n 46) 178.
[106] *LML* (n 46) 73.
[107] See J Finnis, *Natural Law and Natural Rights*, 2nd edn (Oxford, Clarendon Press, 2011) 9–11 and 429–34.
[108] This commitment would only arise if there is a strong version of rationalism that would always and ever deny legal personhood to (permanently or temporarily) non-rational beings. Despite her claim that there are strong and weak versions of all conceptions of the legal person (*LML* (n 46) 167), Naffine rarely actually demonstrates this. As we have seen above, the language of the theorists cited by Naffine to elucidate the rationalist legal person provides almost no support for the existence of a strong version of this view. One theorist cited by Naffine does, however, have an argument which might be extended to support a strong version of rationalism: this is Michael Moore's argument from natural kinds in *Placing Blame* (Oxford, Clarendon Press, 1997) 18–23.

> fully irrational should not attract basic human rights and, of course, the law as a matter of doctrine and practice, protects all human beings.[109]

Why must rationalists claim that legal personhood disappears in the complete absence of reason? Since the rationalist view of the legal person is a view of the paradigmatic, usual, typical, normal or central case of the legal person, why must they extend that view to the non-paradigmatic, unusual, atypical, abnormal or non-central case of the legal person? Of course, if the rationalist conception of the legal person exhausted the category of 'legal person', then rationalists would have to grasp the nettle Naffine proffers. Perhaps, then, I have misrepresented the rationalist view. Yet it is hard to see how: I have simply picked out some of the qualifying words Naffine and the rationalists themselves use when characterising the legal person.

I might, however, have made a different blunder. For although it is true that the rationalist conception of the legal person is limited because it is a view of the paradigmatic legal person, I could have missed another truth, namely, that rationalists must deny legal and moral significance to non-paradigmatic legal persons. The obvious question is, however, why? Rationalists clearly cannot say that the legal and moral significance of non-paradigmatic legal persons derives from exactly the same source as the moral and legal significance of paradigmatic legal persons, at least when speaking of those non-paradigmatic legal persons completely lacking rationality. (Things might be different when speaking about non-paradigmatic legal persons, like children, who have a nascent and developing general capacity for rationality, and adults who had but have now lost that general capacity.) Does that mean rationalists must hold that non-paradigmatic legal persons completely without rationality are legally and morally insignificant? Only if rationalists regard rationality as the only thing that matters for the purposes of law and morality. But why should rationalists think this? Indeed, Naffine notes that rationalists have available a perfectly plausible account of, and a way of distinguishing between, the sources of the moral and legal significance of paradigmatic legal persons, on the one hand, and non-paradigmatic legal persons, on the other. She puts it this way:

> [t]his is the distinction between those whom the law addresses, adult to adult, those to whom it speaks … and those who are intended to receive the benefits of law because they are perceived to have particular needs and interests, that is law's beneficiaries, but who are not necessarily parties to law's adult discourse.[110]

We are now in the territory of claim (ii), and the position just articulated is a direct denial of it. That is, this position holds that legal and moral significance can be determined by factors including legal personhood, but that the same factors need not underpin both paradigmatic and non-paradigmatic instances of legal personhood. It seems more than likely that the moral and legal significance of paradigmatic legal persons—those the law engages with 'adult to adult'—are

[109] *LML* (n 46) 92.
[110] *LML* (n 46) 66.

quite different from those that underpin the moral and legal significance of non-paradigmatic legal persons. Is there an argument to show that rationalists must either confer legal and moral significance only upon paradigmatic legal persons or risk contradiction by conferring such significance upon non-paradigmatic legal persons as well? No such argument is offered by Naffine. So are rationalists inconsistent, as Naffine claims, in failing to deny that non-paradigmatic legal persons have moral and legal significance? It has proved hard to show this. Such inconsistency could arise only in two alternate instances. First, if the rationalist view held that only rational beings can be legal persons or, second, if the rationalist account of the legal and moral significance of the paradigmatic legal person were in all respects identical to their account of the legal and moral significance of the non-paradigmatic legal person. The first claim is clearly contrary to the actual rationalist position, which maintains that rational beings are only paradigmatic legal persons. Furthermore, only if rationalists were committed to this first claim would they be embarrassed by Naffine's observation that current law requires brain death as the principal indicator of the end of human life and, presumably, of legal personhood.[111] As to the second claim, Naffine does nothing to show that rationalists must accept it and, moreover, it seems *prima facie* implausible, for why would rationalists commit themselves to such a limited account of moral and legal significance? If there are two broad types of legal personhood (paradigmatic and non-paradigmatic), then they might well embody different types of moral significance.

(ii) Legal Persons, Legal Fictions and Real Human Beings

The two sites of the legal person—as presupposition and consequence—tell us that legal persons are, *at most*, simulacra of natural persons. The legal person and the natural person are obviously not identical, and this is not just because things other than natural persons can be legal persons. For even when the category of the legal person overlaps with that of the natural person, the overlap is at most partial: the legal person registers few of the manifold features, such as character and abilities, and little of the history and context, that make natural human beings the particular persons they are. The few features the legal person has in common with some actual human beings are plain from the discussion so far: they include the capacities for language and for some level of rational deliberation, as well as the ability to use the outcomes of the latter to inform conduct. We assume that most of our fellow human beings have these capacities to some degree and, indeed, that assumption makes great swathes of our collective life possible. But it is an obvious mistake to assume that each and every one of our fellow human beings has and exercises these capacities all the time. We know that illness, intoxication, age and many other factors undermine the emergence of and ability to exercise these capacities, and that some factors might eradicate them altogether. Hence the legal

[111] *LML* (n 46) 82.

person is sometimes analogous to but also some considerable way short of being a real person:[112] law's person is sometimes a human being that is either not yet, or is no longer, one that has these capacities to the usual extent. Children, the insane, the very aged, the very ill are obvious candidates for this sub-category of non-paradigmatic legal person and natural person. It is also tempting to hold that, even when nothing like a natural person, the legal person is an entity closely related to natural persons or groups of such persons, in the sense that it is the product of the deeds, interests and goals of such persons or groups. Corporations are the lead candidates to occupy this sub-category.

That the central or paradigmatic instance of the legal person has some constitutive features does not, of course, mean that the legal person cannot take different forms, but only that those forms are intelligible by reference to the central case.[113] Intelligibility does not require a number of common features, but does imply some similarity in function across different instances. This accords a higher degree of explanatory importance to the central case of any particular phenomenon than to non-central instances; central instances are also usually more important because they play a greater role in our conduct, processes of deliberation and institutions. That greater role can sometimes blind us to non-central instances and their significance. The claim that the central instance of the legal person is, at best, a simulacrum of real human beings must be tweaked in another way: by 'real human beings' we mean 'the paradigmatic instance or central case of real human beings'. And that means 'contextually situated natural persons, in all their subjectivity and particularity, with reasonable competence in rational, communication and deliberative skills, those skills forming an integral part of a relatively coherent, relatively stable unfolding life-plan'. The connection between the central case of the legal person, on the one hand, and the central case of the human being, on the other, serves as a constraint upon the former: the central case of the legal person is always a shadow of real human beings. Non-central cases are not constrained in that way. They are, however, limited in another sense, since they are intelligible only if expressions of the purposes, goals and aims of real human beings.

The central case of the legal person is an abstraction or, perhaps, a fiction which, in its usual mode of operation, generalises some features that actual natural persons do or should have. The legal person assumes the existence of these features until their non-existence is shown and, even when their absence is proved, that is not always legally significant. The normative force of the legal person resides in what it registers, by way of character and abilities, history and context, about the natural and artificial persons the law judges. As we have already noted, the legal

[112] I use the terms 'real person' and 'natural person' as synonyms and they bear their ordinary meaning.

[113] The 'central case/non-central case' vocabulary belongs to Aristotle, although it was John Finnis's work that reminded contemporary jurists of its utility (see n 107). This vocabulary allows us to paint fine-grained, non-reductive, differentiated and yet still *general* pictures of social practices and institutions.

person therefore functions in much the same way as *LAJ*. Indeed, it is no exaggeration to say that *PaP* is an element of *LAJ* as are some aspects of *PaC*: the former is assumed by *LAJ*, just as it is assumed by the very idea of subjecting human conduct to the governance of rules, while many versions of *PaC* feed into or simply utilise the reasonableness standards that constitute *LAJ*'s uniformity, presumptive identity and limited avoidability components. My claim about the relationship between *PaC* and *LAJ* is qualified—*some* aspects of the former can be elements of the latter—because there is no guarantee that the legal person as realised in all areas of legal doctrine will embody the same elements. Without such a guarantee, we cannot be sure that *PaC* will always and ever be consistent with *PaP* and *LAJ*.

That the legal person and law's judgement are abstract, in the sense that they ignore some or many of the actual abilities and features, as well as much of the context and history, of those to whom they apply, might strike many lawyers as trite and obvious. This apparently pragmatic lawyerly common-sense can, however, be impugned on two quite different grounds. The first is the more superficial of the two but not, for that reason, uninteresting or insignificant. For the apparently uncontroversial claim that the legal person and law's judgement are abstract can be accompanied by another, founded on exactly the same considerations as those informing the abstraction claim, and which lawyers will likely regard as unacceptable: that the legal person and law's judgement are fictions. Lawyers now regard legal fictions as deeply problematic, their suspicion perhaps bred during education, although few contemporary lawyers are schooled in Jeremy Bentham's excoriating critique.[114] Lon Fuller characterised the suspicion well, observing that '[t]he fiction represents the pathology of the law. When all goes well and established legal rules encompass neatly the social life they are intended to regulate, there is little occasion for fictions'.[115] If law's judgement and law's persons are indeed fictions, then it follows that the principal argumentative refrain of this book is a defence of fiction and abstraction.[116] That is worth pointing out right now, for the avoidance of any doubt. Unlike Fuller's late reflections on legal fictions, this book argues that some legal fictions and some instances of abstraction might be virtuous. Moreover, that argument is closer to Fuller's initial view of the nature of legal fictions than the late observation just quoted.

The second challenge to legalism and lawyerly common-sense about the legal person counsels against the errors this mode of thought engenders.[117] Instead of

[114] Some of his complaints are gathered together in LL Fuller, *Legal Fictions* (Stanford, Stanford University Press, 1967) 2–3. Bentham showed unnoticed (by me, at least) skill as a humourist, following his possibly most dyspeptic remark—'in English law, *fiction* is a *syphilis*, which runs in every vein, and carries into every part of the system the principle of rottenness' (*Works of Jeremy Bentham*, Bowring edn, Volume V, 'On the Art of Packing Special Juries' (Edinburgh, William Tait, 1843) at 92)—with a deft 'Let us steer clear of exaggeration': ibid.

[115] Fuller, ibid, at viii.

[116] See ibid, Ch 1, for a rough typology of legal fictions and Ch 2 for the reasons that often support them. Where *PaP*, *PaC* and law's abstract judgement might fit into this schema is unclear.

[117] See J Finnis, 'The Priority of Persons' in J Horder (ed), *Oxford Essays in Jurisprudence: Fourth Series* (Oxford, Clarendon, 2000) Ch 1, s IV (on the US Supreme Court decisions in *Scott v Sanford*

regarding law's person either as, at most, a simulacrum of real human beings or, at least, as nothing but a product of juristic convenience, John Finnis holds that law's persons must first and foremost be regarded as real persons. His starting point is the same as that of Justinian's *Digest*: 'all law is made for the sake of human beings'.[118] From this undeniable truth—which might be finessed with some observations as to how those areas of law not directly made for human beings are surely indirectly made for them, although not perhaps in a purely instrumental sense[119] — Finnis moves to a claim about how we should think about human beings and hence about the legal person. This claim gives rise to an account of what human beings essentially or fundamentally are and that, he says, should inform law: law is made for the sake of this kind of being.

For Finnis, thinking about human beings must begin in the first person perspective of reflection upon what we do, say and think:

> [i]n the act of (say) speaking to my partner in discourse ... I understand my utterance as the carrying out of a choice *I made* and in the same act I am aware of my audible uttering, see the hearers register their comprehension, feel (say) confidence or anxiety, remember a past misunderstanding, and hope my statement will make my point. This experience of the *unity (including the continuity)* of my being—as a feeling, willing, observing, remembering, understanding, physically active and effective mover or cause of physical effects and equally as an undergoer and recipient of such effects—is a datum which philosophical exploration of human and other natural realities can adequately account for only with great difficulty and many a pitfall. Still, prior to all accounts of it, this intelligible presence of my many-faceted acting self to myself is a datum of *understanding*; one and the same I—this human being—who am understanding and choosing and carrying out my choice and sensing, etc., is a reality I already truly understand, albeit not yet fully (explanatorily, with elaboration).[120]

This argument from the internal phenomenology of personhood, from what it is (or feels like) to be a human being, leads to an account of personhood in which continuity over time is a prerequisite and is found, according to Finnis (and to Aristotle and Aquinas before him), in *psyche* (or *anima* or soul). Something like that notion is the only thing that can accommodate the internal phenomenology of personhood in an allegedly plausible account of what it is that persists across or within the arc of a human life:

> [i]n the human animal ... from the very outset of his or her existence as human, it [psyche, anima, soul] is the one essentially unchanging factor, unique to each individual,

(1857), *Roe v Wade* (1973) and *Santa Clara County v Southern Pacific Railroad Co* (1886)). He has expanded his critique of these and other decisions in s II of his 'The Priority of Persons Revisited' (2013) 58 *American Journal of Jurisprudence* 45–62.

[118] Finnis, The Priority of Persons', ibid 1.

[119] Some of the many, many instances: the various Protection of Animal Acts in the UK (from 1911 to 2000); the Town and Country Planning (Tree Preservation) (England) Regulations 2012. Finnis is aware of the point: see ibid, 10–11 and his 'Persons and their Associations' (1989) 63 *Proceedings of the Aristotelian Society, Supplementary Volumes* 257–274.

[120] Finnis, 'The Priority of Persons' (n 117) 13–14; emphasis in original.

> which explains (1) the unity and complexity of the individual's activities, (2) the dynamic unity in complexity—in one dimension, the programme—of the individual's growth as embryo, foetus, neonate, infant … and adult, (3) the relatively mature individual's understanding of universal (e.g., generic) immaterial objects of thought … and (4) this unique individual's generic unity with every other member of the species.[121]

Since this is what persons essentially are, and law is undeniably for the sake of persons, then these are the kind of beings whose conduct, goals, interests and purposes animate the law. We can, however, quibble with both the plausibility condition Finnis sets for any account of human identity (the first-person phenomenological constraint), as well as with the assumed, un-argued requirement that human identity must remain the same across the arc of a life. Not only are there numerous challenges to both, there are also numerous different accounts of what human identity consists in.[122] That said, if Justinian's starting point is accepted, as it surely must be, then some account of the nature of those beings for the sake of whom the law exists, has to be provided. But such an account need not be either substantively or methodologically the same as Finnis's, nor need it be complete: it is no abdication of intellectual responsibility to hold that law is for human beings and that the latter be understood in accord with our best available knowledge and arguments in the human and natural sciences. Furthermore, the move to develop an account of the nature of human beings is, for our purposes, premature, since whatever such an account tells us must still stand alongside what the law tells us. And the law, remember, relates a weak legalist story about the legal person. That being so, there arises a somewhat mundane question: is Finnis's view actually incompatible with that conception of the *legal* person?

It seems not. Finnis does not use the term 'legalism' in his discussion and thus does not take an explicit view on the merits of that general approach to the legal person. He does, however, offer one objection to Kelsen's neither unambiguously nor unproblematically strong legalist conception of the person. It is that Kelsen's 'refusal to treat human persons and their interests and well-being as the point of law' served, in some instances, to 'rationalize judicial abdication from … disciplined and critical concern with the interests and well-being of real people'.[123] Such abdication is found, according to Finnis, in a number of cases, both pre- and post-dating Kelsen's work, which display 'a notable failure of judicial reasoning, of intellectual and moral responsibility in the face of the law's most fundamental

[121] Finnis, 'The Priority of Persons' (n 117) 14. For some of the implications of this view, see his 'Abortion and Health Care Ethics' in H Kuhse and P Singer (eds), *Bioethics* (Oxford, Blackwell, 2006) Ch 1 and 'The Rights and Wrongs of Abortion: A Reply to Judith Jarvis Thomson' (1973) 2 *Philosophy and Public Affairs* 117–45 (both included in J Finnis, *Human Rights and Common Good* (Oxford, Clarendon, 2011)).

[122] For introductory overviews, see J Perry (ed), *Personal Identity* (Berkeley, University of California Press, 1975); AO Rorty (ed), *The Identities of Persons* (Berkeley, University of California Press, 1992). One of the most interesting, relatively recent interventions in this ancient philosophical debate was part three of D Parfit, *Reasons and Persons* (Oxford, Clarendon, 1984).

[123] Finnis, 'The Priority of Persons' (n 117) 6 and 7.

point and meaning: the service of persons'.[124] Finnis may well be right both about the failings of these judicial decisions and the tendency of Kelsen's view to breed such failings. But neither point has any effect at all upon the view espoused here.

Finnis's position would trouble our view only if interpreted oddly or absurdly. One odd interpretation is this: Finnis holds that *any* legalist account of the person breeds the errors he ascribes to the judicial decisions influenced by Kelsen's account. Not only is this interpretation odd because difficult to find in Finnis's text, it is implausible by virtue of the account of the legal person offered here: our weak and qualified legalist conception of the person is in no way incompatible with the view that 'law is for the sake of human beings', that human conduct, interests and goals are law's obvious and pre-eminent core concerns. Our view cannot therefore provide a convivial habitat for judicial abdication from disciplined and critical concern with the interests of real human beings. Note also that neither our view, nor any other view of the legal person, can guarantee against such abdication. An absurd interpretation insists that, despite appearances, Finnis thinks that the legal person can only ever be the kind of real human being he sketches. That this view cannot be ascribed to Finnis is clear not just from (i) the fact that he recognises that 'artificial' persons are assuredly and legitimately part of the law; but also from (ii) the fact that his understanding and general utilisation of Aristotle's notion of the focal case/central meaning militates against the claim that there is only a single instance of this particular concept (the legal person).[125]

The difference between Finnis's and our view of the legal person is not great. Our view holds that the central case of the legal person is a simulacrum of the central case of a real human being. Finnis's view is that the central case of the legal person is the real human being, or possibly the central case thereof. Neither view rules out other, non-central instances of the legal person; nor do these views deny Justinian's undeniable truth. The two views could generate practically significant differences, since Finnis's embodies a specific and fairly detailed picture of the real human being, whereas ours does not. Abortion and euthanasia cases might bring this difference to the fore. Beside this possibility, are there other grounds on which to choose between the two accounts? Descriptive accuracy is one such ground and it seems to me undeniable, on the basis of what we know about all the developed legal systems, that the weak, qualified legalist view of the legal person is embodied in those systems. Our view of the legal person is predominantly the law's view. Whether or not it is the right view is side-stepped here, save only to note that the arguments of subsequent chapters, insofar as they support law's abstract judgement, also support this view of law's person.

[124] Finnis, 'The Priority of Persons' (n 117) 8. I'm not sure that Finnis's charge against Kelsen is altogether fair: see the discussion of the autonomy belief at pp 59–60, for my reasons.

[125] Finnis, 'Priority of Persons' (n 117) s V and fn 62 at pp 59–60.

III. Conclusion

The argument of this chapter is easy to summarise: I maintained that the legal person takes at least two forms (*PaP* and *PaC*), that those two forms and the legal person in general are best understood 'legalistically'; and that both forms are quite closely connected, albeit in different ways, to *LAJ*. Given these connections, it is not unreasonable to suppose that an argument in favour of the latter might well support one or both of the former. That supposition informs all that follows, although with two tweaks. The first is that what follows supposes that arguments in favour of *LAJ* can support those aspects of *PaC* that include reasonableness standards. And the second is that what follows accepts, as a result of the argument in subsection I A above, that *LAJ* presupposes or assumes *PaP*. These two points explain the absence of *PaP* and *PaC* from much of what follows. They disappear not because they are unimportant, but because they are a taken-for-granted background presence.

One final question arises before we return to *LAJ*. Can the legal person be more than presupposition and consequence? Viewed as such, the legal person's role in juridical and general thought might seem to be rather unassuming and modest. I do not think that is a fair characterisation of the role of the legal person, but I do think its role does not go much beyond that of presupposition and consequence. That is primarily because there is no juridical space left for the person in law over and beyond its life as *PaP* and *PaC*. What other way could a conception of the person function in law if not as presupposition and consequence of legal regulation? Alain Supiot is far more ambitious. He invokes law's person in particular, and law in general, as bulwarks against both privatisation and the destabilisation of national cultures, legal systems and economies by transnational corporations. For Supiot,

> [l]egal personality is … simply a means guaranteed by law to enable everyone to realize his or her personality on this earth, in a way that will identify him or her in the eyes of contemporaries and future generations.[126]

What is true of the legal person should also be true of legal systems, says Supiot, since

> [a] legal system does not fulfil its anthropological function unless it guarantees that every newcomer on this earth finds a world that pre-exists them and guarantees their identity over time, while also providing them with the opportunity to transform this world and leave their mark on it.[127]

Supiot's claim that law and the legal person fulfil this stabilising role is a consequentialist one, highlighting an effect of both on human beings and their wider

[126] A Supiot, *Homo Juridicus: On the Anthropological Function of the Law* (London, Verso, 2007) 24.
[127] ibid 37.

social-cum-cultural context. It therefore lends itself to some degree of empirical testing but, even if that level of evaluation is set aside, the claim bears some *prima facie* plausibility. For legal personality surely confers some benefits and protections upon the beings and things to whom it is conferred, a result of which is that they cannot be entirely without legal or moral significance. This is presumably what Supiot has in mind when he observes that '[t]he principle of the inalienability of civic status is the expression of the prohibition that surrounds personality'.[128] That kind of inalienability might plausibly contribute towards the stability necessary for the realisation of one's identity over time. In addition to the role that law's person plays in anchoring actual human beings in context and history, law serves as a means of questioning and holding to account the forces—primarily economic—that can destabilise agents and cultures. Law does this, according to Supiot, because it is a means of interdiction:

> [i]t is a word imposed upon all, and interposed between each person and his or her representation of the world. … [I]t interposes a realm of shared meaning transcending the individual and carrying obligations with it, between people, and between people and the world, and so transforms each of us into a link in the human chain.[.] Law has served many varied purposes in the history of political systems …, but it has served these by subordinating power and technology to human reason … it can temper the most varied forms of political power or technological prowess with a measure of reason.[129]

The precise merits of Supiot's bold argument about law's and the legal persons' anthropological function need not concern us here. The salient point for present purposes is that Supiot's argument about the legal person does not undermine the claim that *PaP* and *PaC* occupy all the juridical space available to law's person. What Supiot does is to highlight, in a way that others might test, an apparently significant, alleged consequence that flows from the 'invention' of the legal person: the creation of a realm of stability and rootedness in a world that might, as economic globalisation and technological development continue, come to have fewer and fewer such realms. That seems most obviously to be a plausible suggestion about the *effects* of the legal person on the wider culture of which it is part and not, of course, a claim about the juridical space that the legal person occupies.

[128] ibid 27. It seems clear from the context that by 'personality', Supiot means 'legal personality'.
[129] ibid xxiv–xxv.

3

Fairness: Responsibility, Impartiality, Equity

'The standard of foresight of the reasonable ... [person] ... eliminates the personal equation and is independent of the idiosyncrasies of the particular person whose conduct is in question'.[1]

Recall the moral jolt I alleged, in chapter one, that some first year law students feel when learning of the decision in *Nettleship v Weston*.[2] Among other things, the case held that the standard of care to which a learner driver must adhere is that of a reasonably competent driver. The decision illustrates law's abstract judgement in action, since the relevant standard of care is one a learner driver—almost by definition—is unlikely to satisfy. The jolt usually manifests itself in the judgement that the decision must be unfair: imposing liability on Mrs Weston for failing to meet a standard she plainly could not meet penalises her for failing to do the impossible. Law students are not unique in arriving at that conclusion; many lay people and some jurists also instinctively feel that something is wrong with the outcome in *Nettleship*. The same feeling arises in other legal contexts. Consider *R v Adesanya*, in which a Nigerian mother was prosecuted for the ceremonial scarring of the cheeks of her two sons. Scarification was and is a normal part of Yoruba culture, the two boys consented to the process, and the scars were unlikely to be permanent. Mrs Adesanya was of unimpeachable character and both she and other members of the Nigerian community in England seemed unaware that scarification was contrary to English law. Mrs Adesanya was convicted under section 47 Offences Against the Person Act (OAPA) 1861.[3] To some, this looks like the epitome of legal heavy-handedness, it being obviously wrong to prosecute and convict for a 'good-faith' offence with no significant bad consequences. The law was blindly applied to Mrs Adesanya in the same way as it would to the perpetrator of any crime.

[1] *Muir v Glasgow Corporation* [1943] AC 448 (UKHL) at 457 (Lord Macmillan).

[2] [1971] EWCA Civ 6.

[3] *The Times*, 16 July 1974 at 3. See also [1983] *Criminal Law Review* at 720–21. There is little evidence to suggest that Mrs Adesanya's case provoked comment at the time, although its general type (a 'cultural defence' case) has since generated much more discussion and controversy: see A Dundes Renteln, *The Cultural Defense* (New York, Oxford University Press, 2004) part I and II. See http://news.bbc.co.uk/1/hi/uk/1076641.stm for one of many alternative examples (last accessed 3rd January 2017).

We are entitled to interrogate the reactions these decisions often provoke and to ask, in particular, what exactly is wrong with *Nettleship*, *Adesanya* and, by extension, with the application of law's abstract judgement (hereinafter *LAJ*). Precisely where and what is the alleged unfairness in these and related cases? There might, of course, be many forms and sources of alleged unfairness here, some of which could be disclosed to us by a well-designed, comprehensive quantitative attitudinal survey or the like.[4] In the absence of such a survey I examine only three ostensibly plausible but quite different bases for the unfairness charge against *Nettleship*, *Adesanya* and *LAJ* in general. The first invokes the notion of responsibility, claiming it is unfair to hold Mrs Weston liable in *Nettleship* because she could not have done otherwise. Since she was a learner driver, she could not (either at all or often) attain the standard of a reasonably competent driver. And ability to do otherwise, it is claimed, is a key component of what it is to be responsible. If the law holds people like Mrs Weston liable when they are not responsible, then that is unfair and morally objectionable.[5]

The second basis for the unfairness charge highlights a problem in *Adesanya* and like cases. It raises a problem of partiality: in convicting Mrs Adesanya, the law not only held her to a standard of which she was unaware, but also to a standard she seemed not to accept.[6] The law was therefore indifferent to Mrs Adesanya and her values, according the latter nowhere near the level of respect routinely accorded to the values shared by the vast majority of the population. This seemingly undermines any claim that law is an impartial means of resolving disputes.[7] The third basis for the unfairness charge indicts both *Adesanya* and its like, on the one hand, and *Nettleship* and its like, on the other. It is an objection to the rigid and unyielding application of the law in circumstances in which equity or mercy requires just the opposite. It holds that the apparent harshness of applying the law to Mrs Weston and Mrs Adesanya could and should have been mitigated, that the law's lack of sensitivity to the circumstances of those caught in its maw is an obvious moral failing. Since *LAJ* is simply a generalised form of rigid and

[4] This kind of empirical work is not popular among jurists and philosophers, although there have been some interesting efforts to advance it and build bridges between disciplines: see, for example, T Tyler, *Why People Obey the Law* (Princeton, New Jersey, Princeton University Press, 2006) and D Miller, 'Distributive Justice: What the People Think' (1992) 102 *Ethics* 555–93.

[5] Although *Nettleship* was not subject to much comment when decided, two contemporary case-notes struck the unfairness chord. WV Horton Rogers' reservations about Lord Denning's judgment were expressed thus: 'the moral notion at the heart of negligence law is too firmly embedded to be overturned by judicial developments' ('Trouble with Learners' (1972) 30 *Cambridge Law Journal* 24–27 at 27). AL Goodhart opined 'is not fairness even more attractive if it can be attained without undue difficulty?' in (1971) 87 *Law Quarterly Review* 444–49 at 449.

[6] I assume in what follows that there are good grounds supporting the 'ignorance of the law is no defence' injunction and therefore ignore it. For some interesting thoughts see: R Goodin, 'An Epistemic Case for Legal Moralism' (2010) *Oxford Journal of Legal Studies* 615–33.

[7] For Dundes Renteln, this and like cases illustrate a 'majoritarian bias in the legal system', there being 'substantial evidence of such bias': above n 3 at 6.

unyielding resort to and application of general rules, this specific complaint is clearly of general import.[8]

Before examining these three unfairness claims, note that some other related objections to *LAJ* are not considered here. I said in chapter one that the burden of this book is not a blow by blow evaluation and attempted rebuttal of all of the many objections aimed at *LAJ*. Instead I counterbalance the weight of these objections by speaking—*regardless of them*—in favour of *LAJ*. This adding of ballast to the argumentative scales discredits the thought that *LAJ* is entirely without merit. But why, then, depart from this script and attend directly to the three objections to *LAJ* just outlined? There are two reasons. First, because I think these three objections are closest to the surface of any common sense or theoretical engagement with *LAJ*, motivating at the outset suspicion about this way of being judged. If that is so, then these objections demand immediate attention. And, second, an exploration of these three objections illuminates the depth of some of *LAJ*'s connections to other fundamental components of legal thought and legal systems. These objections are a prism through which contemporary law's complex nature can be glimpsed.

I. Responsibility

What might it mean to say that Mrs Weston could not have done otherwise and, if true, why should this absolve her from legal liability? This question requires much unpacking, since it not only calls into play the general requirements for liability in tort law in particular and private law in general, but also raises the spectre of how those requirements might be justified. An even broader issue follows on the heels of these two, namely, that of the relation between regimes of legal liability-responsibility, on the one hand, and non-legal (moral, political and other) regimes of liability-responsibility, on the other. We will bump into each issue in what follows.

Let's begin with the general idea of liability-responsibility. By this I mean those conditions that determine whether or not one is in the frame for praise or blame. Most of these conditions relate to what can be called, on an expansive view, human agency, and serve to distinguish our role in bringing about or maintaining situations and circumstances from the role of non-human agents like animals and natural forces. While the conditions for all forms of liability-responsibility will surely have something in common, since they now serve to distinguish between human and non-human agency, they also seem likely to differ from context to context. The conditions for liability to criticism and blame might well differ from the conditions for praise and honour, and the conditions crucial to legal-liability

[8] Given Mrs Adesanya's sentence (a conditional discharge: *The Times*, 17 July 1974 at 4) equity or mercy might well have been at work in the case.

responsibility (usually salient only when legal criticism and blame are being ascribed) may differ significantly from those relevant to moral or other forms of non-legal liability-responsibility (which are in play in situations of praise and blame).

I use the term 'legal liability-responsibility' as shorthand for those conditions almost always necessary for human agents to be in the frame for, but not necessarily recipients of, legal blame and criticism.[9] These conditions assuredly differ not only as between contemporary legal systems—although not massively—and as between different areas of each legal system. However, in the common law legal systems there are roughly three *general* and interrelated conditions for liability-responsibility in private law, although particular areas of private law often supplement and refine some or all of these and even, in rare instances, ignore one or more of them.[10] These refinements, additions and eschewals amount to the *specific* conditions for particular forms of private law liability and are laid out in our textbooks and the cases, statutes and commentaries that they chronicle, evaluate and synthesise. Henceforth I set them aside, but this does not imply that the two sets of conditions are unrelated; far from it. For, although the general conditions of legal liability responsibility provide broader underpinning principles and reaction points for specific conditions, the former must also have a discernible life in our textbooks, cases, statutes and commentaries. We must be able to show not only that these conditions are broadly consistent with large swathes of existing law, but also that they rationally inform (by making intelligible what would otherwise be unintelligible) that law.[11] Both of these plausibility requirements—fit and justification—are open to interpretation and contestation, as will be clear in what follows, but little else is said about them. They are stated here not as a preamble to a discussion of method but in a spirit of methodological candour.

A. The Three Conditions

The first general condition of legal liability-responsibility in private law (hereinafter just 'legal liability-responsibility') is that those in the frame for blame must (i) be

[9] Talk of legal liability-responsibility does not commit one to the view that 'in one of its senses responsibility is virtually identical with liability' (J Raz, 'Responsibility and the Negligence Standard' (2010) 30 *Oxford Journal of Legal Studies* 1–18 at 3, fn 5). The error in regarding liability and responsibility as synonymous is elucidated in HLA Hart, *Punishment and Responsibility*, 2nd edn (Oxford, Clarendon Press, 2008) 215–16. I fail to see how the claim that liability is a 'type' of responsibility entails this elision (Raz, ibid, seemingly thinks it does).

[10] As we will see, the three conditions are closely related, being slightly less abstract versions of those that inform *PaP*: see chapter two, section I A.

[11] These three general conditions are also, I think, in play in criminal law, although I offer no argument to that end. For a more sustained general discussion of the two plausibility requirements, see my 'Method and Fit: Two Problems for Contemporary Philosophies of Tort Law' (2007) 52 *McGill Law Journal* 605–56.

aware of their conduct, or have the capacity to be aware of it; and (ii) some aspect of their conduct must be theirs in the sense that they did it and had reason to do it. There is a link between these two sub-conditions in the notion of intentionality: awareness (or the capacity to be aware) of one's conduct and ownership of some aspects of one's conduct both depend upon it. By 'conduct' I refer to one's actions and omissions and these are not always the same as either the goals or outcomes of those actions and omissions. Goals are those results at which conduct aims and, of course, they may or may not be realised; outcomes are all the consequences and situations one's conduct brings about or maintains regardless of its aims.[12] Awareness of my conduct implies, in the normal run of instances, that I have the standard cognitive and volitional requirements of most human beings: I am able to formulate plans or goals, appreciate at some level that I can manipulate my body and parts of the world so as to try to realise those plans, and thus understand in broad terms something of causality and of the relation between means and ends. To say I am aware of my X-ing implies that X-ing is either a goal of mine, or that I think it a means of achieving some such goal, and thus that I want or have reason to bring X about. We might say that I had X in view or in mind (although the latter might cause howls among some philosophers). It plainly does not follow that I must be so aware of all my conduct, of each and every intervention or refraining of mine in the world. I certainly do not have 'whisker removal' in view or in mind every time I shave: this is often something I do automatically, while half-asleep (and it sometimes shows). But the fact that I am not fully aware of this specific instance of conduct—shaving—says nothing about my general capacity to be aware of this aspect or any other aspect of my conduct. Indeed, it is the fact that I once had to attend very closely to this particular form of conduct that allows me now to do it almost automatically. The point is that my capacity for awareness of my conduct (of whatever kind or type) persists even when not instantiated in particular instances of apparent conduct, just as my capacity to sink six foot putts persists (for some period at least) in the face of some failures to sink six foot putts. If I never again sink a six foot putt, we are entitled to think that I have lost a capacity I once had.

An obvious way of characterising the awareness of conduct, or the general capacity to be so aware, is to say that my conduct is intended (or that I have the general capacity for intentional conduct). For intentional conduct is really just conduct that it is one's goal to perform or that one regards as necessary to the achievement of some goal: my walking down the street to the coffee shop is usually and obviously intentional because I realise it is either the only way, or one of the best ways, to get good coffee. Getting good coffee is obviously a goal of mine but so, too, is the means of realising that goal. The link between intentionality and

[12] There is a general philosophical problem lurking here with regard to the individuation of particular instances of conduct and the re-describability of goals which I sidestep. For a brief overview of the issue, see my *Philosophy of Private Law* (Oxford, Clarendon Press, 2007) 74–78.

goals is a link that rests upon awareness, namely, awareness of some aspect of my conduct, its relation to my goals and the wider world I inhabit. And this same link is a means of determining ownership of my conduct in the face of the question 'what did you do?' For that which I intentionally do, which was my goal or my means of achieving a goal, and of which I was necessarily aware, is in the normal run of events undoubtedly mine. That which I intentionally do, I have reason to do and, that being so, I am owner or author of my intentional conduct. Of course, there can be and often is a difference between what I intentionally do and other situations or events in the world that my conduct causes or effects. In going for coffee, I forget an appointment and also, during my walk back from the coffee shop, bump into and knock over a colleague's young child. There is clearly a legitimate and interesting sense in which I did all these things—all were, for instance, causal consequences of my intentional conduct—but only some of them were intended.

The claim that capacity for and the actual performance of intentional conduct is, generally speaking, a condition for legal liability-responsibility might be contested in two obvious but quite misguided ways. One criticism consists of the production of counter-examples: instances of liability in private law where neither the capacity for, nor actual performance of, intentional conduct is necessary. But the existence of such instances is not fatal to our case, unless there are many. In the absence of a comprehensive survey of private law as a whole I can offer only an assertion: there are insufficient counter-examples to undermine the interpretive plausibility of the intentionality condition, to show it is a bad fit with existing law. My claim about the intentionality condition is not universal, holding that this condition is always and everywhere a necessary requirement for liability, so it cannot therefore be refuted by a single counterexample or even a handful of them. It is enough that the intentionality condition is found and satisfied in a broad swathe of cases in the principal doctrinal segments of private law. Moreover, given what we know about the development of the common law—it is a discursive process, stretched over time, involving the minds of many judges, all of whom may disagree over aspects of one another's decisions—counter-examples and apparent wrong-turns are perfectly predictable. The common law is simply never so neat as to embody perfectly a particular general principle, be it one about the substantive content of some area of law (can merely doing what you are already contractually bound to do be good consideration for a subsequent promise to pay extra?) or about the general conditions of liability-responsibility.

The second objection holds that our emphasis upon intentionality is misconceived. That is because there are very few forms of liability in private law in which the wrong in question must be intentional.[13] Whatever the number of such wrongs, their existence or non-existence has no impact at all on our claim, which

[13] See P Cane, '*Mens Rea* in Tort Law' (2000) 20 *Oxford Journal of Legal Studies* 533–56 for general discussion.

insists only that those in the frame for liability (i) have the general capacity to act intentionally and (ii) did something intentionally which either was a private law wrong or had a private law wrong as an outcome or consequence. There might *seem* to be some instances where even that is not necessary, but the general capacity for intentional conduct is: one may have completely and utterly forgotten one's contractual duties and thus neither acted nor refrained intentionally, yet still be liable for breach of contract. But even here, subject to the details of the contract, liability arises only if one wittingly (intentionally) entered into the contract, was not insane, a minor or acting under some vitiating factor. Intentional conduct is therefore present in the vicinity of the private law wrong.

If awareness and ownership of one's conduct rest upon intentionality, then rationality must also be in play and this is the second general condition for legal liability-responsibility. Intentional conduct is conduct done for a reason; it is also often conduct engaged in as a result of an analysis of the relation between means and ends. I began shaving and continue to shave in order to rid myself of intrusive facial hair; although either a beard or a moustache would disguise my weak facial features, this benefit is more than outweighed by the fact that facial hair simply does not suit me. My goal here (to look less awful than I otherwise would) and the means chosen to achieve it (regular shaving) are therefore the product of a low level process of rational deliberation that characterises vast swathes of everyday human conduct. Furthermore, the ability to understand and process information from other agents and the wider environment assumes some degree of rationality insofar as understanding is impossible without it. If this is what rationality means when taken as a condition for liability responsibility, then it is uncontroversial. However, some degree of disagreement arises among jurists, at least when this question is posed: is that *all* that rationality means in this context? Some jurists—rational minimalists—answer affirmatively, while others—rational maximalists—answer in the negative.

The former hold that the capacity to act for reasons, and what that implies about rationality, exhausts the rationality condition. Within the practical context of legal action, this capacity entails something like 'an ability to offer justifications and excuses … the ability to explain oneself, to give an intelligible account of oneself, to answer for oneself'.[14] It is, in only a very slight variation, a matter of being able to reason practically and 'to be guided by the rules'.[15] Understood thus, the level of rationality required of those in the frame for legal liability-responsibility is not high: having reasons for what one does, being able to express them and being aware of the general context (including rules) in which one operates, requires little by way of reflection upon either the quality of one's reasons or of the information and context in light of which one formulates reasons. Rational maximalists go beyond this requirement and insist, *at least*, that those in the frame

[14] J Gardner, 'The Mark of Responsibility' (2003) 23 *Oxford Journal of Legal Studies* 157–71 at 161.
[15] P Cane, *Responsibility in Law and Morality* (Oxford, Hart Publishing, 2002) at 35.

for legal liability also have (i) the capacity for deliberation and reasoned choice; and (ii) an awareness or understanding of the requirements of law and morality. The former sub-condition goes beyond the minimalist view insofar as deliberation and reasoned choice entail a qualitative assessment, a sorting and weighing, of the reasons for one's conduct. For one sometime rational maximalist, the latter sub-condition necessitates a general understanding on the part of those subject to the law of 'both the system of allocation according to outcomes and how in practice to use causal notions to settle what counts as the outcome of action'.[16] This, too, goes well beyond a minimalist view. Other apparent maximalists are at some points vaguer and at others more expansive when specifying the content of these two sub-conditions.[17]

It is important to recall, when faced with the disagreement between maximalists and minimalists, that both regard rationality (or the capacity for rationality) as a condition of liability-responsibility. It is also possible that both views are correct, in the sense that maximalists and minimalists might both be able to point to areas of legal doctrine that support their claims. That being so, what can safely be said about the rationality condition? Probably only this: that the minimal version of that condition undoubtedly often is, and should always be, a condition of liability-responsibility in private law. Those sceptical about this claim cannot refute it—and for the reasons specified in the discussion of the intentionality condition above—by pointing to areas of doctrine that do not embody it. So, for instance, the fact that in the common law systems insanity seems not to be a defence in tort is no embarrassment.[18] For one thing, it is not obvious that insanity will always undermine the rationality condition as opposed to one or more of the other conditions. Insanity as understood outwith the law is far from being a univocal concept but, where and when one of its instantiations prevents one or more conditions for liability-responsibility being satisfied, then that at least raises the possibility of an exculpatory claim. And the grounds upon which such a claim arises are coextensive with the reasons that provide general support for the three conditions, which we will examine below. These reasons constitute the normative case for the three conditions and do double work: they justify those conditions while at the same time informing our statement and evaluation of the law. Our chronicles of the law are therefore not without a guiding structure or narrative, as they once were. Legal textbooks in the common law world are not the disorderly (albeit alphabetically organised) heaps of judgements and facts that characterised legal knowledge in pre-textbook times.[19]

[16] T Honore, *Responsibility and Fault* (Oxford, Hart Publishing, 1999) at 32. I say 'sometime' because there are remarks that suggest Honore sees himself as a rational minimalist: ibid, at 26, 29 (capacity for 'reasoned choice and action' enough for liability) but note 122 for an interesting qualification.

[17] Hart (n 9) at 227–29. The contest between maximalists and minimalists is an obvious echo of the discussion of the rationalist legal person in ch two, section II B (i).

[18] See J Goudkamp, *Tort Law Defences* (Oxford, Hart Publishing, 2013) 49–58 and Ch 8 for helpful and informed discussion of this issue.

[19] See AWB Simpson, 'The Rise and Fall of the Legal Treatise: Legal Principles and the Forms of Legal Literature' (1981) 48 *University of Chicago Law Review* 632–79 for a magisterial discussion.

Both the intentionality and rationality conditions invoke the notion of capacity and this is the third condition for legal liability-responsibility. Moreover, we have taken for granted a particular interpretation of capacity in the discussion to this point which now requires elucidation and defence. In the words of a compelling treatment of the topic, the meaning of capacity as it has featured so far is a matter of '*can (general)*' as opposed to '*can (particular)*'.[20] With regard to the latter,

> success or failure, on the assumption that an effort has been or will be made, is the factor that governs the use of the notion. If the agent tried and failed, he could not do the action: if he tried and succeeded, he was able to do it. If he will fail however hard he tries, he cannot do it; if he will succeed provided he tries, he can.[21]

By contrast with can (particular), can (general)

> is most commonly used in connection with types of action rather than particular actions. 'Can' in this sense is used to assert a general competence, ability or skill in the performance of some type of action. If a person is a competent golfer, 'he can hole a short putt' must be true; otherwise he would not be competent. What we usually mean by saying that a person can do an action of a certain type is not that he may do it, that it is on the cards that he will do such an action, but rather that he normally succeeds in doing it when he tries.[22]

If the capacity condition for legal liability-responsibility is understood as can (general), then we need not be convinced that someone in the frame for blame was able to do other than they did with regard to any relevant instance of conduct. For, from the perspective of general capacity (which henceforth I use as a synonym for can (general)), capacity to do otherwise does not require the capability to do other than P at the exact time and in the precise context in which P took place. Rather, it requires either the 'general capacity for decision and action' *and* the ability to do other than P in the majority of instances in which conduct of that general P-type is possible (in instances of fault liability); or just the general capacity for decision and action (in cases of strict liability). Suppose that P—the conduct in question—is rightly described as 'driving without crashing'. When faced with a particular motor accident, our question is not 'could the driver have done otherwise than crash at that particular time and in those precise circumstances?' but either 'does this driver have general capacity and usually avoid accidents when driving?' or 'does this driver have general capacity?' If the answer to either of the latter questions is 'yes', the propriety of each question being determined by whether or not 'fault' is a requirement of the wrong, then there is a sense in which it can be said that this driver has the capacity (can (general)) for decision and action and to

[20] Honore (n 16) Ch 7 (originally published in (1964) 73 *Mind* 463–479) 143. Emphasis in the original.

[21] Honore (n 16) 144.

[22] Honore (n 16) 144–45. For critical discussion of Honore's view of capacity, see the essays by M Smith and P Pettit in P Cane and J Gardner (eds), *Relating to Responsibility* (Oxford, Hart Publishing, 2001) chs 1 and 2. Honore's response is at 219–22.

drive safely. The existence of the latter capacity is, of course, perfectly compatible with the driver in question having an accident on a particular occasion or occasions and with the claim that on these occasions the driver could not have done otherwise.

The fact that general capacity can exist when particular capacity (can (particular)) is wanting does not show that the two are independent. Judgements about the existence of some general capacity to X are patently only possible when agents have the particular capacity in numerous instances to do X. If no agent has ever done X, then the claim that any particular agent has the general capacity to do X is dubious but not ridiculous: some agent, somewhere, could be the first to do X. If that agent does indeed do X first, then they clearly had the capacity (can (particular)) to do X; whether or not they have the general capacity to do X depends upon them repeating X a sufficient number of times. If, however, no agent could ever do X, then agents plainly have neither the particular nor the general capacity to do X.

Why should the capacity condition be understood as entailing can (general) rather than can (particular)? Surely those jolted by decisions like *Nettleship* regard them as objectionable for the very reason that Mrs Weston (let us assume) could not have done otherwise in those precise circumstances at that particular time? It is not enough to assume, as up to this point we have, that private law's capacity condition embeds can (general) and not can (particular). For even if that is true—and I think it is broadly true of contemporary systems of private law in both the common law and civil law worlds—it does not answer the present objection, which questions the propriety of regarding capacity as general capacity and embedding that understanding in law. This, it is alleged, is a mistake and the source of the disquiet raised by *Nettleship* and its ilk. But what is the mistake here? It is not that of holding an unreasoned position, since there is a plausible basis for the capacity condition embodying can (general): doing so prioritises the (security) interests of claimants over the (liberty) interests of defendants.[23] By ignoring the particular capacity of defendants, and thus any exculpatory claims that might be built upon its absence, the law protects the interests of those harmed: their claims for a remedy are accorded greater protection and respect than are the potential exculpatory claims of actual harm-doers. This reason is not obviously weak or misguided, but that is not to say it cannot be defeated. If it could be shown that defendants' exculpatory claims and the values those claims embody must, as a compelling requirement of morality or politics, be ranked above claimants' security interests and the values they embody, then the current law would be open to serious criticism. That no such demonstration has yet been provided does not mean that one will never be forthcoming. It does, however, mean that the reason underpinning private law's current view of capacity is as yet undefeated.

[23] Which is itself a consequence of fair terms of social cooperation and a fair division of risks: see A Ripstein, *Equality, Responsibility, and the Law* (Cambridge, Cambridge University Press, 1999) chs 1 and 3 and T Honore, 'Appreciations and Responses' in Cane and Gardner (n 22) 224.

There is another consideration that might inform the jolt felt by some when learning of *Nettleship* which is in one sense related to, but in another categorically different from, that just related. The categorical difference arises from the fact this consideration is metaphysical, rather than solely moral or political, insisting that the metaphysical truth of hard determinism not only shows decisions like *Nettleship* to be wrong but undermines, because incompatible with, the whole basis of all or most of our current judgements about and practices of (liability-) responsibility.[24] So as to support this objection, hard determinism must affirm not just the platitude that everything, including all instances of human conduct, has a cause (who would deny this claim?), but also that the existence and acknowledgment of this truth undermines much of what we currently think and do. The principal difficulty with arguments of this kind is that they either assume a domain free from causal determinism (the realm of much of what we currently think and do) or posit domains of genuine and non-genuine causality. The first assumption runs contrary to the alleged metaphysical truth being insisted upon, while the second quickly becomes enmired in the difficult task of adequately and robustly distinguishing these two domains. These problems are not intended as a refutation of any variety of determinism, hard or otherwise. Rather, everything said here is neutral as to the truth of determinism, having no significant connections to that view.

B. Can the Conditions be Justified?

Why are these three conditions embedded in the law and why should they be? Because conditions like these are necessary if law is in part an enterprise of subjecting human conduct to the governance of rules. (I say 'conditions like these' rather than these exact conditions because the considerations supporting them, as we will see, are not so narrow and precise as to support only one single version of each condition; rather, these considerations can support a family group of like conditions, among which figure the three we have delineated.) Governance by rules implies at least two things: (i) that both addressees and creators of rules *know* in general terms what rules are, what they do and, in particular cases, know how to inform themselves of what rules require; (ii) that addressees of rules can *modify* their conduct in light of rules and that creators of rules also know this and know the limits of this capacity. The 'knowing' and the 'modifying' in that sentence contain the rationale for the three conditions (or conditions like them): only if law is an enterprise of subjecting human conduct to the governance of rules, and only if human beings are able to be so governed, do the three conditions make sense. The intentionality,

[24] Two fine introductions to the varieties of determinism and their alleged consequences are: P Van Inwagen, *An Essay on Free Will* (Oxford, Clarendon Press, 1983) and P French, H Wettstein and J M Fischer (eds), *Midwest Studies in Philosophy Volume XXIX: Free Will and Moral Responsibility* (Oxford, Blackwell, 2005).

rationality and capacity conditions are, in one light, simply more particular manifestations of the general enterprise of subjecting human conduct to the governance of rules. If human beings were incapable of communicating with one another, or were unable to modify their conduct in light of communication with one another, then the three conditions would be pointless. So, too, would be the attempt to subject their conduct to the governance of rules. 'Goading' rather than 'guiding' would be the appropriate way of attempting to bring such beings into line: electric prods (or water cannon, blows, etc) rather than rules are obvious means to that end.

Lon Fuller was crystal clear about some of the broader connections here:

> [t]o embark on the enterprise of subjecting human conduct to the governance of rules involves of necessity a commitment to the view that man is, or can become, a responsible agent, capable of understanding and following rules, and answerable for his defaults.
>
> Every departure from the principles of the law's inner morality is an affront to man's dignity as a responsible agent. To judge his actions by unpublished or retrospective laws, or to order him to do an act that is impossible, is to convey to him your indifference to his powers of self-determination. Conversely, when the view is accepted that man is incapable of responsible action, legal morality loses its reason for being. To judge his actions by unpublished or retrospective laws is no longer an affront, for there is nothing to affront—indeed, even the verb 'to judge' becomes itself incongruous in this context; we no longer judge a man, we act upon him.[25]

That Fuller had in mind the inner morality of law makes no difference to the point, for that morality must also include alongside its eight desiderata versions of the intentionality, rationality and capacity conditions: 'must' because without beings that can satisfy these conditions the overall enterprise is fatuous.

But even if addressees of the law are beings capable of understanding rules and modifying their conduct in light of them—beings capable, that is, of satisfying the three conditions of liability-responsibility—might it not be easier, cheaper and more convenient simply to goad them rather than guide them?[26] Current technology is such that automobiles could be manufactured so as to deliver low-level electric shocks to drivers every time they exceed the speed-limit. That might well be a more effective and efficient means of ensuring safe driving than a schema of requirements-cum-prohibitions with accompanying penalties and a system of enforcement (of both the requirements and the penalties). Surely the most efficient system of regulation is also the best system? Not if we think the notion of dignity is in play here, as Fuller does. For him dignity is a matter of being treated as a responsible being and such a being is, of course, one who at the very least is able to

[25] LL Fuller, *The Morality of Law*, revised edn (New Haven, Yale University Press, 1969) 162–63.

[26] See Hart (n 9) 44 and J Gardner, *Law as a Leap of Faith* (Oxford, Clarendon Press, 2012) 227. For more extended thoughts, see S Darwall, *The Second-Person Standpoint* (Cambridge, Massachusetts, Harvard University Press, 2006) 49–52.

satisfy the three conditions for legal liability-responsibility.[27] Goading of the sharp stick/electrical shock/water cannon/ physical blows kind ignores agents' capacity for agency, their ability to evaluate what to do in the context in which they find themselves and in light of their goals. It makes no effort to engage with agents' deliberative capacity, to communicate with them, to allow them to make one option more salient than another.[28] The point is brought to bear, shock administered, cannon deployed, blow delivered either at the moment at which an agent behaves contrary to the requirement or just beforehand; there is thus very little room to make and act upon a choice contrary to that which is required. Yet law traditionally does build-in a good deal of room for such choice because it normally attempts to engage with the practical reasoning of its addressees. It sets and communicates requirements to its addressees, but it is possible for addressees to ignore these, to make and act upon other choices, albeit at the risk of sanction or other legal consequence. By building-in room for choice, the law treats its addressees as (in Fuller's term) responsible beings, with (in Fuller's term) dignity. In allowing the possibility of choice contrary to its guidance, law also respects freedom. This is freedom to act other than as the law requires, but it is no less a form of freedom for all that.[29]

Finally, the most important question: was it unfair to hold Mrs Weston liable? If by 'unfairness' we mean 'contrary to normatively respectable principles of liability-responsibility', then it seems not. For, insofar as the three general conditions for liability-responsibility in private law have some normative warrant, they count as respectable but not, of course, as necessarily unimpeachable. That being so, it follows that it was not obviously unfair to hold Mrs Weston liable if she could indeed have satisfied those three conditions, namely, that she had (i) the general capacity to engage in conduct for reasons; (ii) the general capacity to engage in intentional conduct (and was indeed the author of some such conduct which had the accident in question as its outcome or consequence) and also, assuming there is a 'fault' requirement in the tort of negligence; (iii) the general capacity to drive more often than not without crashing (although difficulties assuredly arise here with regard to the appropriate conduct description).[30] Of course, absolute

[27] This sense of dignity, which is much the same as that invoked by J Raz in *The Authority of Law*, 2nd edn (Oxford, Clarendon Press, 2009) at 221–22, in some respects overlaps with, but is not identical to, the value-status sense that is the fulcrum of chapter four.

[28] As the salient definitions of goad in the *Shorter Oxford English Dictionary* make vividly clear.

[29] My conception of freedom must therefore make sense both within and contrary to law. An excellent treatment of the former is part II of M Van Hees, *Legal Reductionism and Freedom* (Dordrecht, Kluwer, 2001).

[30] While ch 2 of Honore's *Responsibility and Fault* reminds us of the elusive line between fault and strict liability, he accepts that the liability responsibility requirements for the former are more extensive than for the latter: ibid (n 16) at 15. This is surely right, yet its effect, if any, upon our view of the liability conditions for negligence depends upon our view of the role of fault there (and the way in which fault itself is conceived). I'm inclined to think fault is not a requirement for negligence liability (although there is often, as a matter of fact, fault in negligence cases), but little or nothing in the argument in the text turns upon this.

certainty that the three conditions were satisfied eludes us: the case report contains insufficient information. But, since many potentially pertinent issues were not raised in the case—there was no suggestion Mrs Weston suffered from any cognitive or volitional defects, had a medical condition or was otherwise hobbled in her efforts to drive—it is not unreasonable to assume that she satisfied the three general conditions. So, was it unfair to hold her liable? Not by reference to the law's conditions for liability-responsibility. While legal-liability responsibility is not the only form of liability-responsibility, neither is it obviously morally and politically disreputable.

The latter point is reinforced if it is the case that the general conception of responsibility in play in private law, and of which the three conditions are constitutive elements, is fair. That general conception is best labelled 'outcome responsibility', which

> means being responsible for the good and the harm we bring about by what we do. By allocating credit for the good outcomes of our actions and discredit for bad ones, society imposes outcome responsibility; though often the rewards it attaches and, outside the law, the sanctions it imposes are informal and vague. Under a system of outcome responsibility … [w]e have to take the risk of harmful outcomes that may be sheer bad luck and not our fault; but that does not make the system unfair to people who are likely to be winners overall.[31]

That conception is fair, according to Honore, if three conditions are satisfied. They are

> that the system must in its operation be impartial, reciprocal and over a period, beneficial. It must apply impartially to all those who possess a minimum capacity for reasoned choice and action. It must be reciprocal in that each such person is entitled to apply it to others and they to him. It must work so as to entitle each person to potential benefits that are likely on the whole to outweigh the detriments to which it subjects him. This makes it unfair to apply the system to the incapable, for whom there is no likely surplus of benefit over detriment. But for the capable the three conditions are normally satisfied.[32]

The first two conditions seem relatively unproblematic. By 'impartially' in this context Honore presumably means something like 'non-discriminatory': the system of outcome responsibility must apply to all regardless of differences of rank, status, race, gender and similar matters. Those excluded from the system—children, adults lacking the usual cognitive and volitional capacities—must be ruled out on generalisable, principled grounds. The reciprocity condition is also apparently straightforward, in that all with capacity are subject to and able to invoke the system of outcome responsibility. Viewed in this way, the reciprocity condition might overlap with the impartiality condition insofar as a lack of reciprocity implies a failure of impartiality. If X (or members of group X) are unable to invoke

[31] Honore (n 16) 14–15.
[32] Honore (n 16) 26–27.

the system of outcome responsibility against Y (or members of group Y), then the reasons for this must be generalisable and principled (Y and members of Y are minors, for example). If not, the immunity immediately becomes suspect, apparently resting on improper or unfathomable grounds. Among the former we would include partiality towards Y or members of Y.

The third condition has attracted most comment and, because of this, we must emphasise three points Honore himself makes in the passage just quoted. First, he says 'the system' of outcome responsibility must be beneficial 'over a period'; second, by 'beneficial' he means that '[i]t must work so as to entitle each person to potential benefits that are likely on the whole to outweigh the detriments to which it subjects him'; and third, 'it [is] unfair to apply the system to the incapable'. It is therefore clear that this component of Honore's fairness argument, just like the other two, is both consequentialist and systemic: the *system* of outcome responsibility is fair if, *inter alia*, it benefits those of capacity more, over a period of time, than it burdens them. If the system does not have this effect upon those who use it, then it is *prima facie* unfair (or less fair than it otherwise might be).

There is undoubtedly one interesting difficulty with this argument, but some alleged problems are simply red herrings. One such problem is the idea that benefits and detriments cannot be distributed, at least when they take the form of moral credit and discredit. This assertion supposedly derives from the claim that '[a] person gains moral credit if and only if it is true that she should have it and moral discredit if and only if it is true that she should have it'.[33] That may well be—and perhaps ought to be—true, but the way in which it shows that benefits and detriments (and subsequently moral credits and discredits) cannot be distributed is mysterious. If it is true that X should have credit C, and we ensure than she receives credit C, then we have in some meaningful sense 'distributed' credit C to X. Whether credit C is moral or not seems to make no difference to the possibility of its 'distribution'. Of course, were there something about the domain of the moral that made moral credit (benefits) and discredit (detriments) impossible to distribute, then that would be another matter. But the assertion that 'moral credit and discredit are not resources and they are not distributed'[34] does nothing to support that point: it can only undermine the sketch just offered as to how such credits and discredits might be distributed if (i) there is indeed a qualitatively significant dissimilarity as between moral credit and discredit, on the one hand, and 'resources', on the other; and (ii) that dissimilarity is such as to make distribution of the former impossible or mistaken. The latter might follow from the invocation of an impermeable barrier between the domain of the moral and that of distributive justice—if one thought that these two domains embodied principles and considerations that could not be combined with one another, then one might

[33] A Beever, 'Corrective Justice and Personal Responsibility in Tort Law' (2008) 28 *Oxford Journal of Legal Studies* 475–500 at 486.

[34] ibid.

assert that '[m]oral credit and discredit cannot be distributed unjustly'.[35] Yet that claim requires a good deal of support to be independently plausible—the invocation of Aristotle is not in itself sufficient[36]—and, even if that support is forthcoming, the claim still does not show that moral credit and discredit cannot be *distributed*. The fact that they cannot, as proponents of this argument would presumably insist, be distributed according to principles of distributive justice does not (without more) entail that they cannot be distributed at all. Lottery winnings and kidneys are distributed but not, it seems, according to principles of distributive justice.

If the 'distributability' of benefits and detriments is not the significant problem in Honore's third condition, then what is? Perhaps it is the issue of measuring benefits and detriments 'over a period'. In assessing whether or not the benefits distributed under a system of outcome responsibility outweigh the detriments, much depends upon when that calculation is made. The most obvious but most problematic time would be across the duration of a life, since only such an overview of benefits and detriments ensures an accurate assessment. However, for the agent in question the end of their life is assuredly somewhat late to assess the fairness of the system of outcome responsibility. If a life has already been more or less lived, and it is one in which the detriments of outcome responsibility outweigh the benefits, nothing much can be done to rectify that unfairness. Furthermore, the difficulty of chronicling the whole of a single life, and all its attendant outcome responsibility assigned benefits and detriments, is not insignificant. When extended across the whole of a particular population now living under a system of outcome responsibility, that process is vastly more problematic.

Even though they are not in principle impossible, the notion of whole life outcome responsibility audits is unhelpful. For we live our lives with far less complexity than that, yet still make judgements about how well and badly particular lives are going and have gone. Indeed, it is usually only when something has gone terribly wrong for us—from the death of loved ones, illness and divorce to legal action (a potentially significant detriment under the system of outcome responsibility)—that any kind of serious audit takes place. A life with 'ups and downs' cannot be a bad life under the system of outcome responsibility unless that system has dealt out so many of the latter, or they are of such a magnitude, that they outweigh not just the former, but also the neither up nor down but so-so aspects of that life. We usually know long before the end of a particular person's life whether they are winning or losing as a result of both the system of outcome responsibility and the results of the natural and social lotteries.[37] What underpins this knowledge is, at

[35] ibid.

[36] *Nicomachean Ethics*, 1131 b 12–1131 b 13 and 1132 a 32–1132 a 33 in J Barnes (ed), *The Complete Works of Aristotle* Vol 2 (Princeton, New Jersey, Princeton University Press, 1984).

[37] On the natural and social lotteries see J Rawls, *A Theory of Justice*, revised edn (Oxford, Clarendon Press, 1999) 62–65 (where he speaks of 'the influence of social contingencies and natural fortune'). For a harrowing chronicle of a life of one dealt a poor hand by the social lottery, see A Masters, *Stuart: A Life Backwards* (London, Harper Collins, 2006).

best, an incremental and intermittent series of judgements based upon general human experience yet almost never supported by robust actuarial evidence (or the like). We can and do ask multiple questions about someone's life at a particular time: have they had bad luck? Been ill? Are they struggling with other difficulties? Are they accident prone or beset by calamities? Is theirs a 'troubled' life? Such questions, the fulcrum of neighbourhood chitchat and casual conversation, are our way of making sense of the way someone's life has gone and is going. The questions need not be (and indeed never are) answered by reference to actuarial evidence. But the lack of evidence is felt neither there nor in a more obviously intellectual context where related claims—'[w]e all know people, or know of people, who apparently possess whatever minimum capacity to get by in the world … who nevertheless seem to be life's perennial losers'; 'the well-endowed in terms of natural talents will tend to do better than those who lack such talents'[38]—are made. We might, of course, insist upon a robust evidential basis for such claims although it is difficult to see how it could be reliably accumulated. Moreover, since such claims, and the general human experience upon which they rest, are a common and well-entrenched feature of ordinary life, informing our reactive attitudes and thus our judgement of others, the call for supporting evidence might be regarded as an amusing eccentricity.[39]

The crucial question, then, is this: can such claims inform an assessment of the fairness of a system of outcome responsibility? I think they can and do. They equip us to say, at any point in a particular agent's life, whether or not the system of outcome responsibility is operating to their overall benefit, and we need make no claim about 'the natural order of things' automatically inclining towards benefit overall for such an assessment to be plausible.[40] These incremental and intermittent judgements about how well or badly particular lives are going, and the general human knowledge and experience that they invoke, are also already embedded in our responsibility judgements in law and elsewhere. They condition, for example, decisions as to whether or not agents are fit to stand trial, to give evidence and thus whether they have or lack general capacity. Of course, decisions such as these are also informed by expert testimony, but something must trigger recourse to

[38] The first remark belongs to S Perry, 'Honore on Responsibility for Outcomes' in Cane and Gardner (n 22) Ch 4 at 67. The second is from Beever (n 33) at 485. I take it that this is Beever's own judgement and note that he offers it without any evidential foundation. His apparent criticism of Honore for doing something similar (Beever, ibid, 485) is therefore unfair.

[39] On judgement and reactive attitudes, see PF Strawson, *Freedom and Resentment and Other Essays* (London, Methuen, 1974) Ch 1.

[40] The phrase belongs to J Steele, *Risks and Legal Theory* (Oxford, Hart Publishing, 2004) 96. So far as I can see, she attributes this claim to Honore without warrant. Steele also reiterates the lack of evidence refrain (at 95) but, like all who join it, adduces no evidence to support her sceptical view of the overall fairness of the system of outcome responsibility. In the absence of evidence, and very tellingly for my purposes, she points to some hypothetical instances (95–96) in which outcome responsibility might work harshly. Such instances derive whatever weight they have from the kind of judgements and general human experience outlined above.

such testimony in the first instance. If our incremental judgements and impressions about how well or badly a life is going do not constitute such a trigger, then what does and, more importantly, what can? And, if they are so embedded in our responsibility judgements, then they can be so embedded. Whether or not they are independently morally respectable cannot be tackled in any more depth here; what the discussion so far suggests is that they are not obviously morally disreputable. That must undermine the unfairness claim in play here.

II. Impartiality

What might impartiality mean in the juridical context? I suggest it has at least three dimensions, each of which has some role in other, non-juridical contexts (or so I have argued).[41] If this picture of impartiality captures its most significant features, then there is no significant sense in which decisions like *Adesanya* fail to be impartial.

A. Attitude and Role

Can the commitments that constitute their lives, just like those that constitute ours, be set aside when judges are called upon to be impartial? If this question is directed at all judges' affective commitments, then the answer must be no. It is no more possible for judges to divorce themselves from the commitments that give their lives meaning and value than for anyone else. Impartiality, however, only makes sense against a background of partiality. As a general attitude to life, impartiality might be possible but is certainly not desirable. Judges who embodied it as a general orientation to life would set aside what they know of human kind and their lives. The beings then judging us would know nothing at all of—or be completely alienated from—what standard human lives look and feel like. Expecting real judges to embody such an attitude would be to expect them to live debased lives. Just like us, their commitments and associated experiences make them the people they are; they serve to give them both prior knowledge of human life and ground various pre-judgements and evaluations.

While there is much to be said in favour of being judged by those who have some understanding and experience of life and their fellow human beings, this very understanding and experience can cause difficulty. For the commitments, pre-judgements and values that structure judges' lives might impede attitudinal

[41] W Lucy, 'The Possibility of Impartiality' (2005) 25 *Oxford Journal of Legal Studies* 3–31; this section draws upon 14–25 of this essay and I am grateful to the publishers for permission to do this.

impartiality: their life experiences might be either so limited or of such a kind as to prevent them from adhering to the most minimal requirement of impartiality in the context of legal disputes, namely, an attitude of openness to and lack of pre-judgement upon the claims of the disputants. Ideally, this attitude is but part of a general stance of openness to difference and diversity among citizens, for it is only this that allows judges to go beyond being open-minded about disputants' claims to a more general appreciation of the disputants' general situation and circumstances.[42] To call this empathy is to exaggerate: it is merely a combination of receptiveness to, and willingness to suspend assumptions about, *both* the disputants and their dispute. Moreover, it is the disputants' conduct and the legal nature of their dispute which ensures that judges do not have to do the impossible in order to be impartial, since it is only those of their commitments relevant to the parties and their dispute that judges must hold in check. That judges are capable of suspending at least some such commitments and acting contrary to their pre-judgements is clear from cases in which they lament the decision the law compels them to reach.[43]

The attitude of openness to and lack of pre-judgement upon the claims of the disputants takes institutional form in at least two ways. First, in a concern with the constitution and appointment of the judiciary itself. For the judiciary to be capable of a general stance of openness to, on the one hand, the disputants, their background and situation, and, on the other, the merits of their dispute, it is desirable that individual judges have had not only a range of life and professional experience, but also that, as a group, they reflect the gender, cultural, ethnic and religious diversity of the community in which they work. Calls for a more representative judiciary are therefore calls for a judiciary better able to understand, and less likely to pre-judge, the experience, background and situation of those before them.[44] These calls therefore buttress rather than undermine judicial impartiality.

Second, the attitude of openness is embodied in many requirements of the judicial role. These requirements are found in, *inter alia*, explicit legal doctrine (aspects of which will be noted in subsections B and C), codes of judicial behaviour and aspects of judicial training. In England these codes and training programmes, which include all judges and magistrates, were developed and implemented by the Judicial Studies Board and are now the responsibility of the Judicial College. Beyond training programmes updating judges on, for example, changes

[42] The point belongs to M Minow, 'Stripped Down Like a Runner or Enriched by Experience: Bias and Impartiality of Judges and Jurors' (1992) 33 *William and Mary Law Review* 1201–18 at 1214–17.

[43] See N MacCormick, *Legal Reasoning and Legal Theory*, revised edn (Oxford, Clarendon Press, 1994) at 21, for an example.

[44] Nor are such calls made only by academics. See B Wilson, 'Will Women Judges really make a Difference?' (1990) 28 *Osgoode Hall Law Journal* 507–20 and B Hale, 'Equality and the Judiciary: Why Should We Want More Women Judges?' (2001) *Public Law* 489–504. See also R Greycar, 'The Gender of Judgements: An Introduction' in M Thornton (ed), *Public and Private—Feminist Legal Debates* (Melbourne, Oxford University Press, 1995) Ch 12 and E Rackley, *Women, Judging and the Judiciary* (London, Routledge, 2013).

in various areas of the law such as sentencing and human rights, the College has an Equal Treatment Advisory Committee and issues an Equal Treatment Bench Book for judges.[45] Documents of this kind, which serve to remind judges of the multi-ethnic, multi-cultural and gendered society in which they live and work, reinforce the attitude of openness and lack of pre-judgement that are hallmarks of attitudinal impartiality. Constraints upon judges airing their views on matters of law outwith the court room are also intended to inhibit pre-judgement and the bad consequences, in terms of strategic litigation and related matters, that flow from that.[46] Of course, it is foolish to suppose that constraints, documents and training programmes will make inappropriate partiality *impossible*, but they undoubtedly serve to make it more difficult. More importantly, perhaps, such constraints, documents and training programmes challenge automatic, unreflective assumptions, patterns of thought and prejudgements that covertly thwart attitudinal impartiality.

Finally, an important and obvious constraint upon the attitudinal impartiality of judges must be noted. Although we might want and expect from judges an openness to the claims of the disputants, combined with no pre-judgement of the disputants themselves, that stance is necessarily constrained by the fact that judges decide disputes within the perspective of the law and its constitutive values. This is undoubtedly a role commitment, embodied in judges' duty of fidelity to the law, as well as a matter of attitude. Yet, since this openness is constrained by the values of the law, and since the list of legal values is a relatively closed and slowly evolving one, a tension can arise here. In some instances, for example, legal values could conceivably either inhibit or make impossible openness to particular types of legal claim despite compelling extralegal arguments that they be recognised. Indeed, some legal claims might simply be unthinkable in light of the values and doctrines of a legal system at a particular time.[47] Furthermore, some legal values could be so objectionable as to reduce or completely remove whatever moral and political value attitudinal impartiality may have. Openness to, and a lack of pre-judgement upon, particular legal claims, and the general openness to diversity and difference from which this particular attitude might derive, would be of little value within, for example, the legal system of the Third Reich. The general point here is that impartiality in adjudication, like impartiality elsewhere, exists within the context of partiality: in the case of judges, it is partiality to the rules, standards and values

[45] Equal Treatment Bench Book 2013 (with 2015 amendments) available at www.judiciary.gov.uk/publications/equal-treatment-bench-book/ (last accessed 3rd January 2017). For a general introduction to the Judicial Studies Board and its replacement, the Judicial College, see www.judiciary.gov.uk/training-support/judicial-college/index and www.judiciary.gov.uk/.

[46] An important recent study of extra-judicial writing is S Bartie and J Gava, 'Some Problems with Extrajudical Writing' (2012) 34 *Sydney Law Review* 637–58. See also S Shetreet and S Turenne, *Judges on Trial*, 2nd edn (Cambridge, Cambridge University Press, 2013) at 359–78.

[47] A vivid illustration is the contrast between the early marital rape exemption cases in criminal law and the decision of the House of Lords in *R v R* [1991] 4 All ER 481.

that constitute the legal system. There is no guarantee that these rules, standards and values will always be morally and politically respectable.

B. Outcome Impartiality

Outcomes impartial in the strongest sense are those arrived at *regardless* of: (1) the needs; (2) the status; (3) the past or present conduct of those affected by them; and which (4) impact to exactly the same degree upon those affected by them.[48] It is argued here that, while both needs and status are usually irrelevant to adjudicative outcomes, past or present conduct is almost always relevant; and that equality of impact is present in such outcomes, albeit in an unobvious form. Adjudication is therefore outcome impartial only in a limited or incomplete sense. As will become clear, this is not a cause for regret but, rather, an inescapable consequence of using law and adjudication as a means of subjecting human conduct to the governance of rules.

Although there are a number of processes designed to generate outcomes sensitive to needs, it would be odd to imagine courts resolving disputes and reaching outcomes in a similar, needs-sensitive way. That prospect would conflict with what many expect from adjudication and run contrary to the abstract nature of law's judgment. It would therefore also be a surprise to many were judges to decide particular cases not on the basis of the relevant law, but by an analysis of who would be most adversely affected by the judgement. Holding in favour of the claimant because she would suffer most if the decision went against her, mistakes the law for an altogether more sensitive—and possibly more respectable—means of dispute resolution. Much the same reservation would arise were a court constantly to resolve disputes in favour of the wealthiest or most high status disputants. The law and the courts are supposedly blind to differences in status and needs, treating both mighty and lowly in exactly the same way. The needs and status of the disputants could, of course, be relevant in the circumstances of some legal disputes. Disputes that turn upon the welfare of one or other of the disputants could entail recourse to need, whereas status, taken to refer to personal wealth, might be relevant in the assessment of damages or fines.

The third feature of outcome impartiality—that decisions or outcomes be arrived at regardless of the disputants' or competitors' past or current conduct—can undoubtedly be realised in some contexts. In the adjudicative context, however, it is singularly inappropriate. This is because we conceive of adjudication as a backward looking inquiry into past conduct. This, conjoined with the fact that adjudication is almost always concerned only with the bilateral relationship between the disputants before the court, could well be a defining characteristic of

[48] See Lucy (n 41) at 7–11 for more expansive discussion.

this particular social form.[49] Furthermore, the backward looking, bilateral nature of adjudication is almost always censorial. It is a process of determining right and wrong, the relevant standards and values most often being provided by the law and supplemented by positive morality. The conduct of the disputants is judged according to the law; a *wrongdoer* is usually identified and penalised for or ordered to make good the *wrong* in whatever way the court thinks (legally) appropriate.

Adjudication is, therefore and obviously, judgmental. It judges the disputants' behaviour and character against the rules, standards and values of the law. Not every aspect of the disputants' character and behaviour is in the frame for judgement, the focus only being upon that aspect of their conduct relevant to the alleged legal wrong. That being so, even a blackguard might win his case: if his conduct is legally unimpeachable, then he will succeed even though he is an unprincipled scoundrel. Yet, although adjudication rarely, if ever, extends its judgement to every aspect of the disputants' conduct and character, it always invokes (when done legitimately, at least) the law's values. And the judicial duty of fidelity to law *must* include, if recourse to purposes and values is unavoidable in rule application and interpretation, fidelity to those purposes and values.

This kind of partiality appears unproblematic and, indeed, inescapable. This is because adjudication as we know it is inconceivable without recourse to the values of the law. For that to be conceivable, adjudication would have to be in some sense value-free. Whatever the latter phrase might mean in other contexts, in this context it must, in order to give this putative objection some sense, mean that law has no point or purpose. But, as soon as it is conceded that law is a purposive institution, it becomes unavoidably normative: law in general and the law of particular jurisdictions consists not only of a collection of standards, requirements or prohibitions, but also of a range of purposes that animate them, showing those standards, requirements or prohibitions to be a *system*. The purposes presupposed or explicitly stated by legal standards thus give law its value-structure; without them, law would be literally pointless. And, since adjudication is a matter of interpreting and applying legal standards, requirements and prohibitions, it cannot be impartial as to the purposes or values underpinning those standards and which constitute the law's value structure.

Nor can particular adjudicators, referees, mediators or arbitrators be impartial about the standards, requirements and prohibitions applicable to the competitions or disputes before them. For, if they are to apply and interpret those standards in a rule-governed and not merely habitual way, then they must have a 'pro-attitude' to them and, by implication, to their underlying purposes and values. This pro-attitude is a comprehensive way of referring to the three principal components of Herbert Hart's influential and important account of rule-governed behaviour.

[49] The points about the historical and bilateral nature of adjudication constitute a compelling criticism of some aspects of neo-classical law and economics: see J Coleman, *The Practice of Principle* (Oxford, Clarendon Press, 2001) at 13–24.

The latter differs from merely habitual behaviour because those engaged in it regard the behaviour in question as not merely convergent, but as in accord with a standard for their own behaviour and that of others; they also regard departures from the standard in question as giving grounds for censure and complaint and think such censure and complaint perfectly legitimate. In Hart's richly suggestive summary phrase, those whose behaviour is rule-governed have a 'reflective critical attitude' to the standards (or rules) they follow, apply and interpret.[50]

Why, it may be asked, *must* the behaviour of judges, referees and others who apply and interpret standards be rule-governed in this sense? There is no immediately obvious necessity that it should be an instance of rule-governed behaviour, since we can imagine judges deciding cases in a rule-governed way and judges deciding similar cases 'merely habitually' arriving at exactly the same results in many instances. Yet what we expect of good judges deciding hard cases is *judgement*, where what is meant is not simply a resolution of the dispute, but a discerning assessment of what the law and its underpinning purposes or values require in the particular case. At this point the judge acting merely habitually comes unstuck, since a discerning judgement about what the law requires is only possible on the basis of some *reflection* about the law, its underpinning purposes and their value. Indeed, habitual behaviour and behaviour based upon judgement—upon an assessment of what it is that is required in this particular instance—are probably opposites. Insofar as the judge deciding cases habitually is required to give reasons for her decisions, she is in fact unlikely to be truly acting habitually. Moreover, insofar as judges are required to display consistency across time in their interpretation and application of the law, and therefore in the outcomes they reach in similar cases, they are unlikely to be able to behave merely habitually. This is because habitual 'interpreters' and 'appliers' of standards are unlikely, by virtue of their habitual behaviour, to achieve much by way of reliability or consistency if the cases before them differ.[51] If every case requiring decision were exactly the same in all significant respects as cases already decided, then the decisions of the judge deciding cases habitually might differ little from the judge whose interpretations and applications of the law were instances of rule-governed behaviour.

The partiality of adjudicative outcomes is *at least* double-edged. They are partial in that they judge one or other disputant right or wrong and partial because the values and standards against which that judgement is made are those of the law. These values and standards also need not overlap with those of the disputants.

[50] HLA Hart, *The Concept of Law*, 2nd edn (Oxford, Clarendon Press, 1994) at 57 (page references are the same to the newer, 3rd edn, published in 2012). That Hart thought the operators of a system of legal rules must regard the rules in this light and that they sometimes must, when interpreting or applying such rules, have recourse to the aims or purposes of the rules, is plain from 117 and 127. A still unsurpassed discussion, admirably clear and succinct, is N MacCormick, *HLA Hart* (London, Edward Arnold, 1981) at Ch 3.

[51] The scare quotes are necessary simply because there must be real doubt as to the possibility of habitual rule interpreting and applying.

An apparently necessary consequence of this is that there is yet another way in which adjudicative outcomes are partial, since they do not in any literal sense impact equally upon the disputants.[52] If, as we have seen, those outcomes judge one or other disputant a wrong-doer and either punish him or order him to undo or make good the wrong, then it is *prima facie* implausible to claim that those outcomes impact equally on the disputants. Adjudicative outcomes do not therefore display the fourth feature of outcome impartiality.

There is, however, a viewpoint from which this conclusion seems an exaggeration. It holds there is a sense in which adjudicative outcomes could impact equally on the disputants even in the face of the inequality of impact just noted. This becomes plain once we recall the principal features of *LAJ*, noting that neither law nor adjudication pays much or even any attention to the rich particularity of the parties in dispute. The manifold diversity of particular disputants, with their complex and various traits, personalities, commitments and experiences is usually juridically irrelevant. In the eyes of the law, disputants are formally equal abstract rights-bearers. The equality of the disputants is the 'formal' equality of those with the same capacity to bear rights and of those who, by virtue of their status—as persons and as citizens—have the same bundle of abstract rights (to bodily integrity, to contract, to hold property, etc). Law and adjudication could therefore embody the fourth feature of outcome impartiality on the basis of this conception of equality. But how?

Adjudication rights wrongs; it restores, within the context of a specific legal dispute about some particular right, the abstract legal right of one disputant that has been infringed by the other. The outcome of the case never impacts to exactly the same degree on the disputants because it functions so as to correct the disturbance of the pre-existing equality of abstract rights that obtained between them. The adjudicative outcome impacts more severely on one disputant (the wrongdoer) than the other in order to equalise their formal legal standing. In this way, adjudicative outcomes maintain or restore a regime of equality. It is not bizarre to call this a form of equality of impact, one party having wrongfully obtained an advantage from, or inflicted harm upon, the other that the adjudicative outcome seeks to restore.[53]

Since this account of the way in which adjudicative outcomes might impact equally upon the disputants invokes *LAJ*, it cannot itself support *LAJ*. But it does serve to reduce the implausibility, or increase the plausibility, of the view that some kind of equality of impact is possible with regard to adjudicative outcomes.

[52] It is often assumed that impartiality (and neutrality) must be a matter of equality of impact. See, for example, the essays by A Montefiore (at 6–7) and L Kolakowski (at 72–73) in A Montefiore (ed), *Neutrality and Impartiality* (Cambridge, Cambridge University Press, 1975) and J Raz, *The Morality of Freedom* (Oxford, Clarendon Press, 1986) at 113.

[53] This, of course, is an echo of the sophisticated account of legal formalism in private law defended by E Weinrib, *The Idea of Private Law* (Cambridge, Massachusetts, Harvard University Press, 1995) Chs 1–4.

This kind of equality of impact is complex, so adjudication is not simplistically impartial in this regard. Nor is it obviously impartial in relation to the past or present deeds of the disputants. Adjudicative outcomes therefore straightforwardly embody only two of the four aspects of outcome impartiality.

C. Procedural Impartiality

Procedural impartiality, if it means anything, must at least mean that the *rules* and *practices* of decision-making processes, at a minimum, favour each disputant or competitor equally, or favour neither, or inhibit both equally.[54] In general terms, then, procedural impartiality is a matter of equality of impact and there is no reason to think things are different within the adjudicative context. However, as was noted in the discussion of outcome impartiality, equality of impact is made difficult by the differences between us and it seems that impartial procedural rules must therefore accommodate or mitigate some of those differences. So, in order to ensure that no disputant is disadvantaged by adjudicative procedures, the rules and practices constitutive of those procedures must, in addition to not directly discriminating against disputants, also take account of *significant* differences between them. What is and is not a significant difference is, in the first instance, determined from the juristic point of view, from the point of view of the law and its constitutive values.

One such generic, constitutive legal value is that of participation. This sounds vague but, in concrete terms, it includes at the very least a requirement that disputants understand legal processes and their implications. Within the context of adjudication, procedural rules that made no provision for disputants who did not speak the language of the trial would fail in this respect. Only if some effort were made to address such an important difference between disputants could it be said that the relevant procedures approached impartiality. Understanding the language of the trial, however, implies only a very minimal conception of participation and a more demanding conception could be insisted upon. For participation can be taken to mean genuine involvement—albeit through the medium of legally qualified representatives—in the trial process. Genuine involvement in, as opposed to simple understanding of, the process requires that at least four conditions be satisfied: that disputants have an opportunity to be heard; that they have accurate information about the claims that relate to them; that they be allowed an opportunity to respond to those claims; and that they are made aware of all the relevant administrative requirements.

These four conditions ensure that disputants are not merely impassive observers of the process but engage in it as something like a dialogic enterprise.[55] This kind

[54] See Lucy (n 41) at 11–13 for further discussion.

[55] For Lon Fuller this participation dimension of adjudication also has significant epistemic pay-offs: see his *Forms and Limits of Adjudication* (1978) 92 *Harvard Law Review* 353–409 at 353–72. For a similar refrain, see D Galligan, *Due Process and Fair Procedures* (Oxford, Clarendon Press, 1996) at 4.

of participation seems necessary if law and adjudication are to approach legitimacy in the eyes of those they bind and judge. There must be some sense in which the law, and the processes of adjudication through which it is applied and interpreted, is the disputants' law. It is, and claims to be, the law of *their* community, to bind them as *citizens* and a step towards ensuring this is to involve disputants in the process of resolving those disputes.[56] Of course, highlighting the significance and nature of the disputants' involvement in the adjudicative process should not obscure some difficulties. One is that, as a matter of fact, disputants' involvement in existing adjudicative processes is fairly slight, being filtered through, and perhaps even completely determined by, legal representatives. Another is that the link between dialogic participation in, and the legitimacy of, adjudicative processes is far from obvious. This is particularly so if, when speaking of legitimacy, we have justified political authority (which entails an obligation to obey) in mind. The problem is bridging the gap between accounts of political authority and the requirement of participation.

The four conditions for participation highlight an obvious overlap between the generic rules of natural justice and a concern for procedural impartiality.[57] It is only a contingent overlap, though, since simple observance of the rules of natural justice *cannot* ensure that in all cases those rules impact to exactly the same degree upon the disputants. This is so even though the basis of both the rules of natural justice and the idea of procedural impartiality—some notion of participation—is most likely the same. An obvious illustration that the two do not cover exactly the same ground is this: in many modern legal systems the cost of legal representation is a serious impediment to participation in the adjudicative trial process. If legal representation is available only to those who can afford to pay, and if it is true that legal representation significantly influences disputants' likelihood of success, then those who cannot pay are undoubtedly disadvantaged in the adjudicative process.[58] A concern to ensure that rules and procedures of the adjudicative process impact equally on the disputants would therefore seem to require legal representation for all. However, the rules of natural justice clearly do not require this in all legal or administrative disputes, nor is it contrary to those rules for some forums hearing and resolving disputes to prohibit legal representation, provided the decision to that effect is both properly arrived at and reasonable.[59]

[56] I don't suggest that the law applies *only* to citizens. For an altogether more subtle version of the argument in the text, see RA Duff, *Punishment, Communication, and Community* (New York, Oxford University Press, 2001) at Chs 2 and 3.

[57] The standard treatment of the rules of natural justice is found in HWR Wade and CF Forsyth, *Administrative Law*, 11th edn (Oxford, Clarendon Press, 2014) Pt VI. Also interesting is Galligan (n 55) chs 11–14 (Ch 14 also contains some brief but interesting thoughts on impartiality).

[58] For a general discussion of representation, see Galligan (n 55) at 361–91 and MD Bayles, *Procedural Justice* (Dordrecht, Kluwer, 1990) Ch 3.

[59] Two key cases are: *R v Home Secretary, ex parte Tarrant* (1985) QB 251 and *R v Board of Visitors of HMP The Maze, ex parte Hone* [1988] 2 WLR 177.

Procedural impartiality in adjudication must go beyond simply ensuring that disputants are equally able to participate in the process and that its rules and requirements impact on both to exactly the same degree. This is because a set of impartial rules and practices could easily be thwarted either by those who enforce the rules—officers of the court, administrators and others—or by those—judges or magistrates—who resolve disputes with those rules. The latter could most vividly thwart impartiality by favouring one or other disputant on grounds irrelevant to the dispute. Procedural impartiality must therefore include some obligations upon those adjudicating, refereeing or mediating disputes which, to some extent, simply mirror the expectations disputants have of an impartial process. Within legal contexts there is a range of standard protections against bias or partiality. These include the requirement that judges (and relevant others) hear both sides to the case, that the principal issues in dispute are put before the judges and tested or questioned by the disputants, their legal representatives and the judges themselves, and the prohibition on *ex parte* communications.[60] Furthermore, there are obvious restrictions upon judges (and relevant others) deciding cases in which they have a financial or other interest, or in which they are friends with one or other of the disputants, or in which they are aware of information prejudicial to one of the disputants.[61]

Yet even this might not be enough for a robust conception of procedural impartiality in the adjudicative context. For it might be thought that procedural impartiality here also requires some limitation upon the type of consideration relevant in judicial decision-making. This additional requirement is latent in much of what has already been said about both outcome and procedural impartiality and therefore illustrates one way in which these two features can overlap. Furthermore, the requirement is doubled-sided. In order to see this, the first and almost painfully obvious point is that *adjudicative outcomes are arrived at by reference to the relevant applicable law*, both substantive and procedural. It is the relevant law, of course, that the disputants or their legal representatives put before the court and about which, in hard cases at least, they are usually in dispute. Moreover, the relevant law often has to be applied so as to be consistent with other decisions and more general legal principles; and one of the latter, the principle that like cases be treated alike, serves to uphold impartiality or at least frustrate obvious partiality in judicial deliberations. If legally like cases must be treated alike, then the claimant in *Devenson v Stonoghue* (the legal issue and legally relevant facts being exactly the same as *Donoghue v Stevenson*[62]) must prevail even though the judges dislike her,

[60] On the 'hearing principle' see Galligan (n 55) at Ch 12; Wade and Forsyth (n 57) at Ch 14.

[61] See *R v Bow Street Metropolitan Stipendiary Magistrate and others ex parte Pinochet Ugarte* (No 2) [1999] All ER 577; *Dimes v Proprietors of Grand Junction Canal* (1852) 3 HL Cos 759; and Ch 3 of the *Guide to Judicial Conduct Revised July 2016* www.judiciary.gov.uk/publications/guide-to-judicial-conduct/ (last accessed 3rd January 2017). For helpful discussion of *post-Pinochet* cases, see K Malleson, 'Safeguarding Judicial Impartiality' (2002) 22 *Legal Studies* 53–70 and Shetreet and Turenne (n 46) Ch 5.

[62] [1932] AC 562.

and find her character, behaviour and beliefs suspect. This bulwark against partiality is limited insofar as judges are able to determine what is and is not a legally relevant difference, but it is not illusory. The principle imposes a burden upon the court to say why a putatively like case is not actually sufficiently legally similar to the current case, and that burden at least makes improper partiality more difficult than it might otherwise be, although not actually impossible.

The other side of the requirement that adjudicative outcomes be arrived at by reference to the relevant applicable law can now be made clear. The fact that judgement is made only on the basis of *legal* arguments put before the court protects or promotes impartiality because these factors serve to exclude others. It is the legal arguments disputants put before the court that are important and not, for example, the judges' personal views of the disputants. Judgement must be based on the law and not some assessment, unless it is part and parcel of the law, of one or other of the disputants' moral or social status or virtue. Why? To ensure that disputants are treated in the same way regardless of their character or worth, their moral status, lifestyle or gender, ethnicity or religion. Judgement according to the law therefore treats disputants impartially, not in the sense of taking no position on the rights and wrongs of their dispute, but in the sense of taking no position on the rights and wrongs of their character, commitments, moral standing, etc, except insofar as such considerations are relevant to the interpretation or application of the relevant law. The general point (which again echoes *LAJ*) is that adjudicative outcomes ought not to be determined by judicial empathy with the values, prejudices, principles and conceits of heterosexual, white upper middle class protestant men, except insofar as those values, etc, are immanent within the law. And, if they are, that *is* legitimate cause for regret and complaint from the perspective of most accounts of the values that should or must constitute the law.[63] (It is at this point that an overlap between procedural and outcome impartiality is most pronounced, since a procedural requirement that judges decide cases only by reference to the law can throw into relief the moral quality of the law and its underpinning values.)

Is the decision in *Adesanya* objectionably partial? Would similar decisions in like cases be problematic? The reports of *Adesanya* are too brief to allow a definitive conclusion about the decision's standing with regard to procedural impartiality. However, the fact that (i) no comment was made about any judicial or other lapses of impartiality in the reports (such lapses being undoubtedly newsworthy) and (ii) no appeal was made on those or related grounds, suggest no such issue arose. It is therefore unlikely that those who object to the decision in *Adesanya* are

[63] One such perspective is that of 'public reason'. Philosophers have raised a family of conceptions of public reason, two of the most interesting belonging to G Gaus, *Justificatory Liberalism* (Oxford, Clarendon Press, 1996) and J Rawls, *Political Liberalism*, revised edn (New York, Columbia University Press, 1996) and 'The Idea of Public Reason Revisited' in his *The Law of Peoples* (Cambridge, Massachusetts, Harvard University Press, 1999). The conceptions are similar in that they tell us which considerations public decision-making bodies like courts and legislatures should and should not use.

complaining about that particular type of transgression. Their objection is more likely to be to the *outcome* of the case. Did the outcome of *Adesanya* lack impartiality? In one sense it certainly did. Judgement was *against* Mrs Adesanya: she was held to have broken the law. The law and its underpinning values were held against her, her conduct being contrary to what they required. That this is a failure of impartiality, an instance of objectionable partiality, might underpin Alison Dundes Renteln's judgement that cases like *Adesanya* illustrate 'a majoritarian bias in the legal system'.[64] But judicial partiality towards the law and its underpinning values is unavoidable in most current legal systems, and for two reasons already noted. First, most current legal systems impose a duty of fidelity to the law upon their judges: when fulfilling their judicial duty, they must follow and apply the law. Doing so means that judges cannot be impartial or unconcerned about, or uninterested in, what the law requires. Second, our current understanding of the nature of law application and interpretation in the common law world holds that, in the face of interpretative difficulty, it is always appropriate for judges to have recourse to the point, purpose or value of the law in question to attempt to resolve that difficulty. And that implies judicial commitment both to that task and to those underpinning values.

It is not mad to complain that, when judges do this, their conduct is partial, although it is odd. The oddity is this: is it sensible to complain about judges behaving as they are both expected and required to behave, given the current nature of our legal systems and the judicial duties they impose? Isn't this rather like complaining about dogs barking and cows lowing? That's what they do, after all. Yet this is not to say that there is no plausible complaint here. To see it, however, the original complaint must be restructured, taking Dundes Renteln's majoritarian bias objection not as a gripe about judges upholding the laws (and their underpinning values) of their jurisdiction—that's what they do—but as a complaint about the content of those laws (and/or their underpinning values). This version of the objection nullifies the 'that's what they do' riposte and opens the law up to moral criticism, albeit at the cost of eradicating whatever salience Dundes Renteln's term for this moral criticism—the 'majoritarian-bias'—had. If her complaint is that there are some jurisdictions in which neither the law nor its constitutive values are accepted by everyone bound by them, then she is surely right. Yet how is that a *complaint*? Presumably neither the career mugger who takes my wallet nor the bully who brutalises me accepts that theft and battery are wrong. Their values run contrary to those upheld and embodied in the law. How can that imply that the law should not be applied to them or that the law is in some way morally objectionable? Perhaps in two ways.

The first holds that legal systems should adopt a principle of accommodation with regard to those groups whose values differ from the values of the majority.

[64] See Dundes Renteln (n 3) at 6.

That principle can be either very strong, so that good evidence of difference defeats any legal claim, or quite weak, holding only that good evidence of difference be admitted in court. Furthermore, 'good evidence' in this context will surely include: (i) a demonstration of group membership on behalf of the party invoking difference; and (ii) a demonstration of difference itself, almost always in the form of showing that that difference is embedded in the culture of the group in question. If these two conditions are satisfied in the case of the mugger and the bully, then that evidence either defeats the action against them or is simply admitted for the consideration of the court.[65] Much turns upon how the notion of culture is elucidated here and its exact contours. For example, considerable work needs be done so as to satisfactorily distinguish between the culture of career criminals and terrorists, on the one hand, and that of various religious, ethnic and other groups, on the other.[66] In addition, the principle of accommodation itself requires argumentative support, since it is by no means self-evidently morally compelling.[67]

The second implication invokes, as a condition of authority and legitimacy, genuine consent to all existing laws by all ostensibly bound by them. If some do not consent to the whole system of law, or to particular elements thereof, then either system or elements lack legitimacy. This is therefore a particularly stringent condition and its adoption appears a sure-fire means of denying rather than justifying (or attempting to justify) political authority.[68] That point is not in any way an effort to show that the condition is mistaken—it would be a remarkably feeble attempt—but, rather, a means of highlighting this requirement: that any invocation of the condition must surely be preceded by some explicit preliminary work showing its greater appeal as compared to the various alternatives. Without such work,

[65] The principle and the argument here are a very compressed summary of Dundes Renteln (n 3) chs 1, 2 and 10. Of the many, many discussions of cultural defences, I focus on Dundes Renteln's because it provides by far the best overview. An altogether narrower discussion is M Golding, 'The Cultural Defense' (2002) 15 *Ratio Juris* 146–58.

[66] These groups would have no difficulty in laying claim to a 'culture' as that notion is used by Dundes Rentlen (n 3) 10–12. My invocation of 'criminal culture' is far from a facile *reductio*, although the 'culture' of some areas of criminal activity in some countries may be less formal than was once thought: see, for example, J Aldridge and JJ Medina-Ariza, *Youth Gangs in an English City* (ESRC Report RES-000-23-0615, 2007).

[67] Dundes Renteln's general case for the principle rests upon (i) the un-argued claim that ignoring cultural evidence breaches the law's equal treatment commitments (ibid, 187); and (ii) the invocation of a 'right to culture' (ibid at 15 and Ch 11). While the latter right could legally justify the principle, its moral weight in this context is unclear; for some of the complexities in the notion of juridical equality, see my 'Equality Under and Before the Law' (2011) 61 *University of Toronto Law Journal* 411–65.

[68] The currently dominant view with regard to the justification of authority is philosophical anarchism, which in part holds that 'few if any citizens in existing political societies have political obligations, and existing governments lack the correlative right to command' (A John Simmons, 'The Anarchist Position: A Reply to Klosko and Senor' (1987) 16 *Philosophy and Public Affairs* 269–79 at 269; see also his *Justification and Legitimacy: Essays on Rights and Obligations* (Cambridge, Cambridge University Press, 2001) and 'Philosophical Anarchism' http://papers.ssrn.com/sol3/papers.cfm?abstract_id=1344425 (last accessed 3rd[r] January 2017). The consent condition, as outlined in the text, could inform a philosophical anarchist position.

we cannot properly ascribe the condition to Dundes Renteln. Moreover, once the condition is set aside, the fact that the law sometimes applies to and binds those who do not accept it is less problematic. Yet if this condition and the principle of accommodation are jettisoned, what can be made of the majoritarian complaint?

We might have emphasised the wrong part of the complaint: the objection is not that legal systems contain laws and underpinning values that some reject. Rather, the objection is that some or other of the laws and values in the legal system in question are simply moral mistakes. It is hard to deny that such mistakes have been and still are embedded in our own legal system at doctrinal and procedural levels. But if this is the substance of the complaint, note the difficulty of the task its proponents have set themselves. With regard to *Adesanya*, for example, they must demonstrate that the law applied therein and/or its underpinning values are morally wrong. The same must also be shown of other like cases. The snag is that laws upholding various dimensions of physical integrity do not look like egregious moral errors; some, indeed, suggest that they are moral necessities, part of a crucial minimum content of natural law.[69] There may, of course, be other judicial decisions in which the laws and values invoked are more obviously open to moral criticism; there are also many questions to ask about the morality of some instances of legal enforcement. (Some laws—those prohibiting the use of sundry substances, for example—appear to be enforced far more rigorously with regard to some groups than others.) And while the general critical, moral evaluation of the law and its values is a vital task in any self-aware and self-critical community, it moves us a long way from the current topic. That, remember, is the job of making sense of a specific version of the unfairness charge against cases like *Adesanya* in particular and *LAJ* in general. So far, the attempt to base the unfairness charge upon a failure of either procedural or outcome impartiality seems doomed. The obvious and unavoidable sense in which the decision was partial—partial in the same way that virtually all judicial decisions are partial, being instances in which the law and its underpinning values are upheld and applied—might open the law to moral critique. That critique, however, is surely a general form of moral criticism rather than a specific complaint about partiality.

Is there any remaining way in which *Adesanya* is objectionably partial? Possibly one. In claiming that 'cultural evidence should be admitted into the courtroom …[and that] cultural logic must be taken seriously', while also insisting that 'it is not possible to say how much weight culture should be given in all cases', Dundes Renteln could be making a plea for open-mindedness on the part of judges.[70] Attitudinal impartiality is an important feature of the judicial role and it might be bolstered by the admission of such evidence: it would surely allow a fine-grained understanding of the conduct and agent in question. There can be

[69] Hart (n 50) at 193–200 and D Hume (DF Norton and MJ Norton (eds)), *A Treatise of Human Nature* Vol 1 (Oxford, Clarendon, 2007) bk III, pt II, s ii.

[70] Dundes Renteln (n 3) at 15.

no doubt that, to the open-minded, a fine-grained and detailed story is preferable to a bluntly drawn and incomplete tale. But judges need legal warrant to prefer and admit one type of story over another, and thus to admit or exclude certain evidence. That warrant is found in procedural and substantive legal doctrine. With regard to substantive legal doctrine, the relevant evidence and the level of detail required is specified in the doctrines themselves; there is no general default position in favour of more rather than less detail. If substantive legal doctrine does not require detailed evidence of the disputants' cultural context, then no judge could or would require it. Judicial open-mindedness is thus constrained by the law. One might complain about this, but the complaint—that the law here should take into account more or different evidence—again seems not to be about either majoritarian-bias or partiality. It is instead about the moral standing of the law in question and, as such, it falls beyond our purview.

III. Equity and Mercy

For present purposes, I understand equity broadly and in Aristotle's sense, as 'not the legally just but a correction of legal justice';[71] 'equity is the sort of justice that goes beyond the written law'.[72] Such correction is necessary, thought Aristotle, because law is general (or universal, depending on the translation) and general rules can breed unfairness in particular cases. Such cases are pregnant with potential unfairness, it seems, when they raise issues the creators of those general rules never envisaged and to which those rules were not intended to apply:

> [w]hen the law speaks universally, then, and a case arises on it which is not covered by the universal statement, then it is right, when the legislator fails us and has erred to over-simplicity, to correct the omission—to say what the legislator himself would have said had he been present, and would have put into his law if he had known.[73]

Understood in this way, equity is a matter of interpretation and supplementation. The former involves understanding the current law, that understanding bringing to light a lacuna or related difficulty, while the latter entails going beyond and adding to the law in order to fill the gap or resolve the problem. Aristotle specifies a way in which gaps must be filled and problems resolved—do as the law creator

[71] *NE*, V.10, 1137b11-12. (The abbreviated references are to the *Nicomachean Ethics* (*NE*) (n 36) or the *Rhetoric* (*R*) (with accompanying book, section and line numbers).)

[72] *R*, 1.13, 1374a26-27.

[73] *NE*, V.10, 1137b20-24. The JAK Thomson translation (*The Ethics of Aristotle* (Harmondsworth, Penguin, 1976) at 199) speaks the language of generality: '[w]hen the law states a general rule, and a case arises under this that is exceptional, then it is right, where the legislator owing to the generality of his language has erred in not covering the case, to correct the omission by a ruling such as the legislator himself would have given if he had been present there, and as he would have enacted if he had been aware of the circumstances'.

would have done—but this need not be the only option. Both aspects are echoed in the doctrine of equitable construction, it often being said in addition that Aristotle's account of equity underpins the doctrines of Equity found in common law legal systems.[74] Whether or not these claims are correct is not explored here, for I concentrate solely upon the supplementation aspect of Aristotle's account of equity and use it as one instance of an identifiable general position.

That position's core claim insists there are circumstances in which it is right for judges to go beyond the immediately relevant law when applying and interpreting the law.[75] On this view equity can in principle license both merciful and severe interpretation and application of the law. Many discussions concentrate only upon equity's mercy and ignore its potential for severity, but it is unclear why the grounds that permit supplementation of the law must always and only lead toward mitigation as opposed to aggravation. Any alleged asymmetry here, holding for instance that equity solely inclines towards mercy, must be argued for and not all such arguments are compelling.[76] In what follows only equity's mercy is in play, but not because of any asymmetry assumption; rather, equity's mercy is the only plausible underpinning for the current unfairness claim. The moral jolt felt by critics of *Nettleship* and *Adesanya* is assuredly not informed by the thought that the law applied in the two cases was insufficiently harsh. On what grounds does and should equity's mercy mitigate the law's effect?

There are two incompatible answers to this question. One holds that whatever grounds inform equity's mercy, they are of the same type—let us dub them 'justice concerns'—as at some point inform almost all legal claims. The alternative view denies this, holding instead that the grounds animating equity's mercy are not and cannot be justice concerns, since equity on the one hand, and law and justice on the other, stand opposed to one another. One might be tempted to invoke our two sample cases as a means of resolving this conflict. Take, for example, the sentence in *Adesanya*: the conditional discharge the Court imposed was the most lenient sentence available, that exercise of 'mercy' plainly taking place within the constraints of the law and with a view to justice concerns. Equity's mercy is 'therefore' part of the law rather than an alternative to it. Furthermore, the fact that judgement in

[74] I have benefited a great deal from Dennis Klimchuk's work on this and related issues: see his 'Aristotle, The Earl of Oxford, and the Foundations of the Law of Equity' and 'Is the Law of Equity Equitable in Aristotle's Sense?' www.scribd.com/document/157959929/Klimchuk-is-the-Law-of-Equity-Equitable-in-Aristotles-Sense (last accessed 1st February 2017). I follow Klimchuk and others in using 'equity' to refer to Aristotle's idea and 'Equity' to refer to that area of law that in some jurisdictions is contrasted with 'common law'. Obviously, there are some occasions when I must use a capital when referring to the former.

[75] The position can presumably go beyond judges and include other appliers and interpreters of the law. M Nussbaum, 'Equity and Mercy' (1993) 22 *Philosophy and Public Affairs* 83–125 provides a superb overview of this position's lineage and challenges.

[76] Two such arguments, one compelling, the other less so (made by Nussbaum, ibid, at 85–93), are explored in J Tasoulias, 'The Paradox of Equity' (1996) 55 *Cambridge Law Journal* 456–69. For excellent reflections upon mercy's cousin, forgiveness, see J Murphy, 'The Case of Dostoevsky's General: Some Ruminations on Forgiving the Unforgivable' (2009) 92 *The Monist* 556–82.

Nettleship was against Mrs Weston, she (via her insurers) having to pay damages to Mr Nettleship, shows that the law there allowed no role for mercy. If equity and mercy are integral elements of the law, then where the law allocates them no role, they have no role. But both points beg the question, at least until such time as the exact nature of the considerations informing the availability or unavailability of 'mitigating' grounds in law is scrutinised. The considerations underpinning the sentence in *Adesanya* might, for example, be wrongly characterised as justice concerns, thus leaving room for the independent value of mercy (and its constitutive considerations) to play a role. And the unavailability of mitigating grounds in *Nettleship* could be yet another instance of the law making a moral mistake.

If the compatibility of law and equity were established, in the sense that both are responsive to and bearers of the same type of justice concerns, then that would pose a significant problem for critics of *Adesanya* and *Nettleship*. The problem arises because an incompatibility between law and equity is the most obvious foundation for the current version of the unfairness complaint, the complaint being that the application of the law in these two cases, and in all sufficiently similar cases, is indefensibly harsh. Yet since the law was correctly applied in each case, there being no question of judicial ignorance of the relevant juridical (including presumably equitable) standards, the harshness claim cannot be supported by reference to the internal resources of the law itself. Support for it must therefore come from outside, from morality in general, or from the narrower domain of equity. Because this version of the unfairness charge is tied to an 'incompatibilist' reading of the relationship between law and equity, that is the only reading to feature hereinafter.

Are there any compelling arguments showing that equity and law are incompatible? Two of the most promising are closely related, although each makes its case from a different starting point. One begins from law, the other from mercy.

A. The Argument from Law

The former insists that one feature of law's very form—its generality—prevents it accommodating the considerations that inform equity and mercy. Two points must be noted about this feature, though. First, while Aristotle did indeed highlight it as one factor driving recourse to equity, it is uncertain that he viewed equity in the way we are currently viewing it, as completely independent of and incompatible with law. Our use of Aristotle's remarks as a possible prop for the latter view does not therefore imply that that view is indeed his.[77] Second, and equally obvious, is the point that generality in the juridical context is far from being either a self-evident or univocal notion. The rule of law ideal reminds us that laws must be general, but generality in that context requires little more than that

[77] According to Roger Shiner ('Aristotle's Theory of Equity' (1994) 27 *Loyola of Los Angeles Law Review* 1245–64 at 1258–60), equity for Aristotle plays the role that judgement plays for me in the following couple of paragraphs; it is not therefore impermeably separate from law.

a legal system contain rules and that they not name or be directed against specific individuals.[78] Very narrowly defined, precise legal rules—schedule 2 of the UK Provision and Use of Work Equipment Regulations 1998 tells us, *inter alia*, that regulations 32–35 do not apply to '[a] power press not capable of a stroke greater than 6 millimetres'—do not therefore breach the rule of law's generality requirement. Nor does this generality requirement have any clear generative connection with the snag Aristotle identifies as arising from law's generality, namely, 'the case not covered by the universal statement' or 'the case that is exceptional'.

Such a case is plainly one not easily subsumed under existing legal rules: should one who punches another while wearing a ring be charged with battery with a weapon or with less serious weapon-less battery? Aristotle's intuition here was that the perpetrator 'is innocent really and it is equity that declares him to be so'.[79] Matters are not, I suggest, so clear cut. We could only share Aristotle's intuition if: (i) satisfied that the perpetrator had forgotten he was wearing a ring; and provided (ii) the intuition's effect is limited, saving the perpetrator from the more but not the less serious charge. Furthermore, there is no reason why we cannot share Aristotle's intuition without having recourse to equity—taken as a body of considerations independent of and incompatible with the law—to explain it. For a decision to charge a perpetrator with a less serious offence need be based on nothing more than a judgement about the context of the alleged offence, informed by knowledge of the range of possible charges that could be pressed. Why must that judgement, part and parcel of the everyday working life of any prosecuting lawyer, be described as a matter of equity and thus in some sense incompatible with the law? The latter conclusion could follow if law and judgement (by judges, prosecutors and others) were contraries, but this claim is unsupported in Aristotle and runs counter to ordinary lawyerly experience. We assume that judgement and law often go unproblematically together. Moreover, a similar kind of judgement as is present in prosecutorial decisions like the battery example arises in more obviously legal-doctrinal contexts. Consider, for instance, the choices judges in common law appellate courts often have to make about whether to follow one line of authorities as opposed to another, or to adopt one interpretation of a statutory provision or word rather than another. Such choices are the fulcrum of the appellate court's judicial role and the ways in which they are justified by judges can exhibit better or worse juridical 'judgement'. But, again, we do not need the notion of equity to make sense of this process, nor need we insist that it is in some sense contrary to law.[80]

Aristotle makes another point about law's generality that is different from the two scenarios just sketched, but which can give rise to them. Instead of being an

[78] This is more or less Fuller's view (n 25) at 46–49.

[79] *R*, 1.13, 1374b1-2.

[80] For an overview of some orthodox accounts of adjudication, all of which accept that judges in hard cases have choices, see my 'Adjudication' in J Coleman and S Shapiro (eds), *The Oxford Handbook of Jurisprudence and Philosophy of Law* (Oxford, Clarendon Press, 2002) Ch 6 and part I of my

instance in which law appliers have a choice—should X be charged with offence 1 or offence 2? Should case P or case Q be followed?—it is one in which law-makers use general terms in their regulations because 'a lifetime would be too short to make out a complete list'[81] of every particular instance to which the regulation should apply. If acted upon, this good reason to cast laws in general terms will create some situations of choice for law-appliers. So, for example, since life is too short to specify each and every weapon currently and potentially available to humankind, a time-pressed law-maker will likely be content to prohibit battery with weapons in the most general terms: 'it is an offence punishable by a maximum sentence of 10 years imprisonment to batter another person with a weapon'. A provision like that, lacking any definition section or other guidance, leaves the law-applier with the task of determining what is and is not a weapon. That process is, however, often reducible to either or both types of choice we have already noted: the choice could be a legal-doctrinal one, between different apparently authoritative definitions of 'weapon', or a more context-specific assessment of the seriousness of the conduct in question, with a view to deciding which offence to charge. Both instances are undeniably situations of choice and Aristotle's explanation as to how they might arise is powerful. But, as we have already suggested, it is unclear why the choices law-appliers face must bring forth, or require recourse to, equity. Rather, those choices and the ways in which they are resolved are part and parcel of the normal legal-cum-adjudicative process, highlighting a feature of law as we know it (although possibly not a feature of law as Aristotle knew it).

These arguments from law's generality fail to show the necessity or inescapability of recourse to equity, understood as a body of considerations independent of and incompatible with law. Their failure might, however, be preordained by our interpreting Aristotle's remarks about generality and equity as if directed to one single aspect of the distinctively modern problem of hard-case adjudication, namely, the issue of 'gaps'. Roger Shiner argues that this interpretation of Aristotle is a mistake and he is surely right.[82] Although our previous discussion of Aristotle did indeed use the terms 'gap' and 'lacuna', nothing said there suggested that those are the only hallmarks of hard cases. Such cases are often more complex than that. However, since demonstrating this would take us deep into the territory of how hard cases are and should be both defined and resolved, I adopt a different strategy: I concede Shiner's point, albeit with no admission of liability. Doing so clears space for another argument from generality. This argument, offered by Frederick Schauer, is quite different from those already considered because it does not highlight

Understanding and Explaining Adjudication (Oxford, Clarendon, 1999). Part II of the latter engages with some heretical accounts (mainly second-wave American critical legal studies) which maintain that the nature of adjudication is unavoidably 'political' and perhaps 'therefore' unlawlike.

[81] *R*, 1.13, 1374a33-34.
[82] Shiner (n 77).

> a problem of filling the gaps in the law or of clarifying the uncertainties of the law.[·] Rather it is a problem, as Aristotle was the first to recognize, of correcting the mistakes that law by its very generality necessarily makes.[83]

The argument begins with the undeniable claim that legal rules often incorporate non-universal generalisations and, by doing so, they can produce mistaken results 'where "mistaken" is measured by the result that would have been produced by the direct application of the rule's background justification to the particular case'.[84] Schauer's example is the restaurant rule 'No Dogs Allowed', the justification for which he posits as being the prevention of annoyance to diners. He says that

> [i]f in the case of the rule against dogs in restaurants we were to apply the justification of preventing annoyance directly to the particular cases, we would not exclude well-behaved guide dogs and would exclude not only most pet bears and most pet monkeys, but also many poorly behaved children. Because the 'No Dogs Allowed' rule draws upon a nonuniversal generalization about what creatures are likely to cause interference and what creatures are not, applying the rule instead of the justification will produce errors of overinclusion (excluding the guide dog) and errors of underinclusion (not excluding the child) that would not have been produced by direct application of the background justification.[85]

If it is indeed the case that many laws are just like the No Dogs rule and based upon non-universal generalisations, then the problems of over- and under-inclusion highlighted by Schauer are unavoidable. Furthermore, since the extrapolation from Schauer's simple example to more complex laws seems unproblematic, provided we do not assume that all laws are based upon non-universal generalisations, his point is one all jurists must accept. What does accepting it commit us to? Does it follow that, faced by the problems of under- and over-inclusivity, recourse must be had to an independent non-legal notion of equity? Not at all. Recourse must, of course, be had to something other than the wording of the rule in question and that 'something' can, as Schauer suggests, be an account of the rationale, justification, point or purpose of the rule in question. That is an entirely routine procedure for judges in the common law world, a normal move in the process of justifying adjudicative choices. Why and how does this implicate equity? Why even use that *prima facie* odd term to describe so ordinary and frequent a feature of rule interpretation and application?

It is plain that arguments from law's generality do a poor job of establishing the necessity of recourse to equity, understood (by contrast with Equity) as a body of considerations independent of and incompatible with law. We therefore turn to an argument from mercy, rather than from law's generality, that could provide

[83] F Schauer, *Profiles, Probabilities and Stereotypes* (Cambridge, Massachusetts, Harvard University Press, 2003) 46. Schauer invokes Shiner's argument (n 77) at 46. I am not as confident as Schauer that Aristotle explicitly makes or recognises this argument; the best we can say is that it is not inconsistent with Aristotle's remarks.

[84] Schauer, ibid, 45.

[85] ibid, 45–46.

the necessary support. It is the final argument we will examine which purports to show that law and justice, on the one hand, are incompatible with equity and mercy, on the other.

B. The Argument from Mercy

Nigel Simmonds offers a helpful and admirably clear general statement of the appropriate type of argument:

> [o]n this view, mercy asserts the importance of particularity over and against the abstract universality of justice and law. Mercy may in this way be presented as an essentially antinomian value, amounting to the slippage of the particular from beneath the universal, or the inability of juridical thinking to wholly subjugate what Eliot calls 'the mysterious complexity of our life'.[86]

Asserting the importance of particularity as against law's generality and abstraction is a common theme in much criticism of legal thought and practice, but does not of itself show that law and mercy are incompatible. Even perfunctory familiarity with law shows it to be far from responsive to every kind of reason and every source of information relevant to those caught in its maw. This is in part because legal systems are largely constituted by exclusionary reasons, understood as reasons to ignore the balance of reasons on many issues, and the rationale for this comes close to providing a rationale for law as a means of subjecting human conduct to the governance of rules as opposed to other social forms.[87] Yet the fact that law is not responsive to each and every consideration relevant to understanding and explaining some instance of human conduct cannot show it to be incompatible with bodies of thought and approaches more catholic in the considerations they admit. Morality, ethics and equity might each be responsive to a wider range of considerations in their efforts to explain, understand and justify human conduct than law, but that entails nothing about the nature or quality of those considerations. All of those considerations might be of the same general type—justice considerations, for example—yet only some of them may be relevant in some domains.

The considerations to which mercy attends and is responsive might be qualitatively different from those relevant in law in a substantive or a modal sense. Imagine an instance in which we exercise merciful judgement and call it MJ 1. The considerations upon which we reached MJ 1 are X, Y and Z. Since these

[86] NE Simmonds, 'Judgement and Mercy' (1993) 13 *Oxford Journal of Legal Studies* 52–68 at 59.

[87] On exclusionary reasons see J Raz, *Practical Reason and Norms*, 2nd edn (Princeton, New Jersey, Princeton University Press, 1990) at 35–48, 141–46, Ch 5 and 178–99. The significance of this feature of law for mercy and equity is illuminatingly outlined and discussed in E Christodoulidis, 'The Irrationality of Merciful Legal Judgement: Exclusionary Reasoning and the Question of the Particular' (1999) 18 *Law and Philosophy* 215–41 at 225–36.

considerations cannot be justice considerations, what can they be? They could be substantively different from such considerations in that their content has nothing at all to do with justice: they might perhaps be 'welfarist' considerations. Such considerations are often invoked by parents when asking or compelling their children to conduct themselves in certain ways: 'it's for your own good' is the usual refrain here. But, whatever the exact relationship between these considerations and those of justice, they are plainly not qualitatively dissimilar to those invoked in various areas of law, family law being the most obvious example.

Love and the reasons it generates might be thought both substantively and modally incompatible with those the law registers. Substantively, the reasons of romantic love are rooted in a deep concern with all aspects of a significant other, their very particular and specific otherness being the cause of that concern. Law never registers the specificity of human beings to the extent that lovers do and thus cannot act on the reasons lovers have. Moreover, it might be thought that the reasons lovers have lack a property law's reasons must always or often have, namely, generalisability. If MJ 1 is the judgement of a lover, and X, Y and Z a lover's reasons, then those reasons may be unique to the two lovers and their context. Each lover might, of course, find themselves in love again, but the reasons that drive their conduct then are only the same as those that drove their conduct earlier because they are reasons of love. They are different insofar as the object of love is different, that object in all its rich and enchanting particularity generating reasons unique to it. If love's reasons, arising from a fine-grained appreciation of and commitment to another, are substantively different from law's reasons, and modally different because never or rarely universalisable, then they might be taken as a surrogate for mercy's reasons. And, if mercy's reasons are sufficiently similar to love's reasons, then the similarity can provide a foundation for the incompatibilist reading of the relationship between law and mercy (and equity).

Is that foundation secure? We should not assume so. One reason for caution is that the account of romantic love just offered is far from being either extensive or scrupulous. While I do not mean to imply that the only respectable accounts of romantic love must be philosophical, one thing such accounts emphasise is that love's reasons are reasons nevertheless.[88] Thus, although rooted in a relationship with and understanding of another, those reasons have content that can in some sense be generalised. A lover's reason to make their beloved happy, while undoubtedly and even necessarily rooted in a connection with and appreciation of the beloved, can be generalised because that specific reason is but a token of a type

[88] There is a view that one form of love—agape (love of God(s) and humankind)—is reasonless (or close to being so). A fine overview of some of the philosophical literature is B Helm, 'Love' in the *Stanford Encyclopedia of Philosophy* http://plato.stanford.edu/archives/fall2013/entries/love/ (last accessed 3rd January 2017). Also invaluable is H Frankfurt, *Necessity, Volition, and Love* (Cambridge, Cambridge University Press, 1998) Chs 11 and 14 and Ch 2 of his *The Reasons of Love* (Princeton, New Jersey, Princeton University Press, 2004). For a sustained meditation on the relations between law and love, see Z Bankowski, *Living Lawfully* (Dordrecht, Kluwer, 2001) Chs 6–9.

of reason, namely, the type that accords weight to the happiness of other human beings. Many context- or person- or relationship- specific reasons can look non-generalisable when viewed only from within the domain in which they are in play. But that does not mean that they are truly non-generalisable; a broader view often confirms they are tokens of more general types.

Furthermore, it is worth noting that many of our reasons for conduct are, like reasons of love, rooted in an appreciation of the other. Whether or not I undertake duties to others and the exact nature of those duties often depends upon the circumstances and character of the other: I am loath to lend money to a feckless acquaintance, but always help my clumsy hiking companion to his feet when he falls. The deed and duty in each case is surely a manifestation of a more general concern—altruism, kindness or common humanity—yet that generality does not remove the deed's or the duty's context- or character-sensitive nature. We might therefore be inclined to regard the content of all or most of our reasons, including reasons of love, as generalisable, even when the objects of our love and our duties determine to some degree the exact contours of those reasons.

Numerous critics of mercy have made the same point. They cannot accept, to return to Simmonds's characterisation, that the slippage of the particular from beneath the universal is a result of general reasons having no grip on the particular, because they do not accept that there are non-generalisable reasons in this context. Even when love's reasons are invoked as paradigmatic, critics of particularist accounts of mercy claim to have succeeded in finding general reasons where there are allegedly none. Some of those reasons have come to light in the discussion of what Michael Detmold called the 'particularity void'. He imagines himself a judge having to decide a case he has in a sense already decided.

> [M]y first case turns out to be exactly the case of my exam: A B and C [the operative facts and accompanying law] are proved and the plaintiff seeks damages.... Where A B C the defendant must pay damages. I know this is right. I have done the reasoning. What more is there? Is not my will coiled appropriately, ready to be unleashed? Yes. But what is required to unleash it? Why does it not just unleash itself? ... What is it that gives me pause in the A B C case? It is not that I doubt my conclusion ... It is not that I wish to go off to Halsbury to see if there is something I've overlooked ... I know I've overlooked nothing. It is just that I now have a radically different problem. A particular, practical problem, which universal hypothetical (theoretical) reasoning does not solve. And the whole problem is that no reasoning can solve it. It is particular, about which nothing can be said (anything I *say* will be universal). I am strictly at a loss, and if I keep on thinking I will give no judgement at all. This moment of indecision (a whole realm) is a recurring theme in literature.[89]

How should such a moment of indecision be characterised and, more significantly for present purposes, how might it be resolved? One description, which Detmold does not adopt, is that this is a moment of existential crisis and/or an instance of

[89] M Detmold, 'Law as Practical Reason' (1989) 48 *Cambridge Law Journal* 436–71, 456.

weakness of the will (although not in the technical philosophical sense of conduct contrary to one's best judgement).[90] One's role as a judge is to apply the law and Detmold's indecision bespeaks doubt about, or weakness in the execution of, that role. But, since one is almost never forced to become a judge, voluntarily taking up the role and refusing to perform it looks like self-indulgence: weakness of the will in the sense of sloughing off one's commitments. While this is not the same as the existential crisis supposedly raised by the sheer presumption of one human being sitting in judgement upon another, the force of such a crisis is much the same in its consequences: being affected by either while on the bench must result in retirement (although not necessarily to the bars of Amsterdam).[91] For Detmold, by contrast, the particularity void exemplifies the limits of reason, since nothing the judge says or thinks can fill the gap betwixt thought and action, save for considerations of love.

> I, the judge, ... at the moment of practicality entered the unanswering void of particularity, the realm of love, about which only mystical, poetic things can be said ...; or nothing. Judges enter this realm everyday.[92]

Detmold's attempt to resolve the particularity void by reference to love is the central issue: he suggests considerations of love are mysterious while critics hold that they are as capable of statement, and generalisation, as almost any other kind of reason for conduct. Furthermore, Detmold's critics do so by reference to a literary example he uses, Davout's sparing of Pierre's life in Tolstoy's *War and Peace*. Davout's orders require that Pierre be killed (he is a spy) but Davout does not follow his orders. Davout hesitates, feeling the force of the particularity void, and realises he and Pierre were 'both children of humanity and were brothers'. That realisation constitutes an instance of mercy, leading Davout to spare Pierre's life. Does this, and similar instances, constitute a realm of mystery about which nothing can be said? Scott Veitch does not think so; for him any justifiable exercise of merciful judgement depends entirely upon the criteria used. There are, he says, different perspectives from which to see this. From the point of view of the person who seeks mercy the issue is this: 'To what are they appealing if not something: an argument, strategy, state of mind, situation etc?' From the mercy giver's perspective the 'suggest[ion] that there are no reasons at all (that their granting of mercy is no more than a whim) fails to capture the subtlety of the conditions in which mercy ... [is] appropriate'.[93]

[90] The view of weakness of the will in the text is close to one philosophical view (R Holton, 'Intention and Weakness of the Will' (1999) 96 *Journal of Philosophy* 241–61) that purports to capture common sense.

[91] 'It can't be denied that, for the present moment at least, we have to have judges, don't we? I could not understand, however, how a man could set himself up to perform such surprising function': A Camus, *The Fall* (Harmondsworth, Penguin, 1963) 15–16.

[92] Detmold (n 89) at 457.

[93] S Veitch, 'Doing Justice to Particulars' in E Christodoulidis (ed), *Communitarianism and Citizenship* (Aldershot, Ashgate, 1998) Ch 13 at 232.

On Veitch's view what Davout does in the example is, presumably, something like this: he makes a choice on one ground (fellow-feeling) as opposed to another (the law) and, clearly, these grounds are not in any sense mysterious or unfathomable. Davout is not moved by some ineffable consideration that lies beyond cognition or reason but, rather, is acting on one consideration to the exclusion of another.

So: is mercy (and equity) the realm of mystery and of silence, of the ineffable? Or is it much the same as any other realm wherein reason plays a role? This grandiose issue is not one that can be truly resolved here, in part because there is no obvious way to produce arguments that reduce the weight of all countervailing considerations to zero. Yet one factor seems particularly significant: I cannot help but think that allocating mercy and equity to the domain of the ineffable and mysterious does them no credit, for it associates them altogether too closely with whim and caprice. My intuition is that mercy and equity are more important than that, their importance as virtues depending to some degree upon their being generally intelligible and thus explicable.[94] Whim, caprice or the ineffable escape explicability and intelligibility, occupying the role that 'Act of God' used to play in our explanations of the natural world. The properties of virtues and vices *qua* virtues and vices ought not to depend upon unpredictable and unrepeatable considerations that seemingly pop into and out of existence rather like itches or alleged 'raw feels'.[95] If those alleging that *Nettleship*, *Adesanya* and like cases are unfair have to base their case on considerations of that type, then their case is either not worth stating or is dishonoured in the stating.

This is not to suggest that there are no meaningful or interesting issues in play in the many discussions of the relation between equity and law.[96] One is surely the tension between different modes of ascription and evaluation, or between the many different types of consideration that can be brought to bear within the processes of ascription and evaluation. Law constitutes one such body of considerations. It is not the only one and it is therefore possible and often appropriate to compare the way in which that body of considerations affects our deliberations in particular instances of judgement with the way in which other considerations impact upon our deliberations. Reasons of love might pull in a different direction to reasons of law. But this truism is not well described as presenting a contrast between the general and implacably universal abstract, on the one hand, and the ineffably subjective particular, on the other. For, even if the latter is indeed conceivable,[97] the

[94] I, too, view 'the merciful person as exhibiting a reliable sensitivity to the reason-giving import of certain charitable considerations': J Tasoulas, 'Mercy' (2003) *Proceedings of the Aristotelian Society* 101–32 at 104.

[95] The term, apparently originated by EC Tolman, is often used by contemporary philosophers as a synonym for 'qualia', the latter being purely sensory conscious experiences.

[96] For a striking attempt to reconfigure the relation, see S Coyle, *Dimensions of Politics and English Jurisprudence* (Cambridge, Cambridge University Press, 2013) Ch 13.

[97] For Simmonds (n 86) at 62–65, there is no such thing as the absolute particular, just more or less abstract descriptions of aspects of the world and our conduct.

issue here is more obviously one which throws into relief different contexts of judgement. The alleged contrast between law and equity is thus characterised by Emilios Christodoulidis 'as a switching between contexts of observation' and, we might add, ascription. One context, the realm of mercy, 'is an invitation to think something through' in a presumably open-ended and open-minded way, while another—the realm of law—constitutes 'a reduction … an (exclusionary) reason not to' think things through.[98]

If those troubled by the apparent harshness of the decisions in *Nettleship* and *Adesanya* are contrasting law's judgement with the judgements other domains (such as love, morality or ethics) might generate in those same cases, then there can be no complaint about that. Calling law to account, by contrasting its judgements with those of other domains, is an important means of trying to ensure the law's good moral standing, but there is one respect in which this calling to account can overreach itself. If it is indeed a matter of calling law to account, it must accept law's features and its distinctiveness as one means of subjecting human conduct to the governance of rules. Overreaching occurs when this calling to account in effect replaces law's judgement with other modes of observation and ascription. That may well be an entirely proper and justified substitution, but it is clearly a call to jettison rather than ameliorate law.

*****

Our examination of the three unfairness charges against *LAJ* licenses this conclusion: all three are very difficult to substantiate. Another important point also emerged, although this is only the second time it has been explicitly mentioned: *LAJ* has significant, possibly even very deep connections with two other notions fundamental to modern legal systems. Thus *LAJ* fits snugly with a conception of legal-liability responsibility as outcome responsibility, a conception that underpins much of what we know about substantive legal doctrine. *LAJ* is also in some sense, and in some dimensions, closely related to impartiality, a juristic virtue of the first order. While not identical with impartiality, *LAJ* certainly overlaps with and reinforces it. By contrast, *LAJ* fits ill with the understanding of equity and mercy offered in section III, but that is not a problem. Other understandings of equity's role in relation to law fit better with *LAJ*, although even these views make equity seem a constant irritant to law, never completely integrated but also never completely ignored.

Are these connections significant? Only insofar as outcome responsibility and impartiality are themselves important. Their importance can be measured

[98] The statements quoted are from Christodoulidis (n 87) at 238. The first is taken slightly out of context.

by asking this question: what role would we allocate, if designing a legal system anew, to the alleged virtue of impartiality and to some or other conception of responsibility? If these notions are admitted within the process of legal-institutional design, either as components or parameters, then *LAJ* will also jostle for admission. Not necessarily so, but contingently so, for there are undoubtedly conceivable understandings of both impartiality and responsibility which have no close connections to *LAJ* and its components. The contingency is this: juristic understandings of impartiality and responsibility close to those with which we are familiar will serve as a Trojan horse for *LAJ*. That *LAJ* is part of a web of seemingly mutually reinforcing, very important juristic ideas is yet another indicator of its significance. We turn in the next three chapters to examine another indicator, namely, the ways in which *LAJ* embodies or connects with some of our most important moral and political values.

4

Dignity

'[A]s time went on … the firmer and more widespread became the conviction that birth decides nothing as to the goodness or badness of a man'.[1]

'The root idea of dignity is simply that virtually everyone, regardless of social station, talents, accomplishments, or moral record, should be treated with respect as a human being'.[2]

This chapter argues that law's abstract judgement (*LAJ*) is closely connected to the notion of dignity. To succeed, the argument must show not only the exact nature of the relationship between dignity and *LAJ* but also elucidate the idea of dignity itself. Dignity has a reasonably long and relatively contested history in Western religious, philosophical and juristic thought and section I therefore spends some time outlining both the concept of dignity and two apparently competing conceptions. Section II investigates how different these two conceptions of dignity really are, while section III examines the links between them, on the one hand, and law and *LAJ*, on the other. Section IV offers a brief summary and conclusion.

Although the discussion of dignity in the history of Western thought seems inconclusive, there are two points of which we can be certain. The first is that dignity is embedded within many contemporary legal systems, as a consequence of various international treaties and other commitments and often as an explicit component of domestic legal doctrine.[3] There is, of course, no *a priori* reason

[1] J Burckhardt, *The Civilisation of the Renaissance in Italy* (London, Phaidon, 1945) at 233.

[2] TE Hill Jr , *Autonomy and Self-Respect* (Cambridge, Cambridge University Press, 1991) at 170.

[3] See, for some instances, Universal Declaration of Human Rights, Preamble, Arts 1, 22 and 23 (3); Common Article 3 of the Geneva Conventions and Arts 75 and 85 of Additional Protocol I and Art 4 (e) of Additional Protocol II to the Conventions; and, *inter alia*, the UN Conventions on Slavery (1956), Rights of the Child (1989), Rights of Migrant Workers (1990) alongside the preambles of the International Covenants on Civil and Political Rights, on Economic, Social and Cultural Rights and on the Elimination of Racial Discrimination; European Convention on Human Rights Protocol 13, Preamble; revised European Social Charter (1996), Preamble and Art 26; Convention on Human Rights and Biomedicine (1997), Preamble, Art 1; Art 24 of the Constitution of Japan 1946; The Constitution of the Italian Republic, 1948, Arts 3, 27 and 41; Art 1 (1) and (2) of the Basic Law of the Federal Republic of Germany (1949); Section 10 of the Constitution of the Republic of South Africa (1996). A dated but still helpful overview, from the perspective of English law, is: D Feldman, 'Human Dignity as a Value: Part 1' (1999) *Public Law* 682–702 and 'Human Dignity as a Value: Part 2' (2000) *Public Law* 61–76; more recent overviews are L Ackermann, *Human Dignity: Lodestar for Equality in South Africa* (Cape Town, Juta, 2012) and A Barak, *Human Dignity: The Constitutional Value and the Constitutional Right* (Cambridge, Cambridge University Press, 2015). The essays in part IV of M Duwell *et al* (eds), *The Cambridge Handbook of Human Dignity* (Cambridge, Cambridge University Press, 2014) also provide a useful overview from a number of jurisdictions.

to think that the various manifestations of the notion of dignity in many legal instruments and doctrines are the same: different understandings of dignity could well be embodied in different legal contexts. But nor is there any *a priori* reason to think these various manifestations must be different. In the absence of argument, the issue is an open one. The discussion in section I is an effort to articulate some general, principally philosophical accounts of dignity that might underpin some of the notion's specific legal-doctrinal manifestations, although no effort is made to show that only one such conception dominates.

Why have almost immediate recourse to *general* accounts of dignity, rather than construct such accounts incrementally, by collating and attempting to synthesise dignity's various legal-doctrinal manifestations? There is no compelling answer to this question. Both approaches are perfectly proper and, indeed, in ideal circumstances both should be adopted. Both approaches are compatible, in that each aims to discharge the same task: to identify prospective legal principles. That is the job of elucidating the broader legal propositions that collections of more specific propositions might plausibly embody, such that those more specific propositions can rightly be called a system or unity. Principles are what confer that unity or coherence. The coherence in question is normative, in the sense that it identifies the goal(s) or value(s) or purpose(s) of the allegedly systematic body of propositions; talk of the principles in play in some area of law is therefore usually translatable into talk of the values (or purposes or goals) salient in that same area.[4] There can, of course, be no guarantee that incremental and general approaches will yield the same list of legal principles.

One conception of dignity examined here is proffered as a promising prospective candidate for the role of general and fundamental legal principle in many of the legal systems with which we are familiar: general, because it informs numerous aspects of legal doctrine and legal institutional design; fundamental, since few values are more important. Moreover, this candidate is primarily but not exclusively a *philosophical* conception of dignity, rather than one unearthed solely by an analysis of the various legal provisions that invoke dignity. The choice to begin with philosophical-cum-jurisprudential accounts is principally a result of favouring a general over an incremental approach to dignity. The underlying supposition is that if general accounts of dignity exist, then they are more likely—given what we know of the discipline's ostensible aims—to have been minted by philosophers and legal theorists than by others. When supplemented with incremental, juristic

[4] This view of the nature and role of legal principles belongs to Neil MacCormick: see *Legal Reasoning and Legal Theory*, revised edn (Oxford, Clarendon Press, 1994) chs VII and VIII and his *Rhetoric and the Rule of Law* (Oxford, Clarendon Press, 2005) Ch 10. I think it fits (as MacCormick shows) what most common law judges do, or say they do, when looking for legal principles; it is in important respects at variance with the characterisation of legal principles offered in R Dworkin, *Taking Rights Seriously* (London, Duckworth, 1978) Ch 3 at, eg, 82.

accounts of dignity, which are also often jurisdiction- and sometimes doctrine-specific, we have the prospect of a near-complete understanding of dignity.[5] What follows is, by comparison, very limited, a first step in the attempt to marry general-philosophical and incremental-juristic accounts of dignity.

The second certainty to note is that dignity's presence within many contemporary legal systems tells us nothing about any alleged relationship between dignity and *LAJ*. It only makes the suggestion that *LAJ* and dignity are interestingly connected less implausible than might otherwise be thought. Finally, a caveat: what follows provides a non-sceptical account of dignity's contours. That means it is open to the possibility of dignity marking something distinctive and important about human beings and their condition or, at least, that human beings think it does. Furthermore, the discussion engages hardly at all with sceptics, who insist that dignity is an empty, useless or stupid notion, save only to make four brief points. One is worth making here, at the outset: dignity's embodiment in the law surely raises a *prima facie* presumption in favour of treating it seriously. That presumption entails nothing about the results of so taking the notion, since the inquiry might yield outcomes either sceptical (a 'shibboleth of all empty-headed moralists') or non-sceptical (an indicator 'of what is uniquely human').[6] The other two points are better made once we have a clearer view of the contours of the concept, while the fourth arises only at the very end of the chapter.

I. Concept and Conceptions

The apparent multitude of views about the meaning of dignity suggests that this possibility might be worth exploring: the existence of an argumentative plateau that some, possibly all, apparently competing accounts of the notion share. If there is such a plateau, henceforth dubbed the *concept* of dignity, then it ensures that there is, in broad terms at least, an agreed topic of conversation between many of the proponents of dignity-talk. That is clearly worth knowing. Furthermore, the

[5] The three most interesting and wide-ranging juristic accounts are: Barak (n 3); Ackerman (n 3); and C McCrudden, 'Human Dignity and Judicial Interpretation of Human Rights' (2008) 19 *European Journal of International Law* 655–724. Other helpful general discussions are N Rao, 'Three Concepts of Dignity in Constitutional Law' (2011) 86 *Notre Dame Law Review* 183–271 and R Glensy, 'The Right to Dignity' (2011) 43 *Columbia Human Rights Law Review* 65–142. Some of the most interesting doctrine-specific accounts are: P Birks, 'Harassment and Hubris' (1997) 32 *Irish Jurist* 1–45; D Reaume, 'Indignities: Making a Place for Dignity in Modern Legal Thought' (2002) 28 *Queens Law Journal* 61–94; J Murphy, 'The Nature and Domain of Aggravated Damages' (2010) 69 *Cambridge Law Journal* 353–77; and D Beyleveld and R Brownsword, *Human Dignity in Bioethics and Biolaw* (Oxford, Clarendon, 2001).

[6] See, respectively, M Rosen, *Dignity: Its History and Meaning* (Cambridge, Massachusetts, Harvard University Press, 2012) at 1 (quoting 'Schopenhauer, the Ebenezer Scrooge of nineteenth-century philosophy' (ibid)) and G Kateb, *Human Dignity* (Cambridge, Massachusetts, Harvard University Press, 2011) at 18 (plainly not the Ebenezer Scrooge of twenty-first century philosophy).

existence of an agreed concept of dignity, however abstract, allows us to understand better the differences between the various views in the discussion. Being able to map areas of disagreement, in the face of agreement, helps elucidate what is distinctive about different accounts—henceforth labelled *conceptions*—of an agreed concept. One useful and vivid view of the connection between concept and conceptions in any particular field holds that the discussion must manifest

> a treelike structure. People by and large agree about the most general and abstract propositions about … [X], which form the trunk of the tree, but they disagree about more concrete refinements or subinterpretations of these abstract propositions, about the branches of the tree.[7]

What, in the context of dignity, might be the trunk of the tree?

Although the literature is diverse, it is not implausible to think that the trunk consists of at least three (and quite possibly four) shared precepts. That, at least, is the case with regard to some of the principal accounts of dignity—ancient, pre-Kantian, Kantian and contemporary re-workings—with which we are familiar in the Western philosophical and juristic traditions.[8] Christopher McCrudden has identified and established the centrality of two of these precepts and I simply adopt them, except for this slight amendment: where he uses the term 'value', I use the term 'significance' (the rationale for which will become clear presently).[9] The first precept is that every human being is intrinsically significant, it being no great surprise that different conceptions of dignity appear to invoke incompatible criteria and measures of significance. Humankind's significance is thus unanimously affirmed in the face of disagreement about the exact nature of that significance. The second precept holds that humankind's intrinsic significance should be recognised and respected by others, some forms of treatment being inconsistent with or required by such respect.

The third precept is an implication of the previous two: dignity is primarily an individualist notion that, first and foremost, sets standards for the ways in which

[7] R Dworkin, *Law's Empire* (Oxford, Hart Publishing, 1998) 70.

[8] Rosen (n 6) provides a brisk and engaging overview of the first three strands of dignity talk (alongside some acute observations on the Catholic Church's many views of dignity). For representative instances of each strand, following the order in the text, see: MT Cicerco, *De Inventione* (translated by HM Hubbell) (Cambridge, Massachusetts, Harvard University Press, 1949) Book II, 166, 333; *Defence Speeches* (translated by DH Berry) (Oxford, Oxford University Press, 2000) 'Pro Murena' 67–106; and *On Obligations* (translated by PG Walsh) (Oxford, Oxford University Press, 2000) Book 1, 106, 36–37; Pico della Mirandolla, *On the Dignity of Man* (Indianapolis, Hackett Publishing, 1998 (1486)); I Kant, *Groundwork to the Metaphysics of Morals*, revised edn (edited by M Gregor and J Timmermann) (Cambridge, Cambridge University Press, 2012 (1785)), hereinafter '*Groundwork*' in text and notes, and *The Metaphysics of Morals* (translated by M Gregor) (Cambridge, Cambridge University Press, 1996 (1797)), henceforth '*Metaphysics*' in text and notes. Some relatively recent re-workings of these positions include J Griffin, *On Human Rights* (Oxford, Oxford University Press, 2008) Ch 2; S Darwall, *The Second Person Standpoint* (Cambridge, Massachusetts, Harvard University Press, 2006) at 13–14 and Ch 10; and T Hill Jr , 'In Defence of Dignity: Comments on Kant and Rosen' in C McCrudden (ed), *Understanding Human Dignity* (Oxford, Oxford University Press, 2013). For some informative thoughts on the context of Cicero's view of dignity, see M Radin, 'Roman Concepts of Equality' (1923) 38 *Political Science Quarterly* 262–89, esp 274–83.

[9] McCrudden (n 5) at 679–80. The three sentences that follow in the text paraphrase McCrudden.

other individual human beings should be thought of and treated *qua* individual human beings. That is not to deny that dignity can only be realised and meaningful within a group of human beings—dignity is, after all, relational, a matter of how we are treated and regarded by others. But *indignity*, understood as dignity's opposite, is primarily a form of treatment or series of wrongs to particular individuals: she is denied the vote, I'm required to sit at the back of the bus, and you are subject to public humiliation. Dignity thus has an individualistic basis, even though its realisation is a collective achievement. McCrudden adds a fourth precept to this list, namely, 'the claim that recognising the intrinsic … [significance] of the individual requires that the state should be seen to exist for the sake of the individual human being, and not vice versa'.[10] There can be no objection to this addition, provided we recognise that talk of the 'state'—obviously and pressingly relevant now—may be out of place in some historical epochs. If the state has not always been with us, then this precept has a slightly limited historical relevance.[11]

Those who think there is just a single tenable concept of dignity ('monists'), and those who think we are faced with a welter of utterly incompatible accounts ('pluralists'), will deny the utility of the concept/conception distinction in this context. Yet, while the history and variety of views about the nature of dignity suggest that monism is implausible, it cannot entail the truth of pluralism—not, at least, without substantial further argument. For it remains possible in the face of dignity's history that the various views about it are nowhere near as different as appearances suggest. Some contemporary discussions that provide an overview of dignity's many manifestations seemingly undermine this possibility, for they assume a sectarian, pluralist approach to the notion in which a thousand very different flowers are regarded as blooming.[12] But just because some flowers appear in some respects dissimilar does not mean that they are different species or genera. In what follows, I avoid this assumption; I therefore eschew pluralism about dignity in the strong form which insists that there are many utterly incompatible accounts. A history in which numerous different accounts of dignity have been offered is, on its face, compatible with the moderate pluralism about dignity implied by invoking the concept/conception distinction. On that view, there are competing and thus in some respects different conceptions that nevertheless have important features in common. This moderate pluralist position fits dignity's disputatious history just as well as the strong version. This moderate position is my starting point.

Neither monist nor strong pluralist accounts of dignity are very common, although the former are particularly elusive. It is tempting to tar Immanuel Kant's account with the monist brush, but the fact that he does not address alternative

[10] McCrudden (n 5) at 679.

[11] I have in mind Q Skinner's argument about the state: a lucid and magisterial presentation is Ch 14 of his *Visions of Politics*, volume II (Cambridge, Cambridge University Press, 2002). A briefer treatment is his 'The State' in T Ball, J Farr and R Hanson (eds), *Political Innovation and Conceptual Change* (Cambridge, Cambridge University Press, 1989).

[12] See, for example, the two general collections cited in n 3 (Duwell et al (eds)) and n 8 (McCrudden (ed)) respectively.

accounts of dignity cannot license this move.[13] Kant's account of dignity arises entirely within his framework for moral and ethical thought, its near hermetically-sealed status telling us little about what he thought of other accounts, save that they presumably did not fit within his framework. Pluralist accounts are slightly thicker on the ground and appear to have a contemporary exponent in Michael Rosen. Rosen holds that dignity-talk can refer to at least four quite different notions: (i) a rank or status; (ii) intrinsic value; (iii) measured and self-possessed behaviour; (iv) respectful treatment. While Rosen accepts that, as a historical matter, there has been (and still is) some degree of overlap between these four strands of dignity-talk, it is not a huge step from here to the claim that each strand represents an independent and competing concept of dignity.[14] Indeed, this conclusion seems to follow from Rosen's discussion of various legal manifestations of dignity and their interpretation in the courts. The ubiquity of the notion in legal discourse 'masks a great deal of disagreement and sheer confusion' which arises, Rosen thinks, from the fact that the courts often employ quite different understandings of dignity in different areas of law and, more significantly, in one and the same area of law.[15] He suggests that two of the different strands of dignity talk he identifies are 'very different concept[s]', that there is 'fundamental disagreement' between two others, and that these are 'four … distinct, conceptually divisible strands'.[16] While claims like these lend themselves to a strong pluralist interpretation, they nevertheless constitute too slender a reed to warrant the conclusion that Rosen *undoubtedly* endorses such a view of dignity.

Before turning to the two apparently competing conceptions of dignity—labelled, for reasons that will become obvious, the 'value' and 'status' conceptions—which occupy the remainder of this chapter, a final detour is necessary. For, in order to circumvent the suggestion that dignity is unworthy of further attention, two common but quite misguided objections to the notion must

[13] The *Groundwork* (n 8), is almost entirely free of references to other philosophers; the work of classical Greek and Roman philosopher-sages figures more frequently in *Metaphysics* (n 8). I eschew the practice of Kant scholars to refer not just to free-standing editions of the works in question, but also to a particular work's place in one or other of the 23 Volumes of *Kant's gesammelte Schriften* (Berlin, de Gruyter, 1902). Our principal interest is in the secondary literature and the Cambridge University Press versions of the master-works I refer to are both excellent.

[14] See Rosen (n 6) Ch 1. By highlighting an egalitarian 'break' between ancient and biblical political thought, JA Berman's *Created Equal: How the Bible Broke with Ancient Political Thought* (Oxford, Oxford University Press, 2008) could provide the basis of a pluralist account of dignity, even though the notion does not figure explicitly in Berman's discussion.

[15] Rosen (n 6) at 67. The whole of Ch 2 ('The Legislation of Dignity') seems designed to accentuate the differences between the four strands Rosen identifies. N Rao's 'Three Concepts of Dignity in Constitutional Law' (n 5), is an ostensibly pluralist view also founded upon an extensive analysis of case-law.

[16] The first two quoted phrases are from Rosen (n 6) at 76–77 and 99, while the last is from M Rosen, 'Dignity: The Case Against', in McCrudden (n 8) Ch 7 at 153. See also Rosen's discussion of the 'deep and fundamental' tensions in the notion of dignity in J Waldron, *Dignity, Rank, and Rights* (New York, Oxford University Press, 2012)—hereinafter '*DRR*' in both text and notes—at 90–94.

be set aside. These are my second and third points against dignity sceptics. The objections are closely related, one insisting that the notion of dignity is empty, the other that it is redundant.

For the former to be true, the notion would have to be literally content-less and it is not only the fact that it has been embedded in numerous legal provisions that raises a presumption against this view. There is also a rich vein of thought and scholarship about dignity, two strands of which are examined presently. One is well established, the other ostensibly new. Their very existence means critics cannot help themselves to the claim that dignity is an empty notion without working hard to show that the existing work in the field is without content. The redundancy objection differs slightly from the emptiness objection by accepting that dignity might have some content. The complaint, though, is that the content it has is already provided by other important values, like respect and autonomy. Of course, a great deal turns upon how these values are specified and a full audit of this objection requires a complete elucidation of these alleged alternatives to dignity. In the absence of such an elucidation, note this: the accounts of dignity outlined in what follows sketch the contours not just of dignity but also of cognate notions like respect and autonomy. Exercises in conceptual cartography such as these must surely be examined before the redundancy objection can bite.

A. Dignity as Value

The value conception of dignity demands our attention for at least two reasons. First, it is principally the work of Kant, one of the West's most eminent philosophers, and second, it is still—some 230 years after first publication—subject to lively discussion and debate. That discussion has been particularly vibrant in the Anglophone world over the last 30 or so years and I have therefore decided to concentrate upon a single contemporary 'Kantian' version of the value conception, that articulated by Thomas Hill Jr. Focussing on Hill's scholarship does not imply that it is the only work of its kind relevant to our concerns, although its clarity, scrupulousness and candidly sceptical tone ensures it is among the best and most illuminating of its kind. The problem, rather, is that there are many gifted contemporary philosophers labouring in the Kantian tradition in the Anglophone world, producing excellent work; coming up with compelling grounds for choosing between them is difficult.[17] Since considerations of space and time nevertheless

[17] Even a cursory list must include: C Korsgaard, *Creating the Kingdom of Ends* (Cambridge, Cambridge University Press, 1996); O O'Neill, *Constructions of Reason* (Cambridge, Cambridge University Press, 1989), *Towards Virtue and Justice* (Cambridge, Cambridge University Press, 1996) and *Acting on Principle*, 2nd edn (Cambridge, Cambridge University Press, 2013); A Reath, *Agency and Autonomy in Kant's Moral Theory* (Oxford, Oxford University Press, 2006); A Wood, *Kant's Ethical Thought* (Cambridge, Cambridge University Press, 1999) and *Kantian Ethics* (Cambridge, Cambridge University Press, 2008).

demand that a choice be made, it is convenient that one reason confers greater salience on Hill's work than that of his fellow Kantians. Hill has recently addressed one contemporary critic of the Kantian conception of dignity (Rosen) and, in so doing, has responded to another eminent critic and proponent of an ostensibly different conception of dignity (Jeremy Waldron). In the process, Hill has also cast interesting light on how Kant's work should be understood.[18]

Hill's initial and most thorough account of dignity starts not quite from the beginning, but close to it; he begins with Kant's second formulation of the Categorical Imperative rather than the first. It holds that one should '[s]o act that you always use humanity, in your own person as well as in the person of any other, always at the same time as an end, never simply as a means'.[19] This immediately raises two questions: what is humanity? And: what is it to treat something (i) as a means and (ii) as an end? As to the former, Hill holds that a 'review of Kant's repeated use of 'humanity in a person' in *The Metaphysics of Morals* and elsewhere strongly suggests that … Kant thought of humanity as a characteristic, or set of characteristics, of persons'.[20] Hill shows that Kant mentioned at least five such characteristics, including two different sets of capacities and dispositions: (i) to act for reasons; and (ii) to follow rational principles of prudence and efficiency. Alongside these there is (iii) 'a power to set any end whatsoever' which includes what many other animals lack, namely, the 'ability to foresee future consequences, adopt long-range goals, resist immediate temptation, and even to commit oneself to ends for which one has no sensuous desire'.[21] That power is accompanied by (iv), Kant's claim that 'humanity as rational nature necessarily … includes acceptance ("legislating to oneself") of certain unconditional principles of conduct, that is, categorical imperatives, independently of … punishment and reward'; and the recognition that (v) rational nature 'encompasses theoretical as well as practical reason'.[22] 'Humanity' in Kant is therefore not, for Hill, simply a synonym for humankind or persons; it is more complex than either of those notions, certainly as they appear in ordinary language, and it carries far more weight (and, some might think, baggage).

[18] See n 8 and also his *Dignity and Practical Reason in Kant's Moral Theory* (Ithaca, Cornell UP 1992) chs 2 and 10 (hereinafter, in both text and notes, '*D*'); *Respect, Pluralism, and Justice: Kantian Perspectives* (Oxford, Clarendon Press, 2000) chs 3–5 (henceforth '*Respect*'); *Virtue, Rules, and Justice: Kantian Aspirations* (Oxford, Clarendon Press, 2012) chs 8 and 13 (hereinafter, '*Virtue*'). Of these chapters, those most closely concerned with Kant's texts are *D*, Ch 2; *Respect*, Ch 4 and both chapters of *Virtue*. Note that Hill's references in *D* to the *Groundwork* are to an earlier edition than that cited in n 8, above. I have therefore converted his references into this later currency; there are some slight differences in the translation.

[19] *Groundwork* (n 8) 41. The first formulation holds that one should 'act only according to that maxim through which you can at the same time will that it become a universal law': *Groundwork*, ibid, 34.

[20] *D* (n 18) 39.

[21] *D* (n 18) 40–41.

[22] *D* (n 18) 41.

The first part of Kant's claim that humanity must always be treated as an end and never simply as a means has thus become admirably clear under Hill's tutelage, but what of the second question: what is it to treat humanity not solely as a *means* but as an *end*? One cannot understand what it means to treat humanity as a means, claims Hill, unless one first knows what it is to treat it as an end. This is because treating something simply as a means 'is to fail to treat it in some other appropriate way while treating it as a means',[23] namely, as an end. But the question, 'What is it to treat humanity as an end? … is especially puzzling because "humanity", as a set of rational ends and dispositions, is not the sort of thing which is an end, or goal, in the ordinary sense'.[24] For Hill, the notion of an 'end' in Kant is unpacked by seven distinct but interlinked claims. First, in general terms any end is a ground of self-determination, which Hill regards as a reason for acting. Second, Kant divides ends into those that are relative (ends arising from wants and desires) and those that are objective or ends in themselves ('that hold for every rational being').[25] Humanity is one of the latter. Furthermore, humanity is not an end to be brought about like some or other goal (happiness or wealth, for example) but is, rather, 'an end by virtue of what it is'; 'to say that humanity is an end is not to say that something which does not yet exist should be produced or that the quantity of something desirable should be increased'. Fourth, being an objective end entails that, 'when a person's humanity gives one a reason for doing or refraining from something … that reason takes precedence over other reasons';[26] indeed, Kant's fifth claim is that humanity's status as an objective end is 'the supreme limiting condition in the use of all means'.[27]

The remaining two claims are a little more problematic. The sixth consists of Kant's insistence that objective ends must be conceived only negatively which, if read to imply an absence of any duties to aid others, contradicts what Kant says elsewhere. Hill's solution is to interpret this claim as a reiteration of the third, a different way of saying that humanity and other ends in themselves are not goals to be brought about. The final claim takes us into the territory of the first formulation of the Categorical Imperative, since it requires a plausible reading of Kant's remark that one can in part treat persons as ends 'if one treats persons "as beings who must themselves be able to share in the end of the very same action"'.[28] This cannot mean, in Hill's view, that, for example, one must not 'use a person's services unless that person, quite literally, shared all of one's ends in doing so … that carpenters employed to build an opera house must have among their goals the increased enjoyment of opera'.[29] Rather, it requires only that those used as means

[23] *D* (n 18) 41.
[24] *D* (n 18) 42.
[25] *Groundwork* (n 8) 40.
[26] *D* (n 18) 44.
[27] *Groundwork* (n 8) 49.
[28] *D* (n 18) 44–45.
[29] *D* (n 18) 45.

must be able to adopt the end in question without irrational conflict of will. Thus carpenters who hate opera can adopt the end of building an opera house if that is an obvious way of them obtaining the work and pay they require: their willing of the latter overrides any distaste for this particular musical form. The point here is not, however, about greater wants trumping lesser ones but, rather, about consistency in the maxims for one's actions. In the carpenter's case, the maxim on which he acts—do this for the sake of that—'is such that there is no irrationality in anyone's willing it as a universal law'.[30]

Where does dignity fit into this picture? Humanity (and ends in themselves at large, if the latter constitutes a broader category than the former) is one of the things to which Kant attributes dignity. He ascribes dignity to other apparently different 'things', too, as Hill points out, but on closer inspection most of these seem to be different ways of describing the characteristics constitutive of humanity. So, for instance, persons, rational nature, rational beings, as well as persons who conform to duty and do duty for duty's sake, are all regarded by Kant as having dignity.[31] What, then, is dignity? Kant says it is an 'unconditional and incomparable worth'[32] which, to Hill, means (i) that dignity's value is 'not dependent upon contingent facts'; and (ii) that

> whenever one must choose between something with dignity and something with mere price one should always choose the former. No amount of price, or value dependent on contingent needs and tastes, can justify or compensate for sacrifice of dignity. We may express this by saying that what has dignity is *priceless*.[33]

Things with mere price 'can be replaced with something else, as its *equivalent*; whereas what is elevated above any price, and hence allows of no equivalent, has a dignity'.[34]

To say humanity in persons has dignity is therefore to say humanity has an unconditional and incomparable worth and this, thinks Hill, has some very significant practical implications. Five such implications seem particularly important for our purposes. First, is it clear that Kant's view of dignity requires that 'one would refuse to do anything which damages or impairs a person's rational capacities' because 'humanity is our rationality and capacity to set ends'. Second, 'one who sufficiently valued persons' rational capacities would presumably not want to destroy the persons themselves' and, third, 'since the exercise of rationality is something to be cherished, in trying to influence others one should appeal to their reason rather than try to manipulate them by non-rational techniques'. Fourth, 'valuing highly the setting and rational pursuit of ends even in other persons, one should leave them freedom to set and pursue their ends in a rational (moral and

30 *D* (n 18) 45.
31 *D* (n 18) 47.
32 *Groundwork* (n 8) 47.
33 *D* (n 18) 48.
34 *Groundwork* (n 8) 46 (emphasis in original).

prudential) way'.[35] Finally, if humanity in persons does indeed have unconditional and incomparable worth, then 'certain attitudes and symbolic gestures, and the avoidance of others, might be required'; humanity surely 'should be honoured and respected or at least not mocked, dishonored or degraded'.[36] These implications explain why even those guilty of serious crimes must nevertheless be treated in a dignified way, for no one's humanity can be completely forfeit; they also underlie Kant's prohibition on suicide. One's humanity can, however, fail to come into existence or fall into abeyance insofar as one loses or fails to develop its constitutive characteristics and capacities. In these instances there is something like a precautionary principle at work,[37] demanding respect not just for actual but also for potential and former bearers of humanity: they neither are, nor do they become, morally insignificant features of the universe on a Kantian view.[38]

It seems, then, that the meaning of dignity on the value conception can be easily summarised. It is a matter of humanity's unconditional and incomparable worth. Why, then, the leaden build-up to this statement of what dignity entails? Although generally advisable to cut to the quick, in this instance that is a mistake. For, taken independently of the background argument about the nature of humanity and the distinction between means and ends, Kant's view of dignity as incomparable value can seem both sanctimonious and mysterious.[39] While the former complaint reduces to a matter of taste, the latter is more serious. The mystery arises in part because the value sense of dignity just identified is not the only one in Kant's work.[40] It is, however, undoubtedly significant, as Hill's elucidation of the wider argumentative structure of Kant's remarks makes clear: the value sense of dignity is a vital element in Kant's overall conception of morality. It also provides a clear view of some links between dignity, on the one hand, and related notions, like autonomy and respect, on the other.

On a Kantian view, the latter is the most appropriate affective response-cum-attitude to humanity's incomparable value; without Kantian humanity, there would be nothing worthy of respect. The kind of respect in play is not, however, that which is earned, arising from someone's achievements or other worthy features. It is, rather, 'recognition respect' and is owed not in light of one's deeds, excellences or the like, but by virtue of what one is; being a person, or having humanity, is a ground for such deference.[41] Furthermore, the deference due to

[35] *D* (n 18) 50.

[36] *D* (n 18) 50–51.

[37] *D* (n 18) 50.

[38] See also Hill's discussion in *Respect* (n 18) at 101–09.

[39] Or, according to Waldron, priggish: *DRR* (n 16) at 25.

[40] In *Kant on Human Dignity* (Berlin, de Gruyter, 2011), Oliver Sensen argues that the Circeronian sense of dignity, in which the notion is used to mark status within the order of beings and, in particular, to flag up humankind's high position in that order, fits all 111 uses of the term dignity in Kant's work (see chs 4–5). He may well be right about that but the risk is that although the Circeronian sense fits all uses, it does not do justice to all; nor is it incompatible with value and status conceptions.

[41] See S Darwall, 'Two Kinds of Respect' (1977) 88 *Ethics* 36–49 at 38.

humanity on this view of respect can be regarded as the hallmark of a properly deontological, as opposed to a utilitarian, approach to moral matters, for it guarantees what the latter cannot: respect for the moral separateness of persons. The relationship between dignity and autonomy is complex, but it seems clear that Kant's notion of humanity and its constituents provides the bridge between the two. Autonomy is in part, on Kant's view, a matter of positive freedom and this entails, among other things, 'a deep rational commitment to some principle(s) of conduct as rationally binding' that are 'in some sense necessarily imposed upon oneself by oneself as a rational agent'.[42] That commitment, along with the very idea of binding oneself, is possible only if some of the characteristics constitutive of humanity are in place.[43] Do not, however, assume that dignity and autonomy are identical for Kant. Although there are significant connections between them, the latter is the more expansive and more important notion.

B. Dignity as Status

It is not a great exaggeration to say that the status conception of dignity owes its existence to Waldron. He has developed this conception over the last decade or so and its apparent novelty and originality constitute one reason why it is worthy of attention.[44] The use of 'apparent' in that sentence is not, by the way, a means of slighting Waldron's contribution. Rather, it emphasises both Waldron's claim that the status conception has long been with us and his view of his task with regard to it, that of reminding us of its existence and of the transformation it has undergone. There is another, equally powerful reason why the status conception demands attention: Waldron views it as a direct challenge and better alternative to the value conception. If the latter merits our attention then so, too, does the status conception, its most recent competitor.

Here is a typically clear statement from Waldron as to what dignity, on the status conception, is:

> what I mean by the term … is something like this:
>
> Dignity is the status of a person predicated on the fact that she is recognised as having the ability to control and regulate her actions in accordance with her own apprehension of norms and reasons that apply to her; it assumes she is capable of giving and entitled to give an account of herself (and of the way in which she is regulating her actions and organising her life), an account that others are to pay attention to; and it means finally that she has the wherewithal to demand that her agency and her presence among us as

[42] *D* (n 18) 87.

[43] This much is plain from Hill's remarks at 217–18 of 'Kantian Perspectives on the Rational Basis of Human Dignity' in Duwell *et al* (n 3).

[44] The principal instalments are: 'Dignity and Rank' (2007) 48 *European Journal of Sociology* 201–37; 'Dignity, Rights, and Responsibilities' (2011) 43 *Arizona State Law Journal* 1107–36; *DRR* (n 16); 'How Law Protects Dignity' (2012) 71 *Cambridge Law Journal* 200–22; and *The Harm in Hate Speech* (Cambridge, Massachusetts, Harvard University Press, 2012) Chs 3–5.

> a human being be taken seriously and accommodated in the lives of others, in others' attitudes and actions towards her, and in social life generally.[45]

Stated thus, the substance of this conception is not obviously incompatible with that of the value conception. Waldron's emphasis upon the recognition of agents' ability to control and regulate their conduct is very similar to some of the characteristics Kant regards as constitutive of humanity and thus as bearers of dignity. Indeed those characteristics and the respect they generate encompass most of what Waldron regards as crucial to dignity in the latter part of this quotation: a Kantian understanding of (recognition) respect is just as much a matter of giving, and being entitled to give, an account of one's conduct while having that account, and one's agency in general, taken seriously—'accommodated in the lives of others'—as it is for Waldron. Needless to say, some notion of autonomy surely looms in the background of Waldron's conception of dignity just as it connects with dignity in Kant (although I don't imply by this that Waldron invokes anything like a Kantian understanding of autonomy).

By far the most important difference, for Waldron, between his and the value conception is the notion of status. He holds that any 'good account of dignity will explain it as a very general status',[46] that status being 'normative'.[47] Furthermore, the status human beings currently have is high since 'the modern notion of dignity involves an upwards equalization of rank, so that we now try to accord to every human being something of the dignity, rank, and expectation of respect that was formerly accorded to nobility'.[48] Human dignity currently 'involves universalising, rather than superceding, the connotations of status, rank and nobility that 'dignity' traditionally conveyed'.[49] In an almost Nietzschean moment, Waldron characterises the change that the notion of dignity has thus undergone as a transvaluation of values. What the notion once valued above all else—the incidents of aristocratic status and good patrician bearing—were enjoyed only by a few; what it celebrates now is something akin to that high aristocratic standing, but it is ostensibly ascribed to all. This transvaluation marks a

> sea change in the way 'dignity' is used, enabling it to become a leading concept of *universal* rights (as opposed to special privileges), and bring into the realm of rights what James Whitman has called 'an extension of formerly high status treatment to all sectors of the population.'[...] But we see this only if we understand the *dynamics* of the movement between modern notions of dignity and an older notion of rank. The older notion is not obliterated; it is precisely the resources of the older notion that are put to work in the new.[50]

[45] 'How Law Protects Dignity', ibid, at 201–02.

[46] *DRR* (n 16) 22.

[47] *DRR* (n 16) 18.

[48] *DRR* (n 16) 33.

[49] *DRR* (n 16) 67.

[50] *DRR* (n 16) 33 (emphasis in original). See also 'Dignity and Rank' (n 44) at 219–21, where Waldron illustrates this transvaluation by reference to late-eighteenth-century poetry, and M Tanner's Introduction to F Nietzsche, *Twilight of the Idols* and *The Anti-Christ* (London, Penguin, 1968) at 7.

Another difference between the status and value conceptions Waldron is keen to emphasise is that the former is a significantly legal notion.[51] 'Dignity seems at home in law: law is its natural habitat'.[52] This is not just because, as was noted at the beginning of this chapter, the notion figures explicitly in a range of legal documents, including sundry treaties and constitutions. In addition, Waldron shows how a number of important aspects of legal institutional design, including the argumentative structure of law, the trial process and some of its procedural constraints and requirements, as well as the very idea of being a right-bearer, are premised upon dignity in the sense stated above: all take the agency of the law's addressees seriously, by assuming that they have the ability to control their actions and to give an account of themselves. Legal systems thus 'count on people's capacities for practical understanding, self-control, self-monitoring and the modulation of their own behaviour in regard to norms that they can grasp and understand'.[53] And that, says Waldron, is to value and respect their dignity.

Conscious of the fact that most legal systems recognise a range of different legal statuses, Waldron distinguishes between sortal and condition status. 'Some distinctions of status', he says, 'are still with us … legal statuses that apply to individuals in virtue of certain conditions they are in, that they may not be in forever, or that they may have fallen into by choice or happenstance'. These conditions include statuses like 'infant', 'parent', 'bankrupt' and 'alien'. These tell us nothing 'about the underlying personhood of the individuals who have them'.[54] By contrast, '[s]ortal status categorizes legal subjects on the basis of *the sort of person* they are. One's sortal status defines a sort of baseline (relative to condition status)'[55] and 'represents a person's permanent situation and destiny so far as the law is concerned'.[56] What is that baseline? Once there were many: lord/bondsman, freeman/slave, man/woman, black/white, Christian/non-Christian, to name a few. Now there is only one. Thus,

> the idea behind sortal status is that there are different kinds of person [and] it is precisely this … claim that the principle of *human* dignity denies. There are not different kinds of person, at least not for human persons. … There is basically just one kind of human person in the eyes of the law, and condition status is defined by contrast with this baseline'.[57]

That baseline, in Waldron's view, is a uniformly high and equal status for all, more like the status of lord than of bondsman, of one who can speak for himself rather

[51] He doesn't emphasise the point in all publications: it is up front and central in *DRR* (n 16) and 'How Law Protects Dignity' (n 44), but far less obvious in 'Dignity and Rank', ibid. The fact that Waldron is addressing different audiences surely explains this.

[52] *DRR* (n 16) 13.

[53] *DRR* (n 16) 52.

[54] *DRR* (n 16) 58.

[55] *DRR* (n 16) 58–59.

[56] *DRR* (n 16) 59.

[57] *DRR* (n 16) 59.

than be spoken for, of one who bears rights rather than merely duties; 'it is the status of someone who can demand to be heard and taken into account'.[58]

Can that status be lost or forfeit? Waldron thinks not; or not easily, and this marks another interesting similarity between status and value conceptions. Like the value conception, the status conception holds that criminal wrongdoing does not suspend the requirement that wrongdoers be treated in a dignified way, except insofar as some degree of indignity is unavoidable in answering and paying for one's misdeeds.[59] Dignity must be maintained, says Waldron, in both the process leading to and the mode of infliction of punishment; he endorses James Whitman's thesis that the modes of punishment now most often adopted evidence a 'levelling-up' in the type of treatment meted out to wrongdoers. That thesis is not only broadly correct for Waldron, but also manifests the truth of the transvaluation thesis: 'everyone who is punished is to be punished now as though he were an errant noble rather than an errant slave'.[60] In addition, Waldron accepts something like the precautionary principle that the value conception invokes to deal with potential or lapsed bearers of humanity. So, for example, children have every bit as high a rank on Waldron's account as adults, although only by virtue of being potential adults: '[l]ike heirs to an aristocratic title, their present status looks to a rank that they *will* occupy (or are destined to occupy)'.[61]

Waldron's focus upon law when delineating and understanding dignity does not mean his approach is either non- or anti-philosophical.[62] He does, however, eschew what he regards as a standard philosophical approach, which would be to regard dignity as a moral idea 'and then look to see how adequately or clumsily [it] … has been represented in … statutes, constitutions, and human rights conventions or in … legal doctrines or precedents'.[63] Rather, his inquiry starts with dignity as it is found in those legal sources and works out from there: he still aims to provide a philosophical account—in the sense of elucidating the idea's contours, its moral-cum-political standing and relationship with related ideas—but it is not based first and foremost in a critique or commendation of various philosophical accounts of dignity. Nor is it, in Waldron's view, a stipulative account of dignity's meaning for, although the analysis begins with law, he thinks it captures much of what we mean when we speak of dignity in ordinary language.[64] While Waldron regards the former point as a contrast between the status conception and most other conceptions of dignity, the latter is a commonplace methodological tenet of much contemporary moral, political and legal philosophy.

[58] *DRR* (n 16) 60.
[59] *DRR* (n 16) 64.
[60] *DRR* (n 16) 64.
[61] *DRR* (n 16) 29 (emphasis in original).
[62] Rosen thinks Waldron's approach represents a move 'from politics to metaphysics' and has some doubts about it: *DRR* (n 16) at 80 and 81–84.
[63] *DRR* (n 16) 13.
[64] See 'How Law Protects Dignity' (n 44) at 202. 'Dignity and Rank' (n 44) provides a more expansive discussion of stipulative and non-stipulative usages of dignity (at 209–19).

In other work, Waldron has done even more to demonstrate the embeddedness of the status conception in legal doctrine and legal institutional design. He has attempted to show far more extensively than in *DRR* that the status conception can explain restrictions on hate speech, and how it relates to other important general legal notions like citizenship rights and responsibilities.[65] Given Waldron's starting point, this can only add plausibility to his case for the status conception, but it might engender the following kind of objection. It is that Waldron's case for the status conception is a purely contingent, historically informed one, there being no argument in favour of that conception over and beyond that which shows that it happens to be embedded in legal history and legal doctrine. Critics of the status conception could fully accept the latter point while maintaining that this conception should be rejected. Yet this misrepresents the standing of the transvaluation story about dignity that Waldron tells: it is not intended, in and of itself, to be a normative (moral-cum-political) case for the status conception. Nor does he provide a set-piece master moral or political argument, or series of such arguments, in favour of the status conception.

There can, however, be no doubt that Waldron regards the status conception as morally and politically important. The normative case he provides is incremental, an intermittent list of usually implicit commendations and connections attached to the tale of moral progress that the transvaluation trope unfolds. These implicit commendations might be contested, in the sense that remarks such as these—'the modern notion of *human* dignity involves an upwards equalization of rank, so we now try to accord to every human being something of the dignity … formerly accorded to nobility';[66] 'a good account of dignity … will … generate an account of it as noble bearing'; 'dignity … [is] a high ranking status … assigned now to every person'[67]—could be taken not as direct endorsements of the view expressed, but as mere reportage relaying what certain folk currently think. That is nevertheless false to the overall tenor of Waldron's language and the design of his project in *DRR*: the tale he tells is framed by him, in both the words he uses and structure he adopts, as a good-news story. It is also false to remarks such as this, made towards the end of the levelling-up narrative that dignity's transvaluation embodies: 'our moral views have moved *upward* in this respect, according to all men and women now the moral respect and consideration … [once] accorded [only] to "a much smaller number of white men"'.[68]

Finally, note that the absence of a set-piece moral-cum-political argument in favour of the status conception is perfectly sensible given Waldron's view of moral evaluation and thought. It is that 'a lot of what we call moral thought is not devoted to the establishment of a moral order *analogous* to a legal order, but is in

[65] See *The Harm in Hate Speech* and 'Dignity, Rights, and Responsibilities' both n 44 above.
[66] *DRR* (n 16) 33 (emphasis in the original).
[67] *DRR* (n 16) 22.
[68] *DRR* (n 16) 69 (emphasis in the original).

fact oriented to the evaluation and criticism of the legal order itself'.[69] Political morality, he says, is focussed upon law and any discussion of dignity in political morality thus 'orients itself critically to the place of dignity in the legal system'. Moral and political argument in this context therefore 'involves *immanent critique*, rather than bringing standards to bear that are independent of those the law itself embodies. We evaluate law morally using (something like) law's very own dignitarian resources'.[70]

II. Distinctions without Differences

A. Blurring the Lines

The foregoing sketches generate many questions, one of the most pressing and obvious being: are these two conceptions of dignity genuinely incompatible? There are powerful reasons that suggest they are not. They are the fulcrum of what follows. The first reason takes us back to an issue raised early in section I, about the existence of monist and strong pluralist accounts of dignity. Recall the four allegedly different notions Rosen thinks dignity-talk can invoke.[71] Hill's view is that the value conception embodies all four of these allegedly competing strands. There is no doubt, for Hill, as to the existence of the status strand in Kant's thought. In Kant's view 'every human person has a *status* of dignity, which consists of rights, duties, and respect-worthiness that animals lack'; this is 'the status of equality before the moral law and the status of a moral "lawmaker", that is, a person who shares in the common practical reason that specifies what the basic law requires'.[72] Kant also implies, says Hill, that dignity is a status that can be characterised as having '*intrinsic value* in a sense', the sense being that '[p]ersons with dignity are "ends-in-themselves"' and thus must not be treated merely as means or with indifference; '[t]hey are not "ends to be produced" but exist as beings with a special status and value that Kant contrasts with "relative value"'.[73]

As to the third strand, 'measured and self-possessed behaviour' or 'the idea that one should act in a *dignified* way as befitting one's class and social status',[74] Kant's moral theory had a revolutionary impact. According to Hill, Kant transformed the idea of acting in a dignified way, 'making it appropriate to his conception of all human persons as fundamentally moral equals'.[75] When acting in a way

[69] *DRR* (n 16) 67 (emphasis in the original).
[70] *DRR* (n 16) 67.
[71] See Rosen (n 6) Ch 1.
[72] 'In Defence of Dignity' (n 8) 315.
[73] 'In Defence of Dignity' (n 8) 316.
[74] 'In Defence of Dignity' (n 8) 317.
[75] 'In Defence of Dignity' (n 8) 317. Elizabeth Anderson offers a similar argument, maintaining that Kant's later moral philosophy is based upon the transvaluation of an ethic of honour (and thus

befitting one's class and status, there is only one relevant class for Kant, 'that of human beings with dignity, and the "dignified" behaviour this calls for is whatever in context expresses one's valuing of this status'.[76] Regarding the fourth strand—respectful treatment—

> Kant held that we acknowledge the dignity of humanity by *treating every person with respect*. Respect for the moral law demands respect for every human person, no matter how disliked, useless, or misbehaving. The respect in question is not the special honour and deference we give to those in high office or those who are especially talented or accomplished. It is rather an expressed recognition, appropriate to the context, that the person has the fundamentally equal status and value of dignity as determined by the moral law, that is … [strands (i) and (ii)] above.[77]

The general point here is not an exegetical one, although that is an important issue. Rather, it is this: if Hill is right to claim Kant's view incorporates all four allegedly incompatible strands, then that suggests the general tradition of thought about dignity is not as fractious as Rosen thinks. The presence of the four strands in Kant's thought implies that Rosen mistakes different features of *one thing* for *different things* and it is worth taking this caution to heart. For, although Rosen seemingly embraces a strong pluralist view of dignity, on which there are numerous different and incompatible accounts, the caution also serves as a warning against the moderate pluralist view adopted here. Moderate pluralists might be prone to a very similar mistake, taking different aspects of the *same conception* for *competing conceptions*. Waldron, I think, does this and this mistake constitutes the second reason for doubting that value and status accounts of dignity are indeed competing conceptions.

To see the point, we must examine Waldron's reasons for distinguishing the two. In addition to emphasising the centrality of rank to the status conception, Waldron is keen to highlight other differences that he thinks also illuminate weaknesses in the value conception. I consider two of these alleged weaknesses and then reconsider the relationship between the two allegedly competing conceptions.[78]

The first difference Waldron emphasises between status and value conceptions is that while the latter is stipulative, the former is not. Waldron does a good deal of work to show that the status conception is well rooted in many of our ordinary idioms and understandings, demonstrating its compatibility with some of

of status) from some to all: see her 'Emotions in Kant's Later Moral Philosophy: Honour and the Phenomenology of Moral Value' in M Betzler (ed), *Kant's Ethics of Virtue* (Berlin, de Gruyter, 2008) 123–45 at 131–40.

[76] 'In Defence of Dignity' (n 8) 317.

[77] 'In Defence of Dignity' (n 8) 317–18.

[78] Waldron draws a third distinction between the two conceptions—'[w]e can distinguish the ideas [of value (or worth) and dignity] also in terms of appropriate responses to value and status respectively.[..] The thing to do with something of value is promote it or protect it, perhaps maximise things of that kind, at any rate to treasure it. The thing to do with a ranking status is to respect it and defer to the person who bears it. It is important not to elide this difference' (*DRR* (n 16) 24)—which I ignore. It does not, so far as I can see, amount to a criticism of the value conception.

the principal dictionary meanings of the term.[79] He is surely right about this. But his objection that the value conception is stipulative is not as well founded. Before seeing why, note first this objection's limited range—it hits only at Kant's use of dignity in the *Groundwork*. Waldron thinks that much of what Kant says about dignity elsewhere displays a commitment to, or at least is compatible with, the status conception. So, for instance, in the *Metaphysics*, Kant

> spoke of it [dignity] much more as a matter of status: he talks of the respect which a person can 'exact' as a human being from every other man, and that respect is … a genuine making-room for another on a basis of sure-footed equality and acting toward another as though he or she too were one of the ultimate ends to be taken into account.[80]

In the *Groundwork*, however, Kant holds, as we have already noted, that dignity highlights the unparalleled value of humanity in persons: humanity has a value beyond price that is immune to trade-offs with any other value or interest. About this Waldron complains that,

> although value beyond price and the intrinsic non-negotiable nonfungible worth that inheres in every human being in virtue of his or her moral capacity are wonderful and important ideas, there is no particular reason to use our term 'dignity' to convey them. Wurde [the term Kant uses and which is usually translated into dignity in English], in the sense of the passage in Kant's Groundwork, expresses a type of value or a fact about value. 'Dignity', by contrast, conveys the idea of a type of status that a person may have'.[81]

Neither dignity nor the cognate terms (*Wurde*, dignitas, worth) Kant uses in the *Groundwork*, says Waldron,

> naturally means—or means independently of a technical philosophical usage—the same as 'value beyond price' or 'the intrinsic non-negotiable nonfungible worth that inheres in every human being'. But for a long while some or all of them have been made to bear this sense in moral philosophy.[82]

The general complaint about stipulative definitions is that, no matter how useful they may be in some contexts, they are nevertheless artificial and strained: they do not convey what it is tempting to call the natural or ordinary meaning of the term in question. If this is the substance of Waldron's complaint against the value conception, then the objection is overstated. Two reasons suggest so. First, one sense of dignity in play in the value conception, the sense in which it refers to the worth or value of some 'thing', and which in Kant's *Groundwork* becomes the inestimable or incommensurable worth of humanity in persons, is undoubtedly reflected in ordinary use. By the latter phrase I mean more or less what Waldron means: reports of use one finds in the dictionary. The sources relied upon by our dictionaries and

[79] See 'Dignity and Rank' (n 44) 214–221.

[80] 'How Law Protects Dignity' (n 44) 202. Waldron refers to part II of Kant's *Metaphysics* (n 8), 'The Doctrine of Virtue'. Waldron makes much the same point in 'Dignity and Rank' (n 44) at 211–14.

[81] *DRR* (n 16) 24.

[82] 'Dignity and Rank' (n 44) 213.

like repositories are almost unfailingly literary and some of them either actually instantiate, or are at the very least compatible with, the value sense of dignity. As illustrations of the quality of being valuable, worthy or honourable, the *Oxford English Dictionary* (*OED*) cites, among other sources, Thomas Jefferson's observation that he had recently read no work of 'any dignity' and JS Blackie's remark that the 'real dignity of man' is found in what he is rather than in what he has.[83] Jefferson and Blackie are plainly using dignity to mean 'value' and they are in good company. Translators of Anton Chekov and Albert Camus see the same meaning in play in their work: Camus said the Third Reich was a 'bestial state where human dignity counted for nothing', while one of Chekov's characters reminds us that the world is beautiful, provided we do not lose sight of 'our dignity as human beings'.[84] Both remarks highlight the high value that is or should be borne by humankind.

It might be objected that, while the value sense of dignity has a foundation in ordinary usage, Kant's more specific *Groundwork* sense (dignity as inestimable or incommensurable value) does not. But this seems too fine a distinction to bear much weight. True, none of the users of the value sense of dignity cited in the *OED* and elsewhere obviously seem to have Kant's notion of non-fungible, non-negotiable value in mind, yet all have something of very high value or quality in view. It is far too strained, veering toward the doctrinaire, to insist that what we might call the 'commensurable value sense of dignity', a sense that invokes a *fungible* notion of worth, is a non-stipulative use of dignity, while the 'incommensurable sense', which takes worth to be *non-fungible*, is stipulative.

The second reason why Waldron's stipulation objection is overstated highlights this fact about dignity-talk: some participants move seamlessly between status and value conceptions. Because this fact, without more, is neutral between two competing claims—that those participants are right to move in such a way because the two meanings are not significantly incompatible, and that they are in error to do so—we need reason to favour one or the other. I think we should favour the former, the reason being that assiduous users of the language make exactly that move. There is almost no group of language users as careful, some might even say as finicky and pedantic, as contemporary analytical philosophers. While certainly not a pedant,[85] Hill assuredly qualifies, on most definitions, as an analytical philosopher, and he moves smoothly between value and status meanings of dignity.

[83] See www.oed.com/view/Entry/52653 (dignity) (last accessed 3rd January 2017).

[84] For the Camus quote, see R Zaretsky, *A Life Worth Living* (Cambridge, Massachusetts, Harvard University Press, 2013) 18; for Chekov, see A Partington (ed), *The Oxford Dictionary of Quotations*, 4th edn (Oxford, Oxford University Press, 1992) at 196, 10. Sensen (n 40) at 1, points out that *Duden*, the German dictionary, defines dignity thus: 'value inherent in human beings that commands respect'.

[85] He thus steers clear of the alleged 'narcoleptic pedantry' (H-J Glock, *What is Analytic Philosophy?* (Cambridge, Cambridge University Press, 2008) at 246) of some of his brethren. My use of the term 'analytical' rather than 'analytic' is simply a stylistic and not a substantive choice; I henceforth regard them as synonyms. Another fairly picky group of language users—lawyers—also often lump dignity and status together. For an example, see Hale LJ (as she then was) in *Parkinson v St James and Seacroft University Hospital NHS Trust* [2001] EWCA 530 at [90] ('It affords him the same dignity and status').

Hill does so, moreover, while delineating and reconstructing Kant's value conception, although this will surprise no one familiar with his reply to Rosen sketched at the beginning of this subsection.

For Hill (and in his view, Kant also) value and status are closely related: dignity is not just 'a *value* to be produced but a *status* always to be honoured and respected', while talk of the equal dignity of persons 'refers to their common *standing*'.[86] This willingness to move between allegedly different meanings and thus conceptions of dignity is unremarkable if Hill is right (i) in his claim that 'the cluster of judgements encapsulated in Kant's idea of human dignity includes most of the values we find in appeals to dignity in everyday moral discussions';[87] and (ii) status and value are indeed part of those discussions. The distinction which Waldron attempts to shore up thus seems a will-o'-the-wisp. A good conception of dignity, as Hill suggests, has both value and status components.

This conclusion is also forced upon us by a charitable reading of Kant's most important remarks about dignity, by which I mean at least those found in the *Groundwork* and the *Metaphysics*. As already noted, Waldron's stipulative complaint is directed only against the former; he is well aware of Kant's remarks in the latter that emphasise dignity as status.[88] Yet, rather than complaining about the former and privileging the latter, we could investigate whether or not both sets of remarks can be made consistent, this being possible only if Kant's notion of dignity is fairly complex. Many Kantians—including Hill—think it is, that it has at the very least a value and a status strand, the two being consistent.[89] The moral of this story is that Waldron's stipulative objection is misplaced in a quite different way from that sketched a couple of paragraphs ago. It is not that he mistakes a fairly well-entrenched meaning of dignity for a stipulative meaning, but that he errs by hiving off and making trouble with only one aspect of the value conception of dignity. He is mistaking part for whole.

The second distinction between status and value conceptions, which both Waldron and Rosen take to undermine the latter, is that the latter is 'Platonist'. This objection seemingly extends beyond the *Groundwork* version of the value conception, being an indictment of Kant's general moral philosophy. The epithets 'Platonist' and 'Platonism' are presumably intended to highlight something as embarrassing and mysterious as that allegedly fishiest of Plato's fishy ideas, his notion of Forms that lie behind the realm of appearance. What argument or idea

[86] Hill, *Virtue* (n 18) at 193 and 199 (emphasis mine). See also Ch 11 of his *Autonomy and Self-Respect* (Cambridge, Cambridge University Press, 1991).

[87] *Virtue* (n 18) at 199.

[88] *DRR* (n 16) 25–27. Waldron also refers (at 26) to Elizabeth Anderson's argument about the importance of status in Kant's later moral philosophy (n 75).

[89] For a swift reminder of Hill's view, see his 'In Defence of Dignity' (n 8). Note also Sensen's argument (n 40 at chs 4 and 5) that the status strand, taken in the Ciceronian sense, is the dominant one in Kant.

of Kant's is equally fishy? Waldron suggests that when Kant says 'that the basis of human worth commands respect' he is saying something odd. For

> this is not exactly respect for persons.[..] What commands respect on Kant's account is the capacity for morality; and I agree with Michael Rosen that this is a sort of Platonism;[..] it involves respecting something within a person, not a person him or herself. Our respect for the workings of the moral law within ourselves is subjectively a sort of quivering awe at the way the moral law can strike down our inclinations.[..] Rosen argues that it is quasi-aesthetic ideal, and I am inclined to agree with him.[90]

Rosen's version of the point begins by claiming Kant

> believes that what is intrinsically good is something that is timeless and that right action consists not in trying to bring that timelessly valuable thing into existence or defending it from destruction … but in acting in ways that are appropriate toward it. For Kant, however (unlike Plato), that intrinsically good thing is not independent of human beings—on the contrary, it exists in them as their inner transcendental kernel.[91]

Furthermore, Kant holds that what is intrinsically good 'must be treated in a way that respects the fact of its intrinsic goodness—its dignity' and, in response to the question 'What is this timeless object that is so intrinsically valuable'? Kant answers 'clearly enough in the *Groundwork*: "morality, and humanity insofar as it is capable of morality, is that which has dignity"'.[92]

Given what we already know from Hill's Kantian account of dignity, the centrality and significance of the notion of humanity and its constituent components cannot come as a surprise, although we should remind ourselves that humanity does not mean 'human beings'. What is surprising, from the perspective of Hill's account, is to find humanity cast in the apparently dubious roles of 'inner kernel' (for Rosen) and basis of 'quivering awe' (for Waldron). As to the latter, humanity, insofar as specific human beings display it, is indeed the basis of respect, that which is accorded dignity. The respectfulness that Kant and contemporary Kantians have in mind might be described in flowery terms, but there are less ornate terms available.[93] Furthermore, the occasional floweriness of Kant's language surely cannot be an argument against him; if, in his efforts to emphasise the importance of humanity and the respect it requires, he used expressions that sound odd to the contemporary ear, then so be it. That simply does not engage with the argument itself.

Rosen's description of humanity as human beings' inner kernel is equally mischievous if it suggests that humanity might reside somewhere within us, in some physical space in our bodies perhaps. It doesn't, and neither Kant nor Hill thinks that it does: humanity is not like our appendix or our kidneys. That humanity has dignity, says Hill, is for Kant 'a strong moral claim' and is not reducible to an empirical claim that actual human beings have a certain level of rational and other

[90] *DRR* (n 16) 24–25.
[91] Rosen (n 6) 143.
[92] Rosen (n 6) 144.
[93] See Hill, *Respect* (n 18) 93–94.

competences.[94] Rather, it derives from Kant's model of what it is to be a rational being, those beings being committed by virtue of that status to the moral law and, of course, to the requirement to respect humanity's constituent components. Hill says that Kant thought this model applied to most flesh and blood human beings, but that this is a quasi-empirical belief.[95]

What is it, then, that Rosen thinks Kant and Kantians should be embarrassed about here? If the 'inner kernel' deserving of dignity—humanity and its constituents—is indeed a range of competences actual human beings may or not have, and which are derived from a model of what it is to be a rational being, is that shameful? It is not clear that Rosen would answer affirmatively, his disquiet with humanity and the dignity Kant accords it instead apparently arising from two other sources: (i) from the fact that humanity is valued whether or not it benefits other human beings; and (ii) the supposedly 'timeless' nature of this value. There is a connection between these two sources of worry which becomes clear towards the end of our discussion of the first: I think it is this connection that is the genuine source of Rosen's worry.

As to the first, Rosen says that, although it is natural to think what Kant means when he claims humanity has dignity is 'that the object of moral life should be to act in ways that benefit human beings', this view is wrong: '[a]s Kant makes clear, in his view morality does not take its value from what it contributes to humanity; humanity has value in virtue of being capable of morality'.[96] The embarrassment arises here not with the nature of this non-humanist thought itself, which Rosen broadly accepts, but with one of its implications.[97] For, to make sense of this thought in Kant—the idea that humanity's value depends upon the capacity for morality and not its contribution to humankind—one must accept, says Rosen, the existence of the noumenal realm, a realm only the understanding can think, and in which human beings are free from the causality of the natural world. This is the realm in which duty originates; duty is the core of morality and, of course, one duty all rational beings have is to respect the dignity of humanity. If the noumenal realm is dubious, as Rosen thinks—it is, he says, a 'metaphysical aspect of Kant's ethical thought that most contemporary admirers of Kant try to find ways of deflating or working their way around'[98]—then embarrassment bites at this precise point. Labelling Kant a Platonist highlights this fact.

Rosen is right to say that contemporary Kantians resist recourse to the realm of noumena in their efforts to explicate Kant's account of dignity. Hill's view is that Kant

> did not base his argument for believing in human dignity on premises about noumena, the intelligible world and so on, but rather used those Ideas to reconcile his prior

[94] Hill, 'In Defence of Dignity' (n 8) 321.
[95] Hill, 'In Defence of Dignity' (n 8) 322.
[96] Rosen (n 6) 144.
[97] Rosen (n 6) 130 (invoking Joseph Raz's statement of humanism).
[98] Rosen (n 6) 145.

> moral conclusions (about dignity …, etc.) with the earlier argument that all empirical phenomena must be regarded as governed by natural causes.[99]

For Hill, Kant's case for dignity is neither more nor less than a moral one. The noumenal realm bears no weight in that case, featuring in it merely as part of Kant's wider philosophical position. The question as to which characterisation of Kant's argument is right is a difficult one, the level of textual exegesis required to resolve it being beyond our scope. Furthermore, detailed textual exegesis might not, in the end, help since the point currently divides expert Kant scholars.[100] Before considering how we might progress in the face of this difficulty, a second source of worry must be noted. It is the apparently problematic nature of Kant's 'Platonist' view that humanity's value is 'timeless'.

But what, exactly, is the problem? It is not Kant's view that humanity pre-existed and will outlast human life, thus being a natural part of the fabric of the universe. We can therefore set aside this reading of 'timeless' and, with it, one sense the Platonist objection might have. But there is another sense it might have which follows close on the heels of Rosen's treatment of the first worry. For, although humanity's timeless nature neither pre-exists nor succeeds human life, its existence might depend upon the existence of the noumenal realm. And, insofar as that realm is metaphysically or otherwise suspect, then so, too, is humanity's preeminent status or value. The basis of the second worry is thus exactly the same as the first. The problem is recourse to the allegedly dubious noumenal realm. The issue of the extent to which Kant's arguments in the *Groundwork* and elsewhere depend for their success upon the noumenal realm cannot be resolved here, although one tempting—because seemingly idiosyncratic—strategy is to embrace the substance of the Platonist objection while affirming the Kantian position. The risk, of course, is ridicule: to endorse Kant on the noumenal realm, a realm in some sense free from the causal forces at play in the rest of the natural world, runs counter to the current naturalist temper in most contemporary Anglophone philosophy.[101] Yet the widespread nature of that temper does not, without more, show it to be right, and there are many non-ridiculous arguments ostensibly showing the need to posit or assume something like the noumenal realm.[102] Furthermore, it cannot be said with certainty that alternatives to Kant's position are absolutely free from embarrassment. The distribution of embarrassment in philosophical arguments usually tends toward equality.[103]

[99] Hill, 'In Defence of Dignity' (n 8) 320.

[100] For some different positions, see the sources in n 17, above, and in Hill, ibid, fn 5.

[101] By which I mean a view of philosophy's role as exactly aligned with the natural sciences.

[102] The principal version of Kant's own argument to this end is in third conflict of the transcendental ideas: I Kant, *Critique of Pure Reason*, edited and translated by P Guyer and AW Wood (Cambridge, Cambridge University Press, 1998) A444-451/B472-B479. An excellent overview of the issue for the non-specialist is HE Allison, 'Kant on Freedom of the Will' in P Guyer (ed), *The Cambridge Companion to Kant and Modern Philosophy* (Cambridge, Cambridge University Press, 2006) Ch 11.

[103] Rosen's non-Platonist argument for dignity may be a case in point: n 6 at 140–41.

B. *Entente Cordiale*

Waldron's attempt to distinguish status and value conceptions is not successful. The stipulation objection is the weakest argument, dignity's value strand having a toehold in ordinary language and use just like the status strand. The Platonist complaint is more complex, although an issue it raises—reliance upon ostensibly embarrassing argumentative moves—is not one to which other positions are immune. That neither of these distinctions-cum-objections clearly succeeds raises this question: is it a mistake to regard value and status accounts of dignity as competing conceptions? Hill, our eminent sample proponent of the former, would think so and there are numerous grounds for that thought.

Most obviously, value and status accounts clearly overlap in terms of their content and appear easily combinable. What dignity requires on each account is much the same kind of respect for much the same range of traits and features. Thus the effort to implement and 'operationalise' each conception in real life contexts is likely to generate roughly similar standards and prohibitions. They differ only in the degree of emphasis placed upon status and, as we will see presently, in the biographies they provide for dignity. As to the former, Waldron regards status and its transvaluation as going to the core of dignity, while neither Kant nor contemporary Kantians seem to; status and dignity are related for them, different components of the same idea. This difference stymies any easy amalgamation of these accounts unless Waldron's core claim is weakened. Should it be diluted? One reason, already articulated, suggests so: the failure of the stipulation objection. For, insofar as *both* value and status senses of dignity are rooted in ordinary language and understanding, it is difficult to maintain that one is much more significant or important—because going to the core of dignity—than the other.

Dilution of the core claim allows the combination of status and value accounts into one conception, but we must consider why such a synthesis would be worthwhile. Note first what such a synthesis entails. It generates an account of dignity which holds that what is distinctive about human beings is that their humanity is of inestimable or non-fungible value and that all human beings, either by virtue of their humanity or some other property, have the same high status. Thus humanity and its constituents cannot be traded off as against other values nor are there different ranks within the class of human beings (or beings with humanity). While the basis of the value strand of this conception is clearly humanity and its constituents, the basis of the status strand is less obvious. It could, as intimated, be humanity and thus rest upon the same basis as the value strand; but it need not. The list of other ostensibly plausible bases for the high equal status of human beings is not, however, a long one: autonomy, reason, sentience and the like are properties most often touted as founding the kind of equality claim that the status strand must affirm. Furthermore, not all such candidates can be assumed to be combinable with the basis of the value strand, at least as conceived by Kant. To that degree the latter strand might dominate the status strand. The exact ranking as between value and status strands—higher, lower or equal—is one feature that allows us to distinguish different versions of the value-status conception and, while a complete account of any particular version of that conception must surely rank its strands, no such effort is made here.

Stated thus, the value-status conception is not *prima facie* implausible. There are, however, at least two other considerations that weigh in its favour. The first is that it fits much in the tradition of talk and thought about dignity which is not, of course, to say that the tradition is thick with conceptions of dignity explicitly and self-consciously combining value and status strands. Rather, the two strands often appear in accounts of dignity, the difference or move between them hardly being noted. The fact that both strands appear frequently in the tradition means that explicitly separating and combining them is neither radically innovative nor implausible. There are, however, two additional ways in which this conception provides a good fit with much in the dignity tradition. One is that it embodies the four precepts of the concept and is therefore one branch—a major bough—of the dignity tree. There is no doubt that it endorses the first precept: its content is simply incompatible with the denial of the intrinsic significance of human beings. Equally plain, this conception could not deny that that significance be recognised by others. Its commitment to the third precept follows from its commitment to the first two: dignity is primarily an individualist notion that first and foremost sets standards for the ways in which individual human beings should be thought of and treated *qua* individual human beings. Nor does the fourth precept, tied as it is to the emergence of the state, pose any difficulty for a combined value-status conception. It is just not possible, assuming a commitment to coherence, that individuals could be regarded as mere grist to the mill of the state's survival on this view. This conception is also compatible with a supposedly competing conception of dignity, the Circeronian account, in which 'all human beings are elevated over the rest of nature in virtue of freedom'.[104] Both strands of the value-status conception can comfortably endorse that Ciceronian claim.

As it stands, this 'fit' consideration does nothing to show that the value-status conception has any advantages over its competitors. A demonstration to that end would require an audit of and comparison with each such competitor, something not undertaken here. That lacuna is accompanied by another apparent failing, namely, that our discussion of this conception has been insufficiently critical. To this second limb of the indictment, the plea is 'guilty': there has indeed been relatively little engagement with critical responses to the value-status conception. There are, however, some mitigating factors. My initial aim was to delineate two supposedly competing conceptions of dignity as clearly and sympathetically as possible and that expository task counselled against the introduction of large amounts of critical commentary. Yet it is also true that, in the philosophical literature on dignity, *much* critical commentary relates only to Kant's (value-status)

[104] Sensen (n 40) at 211; he thinks this account is the dominant one in Kant.

conception and *most* of that makes no trouble with what that conception tells us specifically about dignity. Instead it takes issue either with Kant's general approach to ethics and morality or with particular substantive arguments he makes (about the permissibility of suicide, for instance, or about the exact nature of what it is to treat others as means).[105] We have already noted the tendency among critics of Kant to convert specific arguments against some claim he asserts or denies into more general indictments of his overall approach. The discussion has not, therefore, entirely ignored the critical response to Kant's account of dignity.

It certainly has ignored competitor conceptions of dignity. Pragmatic reasons loom large here: space is not unlimited. More importantly, it is difficult to argue that many other existing conceptions of dignity are either significantly different from, or of greater philosophical weight than, the value-status conception. In this regard it is worth noting that three recent philosophical accounts of dignity—those belonging to Ronald Dworkin, Stephen Darwall and George Kateb—are clearly and explicitly derived from Kant or closely related to his view.[106] This is also true of Deryck Beyleveld and Roger Brownsword's ambitious account of dignity that combines legal-doctrinal and philosophical analysis. After delineating two incompatible conceptions of dignity that inform the European Convention on Human Rights (although it is not explicitly invoked therein) and 'the three constituent instruments comprising the so-called "International Bill of Human Rights"', on the one hand, and 'the Convention on Human Rights and Biomedicine and the Universal Declaration on the Genome and Human Rights', on the other, they seek 'a little more philosophical context for … [these] competing conceptions'.[107] Unsurprisingly, they begin 'with Kantian thinking, for it is in Kant's writing that we have not only the seeds of many of our ideas about human dignity but also a serious attempt to ground those ideas'.[108] While not in the end exactly the same as the value-status conception, Beyleveld and Brownsword's account of dignity shares significant similarities with it. It is therefore no great exaggeration to regard the value-status conception as the single pole—either negative or positive—around which contemporary philosophical discussions of dignity rotate.

Furthermore, even if there are philosophical accounts of dignity entirely incompatible with the value-status conception and are in no sense definable by their opposition to it, that fact makes no difference to the argument here. I nowhere claim that the value-status account of dignity is the only one available to us. It is an important, possibly even dominant philosophical conception and, in terms of influence, stands alongside some religious—principally Catholic—conceptions in terms of the attention it receives. However, unlike Catholic conceptions of dignity,

[105] See, for instance, S Kerstein's 'Kantian Dignity: A Critique' in Duwell *et al* (n 3) Ch 23.

[106] See R Dworkin, *Is Democracy Possible Here?* (Princeton, New Jersey, Princeton University Press, 2008) 9–21 and *Justice for Hedgehogs* (Cambridge, Massachusetts, Harvard University Press, 2011) 14, 19, parts III–V and Epilogue; Darwall (n 8); and Kateb (n 6).

[107] Beyleveld and Brownsword (n 5) at 12, 11 and 46 respectively.

[108] Beyleveld and Brownsword (n 5) 46–47; note that they do not rest content with Kant, supplementing his work with that of Alan Gewirth in chs 3–6 of Beyleveld and Brownsword (n 5).

the value-status conception has not as yet been explicitly deployed in the service of a powerful global institutional hierarchy. Its adoption to such ends would be tricky, since it is just not as malleable as Catholic conceptions have proved to be.[109]

The second consideration in favour of the value-status conception is its ability to combine dignity's different life-stories. It highlights dignity's political and legal life alongside its philosophical life, allowing us to appreciate the disjunctions and convergences between the two. That generates a better understanding of dignity's many roles and the various ways in which its meaning can be and has been either stretched or compressed in different contexts. The biography the status strand provides for dignity is rooted in the everyday legal and political struggles that marked the transition, across a number of societies, from feudal to capitalist economic structures and the concomitant massive changes in the social, political and cultural lives of those societies. Some of those changes are still being felt in those societies insofar as a significant axis of their politics involves various struggles for recognition, integration and equality. Waldron's legal examples provide insight into the practical, historically-rooted basis of the status strand. Although it is not the main burden of Waldron's project, these legal-historical snippets (and his evident enthusiasm in bringing them to our attention) show that the move towards a high egalitarian status for all is manifest in the history of the common law. We should not, of course, mistake that process for the realisation of a specific conception of substantive, distributive equality; nor has it been a process that automatically brought lasting and significant social change in its wake. But it is important to appreciate, as Waldron allows us to, that the law bears the marks of dignity's transvaluation, a deeply significant social, political and cultural process occasionally illuminated and distilled in precedents and other legal developments.

By contrast, there is a sense in which, on the value strand, dignity has no biography at all beyond the academy and thus no history. There are two possible reasons for this. One is that this account, although historically rooted in Kant's work, provides a purely and self-consciously 'philosophical' view of dignity that is, on one component of what such an account entails, 'therefore' independent not only of history but of the quotidian disputes about dignity's contours. This view of philosophy as standing above the fray of everyday life, law and politics, while not shared by all philosophers, was at one time fairly common in the 'analytic' philosophical tradition.[110] Whether or not Kant should be placed in that tradition

[109] Rosen (n 6) at 47–54 provides some interesting illustrations. See also the essays by D Hollenbach (Ch 6) and those by J Hanvey, J Soskice, D Walsh, T Beattie and D Gushee (Chs 11–15) in McCrudden (ed) (n 8).

[110] Nailing down the exact constituents of analytic/analytical philosophy is difficult. For a helpful overview of some of the similarities of style, method and concern of some work that can be subsumed under that label see AP Martinich and D Sosa (eds), *Analytic Philosophy: An Anthology* (Oxford, Blackwell, 2001). H-J Glock (n 85), also provides a fine general conspectus, although he thinks the complaint about analytical philosophy's insulation from history is often overstated (see Ch 4). I do not share that view. Note that Kant's own work is not above the fray of everyday controversies about, for example, the permissibility of suicide, sexual continence and use of alcohol: *Metaphysics* (n 8) 176–81.

is a moot point, but some—perhaps many in the Anglophone world—of his contemporary expositors and adherents could be.[111] As such, they provide philosophically rigorous, coherent and defensible accounts of dignity in accord with much of (or perhaps even all of) what Kant said about the matter. On this image of the philosophical enterprise, such an account must also be non-contradictory, aspire to be as general and coherent as possible, and delineate dignity's connections with other important concepts and values. But it need not engage in any direct way with dignity's messy and contested life beyond the philosopher's study and seminar room.

The other reason why dignity's political and legal life rarely registers in Anglophone philosophical accounts is more obvious. Kant's moral and political philosophy, the source of the value account, were rediscovered relatively late by English-speaking analytical moral and political philosophers. That rediscovery, in the United States at least, was roughly contemporary with increasing disquiet among professional philosophers about philosophy's relative insulation from practical affairs.[112] From the 1970s onward, serious attempts were made to combat this insulation, the birth of 'applied philosophy' and the call for philosophy and philosophers to engage with public affairs being hallmarks of a new mood. But the supposed direct engagement with the difficulties and disputes of everyday life commended by this new temper has not, as yet, deeply marked Anglophone Kant scholarship (although its influence has been felt in some quarters). Hence, one does not find much discussion therein of what dignity requires with regard to contemporary controversies.[113] There is no reason why this situation should persist, particularly if the value account must be answerable, as Kant's own account purported to be, to our ordinary understandings of dignity.[114] Where else are such understandings revealed, if not in everyday discussions and disputes (occasionally with legal and political analogues) about what dignity requires in particular contexts? If dignity's value strand aspires to generality, then its generality can be measured by its fit or lack thereof with ordinary understandings.

Why, then, should we separate value and status strands of this conception? So that we do not overlook, punning aside, their different statuses. Each strand captures an important but contrasting aspect of dignity's life-story. The status

[111] Hill locates himself there: *D* (n 18) 2.

[112] I do not mean to imply that there was no Anglophone work on Kant beforehand. There was, particularly on *The Critique of Pure Reason*, although 'such research … was regarded by mainstream analytic philosophers as a historical speciality': K Westphal, 'The *Critique* and Analytic Philosophy' in P Guyer (ed), *The Cambridge Companion to Kant's Critique of Pure Reason* (Cambridge, Cambridge University Press, 2010) Ch 17 at 412. Three of the numerous works I think drove the 'rediscovery' are: RP Wolff, *In Defense of Anarchism* (New York, Harper and Row, 1970) in which Kant is but a background presence, and his *The Autonomy of Reason: A Commentary on Kant's Groundwork of the Metaphysic of Morals* (New York, Harper and Row, 1973); and JG Murphy, *Kant: The Philosophy of Right* (London, Macmillan, 1970). The date of the first issue of the journal *Philosophy and Public Affairs* (*PPA*) was 1971. See the statement of purpose inside the front cover of (1971) 1 *PPA*.

[113] Hill is one of the exceptions: see *D* (n 18) Ch 10; *Respect* (n 18) chs 3, 7 and 8; and *Virtue* (n 18) part IV.

[114] See Hill, *Virtue* (n 18) at 199.

strand provides a reasonably benign genealogy of dignity, tracing its imprint and development in law, politics and everyday life while the value strand is, in some iterations at least, determinedly 'philosophical' and thus ostensibly independent of such matters. Emphasising this reason for separating the two strands might lead to two mistakes. One is to assume that, since there is one good reason for separating the two, there must also be other good reasons. I am not sure there are, but explore the issue no further. The second mistake is to assume that separating value and status strands for this reason amounts to an endorsement of the respective roles allocated to philosophical inquiry, on the one hand, and historical, social, political and legal inquiry, on the other. This separation is dubious, many notable philosophers having reminded us of the significance of philosophy's history and its roots in wider political, social and cultural contexts. Yet, as things stand, the over-labourer view of philosophy—standing above both the other disciplines and everyday life—still has a hold on the academy.[115] A genuinely historically-informed, contextualised type of philosophical inquiry, aware of the resonances and dissonances between our philosophical questions and our quotidian political and legal controversies, will generate a better, fuller understanding of dignity.

Two remaining points need be noted before turning to other matters. First, and directly in response to the point just made, it could be said that this is exactly what Waldron offers: his account of dignity is a historically-informed, contextualised philosophical inquiry into the nature of dignity. I do not deny that it has the makings of such an account, but insist that it is not as yet a fully-fledged instance of such inquiry.[116] Furthermore, fledging demands not just a deepening of the historical aspects of Waldron's project, but also a dilution of the core claim along the lines already recommended. The second point is this: even the less than eagle-eyed reader will have noted, as this subsection progressed, the move from speaking of competing or different 'conceptions' of dignity to talk of different 'strands'. This move marks the realisation that we are, after all, faced with different components of one and the same conception rather than with genuinely competing conceptions. This is not to say that what I've been calling the value-status conception is the only plausible conception of dignity; nowhere near enough work has been done to support that bold and, in light of dignity's history, probably misguided claim. The claim is modest: there is a plausible conception of dignity that contains at least value and status strands. I extend that claim in the following section, which seeks to show that those two strands inform the law and *LAJ*.

[115] By this term I'm treading a path between philosophical 'under-labourers' and 'master-scientists': on both see P Winch, *The Idea of a Social Science and its Relationship to Philosophy* (London, Routledge and Kegan Paul, 1958 (2nd edn, 1990)) at 3–10.

[116] For some observations about the complexities of the historical aspects of the transvaluation thesis, see D Herzog, 'Aristocratic Dignity?' in Waldron, *DRR* (n 16) at 100–17; a broader view is also sketched in Ch 1 of P Rosanvallon, *The Society of Equals* (Cambridge, Massachusetts, Harvard University Press, 2013). J Millar's *Observations Concerning the Distinctions of Ranks in Society* (London, John Murray, 1771), particularly chs I–II and V, looks like a precursor to the kind of project I'm foisting upon Waldron.

III. Connections

Both strands of the value-status conception fit with—in the sense of being embodied in and providing a rationale for—various features of *LAJ* and law. This conception therefore informs the law at both the level of substantive legal doctrines and broader aspects of legal institutional design. For expository purposes, it is best to separate two sets of connections. The first includes those between law, on the one hand, and the two strands of the value-status conception, on the other, while the second contains those between this conception and *LAJ*.

Some of the connections in the first set are sketched fairly briefly below, a number of them having already been touched upon. The claim made in highlighting these connections is that *this conception of dignity is in play in the law in the sense that it can plausibly be regarded as a legal principle.* There is no suggestion that this conception of dignity is the only value or principle in play nor that it is a master value; neither do I claim that all legal systems are always effective in realising and protecting dignity. They uphold it insofar as many of their doctrines and other aspects of legal institutional design embody or presuppose the notion. The examination of the second set of connections takes a little longer than the first, principally because the overlaps are slightly less obvious. Again, there is no claim that dignity is the only principle or value informing *LAJ* nor that it is the most important value. The claim is *that dignity gives normative sense to a number of LAJ's features.* Finally, I identify a particularly interesting feature which the value-status conception shares with *LAJ*. That feature is deeply significant, occupying a role in important accounts of equality and in an equally significant conception of political community; it runs like a unifying thread—sometimes explicit, sometimes implicit—in what follows.

A. Law

Do any legal systems embody dignity understood as the unconditional and incomparable worth of humanity? They *could* do so simply by including a version of that claim in some authoritative legal source—'this legal system holds humanity to be of unconditional and incomparable worth'—but it seems no legal system actually does this. Even explicit affirmations of dignity, such as that in Article 1 of the Basic Law of the Federal Republic of Germany, or Section 10 of the Constitution of the Republic of South Africa, are not direct and unvarnished invocations of dignity's value strand (although the former comes close). Moreover, it would be surprising to find constitutional dignity provisions unambiguously endorsing a single conception of dignity in many of the legal systems with which we are familiar. That is principally because the explicit incorporation into law of such a specific account of dignity (or equality or any similarly general idea) is unnecessary for the purposes of the drafters of such provisions and, moreover, could well be regarded as an inappropriate foreclosing of options on their part. On the latter view, it is the job of the courts and other institutions to elaborate the contours of general juristic notions in particular cases. As undertaken by both the German Federal Constitutional Court and South African Constitutional Court, that process has yielded interpretations of their constitutional dignity provisions that come (albeit not unambiguously) close to endorsing the value strand.[117] Thus, even when constitutional dignity provisions embrace no particular conception of dignity, the courts often end up adopting one such conception simply as a result of the normal process of interpreting and applying such provisions.

Furthermore, the absence of explicit invocations of the value strand in particular legal systems does nothing to refute or undermine a range of connections between it and the law of those legal systems. Legion provisions in numerous legal systems and instruments explicitly and implicitly protect the capacities and characteristics of humanity and, in so doing, embody and respect dignity's value strand. Prohibitions upon torture and demeaning punishment in both domestic legal systems and the Geneva Conventions are two obvious instances. There are also numerous provisions in particular legal systems that purport to be guarantees against destitution and penury, as well as provisions protecting various categories of vulnerable human being. Provisions such as these serve as bulwarks for humanity's constituents, means of ensuring that those capacities and characteristics either get the opportunity to develop or are not degraded. Prohibitions upon consensual slavery contracts and other ostensibly 'undignified' forms of conduct perform a similar function.[118] Most legal systems also contain either prohibitions or constraints upon other forms of behaviour that, while not directly protective of humanity's capacities and constituents, do uphold respect for persons. The prohibition of hate speech, for example, could well be among the consequences of honouring and respecting, or at least not mocking, dishonouring and degrading, humanity's value.[119] Respecting persons is often but not necessarily a way of respecting humanity. Moreover, it seems that many areas of private law, including matters as apparently prosaic as the award of aggravated damages, give expression to the value strand, taken to 'entail[..] the irreducible, intrinsic worth of each human being'.[120]

[117] 'Human dignity shall be inviolable. To protect it shall be the duty of all state authority' (Art 1); 'Every person shall have the right to respect for and protection of his or her dignity' (s 10). For discussion of the South African Constitutional Court's 'Kantian' reading of the latter, see Ackerman (n 3) 99–108; see also 119–38 for discussion of the German Constitutional Court case-law; Barak (n 3) Ch 13; and D Kommers and R Miller, *The Constitutional Jurisprudence of the Federal Republic of Germany*, 3rd edn (Durham, North Carolina, Duke University Press, 2012) Ch 7.

[118] For two much debated examples, see Conseil d'Etat (27 October 1995) req nos 136-727 (Commune de Morsang-sur-Orge) and 143-578 (Ville d'Aix-en-Provence) (Dwarf throwing in France); and *Jordan v S* 2002 (6) SA 642 (CC) (prostitution in South Africa).

[119] Or every citizen's full and equal standing in a political community. On which see Waldron, *The Harm in Hate Speech* (n 44).

[120] Murphy (n 5) at 361. His general argument about the dignitary interest in private law is outlined at 359–62. See *Montgomery v Lanarkshire Health Board* [2015] UKSC 11 at 93 for a recent judicial

Can one accept that these provisions protect and respect humanity's constituents while denying that they embody dignity's value strand? It is true that these provisions do not expressly assert that either dignity or the capacities or characteristics in question are of unconditional and incomparable worth. But the connections just noted, and the practice of superior appellate courts in some jurisdictions, suggest it is dogmatic to insist that only explicit affirmations of the value-strand can count as evidence here.

All of the provisions mentioned in the previous three paragraphs, including swathes of private law, also embody the now uniformly high status ascribed to human beings that marks the status strand of dignity-talk.[121] Prohibitions on torture and demeaning punishment, legal protections for the vulnerable and legal entitlements to the means of (basic) survival, are surely just as much an expression of the relatively high status we now accord to all—or all in a particular jurisdiction—as of the incomparably high value of humanity. (Recall that I speak only of the letter of the law, not its implementation.) It need not be maintained that dignity is the only value that informs or can make sense of these legal provisions. That claim seems just as implausible with regard to, for example, child protection law and aspects of welfare law, as when made in relation to human rights law. For, although some of our most important human rights documents allocate dignity an apparently foundational role in relation to those rights, it seems *prima facie* implausible to insist that all such rights are or must be *derivable* from dignity. The number and variety of our human rights is such that they seem obviously compatible with, and thus capable of being informed by as well as furthering, various different values.[122] This suggests that the attempt to found all such rights on dignity is misconceived, as is the effort to show that dignity is the only value informing and protected by all our laws. As is blindingly obvious, the latter are many and various; it therefore seems likely that the values they embody and serve are equally manifold.

Some broader aspects of legal institutional design draw more obviously upon dignity's status strand than its value strand. Most of these aspects featured in our sketch of the status conception, being the fulcrum of Waldron's discussion. However, rather than treat them in the order he does, it is better to separate them into two categories, since they are not equally important. The first category contains

invocation of dignity in the private law context (standard of care for disclosure of medical risks to patients) and *Obergefell v Hodges* 576 US (2015), where it loomed large in the US Supreme Court's decision on same-sex marriage.

[121] In their accounts of the dignitary interest in private law, both Birks and Murphy move—perfectly predictably, given the argument of this chapter—between value and status strands: see Birks (n 5) at 5–14 (where he claims the Roman wrong of *iniuria* is the manifestation of contempt and a denial of equal respect) and Murphy (n 5) at 361 ('treating them as though they were somehow worth less than oneself, or simply worthless').

[122] I am not alone in thinking this: see Waldron, *DRR* (n 16) at 17. For something close to the contrary position, see Griffin (n 8).

only a single member, it being part of the deep structure of legal institutional design, a presupposition of the legal enterprise. For, if that enterprise is, even if only in part, a matter of subjecting human conduct to the governance of rules, then those rules must have certain properties. They must, at the least, be knowable, intelligible, require only what is possible and be non-contradictory. Furthermore, the creators of these rules must assume that those to whom they are directed also have certain properties: they must be capable of understanding rules and applying them to their own conduct. This idea of self-application—that law works 'by using rather than short-circuiting … the agency of individuals'[123]—is in Waldron's view not only a key feature of legal systems, but also a vital way of respecting agents' dignity. This is because self-control and dignity are, for Waldron, synonyms: recall that dignity on his view is 'the status of … [being] recognised as having the ability to control and regulate … [one's] actions in accordance with … [one's] own apprehension of norms and reasons that apply to [one]'.[124] It seems that, when properly designed and articulated, law cannot for Waldron (or for Lon L Fuller or Joseph Raz) fail to respect dignity.

The second category contains important aspects of legal institutional design that are not quite as fundamental as that just noted. This is because these aspects—having rights understood as protected spheres of choice, the organisation of hearings and the trial process, as well as the option of having one's interests represented in legal action, either in a trial or in other forms of legal process[125]—can differ significantly in the extent to which they are realised in different legal systems. Indeed, we can imagine some legal systems entirely lacking one or more of these features, such as access to legal representation. By contrast, the presuppositions of the legal enterprise are invariant, insofar as that enterprise includes the task of subjecting human conduct to the governance of rules. Although in this sense less fundamental, the current aspects of legal institutional design are genuinely significant means of facilitating self-control. They thus embody and promote dignity and do so in a predominantly egalitarian way. In most legal systems with which we are familiar legal representation, when available, is ostensibly available to *all*; those enmired in legal action as claimant, defendant, ward or accused are *all* not only entitled to speak, but to know the claims and the evidence against them. No one has special rights of audience or other procedural benefits in a trial, such as their evidence being presumed weightier or true, simply by virtue of their status. All stand as equals in the eyes of the law.

Now, while it is plain that the value strand is not incompatible with these two broad aspects of legal institutional design, it is equally obvious that it says little about them. If we start from humanity's incomparable worth we might eventually

[123] *DRR* (n 16) 52.

[124] 'How Law Protects Dignity' (n 44) at 202. Note also the very similar thoughts about dignity articulated by LL Fuller, *The Morality of Law*, revised edn (New Haven, Yale University Press, 1969) at 162–63 and J Raz, *The Authority of Law*, 2nd edn (Oxford, Clarendon Press, 2009) at 221–22.

[125] See *DRR* (n 16) 49–51; 54–55; 61–63.

get close to a conclusion that insists upon a right to representation in trials, but the distance we would have to travel seems huge. This is similar for most other members of the two categories, save for the single member of the first category and the first member of the second category. The assumptions rule-makers have to make about the addressees of their rules, and the idea of a right-holder being one in possession of protected realms of choice, fit quite neatly with some of the characteristics constitutive of humanity and two of its implications. So, having 'a rational nature' and the ability to act for reasons and follow principles, look like grandiose ways of stating the properties a rule-maker must presuppose her addressees to have (if they do not, then the effort to subject their conduct to rules is pointless). One implication of respecting these properties is, as Hill reminded us, that when trying to influence others one should appeal to their reason rather than manipulate them by non-rational techniques.[126] And that, of course, is the essence of self-direction. Furthermore, having protected spheres of choice—having rights, understood as the will theory understands them—is all of a piece with what Hill counts as the fourth implication of humanity having dignity. Respecting humanity is in part a matter of 'valuing highly the setting and rational pursuit of ends ... in other persons' as well as in oneself; thus 'one should leave them freedom to set and pursue their ends in a rational (moral and prudential) way'.[127] Rights as protected spheres of choice are a means of securing that freedom.

B. *LAJ*

One of the most obvious connections here is that between *LAJ* and the status strand. This is because *LAJ* is just another means by which current legal systems embody the high, equal standing or dignity of all. *LAJ* does this by regarding all addressees of the law as identical and by treating them in the same way, with reference to the same standards. *LAJ*'s presumptive identity component cuts against aristocratic and other privilege in the same way as does giving the parties to a trial identical standing. Just as all have a voice and all voices are ranked equally in the trial (at the outset at least), all are presumed equal in terms of their rights, duties and immunities. *LAJ*'s uniformity component cuts against claims that one's particularities or context free one from the law's requirements: all are *prima facie* bound by the same standards. Taken together, *LAJ*'s three components cast immediate suspicion upon any claim to have exceptional or different legal rights or be immune to general legal requirements and duties. And that is also the effect of the transvaluation of status that Waldron regards as the core of his account of dignity: '[w]e are all chiefs; there are no Indians'.[128] Or, in the far less snappy language of

[126] See the discussion at p 132–133 above.
[127] *D* (n 18) 50.
[128] *DRR* (n 16) 60.

LAJ, we are all presumed chiefs and, as a result, bound by the same—chiefs'—rules, with identical duties, powers and immunities.

The connection between *LAJ* and the status strand becomes even more apparent when Waldron, summing up the effect of the transvaluation of status in modern law, characterises it thus: '[i[f I were to give a name the status [sic] I have in mind, the high rank or dignity attributed to every member of the community and associated with their fundamental rights, I might choose the term "legal citizenship"'.[129] Waldron regards this as including much of what TH Marshall subsumed under the heading of 'civil citizenship', one of the hallmarks of which is 'the right to defend and assert all one's rights on terms of equality with others'.[130] That kind of equality of standing is in part what *LAJ* embodies and it is no surprise that, in another attempt to label the high status at which dignity's process of transvaluation has arrived, Waldron calls it 'equality before the law'.[131] *LAJ* is, as I have attempted to show elsewhere, an important component of the complex notion of equality before and under the law; so, too, on Waldron's view, is dignity's status strand.[132]

What, if any, are the connections between *LAJ* and the value strand? While they are plainly not incompatible, it is again true that the latter has relatively little to say about the former. The argumentative distance between humanity's incalculable value and some of *LAJ*'s components seems great; so much so, that the prospect of formulating any satisfactory argument from the former, in support of some of the latter, seems bleak. Think of *LAJ*'s limited avoidability component. Limiting the availability of defences could be regarded as both a consequence of respect for dignity, since it expresses the inestimable value of the humanity of those who suffer as a result of others' conduct, and as a denial of such respect, because it ignores the capacities and context of those whose conduct brought about damage (and thus the degree to which they possess the capacities and characteristics of humanity).

The presumptive identity component, which regards all as having the same legal standing, is more tightly linked to the value strand: it looks, after all, much like an expression of the value of humanity. If all have humanity's constitutive capacities and characteristics, then that *could*—given a copious helping of argumentation—provide a reason why all should stand equally in the eyes of the law. But if it is an open question whether or not all have these capacities and characteristics, then this component of *LAJ* maintains a fiction. That need not be an embarrassment, provided the fiction is derivable from humanity's value or some subsidiary assumptions about its or human beings' nature. The precautionary principle that Hill and Kant espouse with regard to the protection of humanity's capacities and characteristics must be based upon similar considerations. As to the

[129] *DRR* (n 16) 60.
[130] TH Marshall, *Citizenship and Social Class* (Cambridge, Cambridge University Press, 1950) 10–11.
[131] *DRR* (n 16) 61.
[132] See my 'Equality Under and Before the Law' (2011) 61 *University of Toronto Law Journal* 411–65.

uniformity component, it is tempting to maintain that the same standards should apply to all the law's addressees because all are equal in terms of the capacities and characteristics constitutive of humanity. Yet even if this is true, or if there are good grounds for assuming it, the distance between it and the uniformity component remains great. Possession of the same capacities and characteristics is only the first step in the long series necessary to warrant the conclusion that the same legal standards must apply to all. One of the many gaps that must be filled is this: why do those particular capacities and characteristics require or justify that exact kind of treatment? Until this and other gaps are filled, the connection between the uniformity component and dignity's value strand is weak.

C. The Common Thread

Having sketched various connections between dignity and *LAJ*, we can now highlight their common thread. *LAJ* aspires or purports to treat everyone in the same way and it assumes we are all the same. So, too, do dignity's status and value strands: the former ascribes the same high standing to all of us, the latter the same inestimable value. *LAJ* and the status strand do this independently of an audit to establish our similarity: neither is interested in showing, by means of an assessment of our capacities, traits and skills that we are all actually the same; nor in showing, by a comparison of our situations (including family, employment and other aspects of our context), that we are all similarly situated. The value strand assumes we all possess, to the same degree, humanity's constitutive capacities and characteristics: it does not insist we undergo a series of tests before making this judgement, being uninterested in determining and calibrating the differences and similarities between us in terms of our rational and deliberative powers. Similarity in the relevant respects—standing, the capacities and characteristics of humanity, and capacities and abilities underpinning *LAJ*—is assumed or, what in practice amounts to the same thing, differences are ignored.

The assumption of similarity is irrebuttable on the status strand, but not on the value strand, nor under the components of *LAJ*. The high sortal status humanity now has is, for Waldron, absolutely the same for all, although it appears perfectly possible on his view for different jurisdictions to confer greater status on some (citizens) as opposed to others (aliens). Discriminations such as this do not, however, distinguish between those who are morally, politically and legally significant, on the one hand, and those who are morally, politically and legally insignificant, on the other. Rather, they are now usually discriminations within the class of morally, politically and legally significant beings. But it is clear that humankind's high status cannot be sloughed off nor denied, on Waldron's view, without significant moral loss. That the assumption of similarity is rebuttable for Kant and Hill is obvious because they accept that some human beings may lack some, possibly even all, of the characteristics and capacities constitutive of humanity. The capacities presupposed by *LAJ*'s three components, which are in effect those elements of basic responsibility assumed but also to some extent modified by almost all substantive legal doctrines, are taken to be present until the contrary is shown.

What is the significance of the assumption of similarity (or the denial of difference) that underlies *LAJ* and both stands of dignity-talk? This: the reluctance to assess whether or not particular human beings (i) possess or have in sufficient degree the capacities and characteristics constitutive of humanity, or (ii) satisfy the legal criteria of basic responsibility, evidences a commitment to opacity. By that I mean an unwillingness to pry beneath the surface of our assumed agency and hence similarity, to chart and measure the exact details of our particularity. As citizens, we stand together and relate to one another not (although we sometimes do) as intimates whose personal histories are shared and intertwined; rather, we are holders of a status, our entitlement to that rank being, in the normal run of events, taken for granted.[133] To be or become a citizen, full-disclosure is not required; we need not display every aspect of our lives (commitments, capacities, characters, preferences) for inspection and audit. Only some aspects—parentage, place of birth, age, next of kin—are relevant.[134] Similarly, when we stand before a court as ward, claimant or defendant, victim or accused, the only parts of our life-stories in play are those directly relevant to the legal action and the legal doctrines it entails. My sexuality will almost never be relevant in a theft trial; nor is my sexual promiscuity relevant when standing as the victim in a sexual offences trial. My standing as a citizen is likewise usually taken for granted. Hence, when I go to vote, the polling centre staff do not quiz me on my knowledge of current affairs before deciding whether or not to give me a ballot paper; nor do they test my powers of deliberation or ability to project plans, processes and courses of events into the future. They need only know my name, address and polling number.

I am not talking only about privacy here, although that is undoubtedly a manifestation of the commitment to opacity.[135] Opacity includes but extends beyond both the right to have certain information about oneself kept private and the right, identified in some legal instruments, to respect for 'private and family life'. It is more general than both because it goes with us, presumptively at least, into all social, legal and political space: we need not, unless we want to, declare more about ourselves than the bare minimum. This, I think, is a hallmark of our standing as citizens and of most plausible understandings of citizenship. As citizens, we do not have to be transparent to one another in the sense of displaying everything of significance about ourselves and our lives. The contrast is therefore not just between relating as citizens and relating as, for example, friends, family or lovers, but standing as citizens as compared to standing as 'social x-rays', with every aspect of our

[133] See *Groundwork* (n 8) 104 for Kant's observations on the 'dignity' of the status of citizenship.

[134] For a scrupulous analysis of the process of becoming a British citizen, see T Brooks, *Becoming British* (London, Biteback, 2016).

[135] For an illustration of how closely related privacy and dignity have been related in French and German law, see JQ Whitman, 'The Two Western Cultures of Privacy: Dignity versus Liberty' (2003) 113 *Yale Law Journal* 1151–1221; for a South African instance, see *Jordan v S* (n 118).

lives on display.[136] A telling fictional illustration of something close to the latter is found in Dave Eggers's *The Circle*, where Mae, the ostensible heroine, undergoes a transition from opacity at work and in life to that of near complete and constant disclosure called 'going transparent'.[137] This is more than just a matter of being connected to a digital camera; it entails being observed by such cameras at home and in the workplace and informing one's conduct by reference to the content and quantity of social media feedback from one's audience ('zings' in the world of *The Circle*). What if we made 'going transparent' a condition of citizenship in our polity here and now, just as a version of it was a condition of party membership in Oceana?[138] Would that be a good thing?

Neither of opacity's aspects suggests so. Its 'first-person' aspect entitles me to stand among others without disclosure of anything other than the bare fact of my agency, while its 'third-person' dimension requires us, when encountering others, to be content with that. We must:

> adopt … a perspective … external to the person, … holding back from evaluating any of the variable capacities upon which … moral agency supervenes, be they capacities for rational thought or capacities for evaluative judgement or capacities for awareness and understanding of one's place in the world.[139]

A view of citizenship that demands more than this is not one that accords with anything like a liberal view of the way citizens interact with the state. One defining feature of political liberalism is a high degree of caution about state power. That finds expression not just in affirmations of individual rights and liberty, but also in a broader 'attitudinal' concern manifest in thoughts like the state should not snoop upon, or pry into, the lives of its citizens nor humiliate them in any way. Citizens should not be made to beg for state assistance or protection; neither should their private lives—conversations, correspondence and domestic habits—be objects of state surveillance (except in tightly defined circumstances). Their patterns of worship, sexual choices and sartorial decisions are all things that, in a liberal polity, should be left to them.[140] A commitment to opacity is obviously at home in this

[136] I appropriate the phrase from T Wolfe, *The Bonfire of the Vanities* (London, Cape, 1988), but give it a very different meaning.

[137] *The Circle* (London, Penguin Books, 2013) 304. 'The man who is compelled to live every minute of his life among others and whose every need, thought, desire, fancy or gratification is subject to public scrutiny, has been deprived of his individuality and human dignity': EJ Bloustein, 'Privacy as an Aspect of Human Dignity; An Answer to Dean Prosser' (1964) 39 *New York University Law Review* 962–1007 at 1003 (quoted in Birks (n 5) at 3).

[138] 'A party member lives from birth to death under the eye of the Thought Police': G Orwell, *1984* (London. Penguin Books, 1989 (1949)) 240. See also T More, *Utopia* (Cambridge, Cambridge University Press, 2002) Book II: the lives of the utopians are almost completely lived in public.

[139] I Carter, 'Respect and the Basis of Equality' (2011) 121 *Ethics* 538–71, 551. Carter nicely characterises this stance as one of 'evaluative abstinence' at 550.

[140] It might be thought, in light of the many egregious moves in the 'war on terror' in the Western democracies over the last 15 or so years, that this and the previous sentence are intended ironically. They are not.

kind of political view and, indeed, to some extent defines it. It is therefore no great surprise to find that that commitment features in both value and status strands of dignity, on the one hand, and *LAJ*, on the other. Each, whatever their many and varied historical antecedents, has come to prominence hand-in-hand with the rise of liberal conceptions of the polity.

Opacity generates interesting questions, specifically about the depth and nature of its relationship with conceptions of dignity and equality—is it ultimately independent of these notions or simply a component of them? Does it have independent normative appeal or does its appeal derive from its connection to those notions? These questions are not considered here.[141] The claim proposed and defended in this subsection is only that opacity *is an element of* the value-status conception of dignity and of *LAJ*; the status of this claim, particularly what 'is an element of' means, is not further unpacked, save to say that it bears its ordinary meaning. This common thread might not be the only one that runs through these two ideas, but it is the most important one for our immediate purpose. That, remember, was to show that there is an important and interesting relationship between *LAJ*, on the one hand, and dignity, on the other.

IV. Is Dignity a Value?

The value-status conception of dignity is embedded in both the law and in *LAJ*: that much I hope to have shown. In the effort to show that, I sought initially to distinguish two competing conceptions of dignity, there being no claim that these two exhausted the available conceptual space. I concluded, contrary to first impressions and some arguments, that these two conceptions are best understood as different strands of a more complex single conception of dignity (there being, again, no suggestion that this conception exhausts the available conceptual space). Although these two strands provide dignity with slightly different life-stories, they are clearly compatible. I also suggested that the notion of opacity, or evaluative abstinence, is a common thread as between dignity and *LAJ*; that is important in what follows. Opacity figures not only in the conception of dignity just sketched, but also in some of the conceptions of equality explored in the next chapter, as well as in the idea of community articulated and defended in chapter VI.

Finally, I must answer a question that some will think should have been posed a long time ago: why go to the trouble of demonstrating that the value-status conception of dignity is embedded in law and *LAJ*? Most lawyers and ordinary people would need no such demonstration, being entirely unsurprised to learn of the links between law and dignity. Less obvious, perhaps, are the links between dignity

[141] See Carter (n 139), for an excellent discussion.

and *LAJ*, but this is surely only a consequence of the latter either lying beneath the surface of legal doctrine or being so close that we cannot see it. So why spend so much time labouring what for some, perhaps many, is the absolutely obvious? The point is to show, as against its critics, that *LAJ*'s moral value cannot be zero; or, at least, it cannot be zero if dignity is morally valuable and transitivity holds of the relation between dignity and *LAJ*. That, of course, gives rise to the question posed in the heading of this section and the reply to it is my final response to dignity scepticism. I have sought to show that we—current and past inhabitants of the western democracies, at the very least—think dignity is a value. It is embodied in many legal systems and related international documents and declarations. It has also been a topic of philosophical and practical interest to us for a long time and it continues to play a part in contemporary discussion both in and beyond the courtroom and the seminar room. Furthermore, it seems to be the case that dignity does indeed do distinctive conceptual work for us, being related to notions like autonomy and freedom, but not reducible to them. In light of these points, does it still make sense to ask whether or not dignity is a value?

It does. For demonstrating that we regard dignity as a value falls considerably short of showing that it is indeed a value. We might, after all, be mistaken about its status, labouring in the grip of false consciousness. Nothing in this chapter rules out that possibility. Nor do I say anything to those who might pose the question about dignity's value with an eye to its meta-ethical status, where that question is a proxy for discussion of the truth-conditions for values. Questions about the ultimate basis of values, their cognitive status and the ways in which that basis and status might be demonstrated, are beyond our purview. One point is, however, worth making. It is that even the most vociferous contemporary sceptics about dignity do not cast doubt upon the notion's status as a value. They are instead concerned to highlight some of the allegedly baleful consequences of invoking the notion in particular contexts, or to show that our thinking about the notion is nowhere near as coherent as is often thought.[142] Both enterprises are perfectly compatible with the argument offered here and both raise legitimate concerns.

[142] Here is one such sceptic: 'Dignity is surprisingly deeply entrenched in our moral discourse: it is not going anywhere any time soon': Rosen in McCrudden (n 8) at 153. Another (S Pinker, 'The Stupidity of Dignity' www.newrepublic.com/article/the-stupidity-dignity (last accessed 3rdJanuary 2017)), cannot quite bring himself to regard it as useless.

5

Equality

'There are no natural slaves, plebeians, or aristocrats'.[1]

'The year was 2081, and everyone was finally equal. They weren't only equal before God and the law. They were equal every which way'.[2]

What role might equality have in relation to law's abstract judgement (*LAJ*)? This chapter considers a family of related answers to that question. The guiding premise of the discussion is that equality is a *prima facie* plausible normative prop for *LAJ*. This premise seems plausible because *LAJ* undoubtedly embodies forms of equality of treatment in a number of different ways. Its uniformity component holds all addressees of the law to the same general standards. The content of those standards is invariant, being applied to all addressees alike regardless of whether or not they are capable of compliance. The form of equality of treatment that this component embodies is therefore something like equality *under* the law, understood as requiring, at a minimum, that all are governed by the same laws. The presumptive identity component is a means of ensuring equality *before* the law, since it regards all the law's addressees as the same: as abstract beings with formally equal bundles of legal rights and duties, rather than the real human beings they truly are, in all their particularity and difference. The limited avoidability component functions in the same way as the other two, operating to allow excuses and defences only when reasonableness standards are satisfied, whether or not particular defendants can actually satisfy those standards. It thus regards those judged by the law as the same—as having the same capabilities and levels of fortitude—and holds them to the same standards. It is a manifestation of equality before and under the law.

Might *LAJ* be supported by broader conceptions of equality? What follows examines a number of distinct conceptions of equality with a view to their general plausibility, on the one hand, and the ways in which they might relate to *LAJ*, on the other. As to the latter, they do so in two quite different ways. Some of the conceptions examined here say nothing salient about *LAJ*, while two are actually embodied or immanent within it. That, at least, is what I try to show. This approach might be thought absurdly promiscuous, promising an inclusive

[1] E Anderson, 'What is the Point of Equality?' (1999) 109 *Ethics* 287–337 at 312.
[2] K Vonnegut, 'Harrison Bergeron' in *Welcome to the Monkey House* (London, Vintage 1994) 6.

but vague treatment of various incompatible conceptions of equality. What, after all, can be gained from an examination of a number of conceptions of equality: if that process shows that *LAJ* is supported by a number of such incompatible conceptions, then so what? The important task is surely to decide between these incompatible conceptions. While that may indeed be a significant undertaking, it is by no means certain that all the conceptions of equality examined here are ultimately incompatible with one another; the relationship between them is rarely as stark as that. Furthermore, the 'bluntness hypothesis' expounded in chapter one guides the arguments in this chapter, just as it did in the previous chapter. It holds, remember, that aspects of legal institutional design such as *LAJ* might be either normatively over-determined or normatively under-determined. This chapter explores the former possibility.

Finally, note that the conceptions of equality examined here are drawn from the same limited intellectual palette used throughout the book: the existing resources of contemporary liberal political and legal philosophy and the legal systems to which they relate. This bias in favour of the recent rather than ancient has no substantive basis, being founded only upon pragmatic considerations of time and space. The discussion is also completely unoriginal, offering no new argument for, or account of the nature of, equality. It can nevertheless claim to be original in one sense: it seeks to test contemporary liberal political and legal philosophy by reference to its ability to support *LAJ*, an obvious and significant feature of existing legal institutional design.

I. Making Room

This section clears the ground for the next by examining and setting aside three different and ultimately unsatisfactory accounts of equality that might be thought to support *LAJ*. They do not; they lack the wherewithal to act as normative props for *LAJ*. By contrast, section II considers two conceptions of equality that present altogether more promising pathways in the effort to support *LAJ*. The conceptions considered in section II are, in a sense to be elucidated and interrogated at a number of points in what follows, immanent within *LAJ*. Section III ties some of the loose ends arising from the discussion in section II and in chapter four. It also outlines a link with the arguments of chapter six.

A. Equality: Thin and Thinner

Perhaps the thinnest and most formal account of equality insists that like cases be treated alike and different cases differently. Taken as it stands, this principle—henceforth 'the formal principle'—is unhelpful, principally because its most important constituents are left unspecified. That is not to say that the principle is irrelevant or unimportant, since it is surely a vital part of any political and legal conception of equality. But it is to say that the principle, as just stated, does almost no significant work.[3] It requires a catalogue of relevant similarities and differences and that is only likely to flow from substantive normative accounts of the salience of various sets of similarities and differences. Insofar as such accounts are egalitarian, then we would expect them to provide information about both the domain of equality—what is being 'equalised' and why?—and its realisation, as well as generating principles of distribution. But if the formal principle requires a substantive normative theory of some kind or another to be of any use, then there is little point in engaging with it further; we should, rather, engage directly with those substantive theories.

One such substantive theory of equality might exist in the law itself, being presupposed by or immanent within the various general equality provisions found in most contemporary common law systems. These provisions include those found in constitutional documents and legislative provisions such as, *inter alia*, Amendment XIV of the US Constitution, sections 15 and 28 of the Canadian Charter of Rights and Freedoms, Article 14 of the European Convention on Human Rights (ECHR), sections 1–4 and schedule 1 of the Human Rights Act 1998 and section 8 of the ACT Human Rights Act 2004. The idea of equality in these sources is principally qualitative, a matter of 'forms' of treatment—no person shall be denied equal protection of the laws—rather than of distributing amounts of treatment (of the laws?) or other things. Being principally qualitative, the subject matter of these provisions is not easily 'distributed' in any obvious sense, which is not to say that some distributions of some things cannot provide evidence of unequal treatment under these provisions.

It might be thought that, since these provisions invoke a primarily qualitative and institutionally embedded idea of equality, they will be a fruitful source of support for *LAJ*. These juristic statements of equality are not, however, as useful as they might seem. This is mainly because the provisions, in and of themselves, provide relatively little guidance as to the nature of equality and inequality. For, although some laws, policies, procedures and forms of conduct are now clearly invalid under these provisions (such as, for example, the enactment of a legal provision explicitly favouring Caucasians and disadvantaging non-Caucasians),[4] there are nevertheless many instances in which it is hard to be certain. This, at

[3] HLA Hart was more optimistic about the content of this principle and the work it might do (see *The Concept of Law*, 2nd edn (Oxford, Clarendon Press, 1994) 159–160), as was C Perelman in *The Idea of Justice and the Problem of Argument* (London, Routledge and Kegan Paul, 1963) Ch I. For doubts about Hart's optimism, see D Lyons, *Moral Aspects of Legal Theory* (Cambridge, Cambridge University Press, 1993) Ch 2 and L Green, 'The Germ of Justice' *Oxford Legal Research Papers Series* No 60/2010 October 2010.

[4] The key word in the first clause of this sentence is 'now', particularly if we have the history of the XIV Amendment in mind: see W Nelson, *The Fourteenth Amendment: From Political Principle to Judicial Doctrine* (Cambridge, Massachusetts Harvard University Press, 1988) chs I, VII and VIII and A Bickel, 'The Original Understanding and the Segregation Decision' (1955) 69 *Harvard Law Review* 1–65.

least, is so if we have reference to nothing more that the wording of the provisions themselves. Thus it was unclear from the wording of Amendment XIV of the US Constitution, for example, that the University of Michigan Law School's admission procedures, which in some instances prioritised factors in addition to academic merit, denied some citizens equal protection of the laws. It was similarly far from obvious whether equivalent broad equality provisions in other jurisdictions permitted, for instance, differential access to public spaces, schooling, legal advice and differential levels of social security benefits.[5]

In all but the most blatant cases, the courts must necessarily go beyond the literal wording of the relevant equality provisions, in part because of the distance between these general statements ('every individual is equal before and under the law') and specific legal questions (is it discriminatory for the province of Quebec to pay the young unemployed less in benefit than their unemployed elders?). Since the words of this and similar equality provisions give little guidance as to how they should be applied in particular cases, something more is therefore necessary than the bare text. But what is this 'more' and, further, what informs the search for it, gives it traction?

If the provision in question has been litigated before, then in the common law world the precedents will provide some guidance. So, too, might the legislative history of the provision, but there is no guarantee that it will include anything salient. But even textual sources like precedents and legislative history will rarely rationally compel a particular interpretation of an equality provision in a specific case. This is because this additional textual evidence is itself usually subject to a process of elaboration or interpretation. Consider, for example, what courts usually do with precedents cited to them as a guide to the meaning of some or other equality provision. Whether or not such precedents are factually close, they are usually examined (i) with a view to the light they cast upon the meaning of the provision; (ii) with a view to the sense they make of adjacent precedents and legal provisions; and (iii) with a view to their implications in the case at bar and for the future of the area of law in question. Particular precedents might be found satisfactory or unsatisfactory on one or more dimensions. This process is clearly anything but automatic, leaving room for different judgements about 'sense' and 'implications', and thus never determined solely by the precedent(s) cited. If the precedents were indeed determinative in this 'self-interpreting' way, then the case would not be 'hard' and would therefore not be litigated.[6]

[5] A smattering of the vast number of cases must include: *Grutter v Bollinger* 539 US 306 (2003) (US SC)—access to Law School and the XIVth Amendment; *Gosselin v Quebec (AG)* [2002] 4 SCR 429 (SC Can)—differential welfare benefits and s 15 of the Canadian Charter; *Baczkowski and others v Poland*, App No 1543/06, ECtHR 2007—Article 14 (*inter alia*) of ECHR and permission for public gathering.

[6] On what makes a hard case hard, see the slightly different views in N MacCormick, *Legal Reasoning and Legal Theory* (Oxford, Clarendon Press, 1978, revised edn, 1994) 65–72 and chs VI–VIII; and R Dworkin, *Taking Rights Seriously* (London, Duckworth, 1977) (hereinafter referred to as '*TRS*') 81. MacCormick's original view must now be supplemented by his *Rhetoric and the Rule of Law* (Oxford, Clarendon Press, 2005) 49–52.

Moreover, when 'the meaning of the provision' is sought, either in precedents if there are any, or in other textual sources if there are none, what exactly is being sought? The words of the provision are there in the text, so how can its 'meaning' reside elsewhere? And when the implications of applying a precedent to the case at bar are determined to be either good or bad, how is that judgement arrived at? The answer is that the meaning sought, and the basis for judging implications to be good, bad or indifferent is found—as many lawyers would now say—in 'a theory' of the provision in question, by which is meant an account of its point, purpose or value.[7] The process of elaboration in the interpretation of juridical equality provisions is thus one that involves both descent, moving from the general provision to the particular case, and ascent, moving from the general provision to an account of its point, purpose or value. Both aspects of this process are connected in that 'the theory' of the provision indicates the interpretative pathways along which to proceed in particular cases. Note, though, that such theories are not rightly viewed as more abstract than the provisions they theorise; rather, they usually serve to make those provisions more specific, both in terms of their point, purpose or value and in terms of what that account of their point, purpose or value requires in particular cases. Such a theory gives the provision 'depth' or 'body', showing us how to go on applying it, and is thus not best regarded as being solely abstract.[8]

The relative emptiness of juridical equality provisions, conjoined with the process of elaboration involved when the courts apply them in all but the simplest of cases, shows that these provisions cannot easily and explicitly support *LAJ*. The distance from these provisions to *LAJ* is just as far, and just as contestable and problematic, as that from such provisions to, for example, a decision about the legitimacy of differential welfare payments. Furthermore, the fact that *LAJ* is not ubiquitous in legal systems shows it is unlikely that general equality provisions can implicitly support *LAJ*. If such provisions did indeed *require LAJ*, then the doctrinal instances in those legal systems in which the law's judgement is not abstract—some segments of the criminal law, for example—would surely have

[7] Although this process is described in somewhat different ways by jurists in various jurisdictions, its substance is at root the same. Interesting characterisations of the process with regard to the XIVth Amendment of the US Constitution include J Tussman and J tenBroek, 'The Equal Protection of the Laws' (1949) 37 *California Law Review* 341–81; O Fiss, 'Groups and the Equal Protection Clause' (1976) 5 *Philosophy and Public Affairs* 107–77; and L Tribe, *American Constitutional Law*, 2nd edn (New York, Foundation Press, 1988) Vol II, Ch 16. For the interpretation of equality provisions in the Canadian Charter and elsewhere, see A Brudner, *Constitutional Goods* (Oxford, Clarendon Press, 2004) 131–42; D Beatty, *The Ultimate Rule of Law* (New York, Oxford University Press, 2004) Ch 3; and R Sharpe *et al*, *The Charter of Rights and Freedoms*, 3rd edn (Toronto, Irwin Law, 2005) Ch 15. An interesting treatment of the interpretative pathways of the European Court of Human Rights is G Letsas, *A Theory of Interpretation of the European Convention on Human Rights* (Oxford, Clarendon Press, 2007) chs 3 and 5.

[8] The idea of 'knowing how to go on' and its many complications and ramifications (all of which are ignored above) was, of course, a preoccupation of the later Wittgenstein: see L Wittgenstein, *Philosophical Investigations* (Oxford, Blackwell, 1953; 2nd edn, 1958) I, §143–§242.

already come under challenge. That they have not does not entail the conclusion that these provisions cannot support *LAJ*; it does, however, make it unlikely that they can.

In sum, the formal principle provides no support for *LAJ* and the general juridical equality provisions provide little. As accounts of equality, both are deficient, neither telling us enough about what it is that should be equalised, why and how. This judgement might be thought unfair in relation to general equality provisions for, although indeterminate in the ways just specified, they are not completely without content. That content could be expanded and deepened by study of those various jurisdictions' many equality provisions and their multifarious legal-doctrinal and legal-philosophical elucidations. This might be true, but one point is clear: no such in-depth and broad ranging synthesis currently exists. Furthermore, were one to be constructed, it would likely, perhaps even necessarily, make reference not just to the diverse legal materials in the various jurisdictions, but also to the broad jurisprudential and political-philosophical tradition of thought about equality. That tradition, confined only to its Anglophone and relatively recent manifestations, abounds in general and substantive accounts of equality which could inform both juridical equality provisions and undergird the formal principle. It is to three such accounts that we now turn, one being discussed in the next subsection, the other two forming the kernel of section II. Note that the examination of these three accounts does not ignore general juridical equality provisions altogether. Rather, they are taken as a focal point—a repository of *some* of our publicly-stated and institutionally-embodied commitments about equality—that any acceptable account of equality must address. These provisions are not only important markers of past political struggles; they also provide a significant platform for contemporary disputes about the scope and contours of equality. They cannot therefore be ignored.

B. Luck Egalitarianism

A strand of contemporary political philosophy, vibrant for at least the last two decades, holds: (i) that any plausible theory of distributive justice must be egalitarian; (ii) that any such plausible theory must show what, exactly, is to be distributed equally and elucidate the principles of distribution; and (iii) that any such plausible theory must successfully distinguish between the realms of choice and circumstance.[9] This strand of thought, best labelled 'luck egalitarianism', originated as an engagement with John Rawls's *A Theory of Justice* but goes considerably beyond

[9] The principal drivers of this programme and some of their main contributions are R Arneson, 'Equality and Equal Opportunity for Welfare' (1989) 56 *Philosophical Studies* 77–93; 'Liberalism, Distributive Subjectivism, and Equal Opportunity for Welfare' (1990) 19 *Philosophy and Public Affairs* 158–94; 'Luck Egalitarianism and Prioritarianism' (2000) 110 *Ethics* 339–49; and 'Welfare Should be the Currency of Justice' (2000) 30 *Canadian Journal of Philosophy* 497–524; GA Cohen, *On the Currency of Egalitarian Justice* (Princeton, New Jersey, Princeton University Press, 2011) Part

it, taking much more seriously than Rawls the outcomes of the natural and social lotteries.[10] These lotteries illustrate a general truth: one's life chances are significantly conditioned by how one is born, in the sense of one's general state of health and natural endowments, and by where one is born, in the multiple senses of geographical, class and temporal location.

Being born healthy, with the full range of normal natural endowments, into a middle class family in the developed world during a period of peace, does not guarantee that one's life will go well, but it is a huge influence upon one's life opportunities and the overall quality of one's life over its course. Being born then, in that way and in that place, comes close to ensuring that one's life will go better than if one was born in poverty in the developing world, with physical or other ailments, during a period of national or internal conflict.[11] Moreover, the natural and social lotteries deal better and worse hands not just across time and the boundaries of nation-states, but contemporaneously within nation-states. Thus the life chances of someone born now, in the UK, into a single parent family in 'the precariat', are quite different, on most measures, to those of someone born at the same time and place but in 'the established middle class'.[12] The chances of actually

One (hereinafter '*Currency*'); his *If You're An Egalitarian, How Come You're So Rich?* (Cambridge, Massachusetts, Harvard University Press, 2000) chs 6, 8, 9 and 10; and *Why Not Socialism*? (Princeton, New Jersey, Princeton University Press 2009) (hereinafter '*Socialism*'); W Kymlicka, *Contemporary Political Philosophy* (Oxford, Clarendon Press, 1990) Ch 3; E Rakowski, *Equal Justice* (Oxford, Clarendon Press, 1993) Part I; J Roemer, 'A Pragmatic Theory of Responsibility for the Egalitarian Planner' (1993) 22 *Philosophy and Public Affairs* 146–66. Two absentees from this list are R Dworkin, because his account of equality engages with political institutions and structures (see *Sovereign Virtue* (Cambridge, Massachusetts, Harvard University Press, 2000) chs 3 and 4 and his 'Equality, Luck and Hierarchy' (2003) 31 *Philosophy and Public Affairs* 190–98) and P Van Parijs, because he is principally an advocate of basic income (see his *Real Freedom for All* (Oxford, Clarendon Press, 1995) and *Arguing for Basic Income* (London, Verso, 1992)). Cohen's work looms largest in what follows.

[10] The term 'luck egalitarianism' was, I think, first coined by Anderson (n 1) at 289 and endorsed by S Scheffler, 'What is Egalitarianism?' Ch 7 of his *Equality and Tradition* (Oxford, Clarendon Press, 2010) (originally published under the same title in (2003) 31 *Philosophy and Public Affairs* 5–39). On the natural and social lotteries see J Rawls, *A Theory of Justice*, revised edn (Oxford, Clarendon Press, 1999) 62–65 (where he speaks of 'the influence of social contingencies and natural fortune') and Scheffler, ibid 178–82 and 193–200.

[11] The different life expectancy statistics as between the developed and developing world led T Honderich to observe that, 'if one knew only the average lifetimes of these two groups of beings, one would suppose they were different species': *Violence for Equality* (Harmondsworth, Penguin, 1980) 19.

[12] These terms are from the BBC's Great British Class Survey, on which see: M Savage et al, 'A New Model of Social Class? Findings from the BBC's Great British Class Survey Experiment' (2013) 47 *Sociology* 219–50 and F Devine and H Snee, 'Doing the Great British Class Survey' (2015) 63 *The Sociological Review* 240–58. On related ways of categorising social class in Britain, see www.ons.gov.uk/ons/guide-method/classifications/current-standard-classifications/soc2010/soc2010-volume-3-ns-sec--rebased-on-soc2010--user-manual/index.html (last accessed 3rd January 2017) and C Vogler et al, *Social Class in Modern Britain* (Routledge, London, 1993) for a helpful but slightly dated sociological overview. There is no doubt that in Britain social class significantly determines one's life expectancy and life chances: see www.gov.uk/government/publications/mortality-monitoring-bulletin-life-expectancy-and-all-age-all-cause-mortality-and-mortality-from-selected-causes-overall-and-inequalities-update-to-include-data-for-2010 (last accessed 3rd January 2017) and R Webber and T Butler, 'Classifying Pupils by where they Live: How Well does this Predict Variations in their GCSE Results?' *CASA Working Paper Number 99*, December 2005. This is in no sense news: see the figures cited in RH Tawney, *Equality* (London, Allen and Unwin, 1929) 176–77.

being born alive or surviving after birth are also determined, in some developed countries, by social class and ethnicity.[13]

The outcomes of the natural and social lotteries constitute the realm of justice, for luck egalitarians, in part because the hand one receives from them significantly determines one's life chances and is in no sense deserved: it is 'arbitrary from a moral point of view'.[14] Luck egalitarians' efforts to either cancel out or mitigate the consequences of the lotteries have led them to develop principles of justice seemingly unlimited in their jurisdictional range. The latter results from a broad view of the 'currency' that the principles distribute: their content extends beyond Rawlsian primary goods and includes either resources, or welfare, or advantage, or opportunities to access one or more of these. Having formulated principles for the distribution of these 'things', luck egalitarians then apply them to all aspects determinative of the quality of individual lives, such as the distribution of temperament and marriage partners.[15] This preoccupation with what is to be equalised suggests that equality, on this view, is principally a distributive and quantitative notion, concerned with the appropriate distribution of some divisible 'thing' or 'things' in proper amounts.[16] Furthermore, this concern with the 'how' and 'what' of equal distribution seemingly diverts attention from the 'why' of equality. Luck egalitarians assume the case for equality is established, their task being that of determining what equality requires in light of the natural and social lotteries.[17]

Do not, however, assume that the jurisdictional range of luck egalitarian principles is completely unrestricted. The most significant restriction is found in the effects generated by the natural and social lotteries themselves. A world in which those effects—the realm of circumstance or brute luck—have been redressed is a world in which, for luck egalitarians, the demands of distributive justice have been satisfied. Equality's writ runs no further than that. The inequalities that arise in such a world must therefore result from something other than brute luck,

[13] For the difference in US infant mortality rates as between black and white, see the US Center for Disease Control data at www.cdc.gov/nchs/data/nvsr/nvsr61/nvsr61_06.pdf (last accessed 3rd January 2017). The UN Population Division Infant Mortality longitudinal data shows that the US infant mortality rate as between 2005–10 was 5.4, placing it 34th in the world (http://esa.un.org/wpp/Excel-Data/mortality.htm) (last accessed 3rd January 2017). This is a low ranking for an advanced nation and is especially troubling given that the US spends considerably more on health care than many Western European nations. The World Bank estimates that just over 17% of US GDP was spent on health care in 2009, 2010 and 2011 as compared to roughly 9% of GDP in Sweden in the same period; Sweden's infant mortality rate between 200510 was 2.56 (http://data.worldbank.org/indicator/SH.XPD.TOTL.ZS) (last accessed 3rd January 2017).

[14] Rawls (n 10) 63.

[15] Anderson (n 1) at 287–88 (citing GA Cohen, 'On the Currency of Egalitarian Justice' (1989) 99 *Ethics* 906–44, 922–23 and Van Parijs, *Real Freedom for All* (n 9) at 127). Henceforth, my references to Cohen's essay are to the book version (n 9) and, as noted, use the title '*Currency*'.

[16] Thus it is that 'outcomes' (which usually imply a distribution of some or other measurable 'thing' or set of 'things') are of primary interest to many philosophers of equality. See L Temkin, *Inequality* (New York, Oxford University Press, 1993) at 11–12. Temkin notes that some notions of equality might not be illuminated by distributive-cum-quantitative (and thus outcome obsessed!) conceptions: ibid 16.

[17] See Arneson, 'Equality and Equal Opportunity for Welfare' (n 9) at 77.

one obviously salient factor being choice. Inequalities in a just social context that are the product of individuals' choices (or option luck) are of no interest to luck egalitarians because they raise no questions of justice.[18] The distinction between choice and circumstance, or between option luck and brute luck, must therefore be robust: it bears the full weight of the luck egalitarian project. There are serious doubts as to whether it is up to that task.

Two of the most troubling sources of doubt concern, on the one hand, the apparent instability or otherwise problematic nature of the distinction and, on the other, the disturbing consequences its utilisation generates. As to the first, consider this example:

1. Colin and Deirdre are keen winter climbers and hikers. They know their hobby involves some risk but they are not reckless: they pay assiduous attention to weather forecasts before hiking and climbing, setting out only in suitable conditions. Having embarked on a winter hike today in good conditions, they have been badly injured by an avalanche brought on by a sudden deterioration in the weather. They are stranded on a mountain-side and will die without rescue.

Is Colin and Deirdre's situation a matter of choice or circumstance? Our ordinary response would surely be: both. Almost all ordinary, real-life situations are. Our choices are made within a context many aspects of which we do not and cannot control (assume, as luck egalitarians seem to, that that which is beyond our control is that which is beyond the influence of our choices and, therefore, beyond the range of our responsibility).[19] Consider my choice of biscuit in the supermarket. I have no or very little power over the supermarket's decision as to which biscuit manufacturers to contract with and thus which biscuits to stock; nor do I have any power over the structure of national and international grocery markets and thus, for example, over the number and type of supermarkets available to me. Equally, I lack control over—in the sense that I did not choose—my wheat intolerance, but awareness of that condition determines my choice of biscuit. Furthermore, not only do we ordinarily choose between options within contexts like these, over which we have no or very little control—a situation we'll dub 'choice within the web of circumstance'—we also accept that choices can sometimes be fully rationally determined by knowledge of our context. Choosing in light of knowledge of one's context is a hallmark of practical rationality, choosing in ignorance of or

[18] 'In my view, a large part of the fundamental egalitarian aim is to extinguish the influence of brute luck on distribution … Brute luck is an enemy of just equality, and, since effects of genuine choice contrast with brute luck, *genuine choice excuses otherwise unacceptable inequalities*': *Currency* (n 9) at 29 (emphasis mine). The terms 'option luck' and 'brute luck' were introduced by R Dworkin, 'What is Equality? Part 2: Equality of Resources' (1981) 10 *Philosophy and Public Affairs* 283–345 at 292–94 (reprinted as Ch 2 of his *Sovereign Virtue* (n 9)).

[19] '[T]he right reading of egalitarianism … [is] that its purpose is to eliminate involuntary disadvantage, by which I (stipulatively) mean disadvantage for which the sufferer *cannot be held responsible, since it does not appropriately reflect choices that he has made*': *Currency* (n 9) at 13 (emphasis added).

despite it is often a sign of delusion. Yet practical rationality can demand more than that we inform ourselves of our context or circumstances: in some situations it dictates that only one choice can rationally be made in light of those circumstances. Let's label this situation that of 'rational determination of choice'.

Colin and Deirdre's choice seems unlikely to have been the only rationally salient option they could have adopted. It looks instead like the more common instance of choice within the web of circumstance. They presumably chose to go hiking, having been able to choose something else, and with the knowledge that there was much about the context of their choice to hike that was beyond their control. But what, exactly, did they choose? One seemingly undeniable answer is 'to go hiking'. Yet did they choose anything more than that? Did they, perhaps, choose to go hiking and to run any and all risks, of whatever magnitude or type, incidental to hiking in winter? Or might they instead, given their attentiveness to the weather forecast, have chosen to go hiking and to run a moderate or low level of risk incidental to that activity in that context? Moreover, what is it that Colin and Deirdre are running the risk of? Risk of death or, if not that, then risk of serious or slight injury? Or perhaps only risk of high, or moderate, or slight levels of discomfort? The snag here is that of establishing and defending an appropriate description of what Colin and Deirdre chose, assuming they left no written or oral record of what they regarded themselves as choosing. Many might regard this problem as scholastic, given the general truth that ostensibly single instances of conduct can generate multiple conduct descriptions.[20] It cannot, however, be so regarded by luck egalitarians since, as we'll soon see, they seem to think that one lives or dies by one's choices. The correct or most appropriate description of what one has chosen could not, therefore, be more momentous.

Since circumstances, not choices, constitute the realm of luck egalitarian justice, we need be sure that a bright line can be drawn between the two. The prevalence of both choice within the web of circumstance and the rational determination of choice show that we do not ordinarily draw such a line which, of course, is not to say it cannot be drawn. But the fact that choices are ordinarily enmired within circumstances casts doubt upon the rationale for seeking a strict separation between the two. Why do we need such an impermeable dividing line in political philosophy yet manage without it in ordinary life? Luck egalitarians need that line because they seemingly think responsibility tracks choices in a strong sense: subject to the absence of coercion and related conditions, whenever one chooses something one is responsible for that choice and for some or all of its consequences. Now there is a sense of responsibility in which the latter claim is almost always trivially true, namely, the causal sense. Given what we know of causality,

[20] A narrowly focussed but interesting way into the issue is O O'Neill, 'Modern Moral Philosophy and the Problem of Relevant Descriptions' in A O'Hear (ed), *Modern Moral Philosophy* (Cambridge, Cambridge University Press, 2004) 301–16. Also excellent are A Goldman, *A Theory of Human Action* (Princeton, New Jersey, Princeton University Press, 1970) and GEM Anscombe, 'Under a Description' (1979) 13 *Nous* 219–33.

both common sense and scientific, and assuming the usual set of links between thoughts (including choices), conduct and its outcomes, we can say: (i) that one's choices often have causal effects in the world; and (ii) that one is causally responsible for some or all of those effects (and one can be so responsible whether or not one is responsible—in the causal and other senses—for one's choices). However, it seems unlikely that luck egalitarians have only causal responsibility in mind when insisting that responsibility tracks choices. For the latter to be an interesting thing to say, something like liability-responsibility surely has to be in play, understood to entail a normative (usually legal or moral) attribution of, and calling to account for, consequences (some or all of which are also causal consequences).[21] The luck egalitarian claim cannot therefore be merely that choices have causal consequences; it must also be that one is answerable for one's choices and their consequences.

A credo insisting 'where there is choice, there is (liability-) responsibility' is not immediately reducible, but is closely related, to the claim that choice is a necessary condition for responsibility. The latter is not part of our legal and ordinary understandings of liability-responsibility. The most that either understanding is committed to is (i) that choice is *sometimes* an indicator of basic-responsibility, a bundle of cognitive and related features we regard as sufficient to make human beings answerable—'response-able'—for their conduct; and (ii) that choice is *sometimes*, in the guise of consent, a legitimiser of what would otherwise be impermissible conduct.[22] What reason might there be for insisting that choice, contrary to our ordinary understanding, is indeed a general and necessary condition of responsibility?

Making choice a general and necessary condition of either basic- or liability-responsibility implies that it has some especial power or significance. But what could choice signify, over and beyond some degree of deliberation? Perhaps the

[21] The best jurisprudential starting point for discussions of the various types of responsibility is still HLA Hart, *Punishment and Responsibility*, 2nd edn (Oxford, Clarendon Press, 2008) chs II, IV, V and VIII. See also J Gardner, 'The Mark of Responsibility' (2003) 23 *Oxford Journal of Legal Studies* 157–71 and, for a compendious discussion, P Cane, *Responsibility in Law and Morality* (Oxford, Hart Publishing, 2002). That Cohen has something like liability-responsibility in mind when speaking of choice and responsibility seems plain from remarks like this: '[w]hatever number of dimensions the space of disadvantage may have, egalitarianism, on my reading, cuts through each of its dimensions, judging certain inequalities of advantage as acceptable and others as not, its touchstone *being a set of questions about the responsibility or lack of it of the disadvantaged agent*' (*Currency* (n 9) at 19; emphasis mine); see also *Currency*, 121 ('appropriately differential responsibility') and *Socialism* (n 9) at 18 ('for which the agent cannot … reasonably be held responsible').

[22] For this picture of legal-liability responsibility, which I regard as entirely orthodox, see my *Philosophy of Private Law* (Oxford, Clarendon Press, 2006) chs 2–4. D Beyleveld and R Brownsword's *Consent in the Law* (Oxford, Hart Publishing, 2007) provides an excellent overview of consent's role in the law and a Gewirthian account of its normative basis. Close philosophical analogues to my primarily juristic view of choice and responsibility are TM Scanlon, 'The Significance of Choice' in S McMurrin (ed), *The Tanner Lectures in Human Values* (Salt Lake City, University of Utah Press, 1988) Vol 8 at 149–216; Ch 6 of his *What We Owe to Each Other* (Cambridge, Massachusetts, Harvard University Press, 1998); and A Mason, *Levelling the Playing Field* (Oxford, Clarendon Press, 2006) Ch 7.

exercise of a contra-causal power, the significance of which places that instance of deliberation and its consequences beyond the web of causal determination? For choice to carry this degree of significance, we must have a particular view of the nature of causal determinism and the problem it presents. Determinism must negate both basic- and liability-responsibility, on this view, so that the claim 'instance of choice and conduct X is causally determined' is the opposite of the claim 'instance of choice and conduct X is your responsibility'. The problem, then, is that determinism negates responsibility or makes it impossible.[23] An apparent solution to that problem would demonstrate that choice denies determinism and, if all choices could be shown to be instances of contra-causal freedom, then we would have such a denial. Furthermore, we would have a foundation-stone for the claim that one is liable or responsible for—in the sense of having to live with or die as a result of—one's choices and their consequences. One's choices and their consequences can legitimately be ascribed to one, and bear a great deal of weight, because they fall outwith the web of responsibility-denying causality.

If my view of the significance of choice in ordinary-cum-legal thought and practice is correct, choice being an occasional surrogate for basic responsibility and a legitimiser of ostensibly wrongful conduct, then it invites one or other of these alleged objections: it is either compatible with, or says nothing about, the problem of determinism. Both points are true, but neither constitutes an objection. Or, at least, neither constitutes an objection until the alleged problem of determinism has been shown to be a genuine problem. It might be thought a pseudo-problem on these grounds: if determinism is true, then it is true now and presumably has been true forever (if its truth is in the nature of a naturalistic, scientific truth). It is therefore as true of our ordinary-cum-legal responsibility practices as it is of our philosophical thinking: all are determined in the sense of having been caused in the requisite manner. Just as we are caused to adopt and change various practices of calling others to account, we are also caused to doubt the legitimacy of doing so in light of the alleged problem of determinism. But in a world in which everything is caused it is pointless to complain that everything (including our responsibility practices) is caused. So what, then, is the problem of determinism? If it is that causality negates responsibility, then that begs the question, since it simply assumes that the latter must be incompatible with the former. Why assume that, when we have accepted that everything is caused?

[23] If luck egalitarians do not accept this view, then it is difficult to see how choosers within the realm of circumstance lack the power to internalise the costs of the consequences of their choices, whereas choosers beyond the realm of circumstance have exactly that power: see Scheffler (n 10) Ch 8 at 215–20 for pertinent thoughts. Cohen's claim that his view does not imply that there is such a thing as 'genuine choice' (see 'Equality of What? On Welfare, Goods and Capabilities' (1990) 56 *Recherches Economiques de Louvain* 357–82 at 381 and *Socialism* (n 9) at 29–30) might well be true, but it makes one wonder why seemingly genuine choice looms so large in his discussions (the word 'choice' features roughly 55 times in the main text of *Currency* (n 9) often closely associated with 'responsibility'). For Cohen's related thought on 'genuine responsibility' see *Currency* (n 9) 119.

I suggest it is the latter question, and the doubt it raises about the alleged incompatibility between choice and determinism, that explains why determinism almost never registers as a problem in our ordinary-cum-legal responsibility practices. We carry on regardless, principally because the range and content of the problem is unclear. Yet if the problem *causes* us no difficulty there, why should it present greater difficulty within the realm of political philosophy? Luck egalitarianism is perhaps the only strand of contemporary political philosophy that ensnares itself in the problem, doing so as a result of the effort to distinguish, in a sufficiently robust way, between choice and circumstance. Almost all other strands of contemporary political philosophy ignore it. Whether or not they are ultimately right to do so is not a question tackled here. Those strands share with our ordinary-cum-legal thought and practices a lack of interest in the issue and that point is sufficient for present purposes: if we are able, in other contexts, and within other political-philosophical approaches, to avoid this old saw, then we perhaps need special reason to become involved with it. Luck egalitarianism provides no such reason, save for its reliance upon the choice/circumstance distinction. And I am not inclined to regard the invocation of that distinction as providing such a reason on this ground: it is neither clearly drawn nor does it match any distinction we ordinarily use.

Nothing said so far licenses the conclusion that choice and choices are unimportant. The general point, rather, is that we ordinarily accept that choices can be important even when determined by reason and circumstances. That determination causes us no difficulty in ordinary and legal life except when the determining factors are such as to leave only one possible or salient choice, those factors sometimes being the product of wrongful manipulation by other human beings. In those circumstances, the defences of duress or necessity will be available to those facing certain criminal charges, while contracts and other legal undertakings will be unenforceable.[24] Yet these choices having been determined is not what triggers these legal responses; rather, the triggers are the lack of another possible or salient choice and, sometimes, the wrongful manipulation of that choice situation by others. This serves as a significant contrast with the luck egalitarian position on such matters. For, if choices are determined—and that, remember, is in this context simply another way of saying that they are the product of circumstances or brute luck—then they surely cannot have the significance luck egalitarians attribute to them.

What can we conclude about the choice/circumstance distinction? That it is deeply problematic in at least two different ways. First, it requires choices of a kind that are either non-existent or extremely rare in normal life because of the ubiquity of *both* choice within the web of circumstance *and* rational determination

[24] For the availability of these defences and the operation of various vitiating factors in English law, see D Ormerod and K Laird, *Smith and Hogan's Criminal Law*, 14th edn (Oxford, Oxford University Press, 2015) Ch 12 and M Furmston, *Cheshire, Fifoot and Furmston's Law of Contract*, 16th edn (Oxford, Clarendon Press, 2012) Ch 9.

of choice. Moreover, even were such choices to exist, note how odd it would be to place any weight upon them: they would be something like a manifestation of whim, rather than the product of rational deliberation. Second, the distinction seemingly requires choices to be instances of contra-causal freedom in order for them to have any liability-responsibility significance. Regarding this as a very demanding requirement does not beg the question against luck egalitarianism, since it does not assume the truth of determinism. Rather, the point echoes a claim already made, namely, that a solution to the problem of determinism is apparently necessary for choices to bear the significance luck egalitarianism ascribes to them. That hostage to fortune makes luck egalitarianism unique among contemporary accounts of justice. Do we really need to solve the problem of free will and determinism before we can talk meaningfully about justice and equality?

We must now turn to the consequences of utilising the choice/circumstance distinction. Two related results, accepted by luck egalitarians, are that, if one's choices are both 'genuine' and made within a context in which brute luck's effects have been neutralised, then (i) one must bear the consequences of one's choices; and (ii) those consequences fall beyond the purview of justice.[25] Many have thought either (i) or (ii) or both are mistakes.[26] What follows highlights some of the objections to each, noting that they have quite different grounds. The point can again be made by reference to examples. Consider two, set in a world very similar to our own, save that its public conception of justice is a version of luck egalitarianism:

1. The prudent but unlucky investor: after taking expert advice, Annette invested all that she had accumulated from her labour, including the value of her apartment, in a varied portfolio of stocks and shares. She did this as part of a prudent financial plan to cater for her retirement. This plan was executed on 1st March 2007. By 1st March 2009 Annette's portfolio was, as a result of the global financial crash, worthless. The bank with whom Annette had re-mortgaged her apartment repossessed it, she having failed to make monthly repayments for some considerable time.
2. The negligent-cum-reckless motorcyclist: Barry is a young man who has recently passed his motorcycle riding test. Having passed, Barry was legally entitled to ride any motorcycle he wished and he bought a high-powered machine. Within days of buying the bike, Barry had a serious accident, causing himself life-threatening injuries.

Now, if each baleful situation can plausibly be regarded as resulting only from the choices the parties have made in a just situation, then luck egalitarians must say that Annette and Barry (just like Colin and Deirdre in the earlier example) have to bear the consequences of their bad option luck. They must also say that Annette

[25] See *Currency* (n 9) at 29–32 for what genuine choices might look like. Their effect is clear: they 'excuse[...] otherwise unacceptable inequalities' (at 29).

[26] For apparent endorsements of (i) and (ii) see: Rakowski (n 9) Ch 3; and Kymlicka (n 9) at 75; Anderson (n 1) and Scheffler (n 10) chs 7 and 8, seek to show that both claims are problematic.

can have no claim, in justice, upon any assistance with her plight: social housing or any other support cannot be provided to her under that rubric; and that justice provides no imprimatur for Barry's claim to medical assistance. Indeed, it seems that, from the perspective of justice, Annette must be left homeless and Barry must be left at the side of the road. Both could have made different choices—not to invest in stocks and shares, to ride safely and to pay for emergency accident assistance—but neither did. Both must live with, or die as a result of, the choices they made.

Critics hold that the responses luck egalitarianism mandates in these scenarios, and in other related scenarios dealing with bad brute luck, are wrong. The wrongness might, however, be a matter either of justice or of morality. That is to say, the complaint might be that any account of justice that mandates these responses must, by virtue of those responses, be a mistaken conception of justice; or, it might be that following the mandates of justice in these scenarios is a moral error. Some luck egalitarians themselves endorse or hint at the latter possibility, suggesting that the results in these and related scenarios illustrate the limits of our conception of justice. These results show how and when other values must mitigate or cancel the effects of a mistakenly zealous or imperialistic application of luck egalitarian justice. GA Cohen was vividly aware of the possibility of conflict between distributive equality and other values. He held that 'there is something which justice requires people to have equal amounts of, *not no matter what*, but to whatever extent allowed *by values which compete with* distributive equality'.[27] He also noted that a *prima facie* plausible objection to some conceptions of equality is that 'implementing … [them] would involve intolerably intrusive state surveillance'.[28] Our normal intuitive responses to the scenarios, all of which are contrary to what luck egalitarian justice demands, might illustrate exactly this kind of conflict. Our rejection of luck egalitarianism, the choice/circumstance distinction and its consequences in these cases is an instance in which we rightly prioritise other values—humanity, charity, altruism and the like—over equality. This is not an embarrassment for luck egalitarianism but, rather, shows it to have a respectably pluralistic theory of value and a non-imperialistic view of equality's relative importance within that scheme of values.

There is, however, another thought with which these observations are compatible. It is that the claim luck egalitarianism makes with regard to Annette, Barry, Deirdre and Colin—that they must, from the perspective of justice, bear the consequences of their choices—illustrates not the perfectly proper seasoning of equality's claims, but the fundamentally mistaken nature of this conception of equality. For the luck egalitarian responses to these situations are morally wrong: not just *possibly* morally wrong, or *marginally* morally wrong, or morally

[27] *Currency* (n 9) 3 (emphasis mine).

[28] *Currency* (n 9) 7. See also *Socialism* (n 9) at 34 for comment on the conflict between equality and community.

wrong only after a long and hard process of deliberation. They are *obvious* moral mistakes. Leaving Barry bleeding at the side of the road, Colin and Deirdre to freeze to death on the hill, and Annette homeless are instances of moral imbecility. We would regard someone who, at little risk to themselves, was perfectly able to help in these cases but did not, as a moral failure.

It is not reassuring to be told by luck egalitarians that responding to these situations only through the prism of equality is taking equality too far. For the worry here is that this is a conception of equality which must be mitigated *in order to avoid moral imbecility*. And that worry—which is not about limiting equality's range by reference to other values but, rather, about having to limit it by reference to other values *so as to avoid moral imbecility*—looks like a reasonable ground for rejecting this conception rather than mitigating its excesses. The thought is that a conception of justice or equality so morally blind or callous simply cannot be acceptable.[29] Nor is it hard to imagine other conceptions of equality, particularly but not exclusively those emphasising the equal status, value or dignity of all human beings, offering quite different injunctions with regard to Colin and Deirdre, Annette and Barry than those that luck egalitarianism tenders.[30]

Another consequence of utilising the choice/circumstance distinction highlights a conflict between the value of distributive equality, on the one hand, and that of egalitarian respect, on the other. This conflict becomes apparent once we consider how luck egalitarianism might be implemented as a policy goal. The primary goal is, of course, to distribute welfare, or resources, or advantage (or opportunities for one or other of these) in such a way as to ensure that no one suffers as a result of bad brute luck.[31] To do this we must distinguish between those aspects of one's condition—by which I mean everything from the state of one's mind and body to the state of one's bank balance—that result from one's choices and those that are a consequence of one's circumstances. The most obvious way of doing this is by interrogating all whose condition seems different from, in the sense of being unequal to, the majority (assuming there is a majority in a broadly equal 'condition'). So, for example, if I have fewer resources than many others, then that will surely be a cause of egalitarian inquiry on your part: how did this ostensibly baleful situation come to pass? If it is a result of my free and informed gambles or other choices, then your egalitarian concern is misplaced. But if it is a consequence of my inability to obtain gainful employment as a result of my poor cognitive, intellectual and related skills, or a consequence of my physical disabilities, then

[29] For efforts to deal with the broader gripe of which this complaint is a variant, see S Segal, 'In Solidarity with the Imprudent: A Defense of Luck Egalitarianism' (2007) 33 *Social Theory and Practice* 177–98 and K Voight, 'The Harshness Objection: Is Luck Egalitarianism too Harsh on Victims of Bad Option Luck?' (2007) 10 *Ethical Theory and Practice* 389–407.

[30] Richard Arneson's conclusion that the likes of Colin, Deirdre, Barry and Annette 'are owed extra assistance in the name of egalitarianism' ('Luck Egalitarianism Interpreted and Defended' (2004) 32 *Philosophical Topics* 1–20 at 5) might well be true, but that egalitarianism is not the luck egalitarianism Cohen defends. While Arneson's defence of luck egalitarianism (see n 9 for some instalments) is deeply sensitive to the problems that beset that view, it is (perhaps for that reason?) a reinvention of it.

[31] See *Currency* (n 9) 19–20 and 69.

your egalitarian concern is not only rightly triggered. It must also be converted into action to redress this disadvantage.

Although well meant, your egalitarian concern and, in appropriate cases, ameliorative response, both depend upon complete transparency or disclosure on my part. To obtain egalitarian aid, I must flaunt my disabilities while showing them to be unimpeachably a result of bad brute luck. Alternatively, I renounce such aid by confessing to having made poor employment, lifestyle or other choices that have left me in this worse off position. In either case, luck egalitarianism requires a level of disclosure from me that teeters on the brink of being shameful: I must show that I bear the stigma of either my bad choices or my bad circumstances. Doing that involves admissions like, for example, 'I'm less well off than the rest because I'm stupid' or 'I'm less well off than the rest because I made bad choices'. Neither statement looks like the kind of thing an egalitarian should require another human being to say. Why? Because something egalitarians have traditionally assumed and fought for is the idea that 'we'—members of this class or that group—are in some fundamental sense of the same rank and value. And all, as a result, are entitled to and must be accorded the same level of respect and concern.

The transparency and disclosure luck egalitarians would require of some runs contrary to this notion of respect: it is in many instances straightforwardly demeaning.[32] Indeed, this kind of public admission of one's various failings is in many ways worse than the disclosure necessary in current systems of means-tested social insurance benefits. The latter usually only require financial disclosure, employment history and, in some cases, medical reports.[33] Yet the requirement to admit to one's bad choices, or to show that one's disadvantages result from brute luck, as a pre-condition of aid, goes quantitatively and qualitatively far beyond that. It is a matter of what we might call 'life-course auditing', a process of showing which ups and downs in the course of a human life have arisen from choice and which from bad brute luck. But why, it must be asked, should some members of an allegedly egalitarian community be required to disclose such detail of their life-histories and thus risk demeaning themselves in the process? Publicly demeaning conduct is and has been exactly what egalitarians oppose, from segregated public spaces to enforced displays of deference and sumptuary constraints. For luck egalitarians to hold, in response, either that 'victims' be compensated for the pain of disclosure, or that all must make full disclosure regardless of their relative equality of condition, is to miss the point.[34] Shaming some, but compensating them for that, or forcing all to undergo what those who are shamed must undergo, are

[32] It entails, as J Wolff argues, a diminution of one's 'respect-standing': see his 'Fairness, Respect, and the Egalitarian Ethos' (1998) 27 *Philosophy and Public Affairs* 97–122 at 107–10 (hereinafter '*FR*'). Wolff offers further thoughts on the issue of shameful disclosure in 'Fairness, Respect, and the Egalitarian Ethos Revisited' (2010) 14 *Journal of Ethics* 335–50 at 343–46 (hereinafter '*FRR*').

[33] For the conditions on many such benefits in English law, see the Child Poverty Action Group's (CPAG) *Welfare Benefits and Tax Credits Handbook 2014/15*, 16th edn (London, CPAG, 2014) parts 2 and 3.

[34] See Wolff, *FR* (n 32) at 117.

morally eccentric responses to shabby treatment. The right and properly egalitarian response is surely to avoid treating one's fellows this badly in the first place.

This brings us to the last and perhaps most general complaint about luck egalitarianism considered here. It arises not as a consequence of utilising the choice/circumstance distinction nor is it a complaint about the plausibility of that distinction. Rather, it arises from this question: what about *LAJ*? Or, more specifically, what support, if any, can luck egalitarianism give *LAJ*? The answer, I think, is 'none'. This is in part a result of the already noted weaknesses in luck egalitarianism and, in part, because—and this is the complaint—luck egalitarianism is a *purely* distributive conception of equality. That means luck egalitarianism's focus is almost exclusively upon what should be distributed equally—resources, welfare, advantage, opportunities for one or the other, or some combination of them—and the development of principles of distribution.[35] This serves as a double contrast. First, it runs strikingly contrary to the emphasis of many general juridical equality provisions, where, as we have already noted, equality is principally a qualitative notion, a matter of 'forms' of treatment rather than of distributing amounts of 'stuff'. Being principally qualitative, the subject matter of these provisions is not easily 'distributed' in any obvious sense, although, as noted before, some distributions of some things can provide evidence of unequal treatment under these provisions.

Second, luck egalitarianism's near exclusive emphasis upon distribution sets it apart from the history of egalitarian struggle. Fights for equality have never been solely battles for a more equal distribution of some or other thing but, rather, struggles for equality of standing and recognition. Thus the political 'invention' of equality, in 1789, amounted to what Pierre Rosanvallon called 'a visceral rejection of privilege', a challenge to those, and the societies in which they flourished, who saw themselves 'as constituting a distinct order, a nation of the select within the nation … another species of man'.[36] They have been first and foremost campaigns against hierarchy and exclusion, even when ostensibly about the distribution of something as specific as the vote. So, for example, British campaigners for women's suffrage did not regard enfranchisement as the end of their war; it was merely one battle in a struggle to stand fully equal with and be recognised as different from the other 50 per cent of the adult population.[37] Even relatively recent

[35] 'Almost exclusively' because Cohen puts exploitation on the luck egalitarian agenda (*Currency* (n 9) at 5). It seems that Cohen's egalitarianism had, by the time of his death, begun to push beyond luck egalitarianism's emphasis on distribution: see Ch 10 of his *Finding Oneself in the Other* (edited by M Otsuka) (Princeton, New Jersey, Princeton University Press, 2013).

[36] P Rosanvallon, *The Society of Equals* (Cambridge, Massachusetts, Harvard University Press, 2013) 12 (the second part of the quotation is from Abbe Sieyes, *Qu'est que le Tiers Etat?* (1788)).

[37] As Lydia Becker, an early campaigner for women's suffrage, put it: '[t]he keynote of our movement is that woman is the co-ordinate not the sub-ordinate of half of humanity' (1879), quoted in H Blackburn, *Women's Suffrage: A Record of the Woman's Suffrage Movement in the British Isles* (London, Williams and Norgate, 1902) at 170. This might count as a 'struggle for full citizen enfranchisement' of the kind envisaged by GA Cohen, *If You're an Egalitarian, How Come You're So Rich?* (n 9)at 23.

campaigns about equal pay have endorsed many more claims than simply receiving the same pay for the same work. They hit against what campaigners rightly regard as treatment as second-class citizens, whose interests and labour count for less than the interests and labour of others. These citizen-labourers—almost always women—claim a status equal with that of their male brethren, a result of this being that their labour is equally valuable.[38]

Luck egalitarianism's lack of connection with both juridical equality provisions and the history of equality struggles might be explained thus: it is not a 'political' conception of equality, being largely unconcerned with the political and social structure of society and the opportunities for power and advantage they present, maintain and exclude.[39] Yet this does not excuse luck egalitarianism but, rather, indicts it. For, without claiming that a society's political and social structures are the only important determinants of the life chances of its citizens, they are assuredly among the class of such determinants. It is thus not unreasonable to expect them to loom large in theories of equality. *LAJ* is a significant feature of most contemporary legal systems and, being such, it is also an important part of the political structure of the societies in which those systems function. Since luck egalitarianism has little to say about societies' political structures, it comes as no surprise that it is equally quiet about *LAJ*. If luck egalitarianism ignores macro-level political and social structures, it cannot be news to report that it overlooks some of the micro-level components constitutive of those structures.

Why, then, spend so much time examining luck egalitarianism when it has so little to say about the object of our attention? For the reason stated at the beginning of this sub-section, the weight of which, even in light of our selective and narrowly focussed discussion, should now be evident. Luck egalitarianism has been—perhaps still is in some hands—a vibrant strand of contemporary political-philosophical thought.[40] That, of course, presents a puzzle in light of luck egalitarianism's near silence about institutional and structural matters, but it is not one with which this discussion will engage. Before leaving luck egalitarianism, a final point. It is that the arguments offered against that position here do nothing to undermine two other beliefs, namely, that the natural and social lotteries are

[38] See chs 2 and 3 of A Carter, *The Politics of Women's Rights* (London, Longman, 1988) for an overview of the issues.

[39] Recall that, for John Rawls, the 'content [of a political conception of justice] is expressed in terms of certain fundamental ideas seen as implicit in the public political culture of a democratic society. This public culture comprises the political institutions of a constitutional regime and the public traditions of their interpretation' (*Political Liberalism* (New York, Columbia University Press, 1996) 13–14). For an interesting putative explanation of contemporary political philosophy's (including luck egalitarianism's) relative insulation from such matters—the result of a form of neo-Augustinianism—see D Miller, *Justice for Earthlings* (Cambridge, Cambridge University Press, 2013) Ch 10. The absence of a political conception of equality in luck egalitarianism was originally noted by Anderson (n 1) at 312–37; Scheffler (n 10) 202–07 makes a similar general point.

[40] For more additions to the list of doubts, and a compelling argument that luck egalitarianism fails to justify its two distinct—responsibility and equality tracking—limbs, see G Sher, *Equality for Inegalitarians* (Cambridge, Cambridge University Press, 2014) chs 1–4.

important for, but should not be the sole focus of, any respectable account of distributive justice; and that distributive justice is an ideal worthy of pursuit.

II. Two Conceptions of Equality

Before examining the two conceptions of equality that might function as normative props for *LAJ*, we must note the exact nature of that function. My view is that the two conceptions are immanent within *LAJ* and that, of course, stands in need of explanation. The kind of immanence I have in mind is similar to that present in a standard immanent critique of some institution, practice or set of beliefs, where there is a professed commitment to X, but that commitment is either partially observed or completely ignored. The critique there is a matter of holding the institution, practice or holders of beliefs to X, or ensuring that X is explicitly disavowed. However, there is in our public political and legal culture no explicit and unambiguous commitment to either of the conceptions of equality discussed below. Rather, I claim that these conceptions are implicit within—in the various senses of (i) sometimes having elements in common with; (ii) sometimes functioning in the same way as; and (iii) often providing an underlying, unifying normative rationale for—reasonably large swathes of legal materials, understood to include everything from particular segments of legal doctrine (such as the various equality provisions already noted) to broad aspects of legal institutional design like *LAJ*. Many aspects of our public political and legal culture, as well as many of its institutional manifestations, are therefore compatible with, and thus can be informed by, these two conceptions of equality. But I do not think that either conception is anywhere explicitly institutionally affirmed. There are therefore fewer doctrinal hooks from which to hang the claim that these two conceptions can be regarded as legal principles than there are with regard to dignity, for example. While that clearly cannot prevent these two conceptions filling the role of legal principles, their greater distance from the detail of legal doctrine makes their candidature slightly more problematic.

A. The Social and Political Ideal of Equality

This conception of equality might be thought unpromising because inchoate. There is no single, fully worked-out instance of this view, it being a composite picture constructed from a number of different views.[41] Those views do,

[41] I draw principally upon the work of Anderson (n 1); Scheffler (n 10) Chs 7 and 8 and 'Equality as the Virtue of Sovereigns: A Reply to Ronald Dworkin' (2003) 31 *Philosophy and Public Affairs* 199–206; and Wolff, *FR* (n 32). J Wolff and A de-Shalit's *Disadvantage* (Oxford, Clarendon, 2007) could be regarded as a prospectus for the future of *SPIE*'s distributive programme. The work of

however, have something in common—each is a reaction to and criticism of luck egalitarianism—and I regard that as a good, albeit defeasible, reason for treating them together. Moreover, these various reactions, despite their many differences, contain some similar themes and it is these I offer as the core of this position. The quest for a credo that constitutes the social and political conception of equality (hereinafter *SPIE*) can begin with Samuel Scheffler's statement that equality, on this view,

> is not, in the first instance, a distributive ideal, and its aim is not to compensate for misfortune. It is, instead, a *moral ideal* governing the relations in which people stand to one another. Instead of focussing attention on the differing contingencies of each person's traits, abilities, and other circumstances, this ideal abstracts from the undeniable differences among people. It claims that human relations must be conducted on the basis of an assumption that everyone's life is equally important, and that all members of a society have equal standing.... As a *moral ideal* [*SPIE*] ... asserts that all people are of equal worth and that there are some claims that people are entitled to make on one another simply by virtue of their status as persons. As a *social ideal*, it holds that a human society must be conceived of as a cooperative arrangement among equals, each of whom enjoys the same social standing. As a *political ideal*, it highlights the claims that citizens are entitled to make on one another by virtue of their status as citizens, without any need for a moralized accounting of the details of their particular circumstances. Indeed, it insists on the very great importance of the right to be viewed simply as a citizen and to have one's fundamental rights and privileges determined on that basis, without reference to one's talents, intelligence, wisdom, decision-making skill, temperament, social class, religious or ethnic affiliation, or ascribed identity.[42]

This encapsulates the principal themes that unite proponents of *SPIE*. Even though there are more than three such themes, I propose to elucidate them through Scheffler's threefold division between moral, social and political ideals.

The moral ideal embodied in *SPIE* is not one with which any egalitarian would or could disagree. The affirmation, in that ideal, of the equal importance of everyone's life and the equal worth of people are not exact synonyms, but the two can be treated as such for present purposes and labelled the *equal worth* theme. Moreover, they are also undeniable by any professed egalitarian, being part of the definition of that position. The claim that all have *equal standing* does not necessarily follow from equal worth, for we could affirm the latter and also maintain that, given the necessity of certain social, political or economic conditions, some of our number temporarily lack the same status as the rest. Some might, for example, have to abase themselves for a short while or be temporarily forced into certain kinds of labour so as to save all from crisis. But it would be very difficult to maintain

Amartya Sen (particularly but not exclusively *Inequality Reexamined* (Cambridge, Massachusetts, Harvard University Press, 1992)) looms large in (roughly) the second half of Anderson (n 1), as it does, alongside that of Martha Nussbaum (*Women and Human Development: The Capabilities Approach* (New York, Oxford University Press, 2000) and *Frontiers of Justice* (Cambridge, Massachusetts, Harvard University Press, 2006)) in Wolff and de-Shalit, ibid.

[42] Scheffler (n 10) at 191 (emphasis mine).

this subsidiary status for long, just as it was difficult for proponents of slavery to uphold that social and political institution while affirming the equal worth of all humankind. The more comfortable and common position, of course, was to affirm the equal worth of only some members of that class.

The *equal standing* theme is more expansive than the *equal worth* theme in a dual sense: it calls hierarchies into question and emphasises the way one is regarded by, and the place one occupies among, others. A world in which all have equal standing is one in which 'no one need bow and scrape … or represent themselves as inferior'.[43] Equal standing therefore concerns not just one's bare membership of a group (humankind or some smaller gathering), but the nature or quality of that membership: one member's status is exactly the same as that of any other.[44] This theme is probably only worth highlighting as a point of contrast with luck egalitarianism, since almost all other forms of egalitarianism affirm something like it. Moreover, it is not certain that luck egalitarianism denies the equal standing theme; rather, most versions say nothing at all about it. The theme is also a vital element of *SPIE*'s social ideal, according to Scheffler. Few non-sceptical political philosophers, egalitarians or not, would deny the other aspect of the social ideal, namely, that human societies are cooperative arrangements. Egalitarians, though, affirm that human societies are cooperative arrangements among equals and one dimension in which all are the same is the status of their membership: all members stand on the same footing, all enjoy the same standing or status.

The political ideal embodies two themes, one of which is also contained in the moral ideal but which we have not so far noted, the other being unique to the political ideal. Scheffler holds that the moral ideal asserts that 'there are some claims that people are entitled to make on one another simply by virtue of their status as persons', this being narrowed in the political ideal to the assertion that '*citizens* are entitled to make [claims] on one another by virtue of their status as *citizens*' (emphasis mine). Neither assertion is questionable within the egalitarian tradition, although unearthing their basis—showing, that is, the considerations that license them—is by no means an easy task. That task is, in fact, the job of arguing for the normative significance of equality and neither Scheffler nor other proponents of *SPIE* do that; they do, however, issue some promissory notes on the topic while registering how unsatisfactory it is to simply assume, as luck egalitarians allegedly do, that the normative case for equality has been made. We can call this the *entitlement* theme.

[43] Anderson (n 1) 313.

[44] The emphasis upon one's standing with regard to others thus explains the temptation to dub *SPIE* a 'relational' conception of equality (see Wolff and de Shalit (n 41) at 4–8; Anderson (n 1) at 313). For an argument that this 'social status' component of *SPIE* can be combined with luck egalitarianism, see Z Stemplowska, 'Responsibility and Respect: Reconciling Two Egalitarian Visions' in C Knight and Z Stemplowska (eds), *Responsibility and Distributive Justice* (Oxford, Clarendon, 2011) Ch 5.

The second theme of the political ideal can be labelled, following the discussion at the end of the last chapter, the *opacity* theme. It is a matter of being able to stand among one's peers in a group without anything like complete disclosure. One's membership is determined not by a life-course audit of all one's abilities, choices and the circumstances in which the former were exercised and the latter made, but by reference only to 'formal' requirements: place of birth, parentage and the like. For an egalitarian, Scheffler thinks, one's rights and privileges, as well as one's duties and liabilities, should flow from something like this formal assessment of standing or membership and he invokes the notion of citizenship to express the point. That notion, as we will see in the next chapter, is not as unproblematic and simple as often assumed, but there is a thin sense of the term that does the work Scheffler envisages here. That is the 'bare legal' sense of citizenship which, if satisfied, guarantees various rights and privileges in many of the jurisdictions with which we are familiar. Non-citizens often have fewer or different rights and privileges. This theme is again probably only worth emphasising against the backdrop of luck egalitarianism, since most standard egalitarian views take membership of the political community to be a formality satisfied by birth, age or related requirements.

It seems, then, that *SPIE* has at least four themes, some of which are manifest in more than one of its constitutive ideals: that of equal worth, of equal standing, of entitlement and of opacity. Were these themes embedded in an account of the normative power of equality then *SPIE* would look a little less inchoate than it currently appears. Yet there are still some significant gaps. One becomes obvious once we question the rationale for opacity, another when we recall luck egalitarianism's main burden. Whereas the equal worth and equal standing themes seem closely related to, but not entailed by, one another, the opacity theme stands at a remove from them. Indeed, it seems perfectly possible to affirm the former themes while either denying or not affirming the latter. It is easy to envisage luck egalitarians with an interest in hierarchy and exploitation, as well as in the consequences of the natural and social lotteries, doing so. But if the opacity theme does not derive from the equal worth and equal standing themes, then there is little chance of it being derived from or supported by the entitlement theme. How else might it be supported?

It is most obviously supported by reference to one aspect of what Jonathon Wolff called the egalitarian ethos. Such an ethos consists of a commitment to fairness, understood as 'the demand that no one should be advantaged or disadvantaged by arbitrary factors',[45] and to respect. On an egalitarian view, there is a sense in which all are entitled to the latter, and in the same degree, just by virtue of some fact about them: their membership of a group, either large (humankind) or small (a particular polity), for instance. Wolff identifies a number of ways in which one's equal respect-standing can be undermined by others—distrust, lack of

[45] Wolff, *FR* (n 32) 106.

courtesy and shameful revelation—and affirms that egalitarians should set their faces against all of them.[46] An obvious way in which they can set themselves against the latter is by making opacity a hallmark of many social roles and institutional practices. *SPIE*'s opacity theme must therefore be correlated with, in the sense of being derived from, a broader *respect* theme.

While many proponents of *SPIE* complain, as Scheffler does, about luck egalitarianism's almost exclusive emphasis upon distribution, the complaint should not distract from *SPIE*'s own obligation to specify what it is that should be distributed and how. While luck egalitarianism abounds with proposals along these lines, *SPIE* seemingly has none. Can a *distributive* theme be found? One component of such a theme is derivable from *SPIE*'s commitment to equal standing. Implementing that commitment will require, at the very least, a presumptively equal distribution of legal rights: all citizens must, by virtue of their citizenship, have the same bundle of legal rights, duties, powers, immunities and liabilities (hereinafter just 'rights'). If not, how could they be said to have equal standing? The distribution is presumptively equal because some apparent citizens may not, after all, qualify as citizens and some citizens may lose their good standing, forfeiting some rights: those, for example, convicted of offences. Nor does it follow from a presumptively equal distribution of legal rights that all who have identical bundles either get full use from their bundles or end up with equal holdings as a result. Having the same bundle of rights tells us nothing about the levels of utilisation of rights among particular agents nor about the practical benefits they derive from their rights.

Now, insofar as equal standing requires an equal distribution of legal rights, it also requires uniformity, in a sense already familiar to us: it requires that the law judge its addressees by reference to the same general standards. This is not, of course, the full uniformity component of *LAJ*, but only part of it. When instantiated in a system of enforceable legal rights, equal standing cannot allow different legal standards to apply, for example, to people of different ethnicity, gender, levels of wealth or the like. Or, at least, different legal standards cannot be applied to different groups without good legal reason, the types of reason constitutive of that category being compatible with the commitment to equal standing. *LAJ*'s uniformity component holds that, in addition to the same legal standards being applied to all, those standards are also objective. That means that those standards are not particularly sensitive to the capacities and context of those to whom they are applied; indeed, they are often applied regardless of such differences between addressees. This objectivity element of the uniformity component is not quickly derivable from *SPIE*'s equal standing commitment, although it does serve to make the realisation of equal standing easier. For, if the standards applied to all ignore the differences of context and capacity between addressees, then those standards in effect assume that all addressees are the same. And that, of course,

[46] Wolff, *FR* (n 32) at 107–110 and *FRR* (n 32) at 342–46.

serves as a bridge between *LAJ*'s uniformity component, on the one hand, and its presumptive identity and limited avoidability components, on the other.

The latter two components are also interestingly connected to another of *SPIE*'s themes, namely, opacity. In treating all addressees of the law as identical abstract beings, and by basing the availability of exculpatory claims upon reasonableness standards, these components ignore much about the context and the particularity of the people the law judges. In Scheffler's words, '[i]nstead of focussing attention on the differing contingencies of each person's traits, abilities, and other circumstances, [they] … abstract[.] from the undeniable differences among people'.[47] Although opacity is not a specifically distributive feature of *SPIE*, and neither the presumptive identity nor limited avoidability components are uniquely distributive features of *LAJ*, the fact of their overlap is significant. In its light the claim that *SPIE* is immanent within the law in general, and *LAJ* in particular, becomes more plausible. But what more can be said of *SPIE*'s distributive theme?

At least this: it is worth labelling the fact that the equal standing theme requires a particular distribution of legal rights as the 'juristic strand' of *SPIE*'s *distributive* theme. That strand can be distinguished from another, which deals with the distribution of all that does not fall easily or immediately into the former strand. What could we have in mind? Most obviously, perhaps, the kind of very general 'currency'—welfare, resources, advantage or opportunities for one or other of these—the elucidation of which so deeply preoccupied many luck egalitarians. Does *SPIE* distribute that kind of thing and, if so, how? Some proponents of *SPIE* have invoked Amartya Sen and Martha Nussbaum's related ideas of capabilities and functionings as a means of determining a currency for distribution. In the hands of Jonathon Wolff and Avner de-Shalit, these two notions—functionings referring to all those things one requires in order to be or do whatever one has good reason to be or do, and capabilities being 'a set of vectors of functions, reflecting [one's] freedom to lead one type of life or another'—become determinants of social advantage and disadvantage.[48] Having constructed a metric of disadvantage, Wolff and de-Shalit use it to support their argument that egalitarians must ensure that the worst off in society have priority with regard to any distribution.[49] But what is it that must be distributed according to this metric? Wolff and de-Shalit have no single answer since their view is that the notion of disadvantage is plural, having many different axes, and contextual, in the sense that different societies can have various conceptions of what constitutes a minimally good or acceptable life. Thus the currency of egalitarian justice, for Wolff and de-Shalit, is something like this: whatever 'stuff' is necessary to alleviate the position of the worst off in a particular society, judged according to the functionings and capabilities dominant within that society.

[47] Scheffler (n 10) at 191.

[48] Wolff and de-Shalit (n 41) at 37.

[49] On 'prioritarian' forms of egalitarianism, see H Frankfurt, *The Importance of What We Care About* (Cambridge, Cambridge University Press, 1988) Ch 11 and D Parfit, 'Equality and Priority' in A Mason (ed), *Ideals of Equality* (Oxford, Blackwells, 1998) Ch 1.

Elizabeth Anderson also invokes the capabilities–functionings framework in order to construct distributive principles for *SPIE*, holding that '[w]e can understand the egalitarian aim to secure for everyone the social conditions of their freedom in terms of capabilities'.[50] In response to the question 'which capabilities must a society equalise?', Anderson answers thus:

> [r]eflection on the negative and positive aims of egalitarianism helps us meet this … [question]. Negatively, people are entitled to whatever capabilities are necessary to enable them to avoid or escape entanglement in oppressive social relationships. Positively, they are entitled to the capabilities necessary for functioning as an equal citizen in a democratic state.[51]

The currency this approach invokes is therefore just as 'mixed' as that in play in Wolff and de-Shalit's response to disadvantage. That is because the effort to 'guarantee a set of capabilities necessary to functioning as a free and equal citizen avoiding oppression' can range far and wide, covering welfare, resources and much else.[52] Its range is not, however, unlimited, since only that which is necessary for equal citizenship is guaranteed under Anderson's theory of democratic equality. Among such 'necessaries' Anderson includes those things required to function as a human being (requisite levels of sustenance, shelter, etc), who is both 'a participant in a system of cooperative production … and … a citizen of a democratic state'.[53]

These two brief paragraphs illustrate two significant points. First, that proponents of *SPIE* are not silent about what a defensible egalitarianism must distribute in addition to the rights included in the juristic strand; and, second, that there is an interesting convergence among some proponents of *SPIE* upon the capabilities–functionings framework as a means of thinking about what it is that must be distributed and how. But it would be a mistake to assume there is unanimity about the exact what and how of distribution,[54] just as it would be an error to exaggerate the level of detail in the non-juristic strand of *SPIE*'s *distributive* theme. This strand, and the distributive theme as a whole, is probably the least developed component of what, it must be admitted, is a fairly sketchy conception of equality. While the latter thought raises an obvious critical question—why bother with such an incomplete conception of equality?—the former also provides the platform for a critical challenge. It holds that the non-juristic strand is not only underspecified but also indistinguishable from the juristic strand. I'll consider these complaints in reverse order.

As to the latter, it is true that the dividing line between these strands is not particularly robust. It could be collapsed simply by regarding the rights, duties, powers, privileges, immunities and liabilities of the juristic strand as in part

[50] Anderson (n 1) at 316.
[51] Anderson (n 1) at 316.
[52] Anderson (n 1) 327.
[53] Anderson (n 1) 317.
[54] See, for example, Wolff's complaint that Anderson's distributive schema would, like luck egalitarianism, undermine respect: *FRR* (n 32) at 348–49.

constitutive of the functionings and thus capabilities open to agents. They must therefore be distributed in accord with the set of functionings and capabilities we think agents should or must have and, as a result, lack the priority accorded in our sketch of *SPIE*.[55] That sketch placed the distributive theme last, the question of the currency of egalitarian justice—the question of what it is that must be distributed and how—being raised only when equality of standing is achieved. But, it seems, that question can determine the answer to every other: the standing of group members, the value of their lives, the way they relate to one another and the distribution of various rights and liabilities among them can all be fed into the maw of the capabilities–functionings framework. Is *SPIE* therefore just as much a distributive conception of equality as luck egalitarianism?

Yes and no. The point that, in principle, the capabilities–functioning framework determines the distribution of everything is hard to resist. However, it is the case that proponents of that framework, and of *SPIE* itself, hold that some 'things' must be distributed equally to all in advance of any assessment of the nature of various sets of functionings and capabilities:

> [b]ecause the CA [capabilities approach] holds that people are fundamentally equal in dignity [or, in Scheffler's terms, in worth or value], it will sometimes require that entitlements be secured to people on a basis of full equality, reasoning that only this equality is compatible with their equal dignity [or equal worth-cum-value and their equal standing] as citizens. Thus, the right to vote, the freedom of religion, the freedom of speech, and quite a few other entitlements, have not been *adequately* distributed unless they have been *equally* distributed. Any other mode of distribution would set up ranks and orders of citizens.[56]

I take that to be a relatively unproblematic endorsement of the priority of the juristic over the non-juristic strand in *SPIE*'s distributive theme. It is worth noting that a similar priority is affirmed by proponents of *SPIE* who do not explicitly adopt the capabilities–functionings framework, and on much the same grounds. Recall, for instance, Scheffler's claim, at the beginning of the long passage quoted above, that equality is not in the first instance a distributive ideal. That is because, as the rest of the passage shows, Scheffler thinks that other things must be in place for egalitarians—the recognition and guarantee of equal worth-cum-value, on the one hand, and equal standing, on the other—before the currency question becomes live. Although this view is not an explicit endorsement of juristic priority, it is close enough for present purposes.

What are we to make of the vagueness objection, the complaint that *SPIE* is so underspecified as to be unworthy of attention here? I hope the previous

[55] This view seems, in places at least, to animate M Nussbaum's 'Constitutions and Capabilities: "Perception" Against Lofty Formalism' (2007) 121 *Harvard Law Review* 5–97 (the capabilities approach is 'a framework for understanding the foundations of political entitlements and constitutional law': 7).

[56] ibid, 13. This view is not obviously echoed in the discussion of law and political structure in M Nussbaum, *Creating Capabilities* (Cambridge, Massachusetts, Harvard University Press, 2011) at 166–80.

pages give some ground to resist this conclusion, but it would be folly to maintain that *SPIE* is a detailed and well worked-out project. It is a nascent research programme, a conception of equality built upon a critique of luck egalitarianism that not only purports to be truer to the nature of egalitarian struggle and politics than that position, but also to avoid many of that position's difficulties. Whether or not it ultimately succeeds in those aims is not something we can determine here. What is clear, though, is that a number of *SPIE*'s themes—most obviously but not only the opacity theme—are very similar to some of *LAJ*'s components. And by 'similar to' here, I mean this: 'does much the same job as'; so much so, indeed, that *LAJ*'s components can easily be regarded as simple embodiments, in legal-institutional form, of *SPIE*'s principal themes. That being so, the rationale and value of the latter may be extended to the components of the former. That is what is meant by the claim that *SPIE* is immanent within *LAJ*. Having established that, we can now turn to another conception of equality seemingly standing in the same relation to *LAJ*.

B. The Right to Equal Concern and Respect

Ronald Dworkin's right to equal concern and respect is the conception of equality I have in mind.[57] The right holds that

> [g]overnment must treat those whom it governs with concern, that is, as human beings who are capable of suffering and frustration, and with respect, that is, as human beings who are capable of forming and acting on intelligent conceptions of how their lives should be lived. Government must not only treat people with concern and respect, but with equal concern and respect. It must not distribute goods or opportunities unequally on the ground that some citizens are entitled to more because they are worthy of more concern. It must not constrain liberty on the ground that one citizen's conception of the good life of one group is nobler or superior to another's.[58]

Thus, 'individuals have a right to equal concern and respect in the design and administration of the political institutions that govern them'.[59] They should be 'treated with the same respect and concern as anyone else'.[60]

The right to equal concern and respect is far more limited than the injunctions of luck egalitarianism, applying only to the conduct of 'government' and,

[57] By singling out this right for attention, I do not assert that it is the only possible foundation in Dworkin's work that might support *LAJ*. In both *Law's Empire* (Oxford, Hart Publishing, 1998) and *Justice in Robes* (Cambridge, Massachusetts, Harvard University Press, 2006), Dworkin suggests an understanding of integrity that includes a form of equality before the law (at 184–85 of the former and 176–78 of the latter) which could support *LAJ*. I do not explore this pathway further, principally because in each instance the argument is made only in passing and is somewhat inchoate. Dworkin's general statement on integrity is found in Chs 6 and 7 of *Law's Empire*, ibid.

[58] *TRS* (n 6) 272–73.

[59] *TRS* (n 6) 180.

[60] *TRS* (n 6) 227.

presumably, some of its outcomes or consequences. Nor is there any legitimate sense in which the right is exclusively concerned with the quantitative distribution of some 'thing', be that resources, welfare, advantage or opportunities for one or other of these. For, although it can in some circumstances have distributive implications, the right always entails that certain interests of all citizens must be treated in the same way.[61] The right is also clearly more specific than many general equality provisions, principally because it sketches reasonably precisely what must be valued—citizens' ability to formulate and pursue conceptions of the good life as well as their capacities for suffering and frustration. Furthermore, the right tells us how this 'bundle' of interests, which presumably all citizens have, must be treated by government, namely, with both equal concern and equal respect.

It is therefore an exaggeration to claim that this right 'does not have sufficient content to explain the precise nature of the wrongs that are done to people who are not treated with equal concern and respect'.[62] The wrong done by breach of this right is some combination of: (i) curtailment, partial or complete, of some citizens' ability to pursue or formulate conceptions of a good life; (ii) the undervaluing or ignoring of some such conceptions; (iii) the undervaluing or ignoring of the suffering and frustration caused to citizens by either (i) or (ii). Although not compendious, the wrong here is sufficiently clear and substantial to show that the right to equal concern and respect is not empty. That much becomes even more obvious on switching from the negative to the positive register for, if instead of cataloguing the wrongs done by breach of the right, we think instead of the capacities it upholds, it is clear that at the very least the values of autonomy and freedom must loom large.[63] The failure of this specific complaint bodes ill for the more general version with which it is often associated, namely, that which holds that the right to equal concern and respect—hereinafter 'the right' or the '*RECR*'—is so general as to be capable of supporting almost any substantive moral, political or legal position. The mistake here is to *assume* that the right's generality entails contentlessness: if there is any truth at all in this claim, then it must be established on a case-by-case basis. Generality simply cannot of itself generate *a priori* grounds showing that the right is content-free. Furthermore, the supposedly problematic general nature of the right is, for Dworkin, one of its virtues, its generality ensuring that it is compatible with many different and competing normative positions. Dworkin's claim, that any plausible political theory will embody the *RECR*, is therefore only a slight exaggeration, particularly if one confines oneself to large swathes of Western, post-Enlightenment political thought. This effort to elucidate a commonality in the face of difference should not be regarded, without good reason, as dubious.

[61] *TRS* (n 6) 227.

[62] See S Moreau, 'The Wrongs of Unequal Treatment' (2004) 54 *University of Toronto Law Journal* 291–326 at 296.

[63] It becomes obvious in R Dworkin's *Justice for Hedgehogs* (Cambridge, Massachusetts, Harvard University Press, 2011)—hereinafter '*Hedgehogs*' in text and footnotes—that both notions should be subsumed under Dworkin's broad conception of dignity.

One hook from which the previous, misconceived complaint is often hung is the *RECR*'s near-ubiquity. It does a good deal of intellectual and practical work for Dworkin. It was invoked in his early work as a means of making sense of the principal theoretical components of Rawls's account of justice. It played another equally important role, along with the distinction between personal and external preferences, in Dworkin's defence of reverse discrimination, and appeared to be *the* (or one) basis of the normative power of the rights thesis, the most distinctive component of Dworkin's account of hard case adjudication.[64] In his mid-period work, Dworkin argued that the right was the core of any coherent and meaningful liberal political philosophy.[65] His more recent work, ranging over the nature and content of distributive justice to the nature of value and the good life, also invokes a variant of this right.[66] It is, however, unclear how the undeniable fact of the right's frequent invocation demonstrates its vacuity; rather, that fact surely makes the very opposite inference *prima facie* plausible.

But what, exactly, might the *RECR* entail or support? It is probably too demanding to expect a strict entailment between this very general right and a particular concrete feature of legal institutional design such as *LAJ*. Let us therefore content ourselves with examining less rigorous forms of support, if any, that this right might provide for the latter. There is certainly no bar to the right supporting a policy or form of treatment (like *LAJ*) that is not itself obviously a right. For, although Dworkin regards the *RECR* as abstract and fundamental, and therefore a good basis from which to derive other rights,[67] he also claims that the right can support collective welfare claims. Thus he holds

> that particular political rights, *and* the idea of collective welfare, *and* the idea that these function as antagonists at the level of political debate, are all consequences of the fundamental ideal of a political community as a community of equals.[68]

It is this kind of claim that marks Dworkin as a hedgehog in political theory rather than a fox.

Since there is no in-principle barrier to the *RECR* supporting *LAJ*, it remains to determine whether it actually *does* support it. One way in which it surely does so is this: taking the right seriously ensures a form of equality before the law, namely,

[64] *TRS* (n 6) Chs 6, 9 and 12. The right to equal concern and respect 'appeared' to support the rights thesis because there is no explicit claim to this effect in Ch 4 of *TRS* (although the right does appear in passing at 82). Rather, there is a medley of statements that seemingly license this conclusion: see *TRS*, ibid, 101 in conjunction with xii and xv.

[65] R Dworkin, *A Matter of Principle* (New York, Oxford University Press, 1985) Ch 8.

[66] In *Law's Empire* (n 57 above at 222 and Ch 8) and in *Sovereign Virtue* (above n 9 at 1–3, 128, 131 and 184) the right to equal concern and respect became (just) the right to equal concern or equality of concern. In *Hedgehogs* it appears in a form much closer to its original guise: '[a] political community has no moral power to create and enforce obligations against its members unless it treats them with equal concern and respect' (330). It is also expressed in the form of the equal concern principle (one of the 'reigning principles' for government: ibid, 2; 14) and the equal-worth principle (ibid, 14 and 205).

[67] *TRS* (n 6) xiv–xv.

[68] *TRS* (n 6) 368 (emphasis in original).

that citizens cannot be discriminated against or favoured because of their status, conception of a good life, or overall 'worthiness'. *LAJ* ensures the same kind of equality before the law by prohibiting judicial reference to many of the considerations that the *RECR* also embargoes. Like the *RECR* and the opacity theme of *SPIE*, *LAJ* is a way of ignoring many of the differences between citizens. *LAJ* does not register, except when legal doctrine demands, whether a claimant's style of life is worthy or base, whether she is patrician or plebeian, aesthete or philistine. Citizens are treated as if they were the same by *LAJ* and, if it is genuinely successful in doing this, it therefore functions in much the same way as the *RECR*. If we value that right, in part because of the function it fulfils, must we therefore also value *LAJ* because it fulfils the same function?

There are two immediate objections to an affirmative answer. One holds that similarity of function between *LAJ* and the *RECR* cannot justify. Suppose X (the lawful interrogation of those suspected of crime) functions so as to bring about, or bring us closer to, Y (unearthing the truth). The fact that X is justified tells us nothing about Z, which also functions so as to bring us closer to Y. Unless X and Z are either ultimately identical or otherwise closely connected, there is simply no reason to assume that the justification for the former extends to the latter, even though both have the same function. This is apparent if Z in this example were torture. Torture may well have the same function as lawful interrogation, but the considerations that justify the latter are unlikely, in most circumstances, to extend to the former. Furthermore, it might also be the case that whatever value is realised by some particular institution or institutional feature is best realised only in one context or only in a specified amount. It is then possible that the realisation of this value, or an increase in its amount, brought about by another institution or institutional feature, is a bad thing. Thus, the fact that the *RECR* embodies some or other value warrants neither the conclusion that that value is always and ever valuable, nor that its realisation by other means or in ever greater amounts is always and ever valuable.

It is tempting, in the face of this objection, to try to unearth the considerations that justify or support the *RECR*. It could then be determined whether or not those considerations support *LAJ*. If they can, then there is not only unity of function here but also unity of justification. This line of thought might, however, seem to reinforce the first objection and in fact constitutes the second objection, which holds that the *RECR* is without foundation. This objection once *seemed* true, for Dworkin himself hinted that the search for deeper considerations supporting the *RECR* was more or less fruitless. The right might be derived from Dworkin's abstract egalitarian thesis—that '[f]rom the standpoint of politics, the interests of the members of the community matter, and matter equally'—but that thesis itself was difficult to support.[69] Dworkin offered no positive argument in favour

[69] R Dworkin, 'Comment on Narveson' (1983) 1 *Social Philosophy and Policy* 24–40 at 24 (a seemingly related version of this thesis appears in *Sovereign Virtue* (n 9) at 128–29) and 31–35. Another possible Dworkinian ground for the *RECR* could be the value of integrity, for discussion of

of the thesis, thinking it 'too fundamental … to admit of any defense in the usual form', and was content to show just how hard it was to reject.[70] Rooting the *RECR* in the soil of the abstract egalitarian thesis thus promised few or no dividends in the search for normative support. Moreover, the right's abstract and fundamental status—one factor in its favour being its capacity to support and make sense of many other principles of political morality—suggested a foundational role which rendered pointless any effort to find normative considerations that might support it. However, in light of the overall argument of *Justice for Hedgehogs*, we can now see that the second objection is mistaken.

Hedgehogs points to two fundamental considerations that can provide the *RECR* with normative support. They consist of two very general principles which together constitute Dworkin's conception of dignity. The first is that '[p]eople must take their own lives seriously: they must accept that it is objectively important how they live', while the second holds that people 'must take their ethical responsibility seriously as well: they must insist on the right—and exercise … [it]—to make ethical decisions for themselves'.[71] These are ethical principles, for Dworkin, and thus primarily inform the way in which we live our lives. Yet they also have ramifications for morality—the ways in which we must treat other people—and for both politics and law.[72] Indeed, the two fundamental principles of politics that inform the discussion in part five of *Hedgehogs* are not only 'analogues' of the two ethical principles just noted, they are also a disaggregated version of the *RECR*: the requirement 'that government treat those it governs with equal concern, and a further requirement that it respect … its subjects' ethical responsibilities'.[73] Thus the *RECR*, insofar as it realises or is required by the two fundamental principles of politics, can be founded upon a conception of dignity as constituted by the two ethical principles.

It is important not to misunderstand this claim and, to that end, we must reissue a warning already served: there can be no suggestion that 'founded upon' must mean the *RECR* is derivable, in something like a series of strict entailments, from Dworkin's conception of dignity. That is principally because Dworkin 'argue[s] throughout … [*Hedgehogs*] that in political morality integration is a necessary condition of truth', integration meaning that '[w]e do not secure finally persuasive conceptions of our several political values unless our conceptions mesh'.[74]

which see *Law's Empire* (n 57). Of course, non-Dworkinian justifications for the *RECR* are presumably possible. It might, for example, be derived from a conception of autonomy or public reason or from the type of consideration Narveson highlighted (J Narveson: 'Reply to Dworkin' ibid, at 44); it was rooted in a conception of human dignity by Moreau (n 62 at 295–96) which, in light of the argument of *Hedgehogs*, was prescient.

[70] 'Comment on Narveson', ibid, 31. The approach did not persuade Narveson: 'Reply to Dworkin' ibid, 41–44.

[71] *Hedgehogs* (n 63) at 14.

[72] *Hedgehogs* (n 63) 13 for the ethics/morality distinction.

[73] *Hedgehogs* (n 63) 14.

[74] *Hedgehogs* (n 63) 5–6.

'Mesh' might of course include strict entailment but it seems implausible to think it includes only that. The mesh (or integration) requirement might therefore be satisfied, on a non-technical understanding of those words, by dignity providing the *RECR* with an animating ideal, such that it generates answers to the question 'why equal concern and respect?' In part, the plausibility of suggesting dignity for this role will itself be determined by considerations of integration or mesh, but that is all of apiece with Dworkin's view of his enterprise in *Hedgehogs*. It is to provide a series of interconnected interpretations of our most important ethical, moral and political ideals, such that each can be read in light of the rest and each converges upon the others.[75]

What, then, remains to be said about the way in which the *RECR* might support or be immanent within *LAJ*? That the ethical values instantiated or realised by the *RECR* can, as a purely contingent matter, also be realised by *LAJ*. It might be added that this is a desirable situation, provided we can demonstrate either that the values realised by the *RECR* need not be confined to certain contexts only, or that they do not have an optimum distribution or quantity realisable only by that right. If it is morally important that government conduct is not based upon judgements about the worth of different citizens' lives, then *LAJ* is presumptively just as important as the *RECR*. This claim need not hold that similarity of function always and ever justifies, but only that similarity of function justifies in this particular context (*ceteris paribus*).

Some critics of the *RECR* are, however, sure to be dissatisfied with this argument, primarily because they think that the right itself is a fundamentally flawed idea, albeit on grounds quite different to those informing the complaints that the right is either too general to do any useful work or is without foundation. One of these additional objections should be dismissed at the outset. It denies that the right can entail any genuine form of equality, principally because it is alleged that the invocation of 'equal' in the right is empty. Herbert Hart claimed that what is wrong when the *RECR* is breached by, for instance, legislation denying sexual freedom or freedom of worship is the straightforward restriction of liberty. It is 'fantastic' to suppose that victims of this legislation should complain about not being treated with equal concern and respect.[76] Hart clearly does not accept that the denial of sexual freedom or freedom of religion to one group is a form of unequal treatment, in the sense that they are denied a liberty that other groups enjoy. But the ground for his refusal is unclear. For, since it does not seem in any way unnatural to characterise this situation as one of unequal treatment, why should we refrain from such a characterisation? Hart says that 'equal' in

[75] *Hedgehogs* (n 63) 328.

[76] HLA Hart, *Essays in Jurisprudence and Philosophy* (Oxford, Clarendon Press, 1983) Essay 9 at 220. A related version of this objection, which rather mysteriously insists that 'equal' in the right does not flow 'from a conception of equality but from the fact that … [the right refers] to a group with equal claim to have the right', is offered by J Raz, 'Professor Dworkin's Theory of Rights' XXVI *Political Studies* 123–37, 130.

this characterisation is playing an empty role, but he buttresses the point by changing the example. Were a tyrant to ban *all* forms of religious worship, he says, citizens could not complain that their right to equal concern and respect had been breached, since all have been treated in the same (objectionable) way.[77] In part, that is certainly true. Yet this example raises a different issue from that in which some citizens are allowed freedom of worship and some are not. It should not, therefore, guide what we would say in the latter case. Furthermore, the blanket ban on religious worship could indeed be challenged, in normal circumstances, by reference to the *RECR*. This is because it would be unusual for such a ban ultimately to be based upon anything other than a judgement of the unworthiness of a life informed by religious observance. While the wrong here is non-comparative (because all citizens are treated in the same way), it is still plausibly a breach of the *RECR*. For, in displaying zero concern with and according zero respect for this aspect of citizens' lives, this ban denies what the *RECR* assumes, namely, that citizens should be treated with respect and concern by government and that that respect and concern should be equal.

Two related objections might still be tabled by critics. One holds that the *RECR* cannot reliably entail or support anything because it is internally contradictory. The contradiction arises from the conflict between the right's two key components, respect and concern. The other objection, by contrast, concedes that the right may well support *LAJ* in the limited, functional way just noted, but affirms that the right also supports models of judgement incompatible with *LAJ*. The argument that the right is internally contradictory is at best inchoate; certainly it has never been explicitly unpacked. The point is usually made in passing and consists only of noting a possible and plausible difference between respect and concern, namely, that the latter is consistent with paternalism while the former is not.[78] This clearly falls far short of demonstrating that these two notions (and the right they constitute) cannot be combined because contradictory. This would require a demonstration that in every, most or many instances in which the right is in play, its different components pull in opposite directions. That this is not the case in a number of instances is clearly affirmed by Dworkin's own invocations of the right in such different contexts as reverse discrimination, civil disobedience and euthanasia.[79] While it must be conceded to these critics that the *RECR* is certainly complex, that does not show it to be internally contradictory.

For the second objection to succeed, it would have to establish that the opposite to *LAJ*—a form of purely particularistic judgement—fulfils the same function

[77] Hart, ibid, 221.

[78] Raz (n 76) at 130. A closely related version of this objection, briefly but judiciously stated (there is 'on the face of it' a conflict between these two components) is offered by R Sartorius in his essay in M Cohen (ed), *Ronald Dworkin and Contemporary Jurisprudence* (London, Duckworth, 1983) at 208–09. Dworkin's subsequent use of the bare 'equal concern' formulation, in which respect drops out of the picture (see above n 66 for references), could be explained as a recognition of the power of this objection.

[79] See *TRS* (n 6) Chs 8 and 9 and R Dworkin, *Life's Dominion* (New York, Vintage Books, 1993) Ch 7.

as the *RECR*. It seems unlikely that such a case can be made. This is principally because forms of particularistic judgement give free reign to considerations excluded from judicial and other government decisions by that right. On what grounds, for instance, would a form of particularistic judgement exclude a defendant's view of his own superiority as a good reason for risky conduct? Since for this defendant the interests of others are plainly less significant than his own, and since this belief informs his conduct, how can it be excluded as a relevant factor in determining his liability? Similarly, a defendant who accepts the belief, widespread in her community, that it is right to kill her children and herself in the face of marital infidelity would seem, on a particularistic model of judgement, to have grounds for a defence. If such considerations—presumably deeply held and in some sense constitutive of the defendant's identity—are excluded, then the form of judgement in play cannot be exclusively particularistic. The right to equal concern and respect is a tempting and serviceable basis upon which to exclude such considerations, although it is clearly not the only possible basis. Yet the mere fact that the right functions in this way serves to show its incompatibility with models of particularistic judgement.

Since the *RECR* can stand firm in the face of these criticisms, it can also offer normative support to *LAJ*. That support takes the form of providing a broad egalitarian rationale for some of *LAJ*'s features: the reasons why law's judgement is abstract—why it ignores so much about those to whom it applies—can be derived from or found in large part in the *RECR* and the values it serves. Thus *LAJ* can be seen as a legal-institutional manifestation of the *RECR*'s general embargo upon the state making comparative judgements about the worth of citizens' lives or conceptions of the good. That embargo is, of course, hedged about with various rather obvious limits—conceptions of the good contrary to this liberal, egalitarian conception cannot easily be accommodated—but they do not in any way undermine the connection between the right and *LAJ*. Furthermore, there is a great distance between this abstract right and the embargo it entails, on the one hand, and its realisation at the practical level of legal doctrine and institutional design, on the other. But, again, this does not of itself sever the connection. What, then, does it mean to claim that the *RECR* is immanent within *LAJ*? That the rationale and values of the former, in large part at least, can constitute the rationale and values of the latter (in large part at least).

A final point must be noted about the *RECR*. It takes us back to one of the principal issues in the discussion of luck egalitarianism and *SPIE*, namely, that of what should be distributed and how. One complaint against luck egalitarianism is that it is primarily a distributive conception of equality, concerned mainly with the distribution of some 'thing' (welfare, resources, advantage or opportunities for one or other of these) by means of respectable principles. As to *SPIE*, one difficulty is that its distributive component is, on any assessment, underspecified, although some proponents of that position converge upon the capabilities/functionings framework. What does the *RECR* distribute and why? Does it really have any distributive commitments, over and beyond insisting upon an equality of respect and concern? Of course, in Dworkin's hands the right is the basis of equality of resources, his substantive account of equality. But the connection between the former and the latter is, again, by no means a tight series of entailments.[80] Rather, it seems that the *RECR* could function as the foundation for a number of different distributive accounts of equality in much the same way as numerous differently shaped buildings could be constructed upon the same foundational 'footprint'. Is this a problem? Not for our immediate purpose, which is to unearth potential normative props for *LAJ*. But the *RECR* must at some point be translated into a distributive currency, insofar as a distributive programme is a hallmark of any respectable egalitarian position.

III. Difference, Confluence, Connections

Suppose the arguments just offered do indeed show some connections between *SPIE* and the *RECR*, on the one hand, and *LAJ*, on the other. Why might that matter? There are many reasons, but the salient one for current purposes is this: demonstrating these connections is another way of showing that *LAJ*'s moral and political value cannot be zero. Or, at least, it cannot be zero if *SPIE* and the *RECR* are indeed morally and politically valuable. If they are, then that reduces the space for scepticism about *LAJ*. There are, however, at least two grounds for doubting that the arguments offered so far have been successful. One questions whether or not the connections I purport to have established are made out, on the basis that it is ultimately unclear what they consist in; the other holds that the nature of the connections between *LAJ*, on the one hand, and *SPIE* and the *RECR*, on the other, is irrelevant because the very idea of treating *SPIE* and the *RECR* together, as if in some important respects the same, is a mistake. They are chalk and cheese. If that is so, then this seemingly calls into question the utility of highlighting any relationship between them and *LAJ*. I examine each doubt in the order just stated and then, in the remainder of this section, restate the significance of the argument offered above and elucidate another set of connections, this time between dignity, equality of standing and community.

The blanket term I have most often used as a general description of the relation between *LAJ*, on the one hand, and *SPIE* and the *RECR*, on the other, is that the latter are immanent within the former. That term actually covered a range of more particular and slightly different relations. So, for instance, at one point I claimed that the *RECR* can provide a broad egalitarian rationale for some of *LAJ*'s features and, at another point, that *SPIE*'s opacity theme overlaps with two of *LAJ*'s components. These claims are not of exactly the same standing; furthermore, they keep company with other slightly different connections that I have highlighted between

[80] Cohen noted this ('*If you're an Egalitarian …*', n 9 at 165), as did Sher (n 40) at 58 and 70.

LAJ and these conceptions of equality. In the face of this range of connections—not quite a multiplicity but certainly more than two—a critic might well object that the language of immanence is misleading. The use of a single term here is masking a range of different relationships and making matters appear neater than they really are. To that exact charge I plead guilty. I have indeed used a blanket term as a neater way of characterising a range of connections. But those connections are all fairly close and that, alongside a penchant for neatness, explains the usage. Those connections are also, as I hope to have shown, undeniable and that is so whatever language we use to characterise them.

The second objection strikes at the propriety of regarding *SPIE* and the *RECR* as significantly similar. The objection clearly cannot be that they are dissimilar, since that much is apparent from the discussion in section II. The complaint must, then, be something like this: *SPIE* and the *RECR* are so radically different in terms of their argumentative status that they should not be lumped together under any circumstances. The *RECR* is a very general and abstract starting point or axiom for more substantive political positions, principally egalitarian; by contrast, *SPIE* is one such substantive egalitarian position. Since, on this view, *SPIE* and *RECR* occupy different logical space, the effort to show that each one supports *LAJ* cannot illustrate the bluntness hypothesis touted in chapter one. That holds, remember, that various aspects of legal institutional design might be either normatively over- or under-determined. The first possibility is realised if and when some aspect of legal institutional design—*LAJ*, for example—can be supported by or is derivable from one or more value. This chapter, taken in conjunction with chapter four attempts to show that; some conceptions of dignity and of equality seem well suited to act as *LAJ*'s moral-cum-political anchors. Furthermore, this claim is extended by the argument of the current chapter for, in showing that *SPIE* and the *RECR* both support *LAJ*, it also shows that *LAJ* is normatively over-determined *from within the domain of equality*. The objection under consideration would deny this point by denying any significant similarity between *SPIE* and the *RECR*.

It is both possible and plausible to accept, in part at least, some of the substance of this objection while denying it any critical force. The acceptable part of the objection is that *SPIE* and the *RECR* are plainly different and in the sense already stated. That cannot be denied. But why is that difference so significant? We are in the domain of equality, after all. It cannot be denied that both *SPIE* and the *RECR* are deeply, significantly egalitarian. That being so, how can it be a mistake to treat them together? It seems difficult to move from the undeniable truth that *SPIE* and the *RECR* do indeed occupy different logical space to either of these conclusions: (i) that they therefore have nothing in common; and (ii) that they therefore cannot be treated together. Indeed, it is tempting to hold that the difference between *SPIE* and *RECR* adds to the power of our case, in this way: here are two different conceptions of equality—one a substantive but nascent conception, the other a fundamental egalitarian assumption—both of which support *LAJ*. Are two sources of normative support better than one?

Yes, provided they generate independent, non-competitive reasons in support of *LAJ*. Which is to say, these two sources of normative support must be: (i) non-identical (independent); and (ii) one can in principle be affirmed and accepted without denying the other (non-competitive). It is common for reasons to relate in this way. In the effort to satisfy my hunger, it would not be odd for me to pick foodstuffs that are both nourishing and tasty. That these two considerations constitute independent reasons is clear from the fact that they can pull in quite different directions—sometimes nourishing options are far from appetising and tasty ones have little nutritional value. That these reasons are in principle non-competitive is plain from the fact that they can also often pull in the same direction, a nourishing option also being tasty. If both conditions are satisfied with regard to the reasons *SPIE* and the *RECR* generate, then those reasons can cohere with one another in the sense that they can be prayed in aid of something not identical to them, such as *LAJ*. This is true even though it seems unlikely that one can consistently espouse both *SPIE* and *RECR* as part of a single, coherent view of equality. At least, one could not do this without ranking the two, since it seems possible for them to pull in different directions in one and the same instance: recall that in Dworkin's hands the *RECR* seemingly requires choice-sensitive equality of resources and that looks quite different from *SPIE*'s distributive injunctions. Although the issue of whether or not *SPIE* and the *RECR* are combinable in a single conception of equality will be of interest to those building such conceptions, it is of little concern here. Our aim has been to determine whether or not these two conceptions can act as normative props for *LAJ* and the answer is affirmative.

That *LAJ* stands not only at the confluence of two conceptions of equality, but also at the meeting point of those conceptions and the value-status conception of dignity, does not rule out the possibility of *LAJ* having other apparently independent normative props. So, for example, I have tried to show elsewhere that *LAJ* obtains some normative support from two closely related accounts of the wrongs of unequal treatment.[81] This possibility is entirely unsurprising if the bluntness hypothesis is true.

As to the link between dignity and equality, it seems obvious that there is some connection: some philosophers have even sought to derive the latter from the former and many think the two are linked in less stringent ways.[82] For us they look, from one perspective, like different sides of the same coin. The value-status conception of dignity holds that all have exactly the same high status, that being a

[81] See my 'Abstraction and Equality' in C O'Cinneide (ed), *Current Legal Problems* 2009 (Oxford, Clarendon Press, 2009) Ch 2, 22–70 at 51–62 (discussing T Scanlon, 'The Diversity of Objections to Inequality', Ch 11 of his *The Difficulty of Tolerance* (Cambridge, Cambridge University Press, 2003) and Moreau (n 62)).

[82] One of the most interesting attempted derivations is offered by Ian Carter, who suggests that dignity, understood in terms of what he calls 'agential dignity' and 'outward dignity', constitutes one condition for opacity respect, itself a basis for claims of equal treatment: see his 'Respect and the Basis of Equality' (2011) 121 *Ethics* 538–71 at 550–60.

matter of everyone's equal incomparable value. Both *SPIE* and the *RECR* endorse equality of standing and both also have recourse to broadly Kantian conceptions of respect and dignity. Furthermore, opacity, a significant feature of the value-status conception, figures in both *SPIE* and *RECR*. It might therefore seem artificial to separate dignity and equality in the way we have. Tackling each in different chapters serves to obscure the many important and also, perhaps, quite vaguely formulated connections between them. A properly critical interrogation of the relation between the two notions is certainly overdue, but that task cannot be tackled here. There is, however, one reason for treating dignity and equality separately and it is found in my claim, early in chapter four, that the former is in one respect an ineluctably individualistic notion. Equality, in one aspect at least, is principally a matter of standing and one rarely stands alone: equality of standing is a matter of one's relationship within a group. The idea of a group, alongside its relationship with the notion of community, is the fulcrum of the next chapter. The argumentative arc of chapters four, five and six thus moves from individual to group and then to community.

6

Community

'Are we not forty-six million individuals, all different?'[1]

'[T]he concept of community is broad and inherently fuzzy'.[2]

'A community is a group of people united by a bond of reciprocity, a sentiment of joint exploration, and a shared set of hurdles to be overcome and hopes to be realised'.[3]

On the picture painted in previous chapters, law's abstract judgement (*LAJ*) embodies a form of belonging. The model of belonging it manifests is egalitarian and inclusionary, in the sense that *LAJ* assumes that the same standards apply to all, all being taken to have the same bundle of legal entitlements and burdens and all being regarded as the same in important respects. Everyone is taken to have the same high status and value, everyone is presumed to have the same legal standing and all are, initially at least, relatively opaque to one another. Just by virtue of regarding all addressees of the law in these ways, *LAJ* performs an inclusionary role. In actually regarding, or even just aspiring to regard, all addressees of the law as fundamentally the same, *LAJ* and the legal systems of which it is part stand in vivid contrast to feudal legality.[4] Make no mistake: regarding all addressees of the law as the same entails excluding or ignoring a great deal of information about the character, context and conduct of those addressees. But it is also simultaneously and undeniably a matter of inclusion, a lumping together of all before the law's maw.

There is, however, an obvious problem. For to say that 'all' have or are presumed to have the same standing, or that 'everyone' is treated in the same way, is to affirm a relationship without the hard work of delineating who counts as 'all' or 'everyone'. In order to offer an adequate account of belonging, we must illuminate not only the nature of the relationship and why, if at all, it might be thought valuable—respectively the 'what' and the 'why' questions—but also determine who belongs and how they come to belong (the 'who' and the 'how' questions). These four questions are related, and not just in the sense that each requires a plausible

[1] G Orwell, *Why I Write* (London, Penguin Books, 2004) 12.

[2] A Mason, *Community, Solidarity and Belonging* (Cambridge, Cambridge University Press, 2000) 41.

[3] P Rosanvallon, *The Society of Equals* (Cambridge, Massachusetts, Harvard University Press, 2013) 288–89.

[4] As was noted in chapter one, section II A.

answer in order for a model of belonging to pass muster. The answer to one question might determine the nature of the answer to the others in a more demanding way than that, as we will see below.

These four questions structure this chapter. I tackle the who and how questions first, in section I, while the what and why questions, which receive most attention, animate section II. This order of treatment is most salient for the simple reason that we already have some sense of the nature of the relationship that *LAJ* establishes. That is not to say that that relationship is unproblematic and raises no questions—far from it. Yet the who and how questions are, in the context of our discussion so far, altogether newer and seemingly more problematic, although our answer to them is relatively brief and simple. Not only are these two questions natural bedfellows, since the answer to one almost automatically gives an answer to the other, they also have some degree of priority over the what and why questions. That is because any attempted characterisation of a relationship must first surely explain how its parts can come into relation. I treat what and why questions as a bundle because specifying the nature of a relationship quite naturally gives rise to questions about its value, about why it may be worth bringing into being or maintaining.

I. Who and How?

One is caught in the maw of *LAJ*, and thus falls into the relationship it establishes among its addressees, by accident or choice. The accident in question may differ slightly—it may be that of being born and remaining in a jurisdiction until majority or that of straying into a jurisdiction—while the choice is simply that of entering a jurisdiction legally or illegally. Whichever characterisation best fits one's presence in a jurisdiction does not matter much for the purposes of *LAJ*, since it applies to one almost regardless. I say 'almost regardless' because the legal status of one's presence in a jurisdiction can ultimately determine the exact bundle of rights and duties one has, which *LAJ* presumes to be equal; it can also determine the procedures and processes the law uses in relation to one, as well as the remedies one might avail oneself of and the sanctions to which one might be liable, which *LAJ* presumes to be the same for all. Generally, if one's presence in a jurisdiction is illegal, then one's rights and duties, as well as the processes, sanctions and liabilities to which one is subject are not exactly the same as those had by and applied to the legally present.[5] The latter status is usually taken for granted until proven

[5] See R Thwaites, *The Liberty of Non-Citizens: Indefinite Detention in Commonwealth Countries* (Oxford, Hart Publishing, 2014) for discussion of one particularly significant difference. K Kim, *Aliens in Medieval Law: The Origins of Modern Citizenship* (Cambridge, Cambridge University Press, 2000) is a fascinating study of English law's early attempts to police this boundary.

otherwise in any legal action; you are therefore presumed subject to *LAJ*, presumed to have the same rights and duties as all other addressees of the law, presumed to have the same capacities and abilities, and presumed to be subject to the same legal standards as they are.

If being in a jurisdiction is the way in which one is co-opted into *LAJ*'s mode of belonging, then that means of entry depends for its existence upon the fulfilment of two other conditions which, however obvious, are worth pointing out. One, of course, is the existence of a legal system of which *LAJ* is part; we presupposed such a system in the previous paragraph when we spoke of 'jurisdictions'. In the central sense, we mean by this term a (usually functioning) legal system that claims authority over certain issues and persons, often within the confines of a particular place or area. And that brings us to the second condition, namely, the existence of a nation-state. These are often but not always loci of jurisdictions, of legal systems, and the range of the latter often map onto the territorial boundaries of nation-states. The connection between legal systems and nation-states is not a necessary one, since the former can plainly exist in some form without the existence of the latter; we are also familiar in the contemporary world with supranational legal systems that transcend the boundaries of particular nation-states.[6] Since it is also not uncommon to find different legal systems within the confines of single nation-states—think, for instance of federal jurisdictions or those like the UK—we cannot assume a simple one-to-one correspondence between the number of nation-states and the number of legal systems or jurisdictions.

LAJ is a feature of capitalist or bourgeois or mercantile legal systems and they were, and to a great extent still are, products of the nation-state. *LAJ* requires the existence of a legal system and they are normally found within the confines of nation-states. For current purposes, I'll stipulate that the latter, which will often be referred to simply as 'states' or 'the state', refers to bodies united by ties of nationality that succeed in claiming a monopoly on the legitimate use of force in a particular territory.[7] As to legal systems, they are usually recognisable and individualisable, in part at least, by reference to distinct rules of recognition, different systems having different rules.[8] Both issues—about the nature of the state and the identification of legal systems—are much more problematic than this treatment suggests, but those problems are not central to anything that follows.

The answer the two previous paragraphs provide to the how question doubles as a partial answer to the who question, since one reply—'anyone present in the

[6] For the first possibility, see S Roberts, *Order and Dispute* (London, Penguin Books, 1979); on the second, see J Dickson and P Eleftheriadis (eds), *Philosophical Foundations of European Union Law* (Oxford, Clarendon Press, 2012).

[7] The 'state' bit of the stipulation follows M Weber, 'Politics as a Vocation' in HH Gerth and C Wright Mills (eds), *From Max Weber: Essays in Sociology* (London, Routledge and Kegan Paul, 1970) 78, while the 'nation' component tracks D Miller, *On Nationality* (Oxford, Clarendon Press, 1995) Chs 2 and 3. On this view of nationality, there are conceivably many more nationalities than nation-states.

[8] HLA Hart, *The Concept of Law*, 2nd edn (Oxford, Clarendon Press, 1994) Chs V and VI.

jurisdiction'—will almost completely suffice for both. Only 'almost' because the 'anyone' in this answer must be unpacked so as to provide a full response to the who question: in the jurisdictions with which we are familiar, 'anyone' must actually be a legal person and that means either a natural person capable of being responsible ('of majority' is a common short-hand for this; slightly longer-winded is 'of sufficient age to be regarded as legally responsible'), or a corporation.[9] Both answers are rife with contingency and that, to some eyes, might seem dubious. Chance of age and birth, as well as chance of geographical location, may be thought an unsuitable basis for something so significant as the combination of rights and duties, liabilities and powers, standing and treatment that *LAJ* (and the law in general) metes out. Being a few days short of or beyond a particular birthday can have momentous consequences with regard to the legal sanctions one faces. If one is just shy of the age of responsibility and implicated in ostensibly criminal conduct, then that will often mean that one is caught 'only' in the various child welfare procedures that are a significant feature of many regimes of family law. Being days beyond that boundary usually propels one into the 'normal' system of criminal law. The latter may well taint one's life far more severely than the former, a criminal conviction having a more adverse effect upon one's life chances than entanglement with systems of 'child welfare'.[10]

Furthermore, being born either side of a national border can make a huge difference not only to one's overall life-chances—nation Y might, for example, be in the grip of famine and civil war while adjacent nation X is not—but also to the nature and content of the law that applies to one. Nation X's legal system could be characterised by *LAJ* while nation Y's is not. Less dramatic legal differences are clearly the stuff of everyday work and travel for some. Citizens of states within the European Union can move from one state to another on a daily basis for work or leisure and thereby subject themselves to more or less different legal regimes (there being differences in taxation, welfare, health benefits and many other matters as between EU states). Within federal states such changes are also fairly commonplace: the speed limit on interstate highways might be the same in both New Jersey and Delaware, but only the latter has a 'permissive' legal-regulatory regime for large corporations.

The contingencies upon which *LAJ*'s mode of belonging is founded look much the same as those that determine citizenship and nationality, each of which are conditioned in roughly similar ways by chance. Of course, it is possible to make each subject to some kind of formal endorsement at some point. We might, for

[9] See chapter 3, section I for discussion of basic responsibility.

[10] The Swedish cohort study is a fascinating starting point for thinking about the effects of convictions on life chances: see O Bäckman, F Estrada, A Nilsson and D Shannon, 'The Life-Course of Young Male and Female Offenders' (2014) 54 *British Journal of Criminology* 393–410; O Bäckman and A Nilsson, 'Pathways to Social Exclusion: A Life-Course Study' (2011) 27 *European Sociological Review* 107–23; and A Nilsson and F Estrada, 'Established or Excluded? A Longitudinal Study of Criminality, Work and Family Formation' (2011) 8 *European Journal of Criminology* 229–45.

example, insist that when those present in a particular jurisdiction reach a certain age, they must choose whether or not to be citizens or to bear that nationality. While something like this process is used in some states with regard to newly arrived immigrants, it is far from ubiquitous, and it is rarely applied to those born in the jurisdiction.[11] Explicit affirmation is not, it seems, a precondition for either citizenship or nationality in many actually existing states and, if we make it so as a matter of theory, we thereby risk not only making our theory redundant, but also miss a chance to explain something apparently important and pressing about our current practice. Taking that chance does not guarantee we will find an intellectually coherent, normatively compelling justification for current practice.

If little more than presence in the jurisdiction constitutes membership in the putative group 'addressees of *LAJ*', then more must be said about the contingency complaint. And the first additional thing to say is this: what exactly is the nature of the complaint? Our initial statement of it highlighted the alleged *unsuitability* of the factors that determine when and whether *LAJ* applies to one: those factors are *inter alia* contingencies of age, birth and location. But, since we are all born without control over where and when that happens, the complaint cannot be about that ubiquitous condition; it must instead be about the quality or significance of that condition. The contingencies that define it could be regarded as robbing it of any moral power. There are three grounds for thinking this. The first is an echo of Hume's law, a denial that these contingent facts can create any kind of moral status, while the second takes chance and moral salience to be opposites. The former can be dubbed the 'Humean objection' and can be dealt with fairly quickly, while the latter is best labelled 'the chance objection'. The chance objection, together with the third ground for thinking contingency negates moral significance or standing ('the denial of specificity objection'), require more of our time and attention.

As is well known, Hume's law holds that an 'ought' cannot be derived from an 'is'.[12] In the current context, the Humean objection therefore holds that, insofar as the 'fact' of being in a jurisdiction purports to be the basis for the derivation of that series of 'oughts' which constitute the rights and duties which are a component of *LAJ*, then that derivation is a mistake. The point is undeniable but irrelevant. No derivation from 'is' to 'ought' is in play insofar as the fact of one's presence in a jurisdiction marks one's entry into a web of pre-existing normative systems. The 'oughts' that are in part constitutive of *LAJ* exist as a component of one such system and one feels their force as a result of entry. The social world is, on this view, already unavoidably and inextricably normative, not a realm of

[11] For discussion of the British citizenship test, see T Brooks, 'The "Life in the United Kingdom" Citizenship Test: Is it Unfit for Purpose?' at http://papers.ssrn.com/sol3/papers.cfm?abstract_id=2280329 (last accessed 11th July 2016).

[12] D Hume, *A Treatise of Human Nature* (DF Norton and MJ Norton (eds)) (Oxford, Clarendon Press, 2007) Vol 1, Book 3, Part 1, s 1. Some of the classic essays on Hume's principle are gathered together in WD Hudson (ed), *The Is-Ought Question* (London, Macmillan, 1969) and in VC Chappell (ed), *Hume: A Collection of Critical Essays* (London, Macmillan, 1968).

non-normative fact upon which we place a seemingly optional normative overlay. Much can be said about the ultimate basis of the 'oughts' generated by the normative social world, yet there is no need to invoke some non-moral factual realm as their foundation. The strangest thing one needs posit, on such a view, is a relatively unproblematic realm of normative fact.[13] Hume's law need not, therefore, detain us further.

What of the chance objection? It holds that anything over which I lack control—like where and when I was born—has zero moral significance and, by contrast, that everything over which I have (some?) control has some moral significance.[14] Hence the accident of my place and time of birth may well determine the amalgam of rights and duties, liabilities and powers, standing and treatment that I bear and receive, but that of itself has no moral import. The duties imposed or the rights obtained by the sheer chance of my presence in the jurisdiction are morally null, at least until such time as I rationally endorse them.

This line of thought has the paradoxical quality of seeming both intuitively right and intuitively wrong. From the perspective of what I morally deserve, it seems absolutely right, since in one central sense we regard desert as contingent upon our conduct or, at the very least, our aims. What we morally deserve, on this view, is a function of what we have done or of what we tried to do; we receive praise and blame not just for our deeds, but also for our efforts. And, in locutions such as these, we usually mean by 'our conduct' and 'our deeds' something like 'events over which we have had (some degree of) control'. Here we have the opposition between chance and control that seemingly informs the chance objection. Yet it appears equally plain that sheer contingency does nothing at all to undermine some of our moral duties and responsibilities. If, while hiking, I discover an injured fellow hiker, my moral obligation to aid her is in no way affected by the fact that I came upon her by chance; nor would that obligation either arise or vanish if, knowing of her whereabouts, I had avoided her. My obligation to aid is the same whether or not I come upon the party in peril by chance or by design. This apparent paradox is, of course, just that; it is illusory, since our moral standing is sometimes responsive to those situations in the world we have brought about and sometimes not. The moral duties I have to those in peril nearby I have *regardless* of whether or not I have contributed to that situation, whereas the moral duties that arise from the contracts I enter derive almost entirely from the fact that I *entered* into those contracts.

So, if the idea that we can incur obligations as a matter of chance, by simply being in a particular place at a specific time, and the idea that our moral standing is sometimes affected by what we do or control, are both entrenched in our moral

[13] For some alleged problems with the idea of normative facts, see SP Turner, *Explaining the Normative* (Cambridge, Polity Press, 2010).

[14] Lest this view be thought a flight of fancy on my part, recall the discussion of luck egalitarianism in chapter five, section I B.

lives, then the chance objection must be reformulated. It cannot be a blanket objection to chance determining our moral standing, unless it is also a debunking challenge to that common feature of moral experience.[15] Interpreted as consistent with moral experience, it must therefore hold that the package of obligations, rights, etc that *LAJ* imposes and confers are misplaced when categorised as 'being determined by chance'. They must instead be regarded as 'products of choice or other forms of control'. Of course, the complaint cannot then continue along the lines of 'if they are not such products, then they lack moral weight'. Were it to do so, it would take on the debunking role just eschewed. Since moral experience tells us that our moral standing can be influenced by factors beyond our control, and since the chance objection *ex hypothesi* accepts that, the complaint must be one about mis-categorisation.

How can the mis-categorisation version of the chance objection get off the ground? I am not sure it can. It must begin, first, by assuming a close similarity for present purposes between legal and moral duties. It could then claim that our picture of the way in which *LAJ* confers and imposes various duties and rights might be question-begging, ruling out in the very terms of its construction an alternative picture. But what might such an alternative look like? Insofar as the alternative insists that the kind of duties and rights *LAJ* metes out can only come into being as a result of either independent rational endorsement by those they bind, on the one hand, or their involvement (by voting, for example) in the process that creates the law's constitutive of *LAJ*, on the other, then it collapses back into the debunking view.[16] Both possibilities rule out, by stipulation, the possibility of duties arising from chance or, at least, factors beyond our control. Furthermore, there is no reason to think that the view offered here of the ways in which *LAJ*'s duties and rights come into being is incompatible with duties and rights having other bases. Our claim is not an imperialistic one, holding that rights and duties can only come into being as a result of contingency. It is much narrower than that, holding only that this particular set of rights and duties come into being in that way and, in addition, that that broad possibility is not unknown to ordinary moral experience. If the mis-categorisation objection allows that possibility, then what argument can be offered to show that the rights and duties *LAJ* metes out are, despite appearances, not products of chance? If these duties are either the product of a non-contingent divine will, or somehow written into and thence read off the fabric of the universe, then fine: they are assuredly answers to the question. The problem, of course, is

[15] I could be accused of privileging ordinary moral experience and I do, in this sense: I take it seriously until there is good reason to do otherwise. I do not thereby imply that it is uncomplicated or unproblematic. For deft delineation of some of its fault-lines in this context, see S Scheffler, *Boundaries and Allegiances* (New York, Oxford University Press, 2001) at 63–64 and 68–70.

[16] The first alternative is a manifestation of what Scheffler (ibid, 54–59; 68–69) called 'the volunarist objection' to, and 'assimilationist' treatments of, familial, fraternal and similar group- or context-based obligations; the second is close to the view of equality before (or under) the law in R Bellamy, *Political Constitutionalism* (Cambridge, Cambridge University Press, 2007) Ch 2, esp 80–83.

that recourse to answers of either type undermines the general position they are supposed to bolster.

There is one other, slightly strained reading of the contingency complaint that merits attention. It is the denial of specificity objection. What is meant by specificity in this context is that the duties and rights *LAJ* imposes and confers are jurisdictionally limited: it attaches legal and possibly moral priority to those within the jurisdiction. My duties to other members of the alleged group constituted by *LAJ*'s jurisdictional range seemingly trump duties to those outwith the group; similarly, within the group, my rights seemingly trump the rights of those outside the group. The denial of specificity objection holds that our moral duties are nowhere near as narrowly circumscribed or specific as just implied: they are not dependent for their strength or range upon membership of some or other group. David Miller neatly characterised the objection, albeit within the context of nationality, thus:

> [i]n acknowledging a national identity, I am also acknowledging that I owe special obligations to fellow members of my nation which I do not owe to other human beings. This proposition is a contentious one, for it seems to cut against a powerful humanitarian sentiment which can be expressed by saying that every human being should matter equally to us. Each person can feel happiness and pain, each person can feel respected when his or her claims are recognised and demeaned when they are not, so how can it be right to give priority or special treatment to some human beings just because they are tied to us by ... bonds [of nationality]? From an ethical point of view, nationality may seem to give our feelings for our compatriots a role in our practical reasoning that is rationally indefensible.[17]

This objection can easily be extended to *LAJ*. Replacing the terms 'national identity', 'nationality', 'nation' and 'compatriots' in the statement with 'group-identity', 'group', '*LAJ*' and 'group-members' extends the point to a slightly different context, but its force seems just as powerful. How can our moral duties be circumscribed, either by the boundaries of some or other national grouping or by some or other jurisdiction?

This looks like a significant problem, even if we ignore the rather quick assimilation of legal and moral duties that is required to give it force against *LAJ*. Miller's response to it begins by associating the sentiment in question with ethical universalism, a picture of the ethically significant constituents of the world. Chief among them are 'individuals with their generic human capacities' who

> stand apart and prior to their relationships to other individuals. Each person is an agent capable of making choices surrounded by a universe of other such agents, and the principles of ethics specify what he must do towards them, and what he may claim in return from them. Because the principles are to be universal in form, only general facts about other individuals can serve to determine my duties towards them.[18]

[17] Miller (n 7) 49.
[18] Miller (n 7) 50.

On this picture, the kind of limited, context-specific and ostensibly ethical considerations that seemingly underpin our duties to family members, compatriots and the like are insignificant. Or, more accurately, they are insignificant if they do not derive from either universal principles, on the one hand, or from the powers individuals have to create such duties under consent or convention, on the other (the recognition of those powers presumably deriving from acceptance of some or other universal principle). Miller's view is that neither option is genuinely available to the defender of duties of nationality and he is right about that. But that also means neither option is open to defenders of limited duties like those *LAJ* imposes.

It does not, however, follow from this that the denial of specificity objection undermines the argument offered here about the limited context-specific duties to which *LAJ* gives rise. It will follow if ethical universalism is the only view about the ethically significant constituents of the world available. But it is not. An alternative view—ethical particularism—accommodates context-specific duties easily:

> '[i]t invokes a different picture of the ethical universe, in which agents are already encumbered with a variety of ties and commitments to particular other agents, or to groups or collectivities, and they begin their ethical reasoning from those commitments'.[19]

Yet it also accepts the broad humanitarian duties and the sentiment animating them that ethical universalism affirms, the principal difference being that, on the particularist account, the former are only one of two general types of duty and they do not dominate. The duties that arise from our particular context and commitments usually do.

Clearly, ethical particularism constitutes a more favourable habitat for the argument about the nature of *LAJ*'s duties than ethical universalism. What is also equally clear, is that the dispute between particularism and universalism cannot be resolved here (it might not be resolvable at all). Thus, having nailed *LAJ*'s colours to particularism's mast, we can move on to the final point about the how question. If presence in the jurisdiction is enough to confer membership in the alleged group 'those subject to *LAJ*', then it is also enough to create obligations. If *LAJ* does anything, it imposes obligations. Some might cavil at this, albeit for two quite different reasons. The first is this: the fact that the law appears to impose legal (and moral) obligations does not show that it does indeed succeed in imposing genuine legal (and moral) obligations. That point must always be borne in mind and is not incompatible with anything said here. The second cavil is substantive and takes this form: if the legal obligations *LAJ* imposes are also political obligations, then *LAJ* cannot create genuine obligations of the latter stripe because genuine political obligations, including the obligation to obey the law, can only arise from consent. And, *ex hypothesi*, consent cannot always be the basis of *LAJ*'s obligations because consent is not always the basis of one's presence in a jurisdiction.

[19] Miller (n 7) 50.

The most that can be said, on this view, is that the obligations *LAJ* metes out are putative obligations, transformable into genuine obligations only if an argument from consent is available for that purpose. No such argument is, I think, at hand.[20]

Is this a problem? Not unless consent is the *only* means of bringing political (and legal) obligations into being. But there are at least three other ways of attempting to justify political obligation without recourse to consent, each designed to work in its absence. The obligations *LAJ* imposes, if they are to be genuine, must therefore be rooted in an argument from the principle of fairness, from a natural duty of justice or from associative obligation.[21] These arguments are not without difficulties, but nor are they obviously more problematic than, nor always invalidated by versions of, the argument from consent. The latter possibility depends upon *all* versions of the argument from consent also being refutations of *all* arguments from fairness, justice, and associative obligation. They are not.[22]

A brief summary before we turn to the what and why questions. In response to the question, 'who is included in *LAJ*'s mode of belonging?' I've answered, with a few qualifications, 'those present in the jurisdiction'. My response to the question 'how does one come to be co-opted into *LAJ*'s mode of belonging?' is: by choice or by chance. With regard to the latter, I denied that the contingency complaint (in the form of the Humean, the chance, and the denial of specificity objections) is troublesome. Finally, I noted that the obligations *LAJ* metes out are unlikely to be founded upon consent, principally because that notion is in itself problematic, but also because relatively few of those present in a jurisdiction are there as a result of an explicit choice to enter the jurisdiction.

II. What and Why?

A. Three questions

LAJ is a presumptive form of belonging and inclusion. Every adult in the jurisdiction is presumed to have the same value and standing, the same bundle

[20] The classic discussion of consent as the basis of political obligation is sections 95–99 and 119–22 of Locke's second treatise: J Locke, *Two Treatises of Government* (edited by P Laslett) (Cambridge, Cambridge University Press, 1988). Locke's recourse to tacit consent as a means of avoiding the difficulties that flow from regarding consent as the only basis of political authority is richly problematic: see AJ Simmons, 'Tacit Consent and Political Obligation' (1976) 5 *Philosophy and Public Affairs* 274–91 for acute discussion.

[21] One of the best discussions of the former is G Klosko, *The Principle of Fairness and Political Obligation* (Lanham, Rowman and Littlefield, 2004); a classic instance of the second is J Rawls, *A Theory of Justice*, revised edn (Oxford, Oxford University Press, 1999) 93–101 and 293–308, while R Dworkin, *Law's Empire* (Oxford, Hart Publishing, 1998; first published 1986) (hereinafter referred to as '*LE*') Ch 6 is a fine example of the third.

[22] Other potential grounds for political obligation do not loom large in Locke (n 20), but see second treatise, sections 116–17.

of rights and duties, the same powers and capacities, and to be subject to exactly the same legal standards as everyone else. One's inclusion in this group is a result of being present in the jurisdiction, although the legal status of one's presence can determine *LAJ*'s ultimate effect. What more can be said about this form of presumptive belonging? It raises at least three interesting questions, each of which is connected to the broader question of the desirability of this form of belonging. The first is this: do those subject to *LAJ* constitute a social and not just a logically possible group?[23] The second follows on the heels of the first, since 'groupness' is often regarded as a necessary condition for community to exist. The second question, then, is: do those subject to *LAJ* constitute a community?

The third question takes a different shape depending upon the answers to the first and second questions. If both are answered affirmatively, then the third question asks 'is that form of group or community worthwhile, morally and politically speaking?' If the answers to the first and second questions are negative, then the third question takes this shape: even if the form of belonging manifest in *LAJ*'s model of presumptive inclusion is not a worthwhile form of community, is it nevertheless importantly related to worthwhile forms of community? *LAJ* could, for example, be a necessary condition for (although not itself amounting to) a valuable conception of community. I tackle the first question in the next subsection, while the second and third animate subsections C and D.

B. Group and Community

Many philosophers and jurists think communities as well as nationalities and, in some cases, ethnicities are first and foremost groups. All communities are groups, on this view, but not all groups are communities.[24] This thought has some initial plausibility in a context in which groups are assumed to be more than mere collections of individuals and in which communities are regarded as particularly significant groups. If a group is indeed more than a 'mere' collection of individuals, what might it or can it be? Furthermore, what is a 'mere' collection of individuals? Do the people queuing at the bus stop opposite my office constitute a group or are they just a collection of individuals?

For Tony Honore, they can constitute a group only if four conditions are satisfied:

> [t]here must be a common purpose or activity [which must be] known to the active members, and a shared understanding about what is to be done in given circumstances

[23] Such as that of red-headed archdeacons: T Honore, *Making Law Bind* (Oxford, Clarendon Press, 1987) (hereinafter '*MLB*') 54.

[24] See Mason (n 2) at 20–27; for a contrary note, see Miller (n 7), who often speaks of a 'group or community' (at 67) as if the two terms were synonyms, and J Finnis, *Natural Law and Natural Rights*, 2nd edn (Oxford, Clarendon Press, 2011) 150–53.

> by them, or of how to determine what is to be done. The prescription to which the understanding refers must restrict the freedom of at least some members of the group.[25]

The first and second conditions (common purpose and shared knowledge of that purpose) are satisfied by members of the queue, since they do indeed have an obvious common purpose (catching a bus) and they are equally obviously aware that they all (or most of them) have that purpose. They also have a number of shared understandings about what is to be done by them in given circumstances. When the bus arrives all of them will almost always: (i) enter it (rather than, say, climb on to the roof or dangle from the windscreen wipers); (ii) tender money, if necessary (rather than attempting to barter with the driver or conductor); (iii) sit on seats if available (and not on either the floor or on other passengers' laps); (iv) refrain from *inter alia* smoking, lighting fires, cooking and cabaret. That the fourth (prescription) condition is also satisfied seems to follow quite quickly from our statement of the third (coordination) condition, for the shared understandings just sketched are undoubtedly prescriptive and in some sense a restriction of the freedom of some of the bus travellers. Passengers with portable barbeques know better than to try to light and use them.

The bus travellers opposite my office, whom I often join, are not in my experience an eccentric or odd group of such travellers; almost all such travellers behave in the same or similar ways. That is worth noting because Honore suggests that those awaiting trains do not constitute a group, despite the fact that they are for our purposes exactly similarly situated as 'members' of bus queues: they have a common purpose, know that they do, coordinate themselves in much the same ways, and those means of coordination are prescriptive. On the assumption that no relevant difference separates those awaiting buses from those awaiting trains, it seems that Honore thinks neither collection of people constitutes a group. Why is he led to this *prima facie* puzzling view?

One suggestion is found in two closely related remarks. First, about those awaiting a train, Honore says that they

> may have the common aim of catching a train, perhaps even the same train, but that is not enough. If they were to agree on how the places on the train are to be allocated, that might tip the balance.[26]

Second, speaking of train travellers and all the lawyers who work in a particular town, he claims that '[n]one of these collections need share an understanding of what is to be done in given circumstances, or, if they do, their understanding may be too vague to make them a group'.[27] Is this right? Setting aside the lawyers, those awaiting trains and buses surely have more in common than the aim of utilising

[25] Honore, *MLB* (n 23) 38. The insert is necessary to highlight the fact that Honore does indeed think there are four and not three conditions here. For confirmation, see the conditions as laid out at 34.

[26] *MLB* (n 23) 35.

[27] *MLB* (n 23) 35.

a specific form of public transport. As already noted, they know that that is why they are there and all (or almost all) of them structure their conduct on the basis of a range of expectations and conventions that govern how to behave. Equally clearly, those expectations and conventions are prescriptive and liberty-limiting. Of course, the kind of coordination manifest when passengers board buses and trains is not exactly the same as an explicit agreement among passengers about how seats are to be distributed, but neither is it radically different. True, the conventions and expectations by which passengers regulate their pursuit of their goal are never explicitly held up for discussion and agreement. They are obvious methods of prescriptive coordination nevertheless.

It is plain from Honore's first remark that he thinks the train travellers do not have enough in common; from his second remark it is clear that he thinks they lack an understanding of what must be done in given circumstances. He seemingly errs on both counts, apparently having overlooked or down-graded the significance of the various coordination conventions and expectations that govern many aspects of everyday life. When these are brought into view, then those awaiting trains and buses are, on Honore's account, assuredly groups. Might he have other reasons for resisting this conclusion? It cannot be that the purpose bus and train travellers have in common is insufficient to amount to a group purpose because, as is evident from Honore's first remark, he regards that exact purpose as good enough. Despite that, might this shared purpose—catching the train—be thought too vague? There are undoubtedly groups with more demanding and all-embracing purposes (to bring about a global proletarian revolution, for instance), but the path of distinguishing groups from non-groups by reference to the degree of ambition displayed by their purpose (or some such related discrimination) appears richly problematic.

The problem might, instead, concern the conventions and expectations I have emphasised. It could be suggested that these derive not from the specific purpose the ostensible groups in question have, but from the wider culture in which the apparent groups exist. The general rules of manners and etiquette, alongside the principles for simply getting along in everyday life in close proximity to others, set the parameter within which all groups in certain kinds of society exist. To draw upon that parameter as an illustration of the alleged group's commitment to some or other set of conventions or expectations illuminates nothing specific about the group itself. Group conventions and expectations must uniquely relate to the precise purpose, or one of them, that the group has; this might, after all, be the force of Honore's point about the train travellers explicitly agreeing to distribute seats among themselves. That convention derives directly from a specific purpose and not from the wider culture.

This point gains plausibility if we accept that some groups have conventions and expectations which are—or which at first glance seem to be—independent of those in the wider culture. It might be thought, for example, that the conventions and expectations of the Hell's Angels chapter of which I am a member run completely contrary to those of morally respectable society and it is these anti-social conventions and expectations that define the group or capture the point of its existence. Yet the dividing line, if indeed there is one, between my group's 'core' conventions and expectations, and the conventions and expectations of the wider culture, is not so clear-cut. For, while we do engage in activities that some of the ostensibly morally upright eschew, we also have conventions and expectations closely analogous to those in polite society. So, for example, our regular Sunday hell-raising ride into the bucolic countryside is always led by the oldest member of our chapter and it is he, alongside a number of other older members, who decides disputes within the group. Conventions about deference and dispute resolution are clearly not unique to our group, although the content of such conventions may well differ from group to group. Are they therefore part of the wider culture or do they count as group-specific? The fact that there is a plausible sense in which one can answer 'yes' to both limbs of this question shows that the effort to police a boundary between group-specific and general cultural conventions and expectations can be problematic.

Honore's analysis of the nature of groups, and the four existence conditions he identifies, is powerful and important. It allows us to shore up a distinction between groups and non-groups, which we frequently invoke in ordinary life, while also highlighting some difficulties latent in the utilisation of that distinction. By illuminating the basis of that distinction, Honore not only gives us confidence in its use; he also allows us to take a vital initial step in the elucidation and deployment of another seemingly important distinction, that between groups and communities. Furthermore, although our discussion to this point has not touched upon the issue, it must be noted that Honore's analysis draws upon and improves some sociological and philosophical attempts to define groups and elucidate group-membership.[28] Even his apparent misstep about rail travellers highlights two significant points, namely, the sometimes awkward task of distinguishing between specific and general conventions-cum-expectations and the process of mediation between the two. Before turning to the issue of community, a final group-related question arises: do those subject to *LAJ* constitute a group?

To do so, they must knowingly be engaged in a common enterprise and also share prescriptive, liberty-restricting means of achieving it. In 2014 the population of the UK was 64.6 million, those people being subject to at least three jurisdictions: England and Wales, Scotland, and Northern Ireland.[29] Does it make sense to speak of such a large number of people having a shared purpose? Even if we reduce that number by including only those of (roughly) working age (64 per cent of the 64.6 million were aged between 16 and 64 in 2014, giving a rough total of 41 million) and prune that further, following Honore, by counting only 'active

[28] See *MLB* (n 23) Ch 3. M Gilbert's *Joint Commitment* (New York, Oxford University Press, 2013), especially chs 1, 2, 6 and 8, is a recent engagement with many of the issues Honore tackled.

[29] See www.ons.gov.uk/ons/rel/pop-estimate/population-estimates-for-uk--england-and-wales--scotland-and-northern-ireland/mid-2014/sty---overview-of-the-uk-population.html (last accessed 5th January 2017), from which these figures are taken.

members'—those 'who, willingly or not, are already co-operating or benefiting from the co-operation of others'[30]—it is still a very large alleged group. What joint enterprise might they be engaged in or what purpose could they have in common?

I do not think the two formulations of this question are exactly equivalent. Furthermore, the difference between them explains why we are more comfortable holding that a very large number of people might be part of a joint *enterprise* rather than saying that they share a common *purpose*. That is in part because of a linguistic intuition, which I think is reasonably widely shared, namely, that purposes are fairly specific and have limited aims.[31] In ordinary discourse the word 'purpose' is not used as often as cognates like 'aim', 'goal' and 'intention' and even they are not particularly common. If someone wants to know why I am filling a bucket, for example, I will almost never answer 'my purpose is …'; nor will my interrogator normally ask 'what is your purpose in filling the bucket?' The question will usually be a 'why' question—'why are you doing that?'—and the reply a simple statement of a task or aim: 'to clean the windows'. A natural description of my conduct here certainly invokes the notion of purpose, yet it does not use the term: 'he's going to clean the windows' or 'he's cleaning the windows'. The locution 'his purpose is to clean the windows' is just as odd, in ordinary discourse, as is 'his enterprise is to clean the windows', although the basis of the oddity is not exactly the same. True, the term 'enterprise' is probably no more commonly used than 'purpose'. But its meaning is also different in two senses. First, an 'enterprise' is usually a more general (and possibly disparate) form of undertaking than something one has as one's purpose.[32] And, second, an 'enterprise' is almost always plural, involving more than one person and, while one can speak of a number of people having the same purpose (to catch the bus, to beat the opposition), the numerical range of the term seems more limited than that of 'enterprise'. It seems fine to say that the purpose (or aim) of the battalion, or possibly even an army, was to win the battle or the war, yet strange to claim that that is or was the purpose (or aim) of a population of 40 million adults. It also seems non-jarring to say that 40 million adults can be part of a common enterprise described as 'survival', yet odd to describe this as their purpose. It is not just numbers, but also the different resonances of the words 'enterprise' and 'purpose', that explains this.

It is tempting to think that Honore, too, sees this, for he moves from frequently invoking 'shared (or common) purpose' to describe this aspect of what constitutes a group, to characterising that same aspect as a joint or common 'enterprise'.[33]

[30] *MLB* (n 23) 7. See also *MLB*, ibid at 2, 33, 52 and 56–57.

[31] The intuition is confirmed by the *Oxford English Dictionary* in which 'purpose' is defined as '[t]he reason for which something is done or made, or for which it exists; the result or effect intended or sought; the end to which an object or action is directed; aim'.

[32] One of the *OED*'s definitions of 'enterprise' is: 'a bold, arduous, or momentous undertaking'.

[33] 'The difference between a group and a mere collection of individuals lies … in the fact that the members of a group are engaged in a *joint enterprise*' (*MLB* (n 23) 3; emphasis added); 'there must be a *common purpose* or activity' (*MLB*, ibid 38; emphasis added). The former phrase dates from 1987, the latter from 1973.

Yet this thought is confounded by his willingness to use the two terms interchangeably, as in this doubly-pertinent example:

> How do we know if people are engaged in a *common enterprise*? … [I]f the active members[.] of the alleged group co-ordinate some of their actions, this shows either that they accept, willingly or not,[.] a *common purpose*, or that the activity in which they are engaged calls for co-ordination and that they are prepared, willingly or not, to participate in that activity.[34]

This statement not only suggests that Honore lacks the just touted linguistic intuition (and could therefore be accused of ignoring a potentially significant discrimination); it also hints as to how our ostensibly troubling question might be answered. For those subject to *LAJ* assuredly coordinate some of their actions; indeed, they are undoubtedly doing so right now, as I write and as you read. They share and adhere to a great many social conventions and expectations. They have co-existed reasonably peaceably over time and regulate their behaviour when catching buses, trains and planes, going to and returning from work, taking their children to school and their dogs for walks. There are thus many general (don't knock people over; apologise and offer aid if you do) and specific (children must be at school before 8.30) liberty-restricting prescriptions in play in their everyday lives. Some prescriptions relate to membership of fairly small or quite specific groups (the Women's Institute, a political party, the local snooker club), while others—various legal duties and rights—relate to membership of the alleged group 'those subject to *LAJ*'. But are the latter really engaged in a joint enterprise?

If so, the enterprise must be sufficiently general (or vague) as to accommodate all the specific purposes or goals of the active members of the group, while also illuminating an overarching goal that each specific goal either instantiates or is consistent with. What could that be? Survival has already been suggested, its plausibility deriving from the truism that any alleged group's survival is usually a precondition for the achievement of its members' specific goals.[35] Another plausible candidate is slightly less abstract: the common enterprise is that of maintaining the conditions necessary for all or many in the alleged group to be able to achieve whatever specific purposes they have, assuming those purposes are consistent with continued group membership.

Accounts such as these are rare when one considers the joint enterprise which might animate those groups (if any) that are co-extensive with actually existing nation-states. That is not just because many existing nation-states are made up of numerous, ostensibly different groups; it is also because such bare, abstract statements of their joint enterprise are usually submerged beneath narratives of nationality and nation-hood. These narratives often make a virtue of the nation's survival but that survival is usually geared towards other, more ostensibly valorous

[34] *MLB* (n 23) 56–57 (emphasis added).

[35] Honore first mentions survival as being the possible joint enterprise of a group at *MLB* (n 23) 3. Finnis's alternative suggestion (n 24) at 153 is 'the common good'.

goods than that (to be and remain, for instance, 'the land of the free'). This much is clear from an elementary thought-experiment. How would the residents of any existing nation-state with which you are familiar answer this question: 'what, if anything, marks you out as a group?' Their primary answer is, I think, unlikely to be 'the desire to remain as a group' or 'to survive'. Rather, I suspect that the most common answer will invoke accounts, both real and imagined, of national identity and character, themselves frequently drawing upon real and imagined historical events in the nation's history. A nation is first and foremost an imagined community; it is in that form, or as a broader social imaginary, that it animates peoples' lives, often in the most momentous ways.[36] None of which is incompatible with the claim that the joint enterprise unifying such groups is survival or its cognates.

C. Community, Citizenship, Fraternity

Does the fairly thin inclusionary ideal that informs *LAJ* signify anything more significant? Might it, for example, mark an interesting and possibly commendable form of group membership? It could be said to do so in at least two ways, each defining the 'all' that appears in each of *LAJ*'s constitutive claims ('all are subject to the same legal standards') in slightly different ways. I will label these two ways of attempting to expand and deepen *LAJ*'s inclusionary ideal the arguments from citizenship and from fraternity. I take them to have high inclusionary ambition, being efforts to show what it is that could plausibly bind a body of people together within the confines of something like contemporary nation-states and their jurisdictions.

These two apparently different ways of unpacking *LAJ*'s inclusionary ideal are contiguous to *LAJ*, being a good fit in the weak sense of being compatible with it, and also in the stronger sense of being functionally complementary, of doing much the same thing as it. This allows the putative value of both notions, which seem on their face broader than *LAJ*, to be transferred to *LAJ*. Both are ostensibly normative and could well be consistent with a number of values and arguments from first principles; to the extent that they are, they are normatively overdetermined. While some of the normative value of these conceptions might flow from their compatibility with a range of fundamental values, it need not flow from their compatibility with just one such value. Moreover, it is perfectly possible that the arguments from citizenship and fraternity are important and valuable for reasons in addition to those arising from their compatibility with some or all fundamental values.

[36] The term 'imagined' in this and the previous sentence is not pejorative. It captures the thought that large groups, in which members cannot have face-to-face knowledge of one another, must exist as a shared idea: see B Anderson, *Imagined Communities*, 2nd edn (London, Verso, 2006) 6–7. On the broader notion of a social imaginary, see C Taylor, *Modern Social Imaginaries* (Durham, North Carolina, Duke University Press, 2004).

What both arguments have in common is that they embody conceptions of community, those conceptions occupying different points on a spectrum ranging from thin to thick. It would perhaps be desirable but is now impossible to eschew all talk of community because, in much recent political philosophy and jurisprudence, on the one hand, and in ordinary discourse, on the other, the notion tends to confuse more than enlighten. In the academy, the idea became the principal currency of 'philosophical communitarians', on the one hand, and of 'political communitarians', on the other, neither group having offered a particularly helpful or lucid understanding of the idea.[37] Furthermore, in ordinary discourse the idea is often invoked in a vast array of different and frequently incompatible senses—nostalgic, debunking, descriptive, normative, 'statist', 'sub-statist'—such that the exact nature of the claim made on behalf of 'community' is unclear.[38] However, since the notion is so frequently invoked, the attempt to forego its use seems a Canute-like affectation. How, then, do I use the term in what follows? In this (not entirely) stipulative sense: to refer to either the argument from citizenship or from fraternity, each having in common what all communitarian arguments share, namely, they are attempts to elucidate what binds a group together over and beyond the requirements of 'group-ness'. The arguments from citizenship and fraternity are ostensibly normative rather than descriptive and, given that we have *LAJ* in view, must operate mainly at the level of the state. The many different communities that exist at various levels within nations are of interest in what follows only when and if they throw light on the two more general forms of community that are our focus.

These two conceptions of community might seem unfamiliar to some, since the discussion of community within much political (and some legal) philosophy tends to divide conceptions of community along substantive, contemporary

[37] The former are relatively unconcerned with the analysis of either actual communities or of their existence conditions, being more interested in the delineation of (various different versions of) 'the self'. The latter also appear to assume that the concept of community is philosophically unproblematic, their emphasis instead being upon the ways in which actually existing communities can be 'strengthened' or otherwise improved. Fraternity is not entirely absent from either philosophical or political communitarian work. However, in the former the idea is almost always subsidiary to the notion of identity (see, for example, M Sandel's *Liberalism and the Limits of Justice* (Cambridge, Cambridge University Press, 1982) at 31–32 and 147–54; and A MacIntyre, *After Virtue*, 3rd edn (London, Duckworth, 2007) Ch 15). This complaint could also be made, possibly with slightly less justification, against C Taylor's *Sources of the Self* (Cambridge, Cambridge University Press, 1989). A political communitarian classic, in which fraternity features hardly at all, is A Etzioni, *The Spirit of Community* (New York, Touchstone, 1994).

[38] See Mason (n 2) 1–4, for a nice round-up of usages, alongside the usual complaint about the vagueness of the term as used by communitarians (for another instance, from many, of that refrain, see E Frazer, *The Problems of Communitarian Politics* (Oxford, Clarendon Press, 1999) 61). In complaining about 'community', I do not imply that the other terms I use—citizenship and fraternity—are unproblematic. One alleged disadvantage of the latter is its gendered nature: Dworkin, *LE* (n 21) at 437, fn 13. However, that is surely an advantage, since it keeps gender constantly before our eyes. Its gendered nature does create a stylistic difficulty, though, since 'fraternity/sorority' is clumsy. Henceforth, and purely for the sake of readability, I use 'fraternity' to refer to both. Although tempted by a neologism ('sorternity'), it risks bringing to mind a group united by an appreciation of French dessert wine.

political-philosophical lines. Thus we are often faced with a division between 'liberal', 'republican', 'libertarian' (and sometimes other) conceptions of community, as if every substantive current political theory had something direct and explicit to say about community.[39] But some do and some don't. Moreover, some entries in these classificatory schemes are, if taken seriously, just too unwieldy and complex to yield anything like a single coherent view of community. The 'liberal' entry is a prime instance, where the pruning required of that greatly varied tradition of thought in order to generate a uniform view of community amounts to almost complete deforestation. Only one tree is left from what was an intriguing and fairly messy forest. The hunch that informs what follows is that the idea of community need not first and foremost be articulated within the context of particular substantive political theories, that it can be understood independently of them, and that some conceptions of community can draw support from more than one such substantive theory. Conceptions of community need not always and ever match up, in a one-to-one relationship, with substantive political theories. They can cut across those theories, the same conception appearing in more than one.

Finally, note that neither the argument from citizenship nor that from fraternity rests upon an actual feature that each member of the group in question has in common with every other member of the group. Members of any reasonably sized group will, obviously, differ greatly from one another, thus reducing the chances of finding some unifying feature upon which to rest a claim about equality of treatment or standing.[40] Both versions of *LAJ*'s inclusionary ideal must instead rest upon a claim about the way in which members do and should relate to one another within the group.

(i) Citizenship: Thin and Thick

Arguments from citizenship take a polity, now usually envisaged as something like the modern state, as their focus.[41] They characterise the relationship that holds between members, on the one hand, and between members and the polity, insofar as it is distinguishable from members, on the other; that relationship is defined by a fairly specific set of obligations irreducible to the obligations all human beings owe to one another *qua* human beings. These arguments, which cannot by definition apply to those simply present in a jurisdiction but only to 'members', assume

[39] One example: Mason (n 2) Chs 3–6. For a similar move with regard to citizenship (which Mason himself eschews: see his *Living Together as Equals* (Oxford, Oxford University Press, 2012) at 25) see D Miller, *Citizenship and National Identity* (Oxford, Polity Press, 2000) 82–89.

[40] See B Williams, 'The Idea of Equality' in *Problems of the Self* (Cambridge, Cambridge University Press, 1972) Ch 14 at 232–39; M Cavanagh, *Against Equality of Opportunity* (Oxford, Clarendon Press, 2002) at 103–12; and, for a riposte, I Carter, 'Respect and the Basis of Equality' (2011) 121 *Ethics* 538–71.

[41] On this view, then, the idea of 'global' or 'cosmopolitan' or 'transnational' citizenship is nonsense. For one of a number of attempts to show otherwise, see D Held, *Democracy and the Global Order* (Cambridge, Polity Press, 1995); Miller (n 39) at 89–96 is unconvinced.

the existence of all the usual indicia of states: not just states as actual (or claimed) monopoly sources of coercive power, but also as *loci* of legal systems (with constituent bodies of rights and duties and other legal paraphernalia), and as guarantors of certain statuses, conditions and public goods for those subject to their power and influence. Particular arguments from citizenship characterise the relationship between members of the polity, and between polity and members, in different ways, ranging from fairly thin accounts of what that entails to much thicker characterisations of its nature. I'll begin with thin accounts, principally because I want, at the outset at least, to ensure that the argument from citizenship does not collapse into the argument from fraternity.

Perhaps the thinnest version of the argument from citizenship regards *LAJ*'s inclusionary ideal as marking out or replicating most of the parameters of legal citizenship. Legal citizenship, on this view, is the most important aspect of citizenship. It maintains that full members of a polity are marked by the fact that they stand in the same relation before and under the law: all are subject to the same laws and viewed as the same by the law; they are, furthermore, holders of presumptively equal bundles of rights, duties, immunities and powers, all being of the same standing or status. Citizenship, on this view, is equal for all and replaces the various statuses and ranks constitutive of feudal legality. It also extends to guarantee an equal stake in the political organisation of society, since equal citizenship is taken to entail almost unlimited universal suffrage. Citizenship need not, on this view, be an automatically guaranteed status, its award often being subject to conditions. These conditions can be more or less demanding and vary from country to country; they have, of course, varied from time to time.

This thin citizenship version of the inclusionary ideal is impervious to considerations of size by virtue of its almost entirely legalistic status. That citizenship is conceived of as an almost entirely legalistic notion, entailing *LAJ* and some other entitlements and duties specific to particular nation-states, is a hallmark of many modern understandings of citizenship.[42] These understandings sometimes make claims beyond this minimal one on behalf of citizenship, these claims serving to distinguish different versions of modern citizenship from one another. But the minimal claim is common to virtually all modern understandings of citizenship and some such understandings make only this claim. Since, on this claim, citizenship assumes little more than membership in a particular, usually geographically

[42] By 'modern' I simply mean 'not ancient': the conceptions of citizenship in play in the politics and thought of the Greek city states were far richer than many of those in play now, even among contemporary philosophers who hanker after a revival of classical citizenship. The thin, modern view of citizenship includes but can go a little beyond what TH Marshall called civil citizenship: see *Citizenship and Social Class* (Cambridge, Cambridge University Press, 1950) at 10–11. My claim is that Marshall's civil citizenship is an element of virtually all modern (but not early modern: see Kim (n 5) part I) accounts of citizenship, including those that regard it as a moral ideal (see Mason (n 39) at 2 for an instance). For description and analysis of some contemporary, hybrid a-national conceptions of citizenship, which are beyond the purview of this chapter, see D Kostakopoulou, *The Future Governance of Citizenship* (Cambridge, Cambridge University Press, 2008).

and politically specified group—'it is a status bestowed on those who are full members of a community'[43]—there is no difficulty in it being distributed to a vast number of people. While determining membership on such a minimalist or thin[44] account of citizenship obviously implies a clear view of the conditions for membership among those who control access to it, it requires little by way of commonality or common understandings among recipients. Indeed, the fact that there is so little to thin accounts of citizenship generates two apparent problems in the current context. Neither turns out to be especially troubling.

Only a stringently thin view of citizenship, which TH Marshall dubbed forms of 'civil citizenship', is affected by the first alleged problem. Civil citizenship 'is composed of the rights necessary for individual freedom—liberty of the person, freedom of speech, thought and faith, the right to own property and to conclude valid contracts, and the right to justice'.[45] Conceived thus, the thin view of citizenship looks remarkably similar to *LAJ*. It might, indeed, be claimed that the one entails the other and, if they are merely different sides of the same coin, one can hardly provide independent, *additional* moral and political support for the other. The class of reasons supporting one is the same as the class of reasons supporting the other. A thin view of citizenship cannot therefore function as *LAJ*'s normative anchor.

But is the relationship between *LAJ* and the thin view really so close? No. For, although related, *LAJ* and the thin view are not identical. Rather, the thin view is surely an as yet unnoticed additional component of *LAJ*: it articulates, in part at least, the mode of belonging that emerges from a group living under a system of law featuring the presumptive identity, uniformity and limited avoidability components. If the thin view of citizenship is indeed a component of *LAJ*, then it can function as a normative prop for *LAJ* provided one condition is satisfied. It is that the thin view's sources of moral and political support must range beyond those that directly inform *LAJ*. This means that the list of values informing thin views of citizenship must include more entries than just dignity and equality which, of course, seems eminently likely, there being no *a priori* constraints on the sources of normative support available to conceptions of citizenship. The thin view thus seems able to add to the class of reasons available to support *LAJ*, but the exact nature of these reasons depends on the values invoked. Autonomy, non-domination and fraternity are three likely candidates, but there are others.[46] For now, though, I simply note rather than interrogate these potential candidates.

The second putative problem touches upon this same issue, raising again a question about the normative underpinnings of thin views.[47] The problem begins

[43] Marshall, ibid at 29.

[44] Henceforth I mainly use the terms 'thin' or 'thinnest' or 'thinner' to characterise such conceptions of citizenship, although I sometimes also speak of citizenship's 'minimal' claim.

[45] Marshall (n 42) at 10. Marshall also notes, however, that the notion of equality in play in civil citizenship was, for some time at least, not realised in practice: see 33–36 and compare 10–11.

[46] All three feature in subsection (ii), below, although fraternity hogs the limelight.

[47] My shifting from singular (the thin view) to plural (thin views) is not just clumsiness; it accommodates the possibility, unargued for here, that there may be a variety of thin views.

by highlighting one of the most salient features of thin views, namely, that since the conditions for citizenship are legally specified on such views, they can therefore be re-specified by legal change. Citizenship is thus a fairly malleable notion on such views. This emphasis upon the legal malleability of citizenship is, furthermore, one of the principal normative arguments in favour of thin views: they have a clear intellectual advantage over other, thicker views because they mark out distinct conceptual space. Yet this (normative) intellectual virtue might be thought to conceal a (normative) moral-cum-political difficulty. For, if inclusion is *solely* a legal matter, and if the legal requirements for inclusion can be changed willy-nilly (which seemingly follows from citizenship's malleability), then that must undermine whatever moral and political weight thin views might possess.[48] This will certainly be so if and when legal changes in the requirements for citizenship fail to track significant moral and political distinctions. This problem is one reason why, in earlier characterisations, the argument from citizenship was said to be 'ostensibly' normative. Thin versions might, after all, lack any moral-cum-political weight.

There are, however, three reasons that suggest the scale of this problem is exaggerated. First, thin views need not be committed to holding that only legal considerations determine inclusion. Other, non-legal (presumably moral and political) considerations can drive that process as well. Indeed, such considerations can inform the design and construction of the legal determinants of inclusion, since there is no reason to believe that these different types of consideration cannot overlap. The legal determinants of inclusion are not plucked from thin air, nor constructed in a normative vacuum. However, thin views must, if they are to remain distinctive, hold that legal considerations dominate, but that is by no means a controversial claim. The second reason for regarding the problem as an exaggeration is this: its proponents must assume that moral mistakes discredit the moral concept about which they are made. And that is itself a mistake. If I make a mistake about what honesty requires of me in a particular context, that fact no more discredits the notions of honesty and truth-telling than making a multiplication mistake discredits mathematics. That the notion of citizenship is legally malleable, and that it can be changed in ways that may amount to moral mistakes, cannot without more discredit that notion. It simply states the obvious: human beings make mistakes.

The third reason claims that proponents of this problem are at risk of assuming that the contours and details of any particular conception of citizenship are fully morally determined, so that those contours and details follow like straightforward entailments from the moral notion or theory in play. Yet this seems dubious, both in relation to citizenship in particular (which moral notion or

[48] The power of inclusion is often accompanied by a power of exclusion. For an instance of the latter, see British Nationality Act 1981 s 40 and Nationality, Immigration and Asylum Act 2002 s 4.

theory could generate a detailed or complete conception of citizenship?), and with regard to many of our normative concepts in general. Take our concept of responsibility as an instance. It is undoubtedly normative in some contexts and senses, but many of its contours and conditions are consistent with numerous different substantive moral theories (utilitarianism, 'Kantianism', virtue-ethics, for example) and values (dignity, autonomy, freedom and fairness, for example).

The problem does, nevertheless, illuminate a significant pressure point for thin views. For many theorists think it problematic to highlight citizenship's legalistic and malleable aspects to the exclusion of others—particularly those aspects that might give a conception of citizenship greater moral and political depth and thus insure it against excessive malleability. Indeed, the desire to formulate more morally and politically robust conceptions of citizenship is plain in many modern accounts of citizenship.[49] Most of these views do not reject thin views of citizenship but, rather, supplement them. It is the nature of these additional claims that make thicker accounts of citizenship particularly interesting, although some of these claims also serve to blur the line between arguments from citizenship and other forms of argument from community.[50]

These additional claims can take many forms. Yet when they consist of an expansive conception of the role of the actual or would-be citizen not just towards one another but also towards the polity itself, those roles being animated in the polity as part of its own self-conception, then they are on the way to being fraternal views. Although such claims are not necessarily incompatible with thin views of citizenship they often have the effect, when made in conjunction with them, of demoting the legalistic view of citizenship to a relatively insignificant role in the new amalgamated (citizenship plus fraternity) view. Furthermore, when made at the level of nation-states, claims about relations and standing within the group, and about the group's self-conception, are often bound up with narratives of nation-building, national survival and national identity. That supposedly gives them especial significance and can explain their cuckoo-in-the-nest-like tendency.

It makes no sense to regard narratives such as these and their constitutive claims as infinitely legally malleable, even though it is indeed possible for nation-states to attempt to embed creation-narratives, including their conception of themselves, in law. A group's self-conception is, though, difficult to capture in law and not only because the parameters of such a conception can be vague. Such self-conceptions may well change over time and are rarely discoverable in a single

[49] An interesting discussion of some of the ways in which thin views of citizenship have been supplemented is J Carens, *Culture, Citizenship, and Community* (New York, Oxford University Press, 2000) Ch 7.

[50] In some European nation-states such claims have taken primarily political or ethnographic form: R Brubaker, *Citizenship and Nationhood in France and Germany* (Cambridge, Massachusetts, Harvard University Press, 1992) is an informative analysis of two cases.

locus, being widely but differentially embedded in the culture.[51] They are not therefore easily reducible to legal form and thus not particularly legally malleable, unlike thin views of citizenship. Also puzzling is the point of embedding a group's self-conception and other identity-narratives in law. It could be made a crime to contradict, undermine or desecrate such narratives or aspects of them—think, for example, of the crime of flag-burning in some jurisdictions. But it is difficult to see what else the law could meaningfully do here, assuming it is not implementing a policy of racist or related exclusion. There is certainly no guarantee that legally embedding a group's or nation's self-conception in law would insulate that conception from change. Nor would it confer legitimacy upon that conception.

The broader notions that thick views of citizenship often appeal to involve an expansive view of a group's self-conception and that always has, as a component, a commonality of purpose deeper and more robust than that required for the existence of a 'mere' group.[52] A group's self-conception must include, simply as a result of there being a robust commonality of purpose and grounds for distinguishing itself from others, a view of how members relate to one another. Such factors are hallmarks of a *prima facie* fraternal view of community, the principal burden of such views being the elucidation of what unifies members of a group over and beyond the legal technicalities of citizenship.[53] The search for that unifying yet sometimes apparently amorphous 'something', a thicker bond than bare legal inclusion, raises questions like this: are members best conceived as friends, Romans or consumers?[54]

In order for a *prima facie* fraternal view to become genuinely fraternal, a number of conditions must be satisfied. One is that the principle of inclusion utilised in a group must actually extend to all members of the group and that all full-members contribute to, and benefit from, membership. Failure to fulfil this condition often informs an immanent critique of the political and social structure of these societies ostensibly committed to the equal standing of all their members, yet in which some are treated quite differently from others. In such societies, for

[51] A racist group's self-conception is awkward to embody in law simply because legal rules are always subject to interpretation and interpretations can be challenged: see R Abel, *Politics by Other Means* (London, Routledge, 1995) Ch 3 for some of the legal challenges to the pass laws in apartheid South Africa. The courts of the Third Reich were far less receptive to legal challenges to the Nazi race laws, often going far beyond the letter of the law to advance the Nazi programme: see Ch 12 of I Muller, *Hitler's Justice* (Cambridge, Massachusetts, Harvard University Press, 1991) for an outline of this egregious process.

[52] In 'Friends, Romans, and Consumers' (1991) 102 *Ethics* 27–41, Martin Hollis characterises a variety of notional 'Roman' views of citizenship thus: 'The common factor is a *conscience collective*, a shared sense of morally binding incorporation in a collective undertaking, which makes Romans self-consciously Romans or Roumanians self-consciously Roumanians': 35 (emphasis in original).

[53] Some examples: '[l]iberal ideals provide a vision of what we ought to stand for as a people': S Macedo, *Liberal Virtues* (Oxford, Clarendon Press, 1991) at 254; 'it is necessary that the citizen truly see himself or herself as part of a common enterprise' with 'a sense of attachment to place and to people': R Dagger, *Civic Virtues* (Oxford, Clarendon Press, 1997) at 197.

[54] Hollis (n 52).

example, the franchise is limited not on grounds of group membership but by reference to factors, like gender, ethnicity or religion, which are apparently irrelevant to the exercise of the right to vote. Of course, the principle of inclusion can be drawn more or less widely and always stands in need of justification. That full-members of fraternal groups all contribute to and benefit from membership, all also being accorded equal standing *qua* members, leads Ronald Dworkin to suggest that such groups are 'conceptually egalitarian'.[55] Provided it is not misunderstood, this is an important point. For it marks the fact that the formally equal status of all members of a fraternal group is quite consistent with some being more influential or important within it, provided that such 'structure and hierarchy … reflect[s] the group's assumption that its roles and rules are equally in the interest of all, that no one's life is more important that anyone else's'.[56]

Another condition relates to the effectiveness of fraternal claims. They will rarely work if they invoke a conception of the group, allegedly held by that group, which is either transient or newly minted. When invoked as a unifying claim about a group, such a self-conception is unlikely to motivate members of the group to act upon it. It would only generate reasons for action and belief among those whose 'group-ness' it supposedly describes were it especially potent. That is because a group self-conception usually needs a history in order to motivate, thus having had time to be internalised by the group or many in it; only then can it become sufficiently significant and venerated to be acted upon. That, at least, is the case in anything like a group as large as most contemporary nation-states. It is also implausible to think that such a large group could be motivated by a new conception of what unifies it, an original and previously unrecognised self-conception. The newer such a claim, the more likely it is to be regarded sceptically by those in whose name it is invoked.

For fraternal claims, the unity asserted within the group must in the first instance be the group's self-conception. This is in part simply because of the meaning of the words 'fraternity' and 'sorority': in one sense both refer to a body of men or women united by a common enterprise or image of themselves as a group.[57] Genuinely fraternal groups are, however, distinguishable from other groups primarily by reference to their greater level of reflective self-definition and by reference to the normative (primarily moral or political) nature of their self-conception. My membership of a local snooker-club requires almost no reflection on my part about the nature of the club and its image of itself. Quizzed about why I am a member, my answer need be no more reflective than a simple 'I'm a member in order to have access to good snooker tables and cheap beer'. This

[55] *LE* (n 21) 200. Obviously, not all groups are fraternal groups, as some of Honore's examples (n 23) at 38 and 63 make clear. It should also be noted that the claim that genuine fraternities are conceptually egalitarian is compatible with the fact that fraternal groups have existed in non-egalitarian societies.

[56] *LE* (n 21) 200.

[57] See the *Shorter Oxford English Dictionary* definitions.

answer might well be reiterated by every other member of the club about their own membership. The commitment of membership therefore extends only a very short distance, if any, beyond self-interest and brings with it almost no burdens of meaning (about the nature of the group, its commitments and history, etc). But membership of a properly fraternal group brings with it a commitment, actual or apparent, to the group's conception of itself and this conception is, more often than not, a value-cum-virtue laden conception. Hence most fraternal groups have and enforce standards of conduct for members that apply to conduct within and beyond the group.[58] Continued membership is often dependent upon adherence to these standards, commitment to them being part of the group's self-definition. These standards need not be morally and politically commendable, since we know of ostensibly fraternal groups—such as my Hell's Angels chapter—dedicated to nefarious ends, but the articulation and policing of, and unambiguous commitment to, some standards of behaviour for group and member alike is another hallmark of a fraternal group.

The difference between the fraternal conception and the thin citizenship conception of community will be either apparent or real depending upon one's view of the latter conception. Some think that conception both implausible and anachronistic.[59] Whether or not these complaints are justified is irrelevant here, since the complaint animating the whole of our discussion of thin views of citizenship has been that they lack moral and political depth. That difficulty can be avoided either by denying that such views must have such depth (no argument to this end has been explored here) or by supplying it. The latter is usually done by supplementing thin views with other claims which are often fraternal in nature. The potential normative power of the fraternal reading of *LAJ*'s inclusionary idea flows from the normative standing of the conception of community invoked. The task of examining the content of the fraternal conception of community remains outstanding: we have so far only sketched the principal plausibility conditions for any fraternal claim. We must therefore determine whether or not there is a plausible fraternal conception of community with moral and political appeal.

(ii) Fraternity

What kind of self-conception must a group have in order for that conception to inform the equality of standing among members that *LAJ* maintains? More specifically, what kind of fraternity can support or inform *LAJ*? Fortunately, there is an apparently plausible, ready-made answer to these questions. It is found in

[58] This is abundantly clear from the history of fraternities (and only very rarely sororities) such as Guilds: for some Whiggish thoughts on the role and history of Guilds, see the Introduction of JT Smith and LT Smith, *English Guilds* (London, Trubner and Co, 1870) at xiv–xl. A more expansive discussion is A Black, *Guilds and Civil Society in European Political Thought from the Twelfth Century to the Present* (London, Methuen, 1984).

[59] See Carens (n 49) and Marshall (n 42) at 14–18.

Dworkin's idea of a 'community of principle'.[60] Such a community 'insists that people are members of a genuine political community only when they accept that their fates are interlinked ...: they accept they are governed by common principles, not just rules hammered out in political compromise'.[61] Through its embrace of the idea of integrity, such a community 'assumes that each person is as worthy as any other, that each must be treated with equal concern according to some coherent conception of what that means'.[62] And treatment with equal concern is, of course, embodied in *LAJ* insofar as the latter prevents some judgements of personal worth influencing judicial decisions and being inscribed in other aspects of law and culture. As instantiated in constitutional and other equality provisions, *LAJ* is a bulwark against many forms of discrimination; when embodied in doctrines of private and criminal law, it impedes judgement by reference to an assessment of the moral worth of claimant or defendant, except where such assessment is already required by doctrinal rules. It is therefore not too much to claim that, insofar as the three components of *LAJ* exist in private law, criminal law and in various equality provisions, they are functionally co-extensive with Dworkin's right to equal concern.[63]

While Dworkin acknowledges that his model of a community of principle is 'ideal in several ways',[64] this cannot be a reason against it. Not, at least, without an argument showing the folly of idealism. Since idealism is not necessarily a fatal flaw, how should we assess the plausibility of this conception of community? We can do this in three ways. First, we can assess whether or not it satisfies the two broad types of plausibility condition, identified in the preceding subsection, for any fraternal claim. Second, we can consider whether Dworkin's view of a genuine community imports additional conditions into the discussion, determining whether or not those conditions can be added without inconsistency to those already specified. Third, we must attempt to determine the moral weight of a community of principle. This step entails an assessment of whether or not fraternity, understood in Dworkin's terms, can be *LAJ*'s moral anchor or, at the very least, can provide it with a congenial moral habitat.

The first body of plausibility conditions for any fraternal claim includes the requirement that the group in question have a unifying self-conception and this entails an account of the way members relate to one another. That conception is normative, must extend beyond the self-interest of members and must also be conceptually egalitarian. This set of conditions can be called 'substantive' in

[60] Surprisingly, given the topics tackled in Parts Four and Five, this idea features hardly at all in Dworkin's *Justice for Hedgehogs* (Cambridge, Massachusetts, Harvard University Press, 2011): see 311–23 (on associative obligations) and 382–85 (on two models of democracy).

[61] *LE* (n 21) 211.

[62] *LE* (n 21) 213.

[63] See my 'Abstraction and Equality' in C O'Cinneide (ed), *Current Legal Problems* 2009 (Oxford, Clarendon Press, 2009) Ch 2, 22–70 at 44–62.

[64] *LE* (n 21) 214.

order to distinguish it from a second set of 'effectiveness' conditions. The latter conditions hold that, generally speaking, fraternal claims cannot be transient nor can they be newly-minted if they are to be effective. It seems clear that a community of principle satisfies both sets of conditions.

Taking the effectiveness conditions first, the question of whether or not a community of principle's self-conception is transient or newly-minted can only be answered within the historical circumstances of particular societies. Dworkin's view is that the kind of fraternity embodied in a community of principle has some resonance within both the US and the UK. Echoes of it can certainly be found in some of the legal doctrines of these jurisdictions, such as their equality and non-discrimination provisions, as well as in some of their abstract political commitments. The objection that no existing political community is a community of principle must undermine these examples, assuming the objection is not a conceptual or an *a priori* truth. Whether or not a community of principle exists in the real world is an empirical matter and only an investigation of the political and legal structures of actually existing polities will determine the issue. Dworkin has at least pointed to some jurisdictions, and to some of their legal and political aspects, that he regards as approximating a community of principle. Critics must show that this is a mistake.

What of the substantive conditions? Dworkin's community of principle is a group that has a clear self-conception which is in some respects both undoubtedly normative and egalitarian. This self-conception is in part about the way in which members of the group relate to one another: it is, moreover, one in which all full-members not only regard one another as in one sense equals, but also accept that their fates are interlinked. The commonality of purpose in such a community need not extend much beyond the shared commitment that this is—and should strive to remain—a community of principle. This is in principle unproblematic. But there is a related and more pressing difficulty: that of showing that members of a large political community, bounded along the lines of contemporary nation-states, can or do regard their fates as interlinked. This seems a particularly remote possibility if the interlinking of fates required is of the strongest kind, which might well be characteristic of some fraternal groups. In some genuine brotherhoods and sisterhoods the level of concern each has for other members is conceivably the same as that each has for themselves and their family members. This is not the kind of interlinking of fates characteristic of a community of principle, says Dworkin. Rather, what is required is that members

> accept that they are governed by common principles, not just by rules hammered out in political compromise. Politics has a different character for such people. It is a theatre of debate about which principles the community should adopt as a system, which view it should take of justice, fairness, and due process, not the different story … in which each person seeks to plant the flag of his convictions over as large a domain of power or rules as possible. Members of a society of principle accept that their political rights and duties are not exhausted by the particular decisions their political institutions have reached, but depend, more generally, on the scheme of principles those decisions presuppose and

endorse. So each member accepts that others have rights and that he has duties flowing from that scheme, even though these have never been formally identified or declared. Nor does he suppose that these further rights and duties are conditional on his whole-hearted approval of that scheme; these obligations arise from the historical fact that his community has adopted that scheme, which is then special to it, not the assumption that he would have chosen it were the choice entirely his.[65]

Does this view of interlinking fates provide a response to the complaint that this conception of community is worrisomely weak? Not completely. Dworkin's discussion of the nature of liberal community suggests that the interlinking of fates characteristic of a community of principle is very limited. It seemingly extends only to a community's

> official political acts: in legislation, adjudication, enforcement, and the other executive functions of government. An integrated citizen will count his community's success or failure in these formal political acts as resonating in his own life, as improving or diminishing it. On the liberal view, nothing more should be added. These formal political acts of the community as a whole should be taken to exhaust the communal life of a political body.[66]

This is a long way from genuine brother- or sisterhood, but is perhaps all that can be hoped for within contemporary nation-states. Furthermore, although its range appears limited, extending only to 'formal' political acts, this does not mean that the commitment entailed between members of a community of principle to those acts is superficial. Dworkin's view seems to be that this commitment has substantial depth, suggesting a level of evaluative engagement with those formal political acts that goes far beyond either simple awareness or sufferance. This becomes evident once we appreciate the role Dworkinian integrity plays in a community of principle:

> [i]ntegrity expands and deepens the role individual citizens can play in developing the public standards of their community because it requires them to treat relations among themselves as characteristically, not just spasmodically, governed by these standards. If people understood formal legislation as only a matter of negotiated solutions to discrete problems, with no underlying commitment to any more fundamental public conception of justice, they would draw a sharp distinction between two kinds of encounters with their fellow citizens: those that fall within and those that fall outside the scope of some past political decision. Integrity, in contrast, insists that each citizen must make demands on him, and may make demands on others, that share and extend the moral dimensions of any explicit political decisions. Integrity therefore fuses citizens' moral and political lives: it asks the good citizen, deciding how to treat his neighbour when their interests conflict, to interpret the common scheme of justice to which they are both committed just in virtue of citizenship. [...]

[65] *LE* (n 21) 211.

[66] R Dworkin, *Sovereign Virtue* (Cambridge, Massachusetts, Harvard University Press, 2000) 231–32.

> Integrity infuses political and private occasions each with the spirit of the other to the benefit of both.[67]

Although complex and richly suggestive, this is still an incomplete view of Dworkin's picture of fraternity.

The second step in assessing Dworkin's fraternal claim involves determining whether or not the four conditions he sets for a group to create 'genuine fraternal obligations'[68] are compatible with the general plausibility conditions for any fraternal claim. This step might be considered otiose because there are in fact two different enterprises here. On the one hand, there is the effort to specify general plausibility conditions for any fraternal claim; on the other, there is the Dworkinian task of specifying the conditions necessary for obligations to arise within fraternal groups. While correct, this point shows the necessity of the second step rather than its redundancy, since it must be shown that our enterprise and Dworkin's enterprise are not inconsistent. This demonstration is not intended as a specific commendation of Dworkin's conception of community. For, while I am assuming that a good—morally and politically deep—conception of community must provide an account of the way in which a community generates obligations, Dworkin's account is not unique in attempting to do this.[69] Thus, determining whether or not the set of conditions Dworkin specifies for fraternal obligations to arise are consistent with the general plausibility conditions for fraternal claims, is one thing; the job of evaluating Dworkin's account of fraternal obligations is quite another. Furthermore, there is no reason to accept, without additional argument, Dworkin's claim that a fraternal group's ability to satisfy the existence conditions he specifies for fraternal obligations marks it out as a genuine fraternal community. His attempt to 'distinguish … a "bare" community, a community that meets the genetic or geographical or other historical conditions identified by social practice as capable of constituting a fraternal community, and a "true" community, a bare community whose practices of group responsibility meet … [these] four conditions',[70] is drawn in blunt and undiscriminating terms. At first glance, we might think that there are degrees of difference between 'bare' and 'genuine' fraternities or groups, that this is not an all or nothing matter. We might therefore be disinclined to accept this as a means of distinguishing different communities.

Dworkin's four conditions are that the responsibilities of membership in a true (or genuine) fraternal group are regarded: (i) as special to the group; (ii) as being personal to members of the group; (iii) as flowing from a concern each has for every other member of the group; and (iv), that concern being an equal concern for all members.[71] In addition, genuine fraternal obligations must be reciprocal.[72]

[67] *LE* (n 21) 189–90.
[68] *LE* (n 21) 199.
[69] See Dagger (n 53) at 78–80.
[70] *LE* (n 21) 201.
[71] *LE* (n 21) 199–200.
[72] *LE* (n 21) 198.

Only a community of principle, says Dworkin, satisfies all these conditions.[73] Are these conditions compatible with the general plausibility conditions for fraternal claims already identified?

The two sets of conditions overlap at some points. We have already suggested that Dworkin's condition (iv) is a general condition for any genuine fraternity: fraternal groups are, as Dworkin maintained, 'conceptually egalitarian'. Condition (i) is also a general condition for any fraternal claim. Since such a claim is in part one that invokes a group's self-conception, and in some sense therefore illuminates what it is that links members together, it must serve to distinguish this group from others. When Dworkin says that the responsibilities of a fraternal group are special, it is exactly this that he has in mind; these responsibilities hold 'distinctly within the group, rather than as general duties its members owe equally to persons outside it'.[74] Dworkin's claim that fraternal obligations depend for their existence upon some degree of reciprocity among those bound by them is not implausible. Yet, as a precondition that must be satisfied for some fraternal obligations to exist, it is neither incompatible with any of the general plausibility conditions for fraternal claims nor does it throw much light on them. The relationship between the general plausibility conditions and this one need amount to no more than this: that the former must not make the latter impossible. This is also true of the relationship between the general conditions and Dworkin's conditions (ii) and (iii). Does anything in the former serve to thwart the realisation of the latter? It seems not. While the general conditions do not insist that members of a fraternal group must see their responsibilities as personal and as flowing from a concern each has for all other members, neither do they make it impossible for members to see their responsibilities in this way.

The two sets of conditions might, however, be incompatible in a non-substantive, almost epistemic sense. As sketched above, some of the general plausibility conditions for any fraternal claim are clearly in part psychological. That is to say: they are claims about, *inter alia*, how members of the group think about the group and the way in which they conceive of their relation with members and non-members. By contrast, Dworkin maintains that the four conditions necessary for a genuine fraternity 'are not psychological conditions … The concern they require is an interpretive property of the group's practices … not a psychological property of some fixed number of the actual members'.[75] Despite this unequivocal language, note how similar the interpretive property embodied in the four conditions—conditions which require 'the members of a group must by and large hold certain attitudes about the responsibilities they owe one another' and that 'run directly from each member to each other member'[76]—is to actual psychological

[73] *LE* (n 21) 213.
[74] *LE* (n 21) 199.
[75] *LE* (n 21) 201.
[76] *LE* (n 21) 199.

conditions. Why, despite this astonishingly close similarity, is Dworkin loath to call what look like psychological conditions by their name?

One reason might flow from Dworkin's overall interpretive method. Since constructive interpretation is interpretation all the way down, recourse to psychological conditions is just as much a matter of interpretation as any other claim about the social world. Pending a critical assessment of Dworkin's method, this reason must be accepted and can be accommodated within the argument here as nothing more than a simple difference of terminology. What for us are psychological conditions are, for Dworkin, interpretive conditions and nothing of any weight turns on this. A second reason for eschewing psychological conditions in this context is, however, more significant. Dworkin might be worried by 'the Rousseau objection' to such conditions. The objection regards such conditions, not implausibly, as affective ties and maintains that, the larger the group said to hold them, the weaker such ties become.[77] Converting apparent psychological-conditions-cum-affective-ties into an interpretative property is one way of avoiding this objection. Another way, less demanding and certainly consistent with the argument offered here, is to accept the warning the Rousseau objection bears. The objection is, after all, an empirical and not an *a priori* claim which could fairly easily be determined to be either true or false in any particular context. The psychological conditions amongst the general plausibility conditions for any fraternal claim, and those that seem to feature in Dworkin's conditions for a genuine fraternity, are thus always open to the Rousseau objection. Yet simply stating the objection does not show it to be valid in any particular case: that must be established empirically.

The third step in assessing Dworkin's fraternal claim raises this question: can a fraternity, understood as a community of principle, be *LAJ*'s moral anchor? We might doubt this. One reason for doubt is that the link between *LAJ* and this specific conception of fraternal political community is not logically tight. No argument has been provided to show that *LAJ* is compatible only with a community of principle. Indeed, it is likely that *LAJ* will be compatible with, and thus draw normative sustenance from, other types of fraternity. But there is not an extensive family of conceptions of fraternity with which *LAJ* is compatible and from which it can derive support. All such putative conceptions must satisfy the existence conditions for all fraternities, one of which—that genuine fraternities are conceptually egalitarian—should not be ignored in the effort to show that *LAJ* can keep uncongenial normative company. Some *prima facie* uncongenial conceptions of community, such as those embodying caste systems or which are otherwise rigidly stratified, cannot satisfy this condition. Other potential and *prima facie*

[77] See JJ Rousseau (V Gourevitch (ed)), *The Social Contract and other Later Political Writings* (Cambridge, Cambridge University Press, 1997) Book II, Ch 9 at 74: 'The more the social bond stretches, the looser it grows'. The objection as formulated in the text belongs to L Green, 'Associative Obligations and the State' in J Burley (ed), *Dworkin and his Critics* (Oxford, Blackwell, 2004) 269–71. Rousseau features only fleetingly in *LE* (n 21) at 189.

objectionable communities—societies with a very high Gini coefficient, for example[78]—will most likely satisfy many or perhaps all of the general conditions. That *LAJ* is *prima facie* compatible with such conceptions neither undermines the idea itself nor weakens the link between it and a community of principle. The link has to be one which allows the moral and political value of the latter to be extended to *LAJ*.

It is nevertheless true that there are some conceivable communities, ostensibly different from communities of principle, which satisfy the plausibility conditions for any fraternity while also apparently being able to provide normative support for *LAJ*. The political communities envisaged by contemporary republican political philosophers are an obvious example. On one view, a genuine republican community will maximise non-domination and combine the values of liberty, fraternity and equality.[79] Such a community therefore seems a *prima facie* suitable normative prop for *LAJ*. Determining the suitability and evaluating the respective merits of a community of principle, on the one hand, and a republican community conceived in these terms, on the other, are tasks that cannot be tackled here. Rather I simply suppose that these two ostensibly different types of community can support *LAJ* and, unless otherwise stated, will assume that the reasons in favour of a community of principle noted below also support some contemporary republican conceptions of community.

Furthermore, if the suggestion made earlier about the relative indeterminacy of arguments from first moral and political principles is correct,[80] then there is reason to doubt the utility—in this context at least—of assessing the relative merits of a community of principle and a republican community. For it might be the case that both are consistent with and derivable from our most important moral and political values. A general notion of equality, for example, looms large in both a Dworkinian fraternity of principle and recent views of republican community; so, too, does an account of liberty and distributive justice. These notions are conceived in different ways, but the fact that variations of the same values are in play in each conception of community suggests it is unlikely that one or other conception can be dismissed on the basis of its value-content. This also allows us to extend another point about the relative indeterminacy of arguments from first principles: not only do they rarely confer pre-eminent salience on particular aspects of legal-institutional design like *LAJ*, they might also be insufficiently precise to discriminate between one conception of fraternity and another. The conclusion that a community of principle could function as *LAJ*'s moral anchor—but so, too, might a small family of other fraternities—is not an indictment of the argument here. Rather, it illustrates a central argumentative refrain of this

[78] On which see R Wilkinson and K Pickett, *The Spirit Level: Why Equality is Better for Everyone* (London, Penguin Books, 2010) Ch 2.

[79] See P Pettit, *Republicanism: A Theory of Freedom and Government* (Oxford, Clarendon Press, 1997) 110–13 and chs 1–3 of his *On the People's Terms* (Cambridge, Cambridge University Press, 2012).

[80] See ch 1, section II B.

book, namely, that aspects of legal institutional design may well be normatively over-determined.

There is another reason to doubt that a community of principle can be *LAJ*'s moral anchor. It holds that the argument from fraternity, just like the argument from citizenship, is only 'ostensibly' normative. This is because, however conceived, 'fraternity' is not a non-instrumentally valuable property. It looks, rather, like something valuable only by virtue of the other values it establishes, brings about, or facilitates. As stated, this argument does not live up to its billing, since it shows only that a community of principle has instrumental, as opposed to zero, normative weight. Proponents of the argument are confident that one riposte—a demonstration of fraternity's non-instrumental value—will not be forthcoming and they are perhaps right in this sense, for it is quite difficult to discern a plausible sense in which fraternity could be non-instrumentally valuable.[81] It is particularly difficult for non-perfectionist liberals to argue that some or other conception of community is non-instrumentally valuable, as compared to perfectionists in general, either liberal or otherwise. Insofar as political perfectionists cleave to a conception of the good which they hold must be instantiated in the political structure of a community as well as in its non-political life, they are perhaps better able to transfer the moral weight of that conception to conceptions of community consistent with it.[82] Since the notion of a perfectionist liberal is not a contradiction, a community of principle could therefore be justified on perfectionist grounds. Such grounds are, by definition, unavailable to political non-perfectionists.

What is valuable, either instrumentally or non-instrumentally, about a community of principle and similar fraternal communities?[83] The most obvious reply is: such communities expand *LAJ*'s inclusive, egalitarian ideal throughout a community's politics. The type of inclusive, egalitarian treatment *LAJ* attempts to enshrine in law is written large into the political fabric of a community of principle, insofar as such a community regards each member as being as worthy as any other. This injunction, which at this historical moment in the Western democracies might seem trite, appears much less so in historical perspective. There could be no question of inscribing it upon both the political process and the legal systems of feudal societies, without fundamentally changing those societies.

It may seem, however, that this alleged moral advantage of a community of principle is irrelevant here, because this value is one which *LAJ* already embodies.

[81] But not impossible: see Mason (n 2) at 50–56 for apposite discussion. He also offers a related argument in relation to his equal membership conception of citizenship (n 39 at 38–42).

[82] Non-political perfectionists have conceptions of the good life which extend only to personal ethical and moral conduct and belief. While such conceptions undoubtedly have a public life, insofar as they are shared and acted upon by a significant number of people, that life need not be explicitly embedded in political institutions and structures.

[83] I do not consider one of the arguments for a community of principle which Dworkin thinks important, namely, that in such a community law's coercive power is more likely to be legitimate than in other communities (*LE* (n 21) at 190–92). This argument is too closely tied to Dworkin's account of law to be salient in the current argumentative context.

Showing that this value is also instantiated in a community of principle therefore does nothing to increase *LAJ*'s moral lustre. But that is not quite right. For the fact that both *LAJ* and a community of principle embody an egalitarian commitment about the equal worth of all members of the community and of all addressees of the law, is significant if we value that commitment, and in this way. It shows that our having that commitment is not an exception or an aberration. If we espouse it in different contexts—*LAJ*, on the one hand, and as a feature of a desirable type of political community, on the other—then that can increase our confidence in it and add to its normative weight. Indeed, the fact that the commitment is significant and valuable in one, broader context (a community of principle) can add to its lustre in a very specific context (the law), for we can then infer that it is not *sui generis*. Its appeal, its normative weight, might be general and thus transcend particular contexts. This reinforces its importance for us.

There is, moreover, a stronger link running from a community of principle to *LAJ* which can serve to supplement the latter's moral lustre. It is this: the conceptually egalitarian nature of genuine fraternal groups, including communities of principle, requires *LAJ* as a feature of their legal systems (insofar as such groups must have legal systems). We can think again of feudal legal systems to see the point. A legal system as hierarchical and stratified as that of feudal England is straightforwardly incompatible with the idea that no one's life is any more important than anyone else's. Feudal legal systems were marked by the very opposite belief: the lives of some were valued more than the lives of others. A community of principle, and its legal system, is one in which all are, in a clear and unambiguous sense, regarded as the same and in which all should, in one respect at least, see themselves as the same. Their relationship with one another *qua* members of the community is one among and of equals.

Another valuable feature of a community of principle is that the ideas of belonging and non-domination will be well embedded within it. The significance of the idea of belonging may have been lost on Anglophone political philosophers until relatively recently but, in one sense or another, sociologists have almost always regarded it as important. It is also significant to those denied the kind of equal treatment that both *LAJ* and a community of principle embody. Being recognised as an equal in this way is not, of course, an all-embracing, ethically substantive form of inclusion, but it is clearly better than nothing, as many campaigners for equal civil rights have attested.[84] This kind of belonging has as its flip-side an absence of legally enshrined domination: an absence of legally enforced caste, gender, religious and sundry other distinctions. This absence cannot in and of

[84] An intriguing and wide ranging discussion of what agents lack when deprived of recognition, including formal legal recognition, is provided by A Honneth in *The Struggle for Recognition* (Cambridge, Polity Press, 1995) chs 6, 8 and 9 and elaborated at 114–59 of N Fraser and A Honneth, *Redistribution or Recognition?* (London, Verso, 2003). An excellent account of various struggles for legal recognition, combining legal and other narratives, is K Karst, *Belonging to America* (New Haven, Yale University Press, 1989).

itself give rise to a fully respectable, flourishing political community in good moral order. It is, at most, one necessary precondition for such a political community. But this should not lead us to underplay its significance.

Commitment to equal worth and the possibility of belonging in the absence of domination will, for most, be desirable features of a community of principle and other similar fraternal groups. When combined, these features serve to make another desirable property possible: respect and, on the value-status conception, dignity.[85] This is not, remember, respect based upon deeds, accomplishments or skill, whatever their basis, nor upon simple natural endowments. While such factors are often determinants of the esteem in which we hold others, they are not relevant to the type of respect engendered in a community of principle. For respect here means regard for others just because they are human beings who are members (permanent or temporary) of our group. That is in and of itself enough to make them valuable. And that, of course, serves to make difficult the standard types of exclusion and discrimination with which we are familiar.

The fact that the type of respect constitutive of a community of principle is recognition respect, premised not upon people's deeds or achievements but upon the fact that their personhood sets limits upon our behaviour, recalls the notion of opacity.[86] In chapter four I characterised this idea as a reluctance to assess whether or not particular human beings (i) possess or have in sufficient degree the capacities and characteristics constitutive of humanity, or (ii) satisfy the legal criteria of basic responsibility. It also lies behind two points noted in chapter five, namely, the repugnance we feel about shameful disclosure and the presumptive egalitarianism of the social and political ideal of equality, on the one hand, and the right to equal concern and respect, on the other. Opacity evidences an unwillingness to pry beneath the surface of our assumed agency and similarity, to chart and measure the exact details of our difference and particularity. Recognition respect works in a similar way, being meted out regardless of assessments of the range and degree of many of those factors that might be regarded as triggering it. In a community of principle, membership cannot therefore turn upon disclosure of every aspect of our lives (commitments, capacities, characters, preferences) for inspection and audit. One question only—human agent or not?—needs be answered to determine a being's suitability for recognition respect; other equally 'formal' questions such as, for example, 'born "here" or not?' determine membership of particular communities and nation-states. The factors relevant to a determination of inclusion in a community of principle are thus subject to much the same constraints as those at play in the determination of agents' dignity, those that inform *LAJ*'s three components, and those that animate equality of standing in the social and political ideal of equality and in the right to equal concern and respect.

[85] 'A category that conditions subjects' autonomy on intersubjective regard': Fraser and Honneth, ibid, 1. Of course, Fraser and Honneth are speaking of 'recognition', but the differences between that idea and this notion of respect are, for current purposes, insignificant.

[86] I am paraphrasing S Darwall, 'Two Kinds of Respect' (1977) 88 *Ethics* 36–49 at 46.

One remaining consideration pertinent to whether or not a community of principle can be *LAJ*'s moral anchor is this: is Dworkin's account of such a community itself coherent? It is certainly complex, its principal elements being (i) conceptual egalitarianism; (ii) integrity and the sharing of fates; and (iii) the idea of associative obligation. Do these elements ultimately hang together? That they are not obviously inconsistent is clear from the discussion so far, although it is also true that complaints have been made about specific elements. The ideas of integrity and associative obligation in particular have been subject to much criticism and, surprisingly, about the same amount of praise.[87] It cannot be denied that these two elements are problematic parts of Dworkin's case; nor can it be said that these problems are so severe as to undermine that case completely. What Dworkin provides us with, therefore, is a suggestive and intriguing picture of one kind of fraternity which offers a reasonably plausible account of what could unify members of nation-states and is a good fit with *LAJ*.[88] And, while this may not be the only conception of community which can support *LAJ*, it nevertheless illustrates some of the principal features of any morally and politically deep conception of community. In it all stand and relate to one another as equals before and under law in a group united by that egalitarian belief, a belief in the importance of integrity, and by the belief that the group's formal political acts are 'theirs' even when they disagree with some of them. Although not a haven of sensitive moral and ethical concern, such a fraternity *seems* an improvement upon the many hierarchical, rigid, divisive and sometimes genocidal societies known to human history.

D. *LAJ*: Conception of Community or Precondition for Community?

The argument so far shows that *LAJ* can be underpinned by a particular conception of community. This does not rule out *LAJ* being 'merely' a precondition for other conceptions of community, but it does mean that that issue can be set aside

[87] The case against Dworkin's account of associative obligation as the basis of a duty to obey has been put by Green (n 77). A less critical treatment is AJ Simmons, *Justification and Legitimacy* (Cambridge, Cambridge University Press, 2001) Ch 4. For a general defence of the idea, see J Horton, 'In Defence of Associative Obligation: Part One' (2006) 54 *Political Studies* 427–43 and 'In Defence of Associative Obligation: Part Two' (2007) 55 *Political Studies* 1–19; a sympathetic engagement with Dworkin's version of it is S Perry, 'Associative Obligations and the Obligation to Obey the Law' in S Hershovitz (ed), *Exploring Law's Empire* (Oxford, Clarendon Press, 2006) Ch 8. A flavour of both sides of the debate about integrity can be garnered from G Postema, 'Integrity: Justice in Workclothes' (1996/7) 82 *Iowa Law Review* 821–56 and D Reaume, 'Is Integrity a Virtue?' (1989) 39 *University of Toronto Law Journal* 380–409.

[88] Green (n 77) at 283, fn 4, complains that Dworkin says too little about the way in which social and political practice defines a bare community (onto which genuine communities are often mapped). Although textual evidence suggests Dworkin thinks that obligations of justice, and a community of principle, cannot extend to all humanity (*LE* (n 21) at 208 and *Is Democracy Possible Here?* (New Jersey, Princeton University Press, 2006) 48), it has been argued that there is no block to this extension: A Brown, *Ronald Dworkin's Theory of Equality* (Basingstoke, Palgrave MacMillan, 2009) Ch 4 and Part II.

for now. Had *LAJ* been without such underpinning, not being so closely connected to a conception of community, then that issue would be urgently in need of attention. The argument was that those co-opted into *LAJ*'s mode of belonging constitute a group and that that mode of belonging is a morally respectable, fraternal form of community. No argument was provided to show that this form of community is the only morally respectable one available to us; that claim seems, on its face, implausible given the variety of conceptions of community humankind has so far generated. I did suggest that some accounts of community—those that animate thin conceptions of citizenship—often turn into thicker, fraternal conceptions of community and that this occurs under pressure to supplement thin citizenship claims. No argument was offered to show that this is true of all thin accounts of citizenship.

There are many pressure points in the argument of section II and they increase when we include the claims made and defended in section I. Not only will this conception of community, and the *prima facie* jarring claim that 60 or so million people can be part of a joint enterprise, come under attack; so, too, will the suggestion that *LAJ*'s mode of belonging, resting as it often does upon chance rather than choice, is morally respectable and can create moral and political obligations. Such attacks are inevitable if it is indeed true that the issue of associative obligations, the contexts in which they arise, and their supposed weight mark a number of deep fault-lines within contemporary liberal thought.[89] But, even when we succumb to the predictable urge to problematise an argument that in many respects runs against the grain of much contemporary (legal, political and moral) philosophical thought, we must also bear in mind an important duty. That is the duty we have, as actual or would-be philosophers, to try to understand our present as well as our past, to get clear about the nature of our current social condition. In a broad sense that social condition is defined by legal systems and the claims they make and every effort should be made, given the important and sometimes even catastrophic role such systems can play in individual lives, to take those claims seriously. If those claims do not fit with the claims of our reigning philosophies, then it seems clear that the question 'which claims are right?'—or even 'which claims are worth taking seriously?'—must be an open one.

[89] See Scheffler (n 15) 69.

7

Conclusion

'One day humanity will play with law just as children play with disused objects, not in order to restore them to their canonical use but to free them from it for good'.[1]

The abiding motif of the various arguments presented in previous chapters is that law's abstract judgement (*LAJ*) ignores much. What it ignores, and the ways in which it does so, is not, however, well captured in the traditional image of *Justitia*. That image most often tells us that the law has no gaze, for *Justitia* does not see: law and justice are blind. But they are patently not. When we stand before the law, facing its judgement, the law's agents assuredly do see: they register all of those aspects of ourselves and our conduct made relevant by the law, both at conviction and liability stages, and at sentencing and remedy stages. The law sees, yet it almost never attempts to view us in all our detail and context, being satisfied only with glimpses of the real nature, character, experience and milieu of those it judges. This is not to suggest that the law's agents—judges, magistrates, police officers, wardens and the like—deny the humanity and particularity of those with whom they interact. Yet they must often ignore aspects of that double-sided truth, setting aside or placing out of view many of the specificities of those before them. The way the law and its agents actually see us is therefore closer to the way real human beings look when wearing Nicola L's *Red Coat* (*Same Skin for Everyone*).[2] Real people wear the coat and bring it to life, but we see only their broad contours and a few of their features, many of their differences being obscured. The coat offers an impaired or limited view of its wearers and that, rather than *Justitia's* unseeing gaze, is *LAJ*'s vista.

In addition to that motif, the previous chapters highlighted various connections and illustrated a few disjunctions between *LAJ*, on the one hand, and numerous concepts and values, on the other. If *LAJ* is not the exact flipside of the legal person, then it is assuredly closely related to the two principal forms the legal person takes (as presupposition and as consequence). That, at least, was the argument of chapter two. Both *LAJ* and the legal person fail to register many of the features of the real people to which they are applied and both ignore much about the context in which their conduct occurred. Chapter three showed that *LAJ* is closely related to particular conceptions of responsibility and impartiality, these being far from

[1] G Agamben, *State of Exception* (Chicago, University of Chicago Press, 2005) 64.

[2] The *Red Coat* is a performance piece which has been 'performed' all over the world. See http://nicolal.com/category/performance/.

the only understandings of those notions available to us. These conceptions are not, however, obviously morally disreputable, although they are often thought to be so because they overlook much that is allegedly relevant to a full moral or ethical appraisal of people and their deeds. One notion that supposedly rests on such an appraisal is that of equity (or mercy). I argued that *LAJ* is sometimes supplemented by that notion.

At least one fairly complex conception of dignity is embodied within and protected by *LAJ*. That conception, as sketched in chapter four, holds that those with a set of features commonly dubbed 'humanity' are of equally high value and status. Like *LAJ* and the legal person, that conception often ignores much about real flesh and blood human beings, ascribing that value and status regardless of the actual features of existing human beings. *LAJ* is also closely related to two conceptions of equality, while having little at all to do with some others. The relation between those two conceptions and *LAJ*, as chapter five showed, is that the former are immanent within the latter. Each conception of equality emphasises the importance of the way in which one stands in a political-cum-legal community and each cleaves to similarity in the face of difference. Finally, *LAJ* embodies a form of belonging, a conception of community that can appear as simply an extension of the two conceptions of equality central to chapter five. Chapter six unpacked that conception of community, showing that a community with a self-conception like that suggested by a commitment to *LAJ*, and the conceptions of dignity and equality informing it, is a fraternity or community of principle. Chapters four to six also noted that the notion of opacity is a common thread between dignity, equality and community.

I. Immanence and Value

What was the point of highlighting these connections? It was done in the belief that illuminating them deepens our understanding of *LAJ* and also lends it support, in the sense of giving it—or adding to its—normative weight. The explanatory component of this claim seems the least controversial, since it amounts to holding that seeing something in context, or from a broader perspective, can give us a better, fuller view of that 'thing'. When the 'thing' in question is a relatively complex set of institutionally embodied beliefs and practices like *LAJ*, then many perspectives—legal, historical, economic, sociological, political-philosophical—can be brought to bear upon it. My attempt to place *LAJ* in a broader normative (moral-cum-political) perspective is intended to make some of its particular features less troubling than they might appear when viewed up close. The jolt students and others new to law often feel when faced with *LAJ*, for example, seems a good deal less troubling when understood in light of juristic conceptions of responsibility and impartiality. Furthermore, this broader normative perspective prevents us viewing *LAJ* in isolation, helping us to see that it is not a free-standing, single 'thing' or discrete item but, rather, part of a more complex interconnected whole or amalgam comprising, at the least, notions of dignity, equality and community.

In an attempt to capture the nature of that whole, Alan Norrie labels some of *LAJ*'s features an 'architectonic', that being itself part of a 'constellation'. Law's architectonic, for Norrie, includes what I have dubbed law's person or, in his terms, 'abstract legal subjectivity' and 'a morality of form'.[3] This architectonic has a dual existence. It subsists as a quintessentially autonomous legal form yet also intersects with 'social relations, political governance, and ethics'; thus, although 'law is … law' it is simultaneously 'constituted with [or by these] three different dimensions'.[4] Norrie uses the idea of a constellation to throw light upon the way in which law 'is related to [such] specific social, political and ethical contexts'.[5] That idea articulates

> the way in which things which are different and distinct nonetheless 'stand together'.[…] In thinking this relationship of part and whole, different entities, levels, forms and parts of being may be seen as co-embedded with each other, and this co-embeddedness enables their constitutional difference. The co-embedded terms retain their individual importance while being dependent nonetheless on what they are not. A constellation involves the interlocking of distinct entities to provide a sense both of the autonomy of the parts and their co-dependence in the whole. There is a real, intrinsic, relation of the individual terms together with a real, relative autonomy as between them.[6]

Do *LAJ*, dignity, equality and community stand together in a similar relation? I think they do, certainly in the sense of being different—*LAJ* is a social-institutional form, while dignity, equality and community are values—but connected. The 'entities' in play are separate and hence to some degree autonomous, but are nevertheless interlocked or linked.

But aren't these connections—variously described as a matter of embodiment, embeddedness or immanence in earlier chapters—just matters of consistency, different ways of articulating a neither radical nor interesting thought, namely, that this aspect of legal institutional design is consistent with some conceptions of dignity, equality and community? This 'mere consistency claim' does indeed inform the discussion in chapters four, five and six, yet it is the weakest claim in play there. For I take the various claims about embodiment, embeddedness and immanence to be stronger than that. The way in which they go beyond the mere consistency claim can be illuminated by recourse to one aspect of Max Horkheimer's notion of immanent criticism or critique. This is a matter of confronting 'the existent, in its historical context, with the claim of its conceptual principles, in order to criticize the relation between the two and thus transcend them'.[7] The task undertaken in

[3] A Norrie, *Justice and the Slaughter-Bench: Essays on Law's Broken Dialectic* (London, Routledge, 2016) at 7 and 4 respectively.

[4] ibid, 4.

[5] ibid, 15.

[6] ibid.

[7] M Horkheimer, *Eclipse of Reason* (Continuum, London, 2004 (first published 1947)) at 123 and quoted in D Held, *Introduction to Critical Theory* (London, Hutchinson, 1980) 183.

chapters four to six is principally that of articulating the conceptual principles, understood as the values of dignity, equality and community, that give a specific form of sense to *LAJ*. My claim is that *LAJ*—a particular, possibly historically unique legal institutional form—makes normative sense when understood by reference to the conceptions of dignity, equality and community outlined in those chapters. Those conceptions can, of course, count 'merely' as members of broader family groupings of dignity, equality and community, other family members also being able to play the role of animating normative force in relation to *LAJ*. This possibility does nothing to undermine the claim that the specific conceptions of dignity, equality and community discussed above also confer normative sense on *LAJ*; or, at least, it cannot do so unless the task of garnering normative support is a zero-sum game, in which finding that X supports Y necessarily undermines Z's capacity to support Y.

The immanence (or embeddedness or embodiment) claim is stronger than the mere consistency claim in two respects. First, because it insists that the values in play are not merely compatible with, but make normative sense of *LAJ*; and second, because it holds that these values are indeed manifest or contained in that social-institutional form. The latter is an empirical claim, relying not just upon an accurate characterisation of the aspect of social life that is the object of study, but also upon a reliable picture of the animating principles—in our case, the values of dignity, equality and community, in Horkheimer's case usually the values of justice, equality and freedom. Thus '[c]ritique proceeds, so to speak, 'from within' and hopes to avoid, thereby, the charge that its concepts impose irrelevant criteria of evaluation on the object'.[8] The accuracy of this double-sided empirical claim can be determined, in the first instance, by reference to the views of those whose conduct and beliefs constitute the aspect of social life in view. Yet, while the participants' views are the first court of appeal on these matters, they cannot be the final court of appeal, unless those views are taken to be incorrigible.

Characterising the arguments of chapters four to six as instances of immanent critique is misleading in the absence of this caveat: the arguments therein constitute only the first step of immanent critique. There is little in those chapters that could pass as an effort to criticise the relation between the values that ostensibly inform *LAJ* and its realisation of them in practice, that criticism being a prelude to transcending those values and that social-institutional form. This second step is the *critical* element in immanent critique and it is one that Horkheimer, in the quotation above, takes too quickly. For it may well be that the aspect of social life which is the object of study realises very well the conceptual principles (or values) it is said to embody. If that is so, then immanent *critique* is unnecessary. This, however, is not my reason for omitting the second step in those chapters. Although my effort has been to show that *LAJ* forms part of a morally and politically significant and respectable constellation, the case I have made amounts only to identifying

[8] See Held, ibid, 184.

pro tanto reasons in favour of *LAJ*; it thus leaves open the possibility that there might be other such reasons which undermine that case. The *pro tanto* reasons in favour of *LAJ* must be converted into all-things-considered reasons, reasons that outweigh all countervailing considerations, in order to support the judgement that *LAJ* is beyond the realm of immanent critique (or of any critique). And that task lies beyond the range of the current enterprise.

Regarding the later chapters of this book as the first step of an immanent critique, as an immanent excavation of the values informing *LAJ*, will not appease sceptics. Indeed, their question—'how can a demonstration that *LAJ* keeps ostensibly good moral and political company redound to *LAJ*'s normative credit?'—remains pertinent. Since I do not become a good person by being frequently photographed in the company of the great and the good, why should either I or *LAJ* be regarded as morally respectable simply by appearing in morally respectable company? A partial answer builds upon the point just made about explanatory power. It holds that the explanatory advantage of seeing *LAJ* in its wider moral and political context makes an assessment of *LAJ*'s value almost unavoidable. Simply seeing these connections is, in absence of special effort, simultaneously a judgement of the worth of the connected elements. That is because, in part at least, the values in play here are obviously appraisive, signifying a worthy achievement or ideal: that is no less true with regard to community than it is in relation to equality and dignity. That is not to say that one's judgement about the connections between such values and institutional forms like *LAJ* must always be positive, since it is perfectly possible to conclude that these connections are insufficiently strong, or that *LAJ* serves these values less well than alternative institutional forms. Although interlocking webs of connection can, at the very least, lead to either positive or negative assessments, the connections highlighted in previous chapters clearly incline us to the former. The links between *LAJ*, on the one hand, and various values and ideas, on the other, redound to the former's credit not just because those values and ideas are themselves valuable, but also because they are both protected and advanced by *LAJ*. *LAJ* is a carrier or embodiment of those values and ideas, whatever other values or ideas it may embody.

One remaining view of *LAJ*'s connections with dignity, equality and community, altogether more ambitious than those outlined so far, must be noted. On this view an account of the moral and political company that *LAJ* keeps adds to the latter's lustre because it endorses an holistic position about value. Such a position holds that both the worth and truth of each of our values is, either in part or in full, a function of how well each fits with the rest of our values. Ronald Dworkin espoused this kind of view, which he characterised as

> full value holism—the hedgehog's faith that all values form an interlocking network, that each of our convictions about what is good or right or beautiful plays some role in supporting each of our other convictions in each of those domains of value.[9]

[9] R Dworkin, *Justice for Hedgehogs* (Cambridge, Massachusetts, Harvard University Press, 2011) 120.

There are stronger and weaker versions of such a view and, it seems, Dworkin endorsed a variety of the former, holding that 'in political morality integration is a necessary condition of truth. We do not secure finally persuasive conceptions of our several political values unless our conceptions *do* mesh'.[10] If we take 'integration' and 'mesh' in these sentences to amount to something like an 'interlocking framework', then that yields the bold conclusion that a set of values so related is a true set of values.

If we accept that *LAJ* belongs among the values that constitute our political morality, and that it does indeed 'mesh' with dignity, equality and community, then full value holism of the Dworkinian stripe might seem unavoidable. That is a mistake. For the connections outlined in this book need have no meta-ethical significance at all. Charting the links between various social practices and institutions, on the one hand, and values, on the other, is neutral between various philosophical views as to the truth-conditions and exact cognitive status of values. It is not, of course, neutral on the point of the existence of such values and their realisation or embodiment in social practices and institutions and, by extension, their presence in agents' beliefs and conduct. But the exact epistemological status of such values is a topic on which, Dworkin's view notwithstanding, the arguments offered here need take no view. Does this response beg the question against Dworkinian value holism, standing as either an instance of external or internal scepticism? No, because my bracketing of this group of questions is purely pragmatic, not the result of any view, either explicit or implicit, about the nature of moral truth. Furthermore, even if the arguments here did indeed lead to something like Dworkinian value holism, that would not, in my view, be an embarrassment. Value holism is just as plausible an account of the nature of moral truth as some of its principal competitors. It also has the advantage of accommodating what Dworkin calls 'the ordinary view' of morality which holds, *inter alia*, that moral judgements purport to be true, that their truth is not merely a function of community beliefs and nor are they simply determined by our wants.[11]

Finally, note that a warning should accompany the kind of work that this book in part represents, namely, an effort to elucidate the value of some or other aspect of legal institutional design. There is an ever present risk that such work degenerates into a Whig attempt to emphasise the moral glory of our current institutions, viewing them as steps towards the best of best possible moral worlds.[12] For anyone familiar with the law and the often adverse impact it has on the lives of those bound by it, this is sure to appear 'a daring and implausible sanctification

[10] ibid, 5–6.

[11] ibid, 26–28.

[12] Whig theories of history tend 'to emphasise certain principles of progress in the past and to produce a story which is the ratification if not the glorification of the present': H Butterfield, *The Whig Interpretation of History* (New York, Norton, 1965 (first published 1931)) Preface. Whig legal philosophy would presumably glorify as well as ratify the present.

of the actual'.[13] Law is power and its power has great capacity for harm. We must be mindful, therefore, of underplaying *LAJ*'s moral and political shortcomings simply by highlighting those respects in which its moral-cum-political standing is in credit.

II. Taking Stock

Placing *LAJ* in its broader normative context has been an effort to redress the argumentative balance in its favour as against some of the strands of criticism sketched in chapter one. The book has not directly engaged with those strands, save for the exception of chapter three, which tackled three of their sub-components. This lack of engagement is explained principally by the labour involved in outlining *LAJ* and its links with dignity, equality and community. Only now, at the end of the current enterprise, when we have a clear picture of *LAJ* and its ramifications, is a blow-by-blow engagement with some critical responses to *LAJ* possible. And now, of course, is not the time. That said, two points are nevertheless worth making about two such critical responses, one being especially tempting within current legal thought, the other being particularly intractable. The first response is part of the historicist strand of criticism of *LAJ*, while the second is a sub-component of the moral strand.

As to the former, it seems by far the most likely to be invoked against the arguments of this book. Indeed, the book perhaps invites the criticism by holding that *LAJ*, while important in many different areas of legal doctrine at both liability and conviction stages, is not ubiquitous. That very lack provokes the historicist objection, which holds that *LAJ* should now be regarded as significant only as a feature of legal history, current legal systems being in the process of moving beyond it. The zeitgeist, it might be said, is not going *LAJ*'s way.[14] Besides the sociological and historical studies cited in support of this claim in chapter one, there are a number of lines of thought in the contemporary legal academy that make this objection enticing.

Some of these can be lumped together under the heading of 'the regulatory paradigm'. Initially given impetus by the startling rise of law and economics scholarship, first in the US and then elsewhere in the common and civil law worlds, and now sustained by what academic lawyers call 'regulatory theory', this paradigm attaches no special role or importance to law. Within the paradigm, regulation scholarship is 'a broad and open-ended category that can readily apply to many forms of intellectual inquiry concerning the purposive shaping of social

[13] RM Unger, *The Critical Legal Studies Movement* (Cambridge, Massachusetts, Harvard University Press, 1986) 9.

[14] See P Schlag's observations in *Laying Down the Law: Mysticism, Fetishism, and the American Legal Mind* (New York: New York University Press, 1996) at 22–23.

behaviour, particularly state and non-state standard-setting, monitoring and behaviour-modification processes'.[15] Law is just one means of 'purposive shaping' and might not, on a number of metrics, be the most efficient or parsimonious or powerful means of such shaping. If one's task is viewed simply as that of choosing the best means of addressing some specific social problem, then law can come to be regarded as neither a unique nor particularly important item on the menu of means to that end. Viewing law in that way, as one regulatory option or choice among a list of equally salient others, can obscure the features which set that option apart from the rest. One such feature, I suggest, is *LAJ*. And *LAJ*, when combined with the legal person, ensures that law's regulatory stance is unavoidably 'East-coast' rather than 'West-coast', a matter of regulators engaging with—as opposed to by-passing—the practical reason of their regulatees.[16] While the East-coast regulatory stance looks like a dialogue between agents, the West-coast stance is one of efficient problem-solving in which agency merits no special attention.

The regulatory paradigm and the West-coast stance can make *LAJ* seem quaint and anachronistic, a way of regulating human conduct rooted in the past. In a world of smart regulators, *LAJ* need play no significant role, the pockets of legal doctrine in which it figures standing as relics of a less enlightened, less technocratic age. By contrast, those areas of current legal doctrine in which *LAJ* hardly features are exemplars of a properly rigorous, intellectually respectable approach to regulatory design. The cutting edge of current legal thought and practice has thus left *LAJ* far behind. Although tempting, jurists cannot help themselves to this view without undertaking a good deal of work. For one thing, the historical transformation thesis needs to be borne out and that requires some account of those forces driving law's transformation. Moreover, those forces must be shown to be the causal (or other) drivers of the quite specific form of legal change in question, namely, the move from *LAJ* to whatever is said to supersede it. Temptation, in this as in other instances, comes with (intellectual) costs attached.

The seemingly intractable strand of moral criticism of *LAJ* is almost perfectly captured by Karl Marx's thought that bourgeois right is 'a right of inequality':

> [r]ight by its very nature can exist only as the application of an equal standard; but unequal individuals (and they would not be different individuals if they were not unequal) are measurable by an equal standard only insofar as they are made subject to an equal criterion, are taken from a *certain* side only.[17]

[15] B Morgan and K Yeung, *An Introduction to Law and Regulation* (Cambridge, Cambridge University Press, 2007) xiii–xiv. For a narrower view, see A Ogus, 'Regulation Revisited' (2009) *Public Law* 332–46 at 333 ('Without entering into niceties, I take it [regulation] to refer to obligations imposed by public law designed to induce individuals and firms to outcomes which they would not voluntarily reach. Regulation is largely enforced by public officials and compliance is aided by the threat or imposition of some sanction. As such, regulation covers a vast array of state controls over industrial and commercial activities').

[16] A still excellent introduction to the issues here is R Brownsword, 'Code, Control, and Choice: Why East is East and West is West' (2005) 25 *Legal Studies* 1–21.

[17] K Marx, *Critique of the Gotha Programme*, Vol 24 *Marx-Engels Collected Works* 1874–1883 (London, Lawrence and Wishart, 1989) at 86–87, emphasis in original.

Given the undeniable truth that human beings differ from one another in myriad ways, judging them or their conduct by reference to a general, equal standard—an invariant standard applied to all—seems a questionable form of equality or fairness. It is equal or fair treatment that comes at a cost, namely, that of ignoring those variations between agents that explain differential levels of compliance with the standard in question. The standard might, as for the authors of the Gotha programme, be that of an equal distribution of the proceeds of labour among all or, as for us, the general standards of reasonableness the law imposes in tort and related areas. An equal distribution of the proceeds of labour ignores differential capacities for labour, leading to those better able to labour contributing more than those less able; general standards of reasonable care lead to those less able to comply being disproportionately penalised.

This issue is an overarching concern of the book, but there is no sense in which it has been neutralised or overcome in the foregoing chapters. Showing the values that might inform *LAJ* does nothing, in and of itself, to eradicate the concerns and undermine the values underpinning the worry Marx articulates. Naturally, a good deal turns upon how that worry is understood and at least two possibilities are conceivable. One interprets the worry in a minimal way, as simply presenting the thought that 'this situation seems unfair or paradoxical'; another sees it as the precursor of an altogether more morally sensitive conception of appraisal and, consequently, of more morally sensitive conceptions of equality and justice. Marx did indeed offer a more morally sensitive distributive principle in the *Critique of the Gotha Programme* as an alternative to equal distribution of the proceeds of labour, but it is unclear he did so on the basis of alternative, morally sensitive conceptions of equality and justice. For the principle he offered—'[f]rom each according to his abilities, to each according to his needs'—is not explicitly tendered on those grounds, but as being historically appropriate to a society that has moved beyond the division of labour.[18] Yet, whatever its basis, this principle can stand as a template for related standards of ascription and distribution. 'To each according to their culpability' might be invoked as the basis for the distribution of criminal law sanctions, for example, while 'from each according to their ability to pay' could ground decisions whether or not to impose civil law sanctions for wrongs. In order to differ significantly from current principles of legal liability-responsibility, these standards would have to focus entirely upon the culpability and wealth of the very people being judged: in our current legal argot, the standards would have to be subjective, geared exclusively to an assessment of the particular person before the court.

Some contemporary jurists *seem* attracted to the project of reformulating the components of *LAJ* so as to constitute a more morally sensitive means of assessing and distributing culpability. Some of Norrie's work on the criminal law has

[18] ibid, 87. The broader issue here is that of whether or not Marx had a theory of justice. Two excellent entry points to the debate are: N Geras, 'The Controversy about Marx on Justice' (1984) 33 *Philosophica* 33–86 and AW Wood, 'Marx on Equality' in his *The Free Development of Each: Studies on Freedom, Right, and Ethics in Classical German Philosophy* (Oxford, Clarendon Press, 2014) Ch 11.

this appearance. So, for example, he viewed cases like *Chandler v DPP*,[19] on the irrelevance of motive to criminal liability, and *R v Ghosh*,[20] in which the offence may well have been motivated by need, as demonstrations of the law's failure to grasp the full context of the alleged criminal act and to accommodate the alleged criminal's subjectivity.[21] A detailed moral assessment of these instances of alleged wrongdoing would take the wrongdoer's circumstances, character, motives and reasons very seriously and might well, suggested Norrie, lead to exculpation.[22] But the law does not respond to the wrongdoer in this way because, as Norrie observed, one of its functions is simply to protect property and uphold the criminal law. This crime control function would be imperilled by engaging with the alleged wrongdoer in the way allegedly characteristic of moral assessment. Furthermore, this is a baleful situation according to Norrie because the criminal law also holds out the promise of individualised justice. This tension between the functions of the criminal law appears in many different forms and is not circumvented by pointing to instances in which the kind of consideration excluded by the law at one stage (eg, motive in assessment of *mens rea*) is accommodated at another (eg, sentencing). Norrie thought the way to resolve this tension was to endorse, in both doctrine and rational reconstruction, a social constructionist account of the self and subjectivity, one which recognises that agents are products and creators of social structures.[23]

That project, which involves an ambitious reimagining of criminal law's culpability conditions and its conception of agency, is one Norrie no longer endorses:

> my argument is not designed to rationally reconstruct law in a new image, but to probe the character of the existing law and its relationship with morality in the light of and against those approaches which identify an essential homology of the two.[24]

At the danger of putting words in Norrie's mouth, his response to Marx's conundrum is not now that of creating a more morally sensitive criminal law. It is, rather, that of posing the apparent tension or paradox between existing law and its culpability conditions, on the one hand, and a respectable form of moral appraisal, on the other. This is not an unproblematic path, although it is surely less difficult than the road of rational reconstruction. For the scale of rational reconstruction

[19] [1964] AC 763.

[20] [1982] 1 QB 1053.

[21] See A Norrie *Crime, Reason and History*, 3rd edn (Cambridge, Cambridge University Press, 2014) Ch 3; 'Simulacra of Morality?' Beyond the Ideal/Actuality Antinomies of Criminal Law' in A Duff (ed), *Philosophy and the Criminal Law: Principle and Critique* (Cambridge, Cambridge University Press, 1998) Ch 3 at 120–23 (on *mens rea* cases) and 126–29 (on *Alhers* and *Steane*).

[22] Norrie, 'Simulacra', ibid, 127–28.

[23] Norrie, 'Simulacra' (n 21) 131–43.

[24] A Norrie, *Punishment, Responsibility, and Justice* (Oxford, Clarendon, 2000) 232. His view is that he never endorsed this project in the first place, although he did not explicitly rule it out; my reading of his earlier work, particularly the essay cited above in n 21, is that it (i) implicitly endorses that project and (ii) is certainly not inconsistent with it (see my review in (1999) 19 *Legal Studies* 425 at 427–28).

required is ambitious: it is far more grandiose than the recommendation of some or other incremental change in legal doctrine that is a staple of much legal scholarship. It instead entails destabilising the form of law as we know it, as it currently exists in post-feudal, mercantile, liberal societies. Law in those societies has *LAJ* as one of its most remarkable features; the attempt to replace or supersede *LAJ* is therefore in large part an attempt to change the form of liberal or bourgeois or capitalist law. It is not a challenge to the nature of law itself, since law can take many forms; it is, however, a clear challenge to our institutional imagination, because liberal law is the principal form of law we know and experience. Despite his disavowal of rational reconstruction, Norrie's work on popular justice could be a useful starting point for expanding the contemporary legal-institutional imagination, since that form of justice seemingly manifests different styles of ascription, accountability and judgement to those embodied in *LAJ*.[25]

The principal difficulty with the less ambitious response to Marx's conundrum, that of noting an apparent paradox or tension, concerns the point of contrast. On the one hand, we have equal general standards, but what exactly is posited on the other? A more morally sensitive means of judgement is the candidate we have offered, as if that notion were utterly unproblematic and obvious. But it is by no means certain that morality, as understood by ordinary people and many philosophers, always takes the highly context- and agent-sensitive form assumed by this contrast. The more obvious contrast here might instead be that between forms of general and abstract judgement, like *LAJ*, and the supposedly more particularistic judgements that characterise ethical as opposed to moral appraisal. If we take morality and moral appraisal to concern, first and foremost, our duties to others, and the ethical domain as the realm of responsibility for our own lives, then the judgements appropriate to the latter could be qualitatively different from those that are apt in the former. Judgements in the moral domain, just by virtue of its content, might mimic those in law; ethical judgements, since the realm of ethics need not invariably be concerned with our responsibilities to and respect for others, might be more responsive to our context and character.[26]

While there is no doubt that many perceive a conflict between law's judgement and other forms of judgement, it is uncertain that this is a plausible way of understanding it. More must be done for that plausibility threshold to be reached: the ethical pole of the contrast requires fuller specification and it has to be shown to be an appropriate vantage point from which to assess conduct culminating in legal wrongs. Furthermore, there are apparent *moral* critics of *LAJ*—Norrie again comes to mind—who do not espouse anything like the ethical/moral distinction just invoked. The tensions Norrie sees between *LAJ* and other forms of judgement arise from various ostensibly unavoidable antinomies that structure legal thought.

[25] See Ch 3 of A Norrie's *Law and the Beautiful Soul* (London, Glasshouse, 2005).

[26] This contrast between the moral and the ethical I take from Dworkin (n 9) at 25 which in turn derives from B Williams, *Ethics and the Limits of Philosophy* (London, Fontana, 1985).

While some are tempted, on discovering antinomies, to try to resolve or move beyond them, Norrie does not.[27] Uncovering the latent and explicit tensions in our thought, practices and institutions is enough for him; that might also be exactly what the arguments of this book reveal. For, as has often been noted, the attempt to redress the argumentative balance in favour of *LAJ*, to illuminate the values that inform it, need do nothing to undermine the doubts that hang over it. Showing there is something that can be said in favour of *LAJ* does not show that nothing can be said against it. If doubts persist about *LAJ*'s moral or ethical or political standing, then that might be evidence that we are indeed in the grip of antinomy, bound both to affirm and value that which we also suspect and downplay.

My last point is a comment on this chapter's epigraph. Dreams of legal transformation, of transcending law, have perhaps been with us for as long as law and legal thought themselves. Yet should we not, before dreaming, take a good look around and attempt to understand, as best we can, exactly where we are and where we've come from? If we do this not as self-obsessed individual atoms, but as members of societies aware of their long histories and complex institutional forms and social structures, then we will surely better appreciate the value of the latter. We might also better appreciate the value of those institutional forms and social structures that take flight in our dreams.

[27] See Norrie (n 3) Ch 1, 6–7, but note also the 'holistic' turn mentioned at 17 and explored in depth in Ch 9.

INDEX